PHIL NORMAN has been writing on all types of popular culture for press, television and the internet since 1997. He is married and lives in London.

Praise for *A History of Television in 100 Programmes*:

'Norman writes with epigrammic wit, lethal concision . . . and a grasp of both industry politics and political context . . . to be hailed above all is his eye for the particular . . . an acerbic, acute and accurate history, its cynicism tempered by affection and humour . . . celebrates the odd and eccentric' *The Times*

Also by Phil Norman:

*The Great British Tuck Shop* (with Steve Berry)
*A History of Sweets in 50 Wrappers* (with Steve Berry)

# TELEVISION

## A HISTORY IN 100 PROGRAMMES

### Phil Norman

WILLIAM
COLLINS

For Suzy

William Collins
An imprint of HarperCollins*Publishers*
1 London Bridge Street
London SE1 9GF

www.WilliamCollinsBooks.com

First published in Great Britain as *A History of Television in 100 Programmes*
by The Friday Project in 2015

This paperback edition published by William Collins in 2016

1

Copyright © Phil Norman 2015

Phil Norman asserts the moral right to be identified as the author of this work

A catalogue record for this book is available from the British Library

ISBN 978-0-00-811332-2

Typeset in Adobe Caslon Pro by Palimpsest Book Production Ltd,
Falkirk, Stirlingshire

Printed and bound in Great Britain by Clays Ltd, St Ives plc

MIX
Paper from
responsible sources
FSC® C007454

FSC™ is a non-profit international organisation established to promote
the responsible management of the world's forests. Products carrying the
FSC label are independently certified to assure consumers that they come
from forests that are managed to meet the social, economic and
ecological needs of present and future generations,
and other controlled sources.

Find out more about HarperCollins and the environment at
**www.harpercollins.co.uk/green**

# CONTENTS

# INTRODUCTION

*There is no holding down the modern inventor. He rides the*
*waves of the ether with the conquering skill of a master in a*
*celestial rodeo. Give him a valve and there is no holding him. It*
*is almost certain that within a few years we shall have all our*
*entertainment available within our own four walls. Press but*
*the button and a stereoscopic talking film will happen over the*
*mantelpiece.*

'Seen and Heard', *Manchester Guardian,*
1 April 1930

IT HAD AN AURA about it, a presence. By today's standards it was tiny, but it dominated the room in a way its technically superior descendants never quite manage. It catered directly for two of the senses, but in operation it affected them all. The flicker and the glare of the bulbous, grey-green screen. The hum and whine of the tube heating up. The crackle of static when it turned off, the tang of burnt dust in the air when it was repaired. For decades the television set was the most advanced piece of technology to be found in any house. How it worked was a mystery, but it was literally part of the furniture.

It was also an instant portal to a cavalcade of smart, witty house guests with inexhaustible supplies of information, anecdotes, opinions and vibrant sweaters. Miraculous and commonplace at the same time, television occupied a unique position in the national imagination. Detractors claimed it hijacked the national imagination – formerly a cultural Arcadia of chamber music and well-made plays – for its own base ends, but at its best it brought classes and cultures into each other's homes without prejudice. By the late 1960s even the press admitted that TV, coming from nowhere, was beating them at their own game and several new ones of its own invention.

The birth of television in the mid-1920s garnered more fuss than a royal baby. The race to perfect a workable system was matched by the rush to predict imminent social catastrophe. Newspapers, radio, theatre and even the motor car (why drive somewhere you can see at the flick of a switch?) were pronounced doomed many times. Rumour and misconception abounded. Professor A. M. Low worried about the effect on international relations if Americans could use the new device to view their British neighbours engaged in 'frightful' activities, such as drinking cocktails.[1] Meanwhile, R. H. Hill of Oxford University demanded, 'How could one have a bath in comfort if all the neighbours could look in?'[2] Noted physicist Sir Oliver Lodge fretted that broadcasting's electromagnetic waves might make planes fall out of the sky, though he didn't expect TV to become a working reality 'for a good many years yet, perhaps not for a century'.[3]

More usefully, Lodge worried about content, noting that the majority of messages sent by another recent scientific triumph – the transatlantic telegraph cable – were 'rubbishy'. 'It is no use enlarging our powers of communication,' he warned, 'if we have nothing worthwhile to say.'[4] The insubstantial nature of the early demonstrations didn't help – even John Logie Baird provoked a wave of cheap laughs when he based his first telerecording demo around a cabbage.

Initially the preserve of the rich, the take up of TV spread after the Second World War as prices dropped and services improved. Older media, who had originally described it as an elitist fad for well-to-do stay-at-homes, now tried to dismiss it as a pernicious influence on those less stable, less educated than themselves. A snobbish line in the fifties had it that people were raising H-shaped aerials over their houses to make up for all the 'H's dropped inside them.

It may have projected a serene, slightly aloof air on screen, but behind the cameras post-war television was paddling like mad, inventing a new medium on the hoof, often with whatever came to hand. Studios looked less like the glistening caverns of today and more like the shop floor of an engineering works under the stewardship of a hyperactive ten-year-old. A profession was being steadily built through years of committed bodging.

America initially lagged behind Britain, Germany, France, Italy, Russia and Japan in television take up, but soon made up for lost time. NBC's first electronic transmission in 1936, featuring comedian Ed Wynn, ignited an industrial boom that in little over a decade would result in four national television networks broadcasting to over four million set-equipped homes. The US network system, commercially funded and powered by the twin big tickets of sports and vaudeville, was voracious and unstoppable. By the late 1940s its diverse schedule offered programmes that were sombre (*Court of Current Issues, People's Platform*), sophisticated (*Café de Paris, Champaign and Orchids*) and silly (*Buzzy Wuzzy, Campus Hoopla*).

This last category caused unease back in Britain, where ITV's arrival in the mid-1950s threatened the state-run BBC order. The US broadcasts of Elizabeth II's coronation had included grinning appearances by NBC's mascot, chimpanzee J. Fred Muggs, and there were concerns about a similar crassness creeping in to British broadcasting. The Tories championed ITV, Labour vilified it, while Liberal councillor Paul Rose reminded both sides that 'there is always freedom of the knob.'[5]

Technological advance was an enduring obsession, if not always taking place as quickly as predicted: a committee set up in 1943 to prepare for British television's post-war return anticipated the swift invention not only of colour, but 1000-line high definition and 3D.[6] A quarter of a century later, round the clock coverage of the Apollo missions fused the Television Age with the Space Age for as long as the latter held out, and made a star of James Burke, who went on to present the most lavish science programmes ever made, travelling further on a BBC expense account than Armstrong ever managed in a *Saturn V*. On a smaller scale, potting shed innovation was everywhere, from the BBC's home computer sideline to abortive plans in the late 1960s for contestants on *The Golden Shot* to operate the game show's famous crossbow from their own front rooms, via a Golden Joystick in a James Bond-style Golden Suitcase, specially delivered in a Golden Car. The technology, the producers made clear, boasted Golden safety features as 'we don't want any nut shooting Bob Monkhouse.'[7]

Around this time came the first symptoms of two ailments that would dog the medium for evermore. The first was the transformation of the social embarrassment surrounding television among the middle classes into an ironic 'guilty pleasure'. As John Osborne confessed to Kenneth Tynan in 1968, 'When TV is dreadful, it's thoroughly enjoyable. After you've seen *The Golden Shot* a couple of times, it acquires a special horror of its own.'[8] The second, closely related to the first, was nostalgia. In the dying days of 1969, ITV screened *A Child of the Sixties*, taking the temperature of the decade with a rummage in the archive. This sort of thing was nothing new in itself, but for the first time whimsical talking heads were added, including 'the impressions they made on a receptive young mind' – an Oxford undergraduate named Gyles Brandreth. The bar for retro-punditry was set from that moment.

The study of television doesn't have to be so apologetic. Television may not be high art, but many artists have worked in it, regardless of its condemnation as unclean by the world's cultural custodians. Samuel Beckett wrote for it. Kingsley Amis presented a pop music show on it. Carol Ann Duffy laboured in it writing cockney gags for Joe Brown's snakes and ladders game show *Square One* on her way to becoming Poet Laureate.

As a vivid source of graphic reportage, television transformed our relationship with the world at large. When the Vietnam War stopped being a few fuzzy black and white images accompanied by sober paragraphs of text and became an avalanche of explicit, full-colour moving horrors, western populations seriously reconsidered the wisdom of military adventures. Dramatists, meanwhile, found a unique new medium that was more intimate than cinema, more precise than the theatre and which could pluck the hearts of millions. Worries about the creation of a world of antisocial couch ornaments were outweighed by a sense of barriers and borders vaulted by satellite, a shift in the way we looked at the world that wouldn't happen again until the advent of the Internet.

If that arrival meant the writing was on the wall for television's place in the media vanguard, for most it was hard to read. Prestel, the British Post Office's pioneering online data service, was struggling by 1982. Punters predicted that staring at a load of text was so passé in the age of the image it would never catch on. 'Prestel and *The Two Ronnies* . . . have no more in common than the *Financial Times* and Hammond Innes,' reasoned Hamish McRae. 'It would further follow that it is pointless to give people who want to watch *The Two Ronnies* a Prestel set that tells them the time of the trains to Newcastle.'[9] Such faultless logic buoyed TV's unassailable self-image until it was far too late, at which point panic set in.

Factual programmes in particular are acutely conscious of the Internet looking over their shoulders. Current affairs channels pride themselves as vital parts of the democratic machine, but TV could never make on-screen democracy work. In May 1982, *World in Action* tried to atone for the scarcity of news coming out of the Falklands Conflict with a high-tech viewer vote. This consisted of 75 homes being equipped to give instant reaction to the big questions of warfare. The set-up worked fine, but a naively honest on-screen tally of the total votes showed less than half the audience, specially wired in at great fuss, were actually bothering. Viewer participation remains largely a token gesture – and, thanks to premium rate phone lines, often the token that pays for the programme.

Before the Internet took its place as the number one scourge of decent society, television's constant stream bred disdain. A novel takes its place in the literary canon. A film lines up in the cinematic pantheon. Television programmes just float there, then vanish. While films relate to other films at a distance, via elegant homage or the critic's comparative whim, a TV show arrives surrounded by other shows before and after, on other channels, from other seasons. It's an adaptation of this Danish show, a reboot of that long-forgotten space opera, or a strange amalgam of those two 1970s programmes presented by that newsreader who's suddenly all over the place after she showed how game she was, doing that soap opera parody on a charity special. Never mind placing a programme in context, it's an afternoon's work just to pull the thing out of the undergrowth.

Small wonder that early critics, fearful of getting their hands dirty with this suspicious new medium, contented themselves with a few tentative pokes and prods at TV as a whole – muttering darkly about 'admass' and 'diachronic flow', and treating it with the loftiness of the anthropologist. For these early critics, TV could best be understood as the by-product of some industrial process or quaintly exotic lower culture: it was an experimental new plastic from the labs of ICI, or the campfire story of a backward tribe. Aside from the odd accidentally interesting curio, artistic judgement was hardly appropriate. The *Guardian*'s TV editor Peter Fiddick noted that TV's lowly status could lead, at worst, to 'know-nothings writing for care-nothings about stuff that [is] worth nothing.'[10] That was in 1982. Things have got worse since.

So here's an attempt to revisit and revive the history of the idiot's lantern. A hundred programmes have been gathered to chart eighty-odd years of televisual evolution. It is, admittedly, a predominantly Anglophone, western collection. Though the Global Village has lately begun to live up to its name, TV around the world has overwhelmingly followed blueprints drawn up by British and American hands.

A crudely calibrated Hundred Greatest, a solemn Hall of Fame, would give only a fraction of the picture. This book aims to celebrate and mimic the serendipitous joy of that scheduling jumble which, in the days of restricted channel numbers, threw up dizzy juxtapositions daily: an earnest play might be followed by a big broad variety spectacular; a horror anthology that drove children behind furniture followed a sketch show that chewed the carpet. This riotous mix, now slowly disappearing as themed channels and on-demand services take over, may have downgraded TV's importance in the eyes of aesthetes, but gave it a community feel other media lacked. No-one ever turned up at a cinema half an hour early for a screening of *Three Colours: Red* and got thirty minutes of *Slam Dunk Ernest* for their trouble.

This isn't a book about how much 'better' television once was, but how much stranger it used to be – much braver, more foolhardy, unselfconscious and creatively energetic before commerce knocked those fascinating corners off its character. At its best and at its worst, television is brutally honest and charmingly deceitful, sentimentally partisan and coldly dispassionate, obscenely lavish and ludicrously cheap. Its screen bulges with obsessive perfectionists and clueless amateurs, sociopathic monsters and all-round good eggs. It can't be contained by a neat little narrative. It's chaos all the way down.

No countdown of the top hundred shows can do television full justice. But maybe a more varied hundred can make a better stab at exploring it: a rough guide antidote to the standard lists of well-worn greats. What follows is one such alternative trek. Overlooked gems and justly wiped follies, overcooked spectaculars and underfunded experiments are as much a part of TV history as the national treasures and stone cold classics. They can tell us just as much, and sometimes more, about the nature of television, those who crafted it and those who lapped it up. Here, then, are tales of the days when television was at the most exciting, creative stage of any medium: a cottage industry with the world at its feet.

# TELE-CRIME (1938–9)
## BBC

### The original TV drama series.

*When the BBC asks a question, it isn't just a question, it's a 'viewer participation programme'.*

Grace Wyndham Goldie,
*Listener*, 2 March 1939

IN BBC TELEVISION'S BRIEF life before the war, drama meant the theatre: simple studio productions of acknowledged classics or extracts from a show currently running in the West End. These unofficial trailers were either recreated in the studio (with as much of the theatre's scenery as could be blagged) or occasionally and chaotically broadcast live from their home turf. Champions of theatre broadcasts claimed the presence of an audience added atmosphere and upped the actors' game – the fact that the cameras often ended up chasing them about the stage, like a football match filmed by a bunch of drunken fans, was a small price to pay.

Visuals took a back seat at first. Early TV equipment produced low-definition pictures in murky black and grimy white. Faces had to be held in tight close-up to enable recognition, and wide shots couldn't be that wide due to the Beeb's tiny Lime Grove studios. Sets and lighting just about did the job, and nothing more. Directors couldn't cut between cameras – a change of shot had to be done by mixing, which could take several seconds. With all these restrictions, wrote the critic Philip Hope-Wallace, 'the television screen is much less a stage . . . than a checking-board helping us listen to good talk.'[11]

The first step on the road to the modern drama series was taken by what critic Grace Wyndham Goldie, later to run the BBC's current affairs department, called 'an interesting experiment in presentation'.[12] Mileson Horton had made a name for himself in the mid-1930s writing 'Photocrime', an immensely popular series of whodunit photo-stories starring the intrepid Inspector Holt, published in *Weekly Illustrated*. These bare bones procedurals, simply told and visually direct, were just what TV producers were after. Horton was hired to script a series of twenty-minute Holt adventures for the small screen.

Take a typical episode of *Tele-crime*, 'The Fletcher Case'. A man's body is found sprawled on the floor of his bedroom, with a gun in his right hand. It looks like an open-and-shut suicide case for Inspector Holt. Just as he's about to leave the scene, the phone rings. Holt's constable answers: it's the victim's niece. The victim, it turns out, was *left*-handed! Murder! It's a race to the family house to stop the killer striking again. But too late! Another family member has been offed. Holt assembles the suspects and hears their stories.

After fifteen minutes of this, Holt and company fade from the screen, replaced by the gently smiling face of continuity announcer Elizabeth Cowell: 'Well, who *did* do the murder? Viewers have now all the evidence necessary to detect the criminal.' There follows a few moments' reflective pause for the audience to flex their minds, then it's back to the house for a rapid denouement.

The guess-the-culprit interval was an early bit of audience participation that didn't last the pace (although it was revived for Jeremy Lloyd and Lance Percival's 1972 panel game *Whodunnit?*). The rest of *Tele-crime*, though, set the mould for the detective series, the backbone of popular TV drama ever since.

The crime thriller, like most genres, is a self-concealing art: done well, the writing and direction are taken for granted; done badly, they're sitting ducks. 'In an affair of this kind,' observed Wyndham

Goldie, 'nobody expects any depth or subtle characterisation, but the people in the story must be made just sufficiently interesting for us to care which of them is hanged.'[13] Television evolves not with quantum leaps of genius, but by continuous tinkering. *Tele-crime* may have long vanished into thin air, but look at the foundations of any current drama series and you might just glimpse the smudgy, over-lit face of Inspector Holt.

# COOKERY (1946–51)
## BBC

### The first celebrity chef.

THE FIRST PERSON TO sling a skillet in the studio was French restaurateur, novelist and boulevardier Xavier Marcel Boulestin. He essayed suave hob-side demonstrations wearing a double-breasted suit during the BBC's 1930s infancy in programmes like *Bee for Boulestin* and *Blind Man's Buffet*. However, the cult of the celebrity chef – the omnipresent gastronome as relaxed in front of the camera as at the oven door – began with Philip Harben.

Rotund, neatly bearded and rarely seen out of an apron, Harben emerged from the post-war landscape of ration coupons and meat queues to become an ever-present face on TV via his first series, the sensibly-titled *Cookery*. Harben rustled up austerity lobster vol-au-vents and welfare soufflés for the vicarious pleasure of families struggling on one slice of condemned corned beef a week, but few recognise just how many aspects of the twenty-first century tele-cookery landscape owe him their existence. Without Harben, we may never have witnessed these culinary devices:

THEATRICALITY – The son of film actors, Harben knew how to put his recipes, and himself, across to best effect in the muffled turmoil of early television, keeping the stream of patter going as the sheets of flame leapt from his flambé pan. 'He stands almost alone,' remarked an awed Reginald Pound, 'a precision instrument of self-expression.' [14]

MERCHANDISE – Not content with putting his grinning, bearded face on jars of Heinz pickle and packs of Norfolk stuffing, Harben supplemented his meagre BBC salary with the launch of Harbenware, heavy gauge saucepans with a special 'Harbenized' non-stick coating, bearing labels festooned with his grinning, bearded face.

BACK TO BASICS – The ridicule endured by Delia Smith for demonstrating how to boil an egg was nothing new to Harben, who devoted the lion's share of one programme to making a cup of tea. Pot-warming temperatures, infusion times, even the height from which to pour the water onto the leaves were discussed at rigorous length.

NATIONAL AND INTERNATIONAL DISHES – Harben got away from the standard Mayfair dinner party aspirations of TV cookery to celebrate Britain's regional food in 1951's *Country Dishes*, rustling up everything from Cornish pasties to jellied eels. If technology had allowed him a global culinary excursion he'd have made one – instead he brought the resident chef from NBC's *Home* show to the UK for a national dish swapping session in 1955's *Transatlantic Exchange*.

SLUTTY INGREDIENTS SCANDAL – Delia's controversial dalliance with frozen mash and other timesavers was pre-empted in 1954 when Harben rustled up *sole bonne femme* using haddock and milk instead of the traditional Dover sole and wine. An outraged telegram from catering students at Blackpool Technical College reached the Director General within hours. 'The BBC permits Harben to clown with classical French dishes in a way which exposes the British kitchen to a justifiable scorn,'[15] they raged. Whatever, they demanded, would the Americans think if this got out?

NUTRITIONAL CRUSADE – Getting the nation eating properly was another Harben innovation. This being 1949, however, the problem was that folk weren't eating enough. Specifically, Harben attacked the 'sparrow-sized breakfasts' of Britain's working men. 'We cannot stay a first-class power if we give up eating a first-class breakfast,'[16] he told the press, encouraging British men to get up earlier and fry their own bacon if necessary. Harben's Great British Breakfast was possibly unique in food campaigns for also recommending a few post-prandial minutes with a newspaper and a cigarette.

PRIMADONNA ANTICS – Every great TV chef must exhibit a total lack of humour at a crucial moment. Harben set the template in 1957 on the set of *The Benny Hill Show*. He'd sportingly played the stooge before to the chaotic Mr Pastry and rebarbative Fred Emney, but Hill took a step too far. 'They submitted a sketch to me which I considered degrading. The whole thing indicated that I couldn't cook. That's no joke to me.'[17]

MOLECULAR GASTRONOMY – Beating Heston Blumenthal by over forty years, Harben stocked up on microscopes, slide rules and calculus tables for his 1964 ITV series *The Grammar of Cookery*. With technical advice from microbiologist A. L. Bacharach and editions called 'The Three Faces of Meringue' and 'Egg Liaison', he took cookery to new heights of sophistication. 'If you are a great cook, madam,' he claimed, 'you are a singer of songs, a poet, an actress, a painter, a pianist. You are Maria Callas, you are Cilla Black, you are Vanessa Redgrave all rolled into one. And the world is at your feet.'[18]

# CAVALCADE OF STARS (1949–52)

## DuMont (Drugstore Television)

### Vaudeville begets the sitcom.

As television progressed from esoteric technology to world-wide medium-in-waiting, one question dominated: what the hell are we going to put on it? The *Manchester Guardian* held a competition asking just that in 1934. Winning suggestions ranged from high mass at St Peter's to a chimps' tea party, 'MPs trying to buy bananas after hours', and 'Mr Aldous Huxley enjoying something'.[19]

In America, such wild fancies became real. There was the 1944 show that led one critic to gush, 'This removes all doubt as to television's future. This is television.'[20] 'This' was *Missus Goes A-Shopping*, a distant ancestor of *Supermarket Sweep*. A more solid solution to the content problem was sport. Entire evenings in the late 1940s consisted of the sports that were easiest to cover with the new stations' primitive equipment: mainly boxing and wrestling. On the other hand, figured New York-based programmers, there was a whole breed of people who were past masters at filling an evening with entertainment off their own bat. They were just a few blocks away, doing six nights a week for peanuts.

Vaudeville stars like the Marx Brothers had dominated pre-war cinema comedy, touring a stage version of each film across America to polish every line and perfect every pratfall before they hit the studio. Television wanted vaudevillians for the opposite quality: bounteous spontaneity. The big, big shows began with NBC's *Texaco*

*Star Theatre*, hosted by Milton Berle. Through a mess of broad slapstick, elephantine cross-dressing and taboo-nudging ad libs, Berle became the first of television's original stars, with his loud and hectic shtick penetrating the fog of the early TV screen like bawdy semaphore from the deck of an oncoming battleship. No marks for élan, but plenty for chutzpah.

Other broadcasters followed suit, including DuMont. The odd one out of the networks, DuMont originated from TV manufacturing rather than broadcast radio, so had to search harder to find celebrities, and struggled to keep them. *Cavalcade of Stars*, their Saturday night shebang, was a case in point. It was originally hosted by former *Texaco* stand-in Jack Carter, then Jerry Lester, both of whom were poached by NBC as they became popular. Desperation was setting in when they came to Jackie Gleason. Gleason, having bombed in Hollywood, was working through the purgatory of Newark's club circuit when DuMont offered him a two-week test contract. Gleason had worked in TV before, starring in a lacklustre adaptation of barnstorming radio sitcom *Life of Riley*, so had his reasons to be wary. But that was someone else's script. *Cavalcade* was 100% Jackie.

Every show needed a sponsor. *Cavalcade*, lacking the might to pull in big time petroleum funds, was sponsored by Whelan's drugstore chain. Each edition was preceded by a strident, close-harmony paean to the delights of the corner pharmacy, under the bold caption 'QUALITY DRUGS'. Then on came The Great One in imperial splendour with a retinue of his 'personally-auditioned' Glea Girls. Often he'd daintily sip from a coffee cup, roll his eyes and croon 'Ah, how sweet it is!', his public chuckling in the knowledge that the cup wasn't holding coffee. After his opening monologue – a combination of double-takes, reactions and slow-burns as much as a string of verbal gags – he'd request 'a little travellin' music' from his orchestra, and to the resulting snatch of middle eastern burlesque, he slunk around the stage in a possessed belly-cum-go-go dance before freezing stock still and uttering the immortal line, 'And awaaaaay we goooo!' After all that, the programme actually started.

This indulgently whimsical ceremony wasn't unique to *Cavalcade*, but on Gleason's watch it grew into a kind of baroque mass, initiating the audience into his comic realm. The logic of replicating the communal aspect of stage variety on such a private, domestic medium seems odd today, but a large proportion of Gleason's working class audience, unable to afford their own TVs, watched *en masse* in the bars and taverns of the Union's major cities (DuMont's limited coverage never reached the small towns), creating their own mini-crowds who joined in with gusto. Vaudeville's voodoo link with the audience could cross the country this way. Performer and punter were in cahoots.

*Cavalcade* wasn't all Pavlovian faff. The main body of the show boasted as much meat as that of its star. Dance numbers and musical guests were interspersed with extended character sketches taken from life – Gleason's life. At one end of his one-man cross-section of society was playboy Reggie Van Gleason III. At the other, Chaplinesque hobo The Poor Soul. Somewhere in between came serial odd job failure Fenwick Babbitt and The Bachelor, a pathos-laden mime act in which Gleason would prepare breakfast or dress for dinner with all the grace and finesse you'd expect from a long-term single man, to the melodious, mocking strains of 'Somebody Loves Me'. Hobo aside, Gleason had lived them all.

Gleason's fullest tribute to his Bushwick roots was the warring couple skit that became known as 'The Honeymooners'. Gleason played Ralph Kramden, a short-fused temper bomb of the old-fashioned, spherical kind; a scheming bus driver with ideas beyond his terminus. He lived with his more grounded wife Alice in a cramped, walk-up apartment at 328 Chauncey Street, a genuine former address of Gleason's and possibly the most accurate recreation of breadline accommodation in TV comedy. In this washboard-in-the-sink, holler-up-the-fire-escape poverty, Kramden and his unassuming sewage worker neighbour Ed Norton (Art Carney) sparred, plotted and generally goofed around. The working-class-boy-made-good was talking directly to his peers about life as they knew it, as surely as if they were sat at the same bar. The aristocracy of executives and sponsors that made it technically possible didn't figure in the exchange at all. They delivered the star, and then made themselves scarce until the first commercial break. It would be television comedy's struggle to preserve this desirable set-up against tide after tide of neurotic, censorious meddling from above.

*Cavalcade of Stars* became DuMont's biggest show. Naturally, this meant Gleason was snapped up by CBS within two years. His fame doubled, and that of 'The Honeymooners' trebled. It broke out to become a sitcom in its own right, but oddly never achieved quite the same level of success outside its variety habitat. Meanwhile Sid Caesar, Imogene Coca and a stable of future comedy writing titans seized the vaudeville crown with NBC's *Your Show of Shows*.

Gleason himself wasn't immune to the odd misstep. In 1961 he hosted the high-concept panel game *You're in the Picture*, in which stars stuck their heads through holes in paintings and tried to determine what they depicted. The première bombed so hard that week two consisted entirely of Gleason, in a bare studio with trusty coffee cup to hand, apologising profusely for the previous week. He was reckless, chaotic and hopelessly self-indulgent, but he instinctively knew when he'd failed to entertain. He was also relentlessly determined, signing off his marathon *mea culpa* with a forthright, 'I don't know what we'll do, but I'll be back.' Television couldn't wish for a better motto.

# CRUSADER RABBIT
# (1950–1)

## NBC (Television
## Arts Productions)

### TV's first bespoke cartoon.

AMERICAN CARTOONS DOMINATED FORTIES cinema. The heart-on-sleeve perfectionism of Disney and the demolition ballets of Warner Brothers were known, loved and merchandised throughout the world. But when television began to look like a viable proposition, the animation giants kept their distance: too small the screen, too monochrome, and most important, too cheap the going rate. It might be good for the odd commercial or as a place to dump black-and-white shorts even the dankest fleapit would no longer touch, but cartoons made especially for TV? The idea might have seemed a joke to the main animation studios, but there was a gap in the media market waiting to be filled. This one snugly accommodated an adventurous animal.

*Crusader Rabbit* and his faithful sidekick Ragland T 'Rags' Tiger were a pairing in the short-smart/big-dumb cartoon tradition that had its origins in Steinbeck's *Of Mice and Men*. Their creator was Alex Anderson, nephew of the self-styled Woolworth of cinema animation, Paul Terry. Anderson reduced his uncle's cheap and cheerful formula even further, basing his methods on a sequence in Disney's behind-the-scenes cartoon feature *The Reluctant Dragon* which showed an embryonic cartoon in animated storyboard form – simple cuts from one still drawing to the next, smartly timed to the soundtrack. Anderson took the idea and applied it to a finished series.[21]

Together with old friend Jay Ward handling production duties, Anderson formed Television Arts Productions. Equipped with an army surplus Kodak film camera and several veteran draughtsmen, TAP began production, leaving no corner uncut. Single poses lasted on screen for anything from one to fifteen seconds, and loops of motion were reused with shameless regularity. Verbal gags did most of the work, but mouth movements were minimal – in the pilot, a fast-talking radio announcer blatantly hides his behind a sheet of paper.

The pilot impressed NBC enough to commission a series, at $2,500 per episode – in the labour-intensive animation world, about as cheap as you could get. *Crusader Rabbit* rode out, sponsored by that great friend of early TV innovation, Carnation Evaporated Milk, at 6 p.m. on 1 August 1950. The show aired every weekday for the best part of a year, pitting the tenacious pair against adversaries Dudley Nightshade, Whetstone Whiplash and Achilles the Heel.

As production stepped up, Ward's talent came to the fore. While Anderson supervised the visuals, Ward took charge of the dialogue recording sessions, coaching the voice talent and editing to keep things as snappy and fast-moving as possible. This was a practical necessity – with budgets this tight, editing in sound only made economic sense – but it gave a quickfire ebullience to the otherwise static show, emphasising verbal gags in a way which would shape Ward's later output and TV animation in general.

It also instigated a less happy animation tradition. Jerry Fairbanks, Television Arts' commercial partner in the *Crusader Rabbit* venture, turned out not to be as financially secure as he claimed. An uneasy NBC sequestered all 195 *Crusader Rabbit* cartoons as collateral.[22] Ward and Anderson found themselves without a franchise, their stake in the original and rights to the characters having been legally spirited away. This sort of custody battle, with the creators forever on the losing side, would become a feature of TV cartooning, where the bottom line drags heavily. *Crusader Rabbit* would eventually be reborn, via other hands, in 1957.

Ward started afresh, in tandem with cartoon veteran Bill Scott, to create a plethora of wisecracking properties that took *Crusader Rabbit*'s chattering statue model and upped the wit, tempo and volume. This began with a blockbuster that aped its progenitor's character template – *The Adventures of Rocky and Bullwinkle*. Meanwhile William Hanna and Joseph Barbera, ex-MGM animators who brought *Tom and Jerry* to life and were briefly engaged by Ward for a legally embargoed *Crusader Rabbit* revival, borrowed the limited animation style for their own work. *The Ruff and Reddy Show*, in which a smart little cat and a big stupid dog engaged in pose-to-pose capers, was followed by *Huckleberry Hound*, *Yogi Bear* and flatly coloured, ever-blinking cartoon versions of sitcoms like *The Honeymooners* (*The Flintstones*) and *Bilko* (*Top Cat*). Even Uncle Paul Terry was lured to the small screen for, among others, *Deputy Dawg*. Vast empires of severely restricted motion conquered television with phenomenal speed – sideways on, with feet reduced to a circular blur, passing the same three items of street furniture every five seconds.

# THE BURNS AND ALLEN SHOW (1950–8)

## CBS

### Still in its infancy, the sitcom goes postmodern.

*You know, if you saw a plot like this on television you'd never believe it. But here it is happening in real life.*

George Burns

THE COMEDIAN WILL ALWAYS beat the philosopher in a race – he's the one who knows all the short cuts. In the case of post-modernism, that enigmatic doctrine of shifting symbols and author-less texts, the race was over before half the field reached the stadium.

George Burns and Gracie Allen were a dedicated vaudevillian couple. In 1929, the year before father of deconstruction Jacques Derrida was born, they were making short films that began by looking for the audience in cupboards and ended by admitting they'd run out of material too soon. While Roland Barthes was studying at the Sorbonne, Gracie Allen was enlisting the people of America to help look for her non-existent missing brother. A decade before John Cage's notorious silent composition *4'33"*, Gracie performed her *Piano Concerto for Index Finger*. And a few years after the word postmodernism first appeared in print, Burns and Allen were on America's television screens embodying it.

*The Burns and Allen Show* began on CBS four years after the BBC inaugurated the sitcom with *Pinwright's Progress*. In that time

22

very little progress had been made. Performances were live and studio-bound. Gag followed gag followed some business with a hat, and the settings were drawing rooms straight from the funny papers. Burns and Allen's set looked more like a technical cross section: the front doors of their house and that of neighbours' the Mortons led into rooms visible from outside due to gaping holes in the brickwork. The fourth wall literally broken, George (and only George) could pop through the hole at will to confer with the audience. If anyone else left via the void they were swiftly reminded to use the front door. 'You see,' George explained to the viewers, 'we've got to keep this believable.'

While Burns muttered asides from the edge of the stage, Allen stalked the set like a wide-eyed Wittgenstein, challenging anyone in her path to a fragmented war of words. From basic malapropisms to logical inversions some of the audience had to unpick on the bus going home, Gracie would innocently get everything wrong in exactly the right way. She sent her mother an empty envelope to cheer her up, on the grounds that 'no news is good news'. She engaged hapless visitors in conversation with her own, unique, logic ('Are you Mrs Burns?' 'Oh, yes. Mr Burns is much taller!'). Gracie was, admittedly, a Ditzy Woman, but this was the style in comedy at the time – Lucille Ball played a Ditzy Woman, and she co-owned the production company. Besides, Gracie's vacuity could be perversely powerful – she was frequently the only one who seemed sure of herself. In her eyes she ranked with the great women of history ('They laughed at Joan of Arc, but she went right ahead and built it!').

While Gracie defied logic, George, in his mid-fifties but already the butt of endless old man gags, defied time and space. With a word and a gesture, he could halt the action and fill the audience in on the finer points of the story while Allen and company gamely froze like statues behind him. During Burns's front-of-cloth confabs the viewer's opinion was solicited, bets on the action were taken, and backstage reality elbowed its way up front. The story's authorship was debated mid-show: 'George S. Kaufman is responsible for tonight's plot. I asked him to write it and he said no, so I had to do it.' When a new actor was cast as Harry Morton, Burns introduced him on screen to Bea Benaderet (who played his wife Blanche), pronounced them man and wife, and the show carried on as usual. On another occasion, George broached the curtain to apologetically admit that the writers simply hadn't come up with an ending for tonight's programme, so goodnight folks.

Even the obligatory 'word from the sponsor' entered the fun. The show's announcer was made a regular character: a TV announcer pathologically obsessed with Carnation Evaporated Milk, 'the milk from contented cows'. These interludes, knocked out by an ad rep but fitting snugly within the framework provided by the show's regular writers, exposed the strangeness of the integrated sponsor spot by embracing it. The show kept on top of the sponsor, and the sponsor became a star of the show – a very sophisticated symbiosis.

In October 1956, Burns gained a TV set which enabled him to watch the show – the one which, to him, was real life (the Burns and Allen played by Burns and Allen in *The Burns and Allen Show* were the stars of a show of their own, the content of which remained a mystery). He could sow mischief, retire to the set, and watch trouble unfold at his leisure. When he tired of that, he could switch channels and spy on Jack Benny. Burns's fluctuating relationship to audience and plot (of which, he said, there was more than in a variety show, but less than in a wrestling match) was a deconstructionist triumph.

Ken Dodd questioned Freud's theories of comedy, noting the great psychoanalyst 'never had to play second house at the Glasgow Empire'. Burns and Allen, graduates of vaudeville, would have agreed. The self-awareness that high art lauds as sophisticated was part of the DNA of popular entertainment from the year dot – that is, about a day after George Burns was born.

# THE ERNIE KOVACS SHOW (1952–61)
## DuMont/NBC/ABC

### TV's visual gag pioneer.

MOST MODERN COMEDIANS APPEAR on TV. Very few use it. In Britain there have been Spike Milligan, the Pythons, Kenny Everett and Chris Morris. America boasted George Burns, the *Laugh-In* crowd, David Letterman and Garry Shandling. But most of all it had the quintessential TV comedian: the cigar-sucking, second generation Hungarian Ernie Kovacs.

Like many TV comics, Kovacs began as a nonconformist local radio DJ, before becoming a continuity announcer on Pennsylvania's regional NBC affiliate station. His first on-screen stint came in 1950 as eleventh hour stand-in on cookery show *Deadline for Dinner*, where a talent for off-the-cuff wisecracks impressed management enough to give him the blank canvas of a ninety-minute morning programme. In 1950, the 7.30-to-9.00 a.m. weekday slot was uncharted terrain, so Kovacs had free rein to improvise as he wished. He goofed around to music, toyed with random props and chatted calmly to the viewers, seemingly unaware of a live panther squatting on his back. At a time when comedy was ruled by repetition and ritual, Kovacs insisted on constant innovation.

*The Ernie Kovacs Show* proper first appeared on the DuMont network, in front of an audience of 'twenty-three passing strangers'. Kovacs preferred to work without a full studio audience for one very good reason – he was determined to use the medium in every way possible, so a lot of his gags only worked on the screen. Atmosphere came from the camera crew, who could laugh (and heckle) as heartily as anyone.

He exploited the basic video effects of the day – wipes, super-impositions and picture flips – to make characters fly off screen, expose the contents of his head or superimpose it onto a small dog. He would walk off the edge of the set and give viewers an impromptu guided tour of the studio paraphernalia. With his technicians he made an inverting lens from mirrors and soup cans, built a cheap upside-down set and walked on the ceiling. Or he simply stuck a child's kaleidoscope in front of the camera, accompanied by some music. In an unexplored medium he broke ground with every step – usually accompanied by a discordant sound effect. His work is most often compared to Kenny Everett's, but he pre-empted others. His interest in the personalities of puppet animals is reminiscent of early Vic Reeves (sample stage direction: 'Trevor the stuffed deer is vacuumed – laughs.'[23])

After the DuMont network collapsed, Kovacs returned to NBC to occupy a variety of slots, culminating in his first prime-time gig, an 8 p.m. Monday night spectacular from a real theatre, with a real audience. The show also came with a real budget that Kovacs didn't hesitate to spend with alarming profligacy: huge song-and-dance numbers were choreographed, incorporating giant flights of collapsible stairs; Boris Karloff was paid top dollar to recite the alphabet. The transition from backroom 'improv' to gargantuan showcase came surprisingly easily to him.

One sketch from these shows was far ahead of its time. To the thunderous accompaniment of drum rolls and the clatter of tele-printers, Kovacs appeared as a self-important newsreader, employing primitive in-camera effects to lampoon the already excessive presentation of TV news decades before the likes of Chris Morris. One sketch, 'News Analyst', is uncannily modern in its approach:

KOVACS: Good morning. This is Leroy L. Bascombe McFinister . . .

*[Picture is wiped inward, leaving tiny vertical slit in middle through which we glimpse Ernie.]*
KOVACS: . . . with the news.
*[Wipe widens to full set.]*
KOVACS: Behind the news.
*[Picture tilts right.]*
KOVACS: News flashes and news highlights.
*[Tilts upside down.]*
KOVACS: Events of the day and events of the night.
*[Picture spins 360 degrees to left.]*
KOVACS: Brought to you . . .
*[Picture spins to right, ends upside down.]*
KOVACS: . . . as they happen . . .
*[Picture spins upright.]*
KOVACS: . . . when they happen.
*[Tilts to right, then back.]*
KOVACS: News!
*[Tilts to left, then back.]*
KOVACS: From all over!
*[Shot of spinning world globe – hand reaches in and stops globe.]*[24]

(This complex, frenetic high-tech skit was, astoundingly, performed live.) The final NBC Kovacs show climaxed with a dance number that had close to 100 people and animals on stage, ending with the destruction of the set as the credits rolled, while perspiring executives picked up the tab.

Kovacs simultaneously subbed for Steve Allen, hosting the Monday and Tuesday editions of *Tonight*. His effects-heavy fantasies didn't sit well in a show built around talk and the expense of the more elaborate gags made his tenure brief. But it did incubate two of his most famous routines: Eugene, a featherweight tenderfoot whose every action caused loud, incongruous sound effects; and the tilted room, a set built on a slant which a prism lens restored to the vertical, rendering everything from olives to milk prone to hare off in bizarre directions as the hapless Eugene looked askance.

In January 1957 Kovacs was parachuted into a prime-time slot following a much-publicised Jerry Lewis special. Spotting a potential big break, he put everything into devising a speech-free showcase of his very best material. The 'No Dialogue' show was meticulously executed, including a perfected and expanded tilted room sketch. This was crafted comedy in the fullest sense, and won plaudits galore. Another equally precise special, *Kovacs on Music*, featured the comedy debut of André Previn. Kovacs had finally made the big time, but his pinnacle was precarious. The early experimental spirit of US TV was being rapidly eroded as big money entered the equation, and ratings became the only thing that mattered.

Kovacs was obliged to switch again, to ABC, for a series of specials and a quiz show, *Take a Good Look*. The quiz show featured his most expensive gag of all – as a used car salesman slaps a car on the bonnet, it falls through a hole in the ground, creating a bill of thousands of dollars for a thirty-second quickie. The specials were recorded with a dedicated crew in marathon all-weekend studio lock-ins. Alongside familiar routines, he created elaborate and rather elegant musical ballets of office equipment and other inanimate objects. His disdain for network top brass made itself felt in satirically amended end credits.('Associate Producer (That's like STEALING money!)')

These shows won Kovacs his only Emmy, for 'outstanding achievement in electronic camerawork'. He died in a car accident shortly after recording the eighth, which was shown in tribute a fortnight later. Like the experimenters who followed him, Kovacs remained on the fringes of television, distrustful of its grandees and eager to undermine and mock them at every opportunity, finding door after door slammed in his face as a result. As a career model for fame-hungry comics, he was as lousy as they came. As a master craftsman, he was among the greatest.

# THE PHILCO-GOODYEAR TELEVISION PLAYHOUSE: MARTY (1953)

## NBC (Showcase)

### TV drama mines the mundane.

*I am just now becoming aware of this marvellous world of the ordinary. This is an age of savage introspection, and television is the dramatic medium through which to expose our new insights into ourselves.*

Paddy Chayefsky, 1956

As TELEVISION BEGAN COLONISING the lounges of urban America, Hollywood started to panic. Playing to their strengths, the big studios began turning out product that emphasised the things TV couldn't provide: colour, star power, and most of all, size. The big screen was filled with big names in big adventures; pageants, epics and melodramas in which the safety of lives, societies, even the world hung in the balance. The challenge was made: fit that lot into your ten inches of bulbous glass.

Many programmes valiantly, if foolishly, tried to compete. Wiser heads moved in the opposite direction. Paddy Chayefsky, scion of a Russian Jewish family in the Bronx, was one of the first and best writers to size up what the small screen could and couldn't show. A moderately successful playwright, he moved into television in

29

1952 when the US government lifted restrictions on new TV stations, causing audiences to rocket. As Chayefsky saw it, 'television, the scorned stepchild of drama, may well be the basic theatre of our century.'[25]

TV imitations of cinema condemned themselves to a lazy, second rate status, the lack of resources perpetually showing them up. 'You cannot handle comfortably more than four people on the screen at the same time,' he wrote. 'The efforts of enterprising directors to capture the effect of five thousand people by using ten actors are pathetic.'[26] From his very first TV efforts, Chayefsky took a clear look at how life could convincingly be crammed into that tiny box.

It was during the rehearsals for *The Reluctant Citizen*, a play about an elderly Jewish immigrant, that Chayefsky found the scenario for his greatest TV work. Due to the cost of Manhattan real estate, NBC augmented their rehearsal studios at 30 Rock with any spare bit of space going in the city. Hotel ballrooms in daylight hours were a prime source. While mooching around one of these during a break, Chayefsky's eye fell on a sign put up for a singles night: 'Girls, please dance with the man who asks you. Remember, men have feelings too.' This intimation of painful male shyness caught Chayefsky's imagination, and he soon began writing 'the most ordinary love story in the world.'[27]

Rod Steiger played the title role, a good-natured but reticent Italian-American butcher in the Bronx shamed by friends, family and customers for his enduring single status at thirty-six. ('I'm a fat, ugly little guy and the girls don't go for me, that's all.') One night he's all but forced into going to a singles dance by his domineering mother. ('Why don't you go to the Waverley Ballroom? It's loaded with tomatoes!') The evening looks like being yet another slog of rejection and heartache, until a lairy guy offers him five bucks to take 'a real dog' off his hands. Marty is disgusted by the idea, but finds the girl in question, Clara. He asks her, genuinely, for a dance and they bond over their shared misfortunes. ('You don't get to be good-hearted by accident. You gotta be kicked around long enough and hard enough, then you get to be like a real . . . a professor of pain, you know?')

The rough, natural dialogue with its repetitive, drowsy poetry was a revelation. The final scene, in which Marty finally plucks up courage to spurn his deadbeat pals, phone Clara and ask her out, was partly improvised by Steiger when the real dialogue slipped out of his head on the night. It fitted in seamlessly. His performance impressed director Elia Kazan enough to land him a part on *On the Waterfront*, and a star was born. Cinema may have had TV looking over its shoulder, but 'movie star' remained the top job.

'The basic limitation of television is time,' thought Chayefsky. 'Television cannot take a thick, fully woven fabric of drama. It can only handle simple lines of movement and consequently smaller amounts of crisis.'[28] That said, *Marty* packed a great deal into well under an hour. Its wonderfully minimal effects included an exterior shot of the ballroom made from cardboard and light bulbs. When Marty followed the distraught Clara out onto the ballroom fire escape and asked her to dance, the tender moment was undercut by some incidental laughter from elsewhere in the building. *Marty* was a basic affair, but basic didn't mean simple.

Two years later *Marty* became the first TV drama to be remade for the big screen. With Ernest Borgnine in the lead, real Bronx locations and an expansion of the 'cantankerous aunt' subplot, it was a mighty success and took several Oscars, including Best Picture and Screenplay. Chayefsky had achieved that rarest of fames: the TV writer as household name. In a Nat Hiken comedy sketch, Phil Silvers played one half of a pretentious theatregoing couple who mistake the apartment of a dysfunctional, blue collar family for an off-off-Broadway venue. As they settle on the sofa, the nonplussed residents start squabbling at top volume. Silvers knowingly remarks to his wife, 'obviously by Paddy Chayefsky'.

The TV networks moved their centres of production across country to Hollywood, and Chayefsky fell out of love with the medium he'd championed. The easy, trusting commissions he'd had in the early years gave way to the business-driven pseudo-science of corporation men, with whose ideas the writer was expected to compromise willingly. Many of Chayefsky's pitches got no further than the pilot stage, including a 1965 sitcom version of *Marty* starring Tom Bosley.

Another grounded project was *The Man Who Beat Ed Sullivan*, about a hick Ohio entertainer whose marathon variety show becomes a national sensation. (Chayefsky didn't help his case by insisting that the variety show within the play should actually be a full-on, three-hour spectacular in itself.) It wasn't until 1974 that Chayefsky arranged his televisual disaffection into a film script about a suicidal newsreader, a power-crazed producer and a corporate conspiracy: his valedictory masterpiece, the cellar-dark satire *Network*. It was a damning testimony against the medium's worst excesses by one of its pre-eminent craftsmen; television's finest humane miniaturist denouncing its increasingly inhuman gigantism. Promoting the film, Chayefsky had three sad words for his *alma mater*: 'Television? Forget it.'[29]

# SMALL TIME (1955–66)
## ITV (Associated-Rediffusion)

### Giants of children's television assemble.

CHILDREN HAVE ENJOYED A special relationship with television since the very first transmissions. The BBC gave them their own playground in the schedules with *Watch with Mother*, in 1950, where they could enjoy the company of clattering puppet mules, unintelligible folk assembled from garden implements and the very biggest spotty dog you ever did see – all chaperoned by jolly matriarchs dispensing orotund vowels through shatterproof smiles. With its sailor suits and spinning tops and crumpets on the trolley, it was childhood as the Edwardians would have recognised it: the childhood, more or less, of the programme makers, handed down like a careworn teddy bear. When ITV arrived a few years later, its TV crèche was decorated in unmistakeably bolder, more modern style.

Beginning as a fifteen minute segment in Associated-Rediffusion's weekday *Morning Magazine* line-up, *Small Time* soon gravitated towards its natural teatime home, and grew into a proving ground for a vast swathe of children's TV talent. Many of the segments – *Booty Mole, Snoozy the Sea Lion, Gorki the Straw Goat* to name a few – would live on only in a few very keen baby-boomer memories. A few, though, added up to as great a legacy as one TV slot could hope to spawn.

*The Adventures of Twizzle* starred a Pinocchio-esque boy puppet who could extend his limbs at will. The stories, from the pen of Roberta Leigh, were brought to life by puppeteer Joy Laurey, but of more historic note was the show's producer, future 'Supermarionation' chief Gerry Anderson. Another artificial lad, *Torchy the Battery Boy*, arrived a few years later courtesy of the same team. The results could only be described as 'sub-marionation': strings were thick as mooring cables, movements spasmodic. But this was the style, or lack of style, of the times. 'Production values' existed neither as jargon, nor as values. The job was done with the means to hand: nothing more and nothing less.

Puppets of the glove variety formed the second line of teatime attack. These were several degrees sprightlier, and occasionally wittier, than their dangling cohorts. Pussycat Willum, a doe-eyed kitten, became *Small Time*'s eager, if slightly mawkish, figurehead. But the strand's undoubted star turns were Ollie Beak and Fred Barker. This portly owl and calcified dish mop of a cockney dog were the creations of Peter Firmin, operated by Wally Whyton and Ivan Owen respectively. Their main human foil was Muriel Young, announcer on Rediffusion's opening night and a primly tolerant foil for the duo's impromptu shenanigans. More raucous yet were *The Three Scampis*: Bert Scampi (operator Howard Williams) and his animal pals, hedgehog Spike McPike (Wally Whyton) and aristocratic fox Basil Brush (Ivan Owen). Again, Firmin was the man behind the sewing machine.

Firmin had been introduced to television by Rediffusion's young stage manager and part-time prop maker, Oliver Postgate. In 1958 Postgate, tiring of organising other people's programmes, created one of his own. *Alexander the Mouse* was a whimsical tale of a rodent with royal aspirations, set behind the skirting board of an old house, the first of what would be a long line of wistfully remote Postgate worlds. Firmin painted the characters and sets, which were stuck to metal strips and 'animated' live on air by dragging magnets about under the table. This attempt to undercut even the ultra-cheap *Crusader Rabbit* production technique had the catch that, according to Postgate, 'hardly a programme went out without . . . a hand coming into shot or a mouse coming adrift.'[30]

Postgate's next attempt, the Willow Patterned *Journey of Master*

*Ho*, took a more conventional approach to movement. Cut-out figures were manipulated in stop motion in a makeshift studio in Postgate's North Finchley back bedroom, shot and edited on a 16mm film rig made of Meccano and string for £175 per ten minute episode. In 1959 he reunited with Firmin to create their first classic story. *Ivor the Engine* was a gloriously melancholy tale of the sole locomotive of the idyllic Merioneth and Llantisilly Rail Traction Company Limited. Firmin's watercolour evocations of the Welsh mountains were exquisite, but the tone Postgate's narration took, hitting a plaintive, nostalgic note halfway between John Betjeman and Dylan Thomas, was the greatest innovation. Moving away from the stiff-backed, once-upon-a-time scene-setting of previous children's programmes, Postgate injected poetry and personality, trusting small children to engage with something more than a bland narrative of mild peril that ended in time for supper.

As the sixties ran on, *Small Time*'s big talents slowly dispersed to the four corners of television: Anderson and company to forge a puppet dynasty, Postgate and Firmin to carve a homely niche in animation, Brush to Saturday night ubiquity, and Young to produce acres of glam rock television. The strand's last significant signing was Pippy the Tellyphant, a pantomime elephant operated by husband-and-wife team Jimmy and June Kidd, which cost an unprecedented £300 to construct. Pippy provokes few nostalgic reveries these days, while her cheaper, humbler companions, strapped for cash but bursting with ideas, have taken their place in the TV annals. The hearts and minds of millions were won over with cardboard and felt.

# THE PHIL SILVERS
# SHOW (1955–9)
## CBS

### Sitcom comes of age.

*'Andrew Armstrong, Tree Surgeon'? That's a television idea? Well,
who knows. Look what they did with a fat bus driver.*
Bilko's Television Idea, 12 February 1957

BY THE MID-1950S, SITCOM was already being dismissed by
critics as a fad on the wane. It had come a long way in the few
short years since its simple beginnings, from the down-to-Earth
compactness of *The Honeymooners* to George Burns hurdling the
fourth wall and Lucille Ball's international stardom with *I Love
Lucy*. Despite this tide of invention, or perhaps because of it, when
inspiration began to flag for so much as a season, critics sprang
up to predict the death of the American sitcom. The trouble was,
as John Crosby observed when hailing *The Phil Silvers Show*, 'every
time you start to count out situation comedy as a dead duck,
something comes along.'[31]

Master Sergeant Ernest G. Bilko was a new kind of sitcom hero,
eight times smarter than the average viewer could hope to be, and
a thousandth as honest and hardworking as they claimed to be.
Bilko's essential good nature, fatherly love of his reprobate army
platoon, and Phil Silvers' winning smile were all trotted out as
redemptive justifications for the popularity of this good-for-nothing

snake, but it was simpler than that. The double-crossing, dissembling, greedy slacker had the American dream down pat – his country was the one serving him.

Though it was, like all sitcoms, an ensemble effort, Bilko had two major creative forces. The fast-talking vaudeville comic Phil Silvers had steadily built up a solid but unspectacular profile since the war, specialising in sketches that showcased his knack for speedy patter and swift ad-libs, usually playing against a taciturn and bewildered stooge. He was paired by CBS executive Hubbell Robinson with writer Nat Hiken, who had moved from local radio comedies to TV variety sketch shows. Steeped in the desperately inventive chicanery of the Broadway milieu, especially its notoriously disingenuous press agents, Hiken saw Silvers in a similarly underhand role. After considering set-ups ranging from baseball team manager to stockbroker to Turkish bath attendant, they settled on the immortal master sergeant.[32]

Initially titled *You'll Never Get Rich* after the lyric from the song 'You're In the Army Now', Hiken's creation was to its rival sitcoms what Bilko was to his rival sergeants. Previously, one plot reversal had been considered quite enough for the average sitcom's twenty-four minutes. Hiken put in at least one more, sometimes two or three. Hitherto simple plots of swindling and misapprehension doubled and quadrupled before the viewer's eyes, finally to be snapped shut again by some spectacularly deft sewing up of strands in the closing seconds. At script meetings, Hiken had a compulsive habit of creating little origami animals as he outlined a plot.[33] Whether it was incidents at an army post or scrap paper, the skill was the same – artfully precise manipulation.

The cast ranged in experience from seasoned actor Paul Ford as Bilko's just-dumb-enough colonel, to complete non-professionals – filthy nightclub comic Joe E. Ross played childlike Mess Sergeant Rupert Ritzik, and hopeless slob Maurice Gosfield played hopeless slob Private Duane Doberman. The bulk of the lines inevitably went to Silvers, but there was a fine balance at work here: Bilko's corporals Henshaw and Barbella oscillated between willing henchmen and disapproving moralists; the excitable Private Paparelli could often out-talk his sergeant; the chorus of rival sergeants occasionally got one over on their nemesis. The scenes when Bilko and Colonel Hall were alone together remain among the best in sitcom, a perspicacious fox inexorably pulling the wool over the eyes of a sappy bloodhound.

Hiken assembled a crack team of writers around him, including a young Neil Simon, but his obsessive nature meant he could never leave a script alone, often rewriting it into a completely new show. The Writers Guild, suspicious of the prevalence of Hiken's name on the credits, tried to lobby for the other writers, only to be told by those writers that he really did have significant input to almost every programme.[34] Hiken also made regular appearances on the studio floor to fiddle with minuscule details of staging. With so much depending on one man, it was inevitable that later seasons began to slip from the early stratospheric heights.

The decline showed in the increasing use of guest stars. Where previously celebrities would be satirical inventions like inane comedian Buddy Bickford or rock 'n' roll sensation Elvin Pelvin, now the real-life likes of Ed Sullivan, Mickey Rooney and Kay Kendall would turn up. Setting the pattern for countless comedies hence, it began as a display of the show's popularity and became a sign of flagging inspiration. The quality level remained high, but the platoon's move for its final season from Fort Baxter, Kansas to the Californian heat of Camp Fremont held a sad irony.

US television's big east-to-west move would affect sitcom as much as drama. Though set in Kansas, Bilko was really a New York show, drawn from the Broadway melting pot, infused with Jewish humour and recorded at the old DuMont studios. Over the next few years sitcoms would become slower, simpler and sillier. The dialogue was less snappy and the characters less smart as network bosses sought to woo Middle America. *The Phil Silvers Show* merely opened with a cartoon; shows like *Gilligan's Island* and *Mr Ed* (the latter backed by George Burns) were cartoons themselves, often not particularly good ones. Add a plethora of

Hollywood-produced 'adult' western shows and the cosy croon of Perry Como to the evening schedules, and the televisual tide was decisively turning from Hiken's satirical high water mark. Those critical jeers began to look less precious and more prophetic with each new season. Bilko could outsmart anyone, but he couldn't cope with being out-dumbed.

# A SHOW CALLED FRED (1956)
## ITV (Associated-Rediffusion)

### Television comedy explodes.

*TV isn't like films, radio or the stage. It has bits of all three in it, of course. But it is something demanding a new approach.*
— Terry-Thomas, *Answers*, 6 October 1951

COMIC GENIUS HAS THE habit of springing up in several places at once. About the time Ernie Kovacs was conducting his early Pennsylvanian experiments, Terry-Thomas, the gentleman's gentleman comic, was regaling BBC audiences with *How Do You View?* Written by Sid Colin and Talbot Rothwell, this loose assemblage of sketches and monologues pioneered countless bits of televisual business: the deadpan nonsense interview (conducted by linkmen Leslie Mitchell and Brian Johnston); mock home movies; the constantly-interrupted speech; and the random foray off the set and around the cameras, booths and assorted detritus of the studio, just for the hell of it. Its success in those sparse early days was considerable, although critics were snooty. 'I should not care to say,' ventured a confused C. A. Lejeune, 'whether the presentation is more formless or the material more inept.'[35]

While 'T-T' was in his pomp on TV, the BBC Home Service was plagued by an infestation of nits. *The Goon Show* didn't so much break the rules of radio comedy as blithely caper on to the air in complete ignorance that any existed in the first place. With its cast of vocal grotesques and relaxed approach to the laws of cause and effect, it became an unhinged institution to a nation still recovering from the similarly lunatic privations of war. Two Goons – writer Spike Milligan and voice-of-them-all Peter Sellers – joined forces with young American director Richard Lester to translate their formula to independent television, in the form of *The Idiot Weekly, Price 2d.*

The fusty periodical of the title, inspired by the florid world of *Daily Express* humorist Beachcomber, provided an extremely tenuous jumping-off point for a bewildering array of skits, with Sellers playing Edwardian schoolmasters and gentleman boxers, 'Footo, the Wonderboot explorer' and even much-loved Goon character Bluebottle. Blackout gags included an expectant audience sat before a curtain, which was raised to reveal another audience, facing them. Singers like Patti Lewis got a custard pie in the face. This time, the critics had caught up with the viewers: even the *Daily Mail* dug this 'bubble of nonsense which stayed miles above the surface of reality.'[36]

A few months later the same gang made *A Show Called Fred*, which scrapped the magazine trappings and intensified the lunacy. As the *Daily Mail* noted, *The Idiot Weekly* 'made a few grudging concessions to the audience, in as much as it was possible to follow the jokes by the ordinary, accepted sense of humour. *Fred* makes no concessions at all.'[37]

A typical edition of *Fred* began with Spike, dressed in rags, mooching around the Associated-Rediffusion studio corridors: a parody of the Rank Films gong (which Terry-Thomas also lampooned) and credits for 'the well-known Thespian actors' Kenneth Connor and Valentine Dyall (usually clad in bow tie, dinner jacket and no shirt). There would be mock interviews with insane individuals, often called Hugh Jampton, commercials for 'Muc, the wonder deterrent', and viewer query slot 'Idiots' Postbag', presented in front of a projected backdrop of open sea, or a burning building. ('Dear sir, do you know what horse won the Derby in 1936?' 'Yes, Mr Smith, I do.')

Even by the primitive standards of the day, the thing was heroically shoddy. Backdrops wobbled and frayed at the edges, costumes
were either half-complete or non-existent, and in the frequent
pull-out shots to take in backstage crew and chunky EMI cameras,
the floor was visibly covered in studio junk. As with Kovacs's shows,
laughter came from the camera crew rather than an audience. *Fred*
ended with an extended parody of the various po-faced dramas
with which it shared the schedules. Soap opera *The Grove Family*
became 'The Lime Grove Family': 'Mum' cooked roast peacocks'
tongues on baked mangoes in the piano, whereupon 'son' hit her
with a club, and was reprimanded by 'dad', saying, 'You mustn't hit
your mother like that. You must hit her like *this* . . .' Their version
of *The Count of Monte Cristo* featured the first appearance of the
famous coconut-halves-for-horses'-hooves sight gag and ended
with the destruction of the already threadbare set, a rousing chorus
of 'Riding Along On the Crest of a Wave', and Valentine Dyall
doing the dishes in the studio's self-service canteen.

Descriptions like this are hopelessly inadequate. As Bernard
Levin put it, 'if you do not think that is funny it is either because
I have failed to convey its essence or because there is something
wrong with you.'[38] Peter Black agreed: 'This show has built up in
three weeks a following that has gone beyond enthusiasm. It is an
addiction.'[39] Critical credentials notwithstanding, these men were
television comedy's first fanboys.

When stuff like *Fred* appeared on the continent, it was Absurdist
theatre, afforded its rightful place in the cultural pantheon. Over
here it was just British rubbish. Bernard Levin tried to redress
matters, asserting that the *Fred* team 'have done television a service
comparable to that rendered by Gluck to opera, or Newton to
mathematics.'[40] Philip Purser claimed *Fred* was 'roughly equivalent
to the revolution in the theatre promoted by Bertolt Brecht; and
not entirely dissimilar.'[41] It certainly created its own version of
Brecht's Alienation Effect. 'I had to make a very real effort of will
on Wednesday,' recounted Levin of trying to watch *Gun-Law*, the
bog-standard western which followed *Fred*, 'to convince myself

that this was not meant to be funny. For a long time I could not stop expecting Mr Spike Milligan to put his mad, bearded head round the corner of the screen with some devastating remark about the shape of Sheriff Dillon's face.'[42]

Milligan's TV year ended with *Son of Fred*, available for the first time in the north, with cartoons by Bob Godfrey's Biographic Films, mocked up technical breakdowns and Gilbert Harding's Uncle Cuthbert playing the contra-bassoon while suspended from wires in a wheelchair. ('Kind of an aerial fairy,' he explained.) It also inaugurated the grand tradition of putting jokes in the *TV Times* listings. ('Frisby Spoon appears without permission.') In 1963 a compilation, *The Best of Fred*, was presented to a public that, claimed ITV, had now 'caught up' with Milligan's anarchic humour, with Milligan and Dyall reminiscing over the show's distant heyday in between clips. Innovation had become nostalgia.

Lester would go on to give the Beatles silly things to do on film. Milligan inaugurated the *Q* series in 1969, which took his illogical methods down increasingly strange paths. Meanwhile his former co-Goon Michael Bentine cooked up a more technically elaborate version of the same mayhem for the BBC's *It's a Square World*. But *Fred*'s place in history would be secured by countless other hands. All around the country, short-trousered future members of *Python, The Goodies* and other anarcho-comic collectives were watching closely and making mental notes. As Peter Cook would later note, Milligan 'opened the gate into the field where we now all frolic.'[43]

# MY WILDEST DREAM (1956–7)
## ITV (Granada)

### The comedy panel show outstays its welcome

*A panel of celebrities, of one kind or another, are asked in turn to identify somebody they have met in the past. One of the particular eccentricities of television was shown up in this programme – the choosing of a 'celebrity' for the panel with no qualification or aptitude.*

Review of *Place the Face*,
*Manchester Guardian*, 9 July 1957

THE PANEL SHOW WAS a mainstay of television right from the beginning, for reasons both cultural and commercial. The cultural: since the nineteenth century the parlour game, a relaxed after-dinner orgy of banter and one-upmanship, was the icing on the middle class party cake, a civilised letting-down of the hair. The commercial: it's cheap. It's wit without a script, drama without a set, sport kept safely indoors. A prestigious panel show will have the country's greatest two-dozen raconteurs fighting to appear on it. For a less prestigious one, a hundred dim bulbs will tear each other to pieces. Get the initial ingredients right, and it keeps itself afloat with minimal effort – it's the perpetual motion format.

The cosy, chatty panel game established itself as a national comfort blanket on radio during the war. The BBC Home Service's

*Brains Trust*, in which clubbable eggheads like Kenneth Clark and Jacob Bronowski debated esoteric enquiries sent in by the public, reached nearly a third of Britons and made highbrows into stars. At the same time, the ease of it all bred suspicion. In 1942, questions were asked in the Commons on whether the *Trust* participants' fees of £20 per session 'for attempting to answer very simple questions' was public money for old rope.[44] It was certainly valuable old rope: in 1954, *One Minute Please*, predecessor to the long-running *Just a Minute*, became the first BBC panel format sold to the USA when Dumont bought the TV rights for $104,000.[45]

On television, two shows dominated. Vocational guessing game *What's My Line?* began on CBS in 1950 and hit the BBC the following year, augmenting the elitist 'wits' enclave' with a celebration of honest (but preferably amusingly odd) everyday work. In 1956 Princess Margaret attended an edition, watching from a special 'royal box' rigged up in the stalls. Then there was the loftier *Animal, Vegetable, Mineral?* This was an archaeological quiz that challenged academics to identify cuttlefish beaks and Tibetan prayer wheels, employed a young David Attenborough on its production team and invited viewers 'to follow the fluctuating course of the contest as the experts grope towards the right solution, and perhaps enjoy a nice cosy feeling of superiority meanwhile.'[46]

Its star turn was archaeologist Sir Mortimer Wheeler, whose powers of observational deduction were second to none, though this wasn't what made him such a draw. With a florid, expressive face, aided by an atavistic moustache made for twirling, he'd frown intensely at a flint axe or quern – hum, ha, squint, peer – then, in a cartoonish light bulb moment, all but leap in the air as the penny dropped. This showmanship was aided by the custom of lunching the panel, together with chairman Glyn Daniel, at a Kensington restaurant prior to live transmission. Occasionally, the team lunched too well: Daniel on one occasion lost complete track of the scores, decided nobody really cared anyway, and later, staring down the camera lens, used one of the objects – an Aboriginal charm – to put a hex on 'the viewer who sent me a very silly letter.'[47]

This element of risk cast a long shadow over the format's early days. Panel regular Gilbert Harding built a reputation for rudeness that frequently tipped over into outright disdain, such as his notorious claim to a *What's My Line?* contestant that 'I'm tired of looking at you.' In 1954 the BBC, in a fit of panel game mania, commissioned several shows based on viewers' ideas. Results included *Change Partners*, in which the panel had to sort eight married challengers into their constituent couples, working out who was shacking up with whom by asking them to recall marriage proposals, ruffle each others' hair in an affectionate manner, etc. A year later they apologetically axed all their panel shows, except *What's My Line?* [48]

ITV rushed in where the Beeb now feared to tread. In 1956 Granada converted an old BBC radio format into a prospective early evening panel hit. The panel took its cue from *Does the Team Think?*, Jimmy Edwards's pastiche of *The Brains Trust*, which consisted of four comedians battling to out-gag and upstage each other. For *My Wildest Dream* the urbane Terry-Thomas led the panel, with his three 'dreaming partners' Tommy Trinder, David Nixon and Alfred Marks. Acting as 'peacemaker' was Kenneth MacLeod. It's worth taking a close look at this particular programme, which handily features all the symptoms of lazy thinking, over-egged whimsy and misplaced trust in star power that marked out the format at its worst.

The panel's objective was to determine, by diligent questioning, the secret fantasies of the humble folk wheeled before them. Inevitably, since most people's fantasies tended towards the predictable ('win the pools', 'go out with Marilyn Monroe'), a bit of creative bending of the rules crept in. Hence a woman appeared claiming she wanted more than anything to put a mouse in a guardsman's boot, while another contestant longed to tickle a point duty policeman under the arms. Such bewildering dollops of 'unbelievably fatuous' [49] whimsy would, the producers hoped, be spun into comedy gold by the dreaming partners.

This turned out to be optimistic. What happened was that four comic minds, all too aware of the humourlessness of the situation, trod water ever more frantically until panic set in. One reviewer captured the mood of an early edition. 'Last night there were intolerable bouts of shouting by all four of the panel and the chairman, and one at least of the challengers was made the butt of what could hardly be called humour. It did remain a little doubtful whether some of the quarrelling was genuine or faked because it seems to come to a peak each time before a break for advertisement.'[50] Shouting, bullying, artifice: these vices would prove hard to suppress. *My Wildest Dream* was 'not merely negatively silly but is positively revolting.'[51] It started to appear later and later in the evening schedule, and the panel calmed down a bit, but the brickbats continued to the bitter end. ('The most actively unpleasant panel show in commercial television.'[52])

A second wave of panel shows in the seventies was more self-consciously refined. BBC2 games like *Face the Music* and *Call My Bluff* were all drawing room erudition and cravatted anecdote. Once again many entries were wireless in origin (in this case Radio 4), but the TV transfer brought certain behavioural tics to the fore. 'On *Face the Music*,' noted Clive James, 'Bernard Levin takes a sip of water after getting the right answer. It is meant to look humble but screams conceit.'[53] This extra level of gamesmanship was often in danger of edging the nominal subject of the programme out of the frame entirely.

The third wave began in the nineties with *Have I Got News for You* and its many derivatives, and this time it stuck. A few years' craze became several decades' industry. Where once strutted eccentrics who'd fallen into the role (Gilbert Harding, Nancy Spain, Lady Isobel Barnett), 'panel show contestant' was now a fully furnished vocation for comedians with the right voice, cultural references and agent representation. Precious little else had changed, though. In 2014, BBC Director of Television Danny Cohen tried to redress the archaic gender balance of the genre by outlawing all-male editions. Bow ties became polo shirts, but the panel show remained essentially a gentlemen's club.

# OPPORTUNITY KNOCKS (1956–78)

## ITV (Associated-Rediffusion/ ABC/Thames)

### The talent show girdles the globe.

THE HARD-BITTEN, SELF-MOTIVATING MEN and women who work the reality talent contests would have no need of anything as mimsy as a patron saint, but come the Judgement Day Live Final they'd be granted the protective arm-round-the-shoulder, whether they wanted it or not, of Hughie Green.

A juvenile song-and-dance man turned compère, stunt pilot and international aerospace hardware salesman, Green created radio talent show *Opportunity Knocks* in 1949 for the BBC Light Programme, though its brash tone proved too gamey for Broadcasting House. Sensing foul play in the cancellation, Green expensively sued the BBC, lost, and took the format to Radio Luxembourg for a two-and-a-half-year stint, before presenting a TV version to Associated-Rediffusion, where he presented a trial run in the summer of 1956, during which time he was declared bankrupt. The motley assortment of talent he initially offered was summed up by Bernard Levin: 'Nobody on the edition I saw actually made a model of Wembley Stadium out of butter, but there was a man who spent his entire time hopping.'[54]

The following January, at the height of its Reithian pomp, the BBC broadcast *It's Up To You*, a fortnightly talent parade from their northern studio. A panel of judges poured praise and scorn on a line-up of eccentric amateurs including, in the first edition, a man from St Helens who tied his braces round his neck and sported a lemon in his left ear, leaving the panel bewildered. 'The thing I found distracting about this man,' complained one judge, 'was the lemon in his ear.'[55]

Over on the commercial channel, Hughie was permitted to take show business as seriously as he liked. His contestants were no half-daft party tricks but honest folk with an honest hunger for fame and, on occasion, the talent to honestly acquire it. Success was determined by a postal vote, with a touch of immediacy provided by the mysterious 'clapometer', which purported to measure the level of the studio audience's applause. Green's default mode of address was a transatlantic unction so treacly its hapless recipients found themselves bogged down to the point of immobility. As one critic remarked, the effect of the Green charm offensive was to leave 'you feeling – for all the smooth assurances that we were watching new talent get its biggest break – that it was the impresario we were expected to admire'.[56] The pattern was set for *New Faces* and its twenty-first century descendants. Many contestants went on to carve decent careers for themselves (Les Dawson, Pam Ayers, Paul Daniels, Su Pollard, Lena Zavaroni and Freddie Starr among them) but the acts were increasingly a means to an end – that end being the furthering of the talent show brand and those behind it.

A man of colossal ambition, Green found national dominance unsatisfactory. In 1970, after two successful international editions of the show with Norway, Sweden and Denmark joining the UK via crackly satellite feeds, he announced his determination to tackle 'probably the biggest challenge television light entertainment has had to face': the creation of a global TV talent show. 'A communication satellite would mother a world star,' he predicted, biblically. On New Year's Eve 1973 he hosted the *Opportunity Knocks Concorde Special* from the flight deck of the supersonic craft as it zipped over the Bay of Biscay, though the acts themselves were, disappointingly, located in the usual studio.

The following year megalomania set in for keeps, as Green commandeered his own show to deliver an unbalanced anti-union rant, pushing the boundaries of celebrity privilege out of sight. It was only natural that Hughie's global stardom should peak with 'a 13,500 mile link-up via the Indian ocean satellite'[57] as OppKnox HQ, London joined its newly-created sister franchise at the Channel 7 studios in Sydney, and Hughie's Aussie counterpart Johnnie Farnham (like Hughie, a former cabaret man with national smash hit 'Sadie the Cleaning Lady' under his belt).

With a studio complete with audience and full orchestra apiece, Hughie and Johnnie batted the banter back and forth across the heavenly void, with plenty of well-wrangled applause to cover the time delay. Five previously successful contestants from each country, including Pam Ayers and Frank Carson for the Brits, competed for the special Satellite Trophy. A brave new world beckoned, a globe unified in the name of talent. Nation shall mark spinning plates out of ten unto nation.

Within two years, all the gimmicks used up, *Opportunity Knocks* came to an end. (A BBC revival in the late '80s featured Bob Monkhouse as compère and introduced the telephone voting system.) Green didn't stay down for long, though. He returned in 1980 as 'adviser' to London Independent Television, one of the many consortia tendering bids for the 1982 ITV regional franchise renewal. LIT's typically immodest bid – it was planning to replace both Thames and London Weekend – included *Crossroads* five days a week, a breakfast programme, *Good Morning London*, and a familiar-sounding entertainment programme called *Talent Scouts*, identity of host to be confirmed. Today's TV talent magnates, powerful as they are, remain little more than tribute acts to the great Hughie.

# THE SINGING RINGING TREE (1957)

## BBC1 (DEFA)

### The garish Euro-fable that haunted a generation.

CHILDREN'S ENTERTAINMENT CARRIES TWO schools of thought. The first, which dominates thinking in Britain and the United States, exalts the carefree state of childhood above all else. Fun, jokes, songs and slapstick are the order of the day – kids will have enough time to learn the dry reality of life when they grow up. Let's name this school after one of its early popular manifestations, a manically droll panto caper initiated by the BBC in 1955: the School of *Crackerjack*. Its opposite number takes the view that life can be harsh, and children need to be prepared for that. Fantasy is good, but always tinged with a melancholy, even morbid, edge. This school was represented in Britain by Oliver Postgate's thoughtful stop motion tales, but was mainly prevalent in Europe, especially the part near the Iron Curtain: the *Singing Ringing Tree* Movement.

*Das Singende Klingende Bäumchen* was a film made by DEFA, the state film studio of the German Democratic Republic in Potsdam, a loose adaptation of the Brothers Grimm fairy tale *The Singing Springing Lark*, packed with spoilt princesses, dashing princes, evil dwarves and supernatural inter-species transformations. Appropriately enough, it looked like nothing on Earth. Magical forests were rendered in those am-dram materials, papier mâché and plywood. Rustic architecture bulged, twisted and kinked as if grown from seed, and floral forms rippled with a coating of fresh porridge. Lawns had the feel of a grocer's window display, flames were unapologetically papery and those distant hills it took the prince three days on horseback to reach were nevertheless eclipsed by his shadow – or rather one of his four shadows. Then there was the musical score, which began in syrupy orchestral mode but soon veered off into grating organ leitmotifs that would have had members of Throbbing Gristle asking for the night light to be left on.

Even if they couldn't put it into words, kids could sense the wrongness of this world. For many, it added to the appeal, the laissez-faire approach to storytelling mimicking their own, ever-changing, playground adventures. For others, the claustrophobic kingdom, rendered in a queasy palate of jade greens, sunburst yellows and atomic puce gave the nightmare fable a feverish sheen as enervating as it was compelling. But whether you willingly dived into this bumper colouring book, or warily regarded it through a glass of Lucozade darkly, you were, in the old-fashioned, malevolent sense of the word, enchanted.

Despite jeers from the state's Marxist-Leninist film critics, who deplored its 'positive depiction of a reactionary society', it became one of DEFA's biggest successes in its native country. It would have stayed there if it hadn't been for the BBC's progressive yet cash-strapped children's department, recently rechristened 'family programming' and which by 1964 was scouring the continent for schedule fillers more affordable than the USA's premium product. Heavily subsidised and going for a song, *The Singing Ringing Tree* fitted the bill perfectly. Peggy Miller sliced it into three twenty-minute segments with an overdubbed storybook narration read by *Late Night Line-Up* presenter Tony Bilbow, whose measured tones faded in and out over the forthright declamation of the German actors, a reassuring presence in a world of antlered horses and giant ice-bound goldfish.

While other imports had their fans, like the cheery *Heidi* and wistful *The Boy Who Loved Horses*, nothing came close to *The Singing*

*Ringing Tree*'s high contrast discomfiture. It returned to the BBC every couple of years under the tenure of children's department head Monica Sims, who consulted child psychologists to help determine the limits of child-frightening television. She concluded that 'sometimes quite frightening experiences in fantasy programmes are far enough divorced from their own surroundings not to frighten them too badly . . . they get a frisson from it, but they know it isn't actually happening here.'[58] The Ruritanian cake-in-the-rain trappings of *The Singing Ringing Tree* certainly passed the anti-realism test, and the three-part wonder remained a fixture until 1980.

Along the way, it picked up many companions. From Yugoslavia came equine romance *White Horses*, with a Jackie Lee theme song that made the top ten. France provided the more boyish contingent with overcast swashbuckler *The Flashing Blade*. Some series played up to national stereotype: West Germany's *The Legends of Tim Tyler* was a mordant modern fable about a boy who traded his laugh with a sinister millionaire, while the Dutch *Children of Totem Town* concerned an experimental hippie commune for kids. Towards the end, they were just insane, like Spain's *Oscar, Kina and the Laser*, in which a boy genius invents a talking laser, then flees with it and his pet goose in tow. But perhaps the most potent was Czechoslovakian parable *The Secret of Steel City*, a tale of two rival kingdoms, one democratic and peaceful, the other totalitarian, heavily industrialised in High Victorian manner, and preparing a super freeze weapon to conquer their neighbours. Even its knee-high audience could see through the feathered hats and Jules Verne steamship paraphernalia to the Cold War allegory beneath. The garnish of fantasy could let you slip subversive education to the kids, as well as scare them witless.

# SIX-FIVE SPECIAL
# (1957–8)
## BBC

TV's first rock 'n' roll smash hit.

*I knew we were in for some laughs when, at our first recording session, we were instructed to play out of tune because, in the words of Mr Good, 'it doesn't sound fascist enough'.*
Benny Green recalls his tenure in Lord Rockingham's XI,
*Daily Mirror,* 27 January 1979

HERE'S AN INSTRUCTIVE EPISODE in the history of media hiring practice. Back in the mid-1950s when he undertook the BBC training course for junior producers, Jack Good made a bizarre mock advertisement as his graduation piece: a promotional spot for luxury coffins, which featured boxer Freddie Mills throwing Chelsea pensioners off the cliffs at Beachy Head.

Anyone exhibiting such jubilant bad taste these days (and allowing for the moral inflation of the last sixty years, its contemporary equivalent would have to be quite something) would be shown the door by the men from compliance. Instead, Good was given a free pass to create a sizeable chunk of youth TV, in the same casual manner. 'These fat guys at the BBC said, "You look like a young chap, put something together with mountain climbing, fashion for girls, that sort of thing,"' Good recalled. 'I thought, I'll put rock 'n' roll on.'[59]

The *Six-Five Special*'s arrival was fortuitously timed. Not only did it coincide with Bill Haley's first, epochal tour of the UK, it got first dibs on the brand new teatime slot. The 6-7 p.m. hour was previously a televisual dead zone by government decree, to allow parents to get younger children to bed, and older ones to do their homework. Into this oasis of orderly sobriety, Good brought unbridled anarchy.

'This is basically a programme for young people,' admitted the *Radio Times*, 'but the term is relative. Rock 'n' rolling grandmothers and washboard-playing grandfathers are welcome aboard the "*Special*".'[60] The Beeb intended rock 'n' roll to be just one element of a varied magazine programme featuring sports coverage and other healthy outdoor activities, but Good knew the kids just wanted music.

For the first edition, conventional sets were built in Hammersmith's Riverside Studios. Shortly before the live transmission, Good had the sets dismantled, leaving a bare studio in which guest stars, house band The Frantic Five and presenters Josephine Douglas and Pete Murray mingled informally with the audience of jiving teenagers. ('A hundred cats are jumping here!') The cameras lingered on the exuberant dancers as much as on the acts, and prizes were offered to couples who 'cut the cutest capers'.

Square folks were aghast. 'I feel thoroughly disgusted that the powers-that-be give time to exhibitions such as this. I cannot imagine that any decent-minded girl would permit herself to be pulled around in such a way, even to the extent of allowing herself to be thrown at times over the shoulders of the males taking part,' fumed an outraged citizen of Penarth.[61] Success was assured.

Early editions established the format, with Tommy Steele a regular draw. Ten shows in, shaggy-haired, surly 'Six-Five Specialist' Jim Dale arrived, graduating from warm-up man to main attraction. Uneasy with what he saw as the forced adulation the audience lavished upon him, he adopted a serious, unsmiling countenance as a defence mechanism. The twelve-million-strong audience, seeing their own youthful sullenness transformed by the cameras into cool belligerence, adored him even more, and television began following the movies in turning previously mortifying awkwardness into an alluring detachment.

Good soon became restless, feeling restricted by the 'jolly, hearty' element imposed on his programme (Freddie Mills's 'healthy activity' spot was fine, but ramrod-backed guests such as Regimental Sergeant-Major Ron 'Tibby' Brittain quashed the groovy mood somewhat). The nugatory wage the BBC paid him didn't help matters either. He upped sticks in 1958 for the more indulgent, independent pastures of ABC, the weekend-only independent broadcaster for the midlands and the north. 'I want to bring a breath of excitement to television,' he claimed in the publicity for *Oh Boy!*, 'the fastest, most exciting show to hit TV' which launched directly opposite the *Special* in June of that year.

Escaping the Beeb's square tendency, Good made *Oh Boy!* about the music only – up to eighteen numbers in forty minutes with minimal fluff in between, accompanied by a wilder house band, Lord Rockingham's XI. Thirteen weeks in, it was netting five million viewers, helped by hot footage of Cliff Richard that was condemned in the press. 'His violent hip-swinging during an obvious attempt to copy Elvis Presley was revolting – hardly the kind of performance any parent could wish their children to witness,' raged, of all institutions, the *NME*. 'Remember, Tommy Steele became Britain's teenage idol without resorting to this form of indecency.'[62]

Most of *Oh Boy!*'s viewers were poached from *Six-Five*. Good played up the inter-channel rivalry wherever he could, issuing dire warnings of industrial espionage: 'Remember that spies are every-where – ours as well as theirs – and a source of leakage will not remain hidden for long.'[63] The *Special* rattled on without Good on the footplate, but the strain was beginning to show. A hasty September revamp went for all-out, show-stopping gigantism. A lavish new set – 'the biggest in European TV' – was built. Three new house bands were hired. Six female hosts – the '*Six-Five* Dates' – shared presentation duties. Rock and skiffle were jettisoned in favour of beat music. It was all to no avail, and the *Special*'s journey ended on relatively desultory ratings of four and a half million.

Good's innovations continued on the other side with *Boy Meets Girls*, featuring Marty Wilde and the sixteen Vernons Girls in a setting Good promised was 'less frantic and less noisy than *Oh Boy!*' The show's main historical claim was the British debut of Gene Vincent, in a career doldrums after 'Be-Bop-A-Lula', whom Good remodelled in a leather-and-medallion rebel biker image, even, according to legend, egging him on to accentuate his motor-bike injury with the off-stage exhortation, 'Limp, you bugger, limp!'

When he tired of that, he went off in the opposite direction with *Wham!*, introducing 'The Fat Noise', a gargantuan house band which produced 'the fattest, roundest sound that has ever come to television.' But nothing was working, and Good departed for the USA, to finally hit real paydirt at the ABC network with *Shindig!* and set The Monkees on their path to self-destruction with the chaotic TV special *33 1/3 Revolutions Per Monkee*.

Good returned to the UK sporadically throughout the next few decades, engineering various *Oh Boy!* revivals to put a spring in the step of middle-aged Teds, but he became increasingly estranged from contemporary pop with every slight return. Finally, in 1992, Jack Good left the music television business he'd been instrumental in creating, in as unexpected a way as he'd entered it – he joined a Carmelite hermitage in Texas.

# THE STRANGE WORLD OF GURNEY SLADE (1960)

## ITV (ATV)

### The sitcom eats itself.

*Who and what is Anthony Newley? . . . This brown-haired, blue-eyed searcher after truth hovers and flits in and around and above the world of show business like a creative helicopter.*
*Radio Times*, 9 November 1961

THOUGH IT STILL HANDLED rock 'n' roll with all the aplomb of Stan Laurel taming a cobra, television did as much as cinema and radio combined to bring big, brash all-round American entertainment to the chilly front rooms of ration-squeezed Britain. The size, confidence and polish of those variety showcases were swiftly imitated by home-grown entertainers who got their suits reupholstered, their smiles re-pointed and their accents suspended somewhere between New England and the Old Kent Road. The alien sheen of these imitation Yanks – the brittle charm of Brucie, the oily palms of Michael Miles, the messianic humility of Hughie Green – caused amusement and unease among viewers accustomed to the polite cough and the if-you-please of English stage tradition.

Comic and singer Anthony Newley, from out of the Hackney Marshes via the Italia Conti stage school, acknowledged the incongruity of the transatlantic manner. He developed a penchant for running a self-deprecating commentary on his own act. On a UK tour to promote his film *Idol on Parade*, he stood by the screen as the opening credits rolled, talking them down, one by one. ('"Directed?" The director couldn't direct traffic! "Photographed by?" He nipped out to Boots the chemist . . .'[64]) Television, the most self-referential medium yet hatched, snapped him up.

Newley's TV accomplices were writers Sid Green and Dick Hills, who had constructed specials for Sid James, Roy Castle and, disastrously, Eamonn Andrews. Initially billing themselves as the grand 'SC Green and RM Hills', they soon relaxed into 'Sid and Dick', names more appropriate to their modern, laid-back writing style. 'They admit cheerfully that they belong with the coffee shop and back-of-the-envelope script writers,' reported the *Mail*, 'rather than the agonised pacers around kidney-shaped desks in grey flanelled rooms.'[65]

Newley's attitude to comedy writing was similarly easygoing. 'How do I define humour?' he pondered at the behest of the *TV Times*. 'I don't. I wouldn't dare.'[66] After two reasonably successful *Saturday Spectaculars* for Lew Grade's ATV in early 1960 – one featuring copious amounts of Peter Sellers – Newley, Hills and Green tackled the still maturing world of the sitcom, applying their skills in the same sideways-on manner. Given carte blanche to fill six half-hours how they fancied, they wrote, designed and shot the whole series in seven weeks. Newley was keen to point up the trio's ground-breaking intent. 'We hope to achieve humour without setting out to be deliberately funny.'[67]

An estimated twelve million viewers settled down at 8.35 p.m. on 22 October for the first episode of *The Strange World of Gurney Slade*. What they saw went roughly like this. We open on the front room of a terraced house, wherein Gurney Slade (Newley) is an unwilling participant in a *Grove Family*-style domestic soap with the feeblest acting and script known to man, all hurriedly-discharged paragraphs of backstory and leaden lines of chirpy banter. When the cue finally arrives for him to speak ('Will you have an egg, Albert?') he silently gets up, puts on his coat, moodily strutting past the floor manager and off the set, leaving the other actors mugging desperately. There's even a cartoon sound effect as he smashes through the fourth wall.

The liberated Gurney wanders the streets aimlessly for the next twenty minutes. He despairs of the state of the medium. ('"How'd you like your egg done, dear?" The Golden Years of British Entertainment! So much for Shakespeare and Sophocles.') He reads minds. He chats to animals and the inanimate. He has conversations in invented languages. ('Flangewick?' 'Clittervice!' 'Hendalcraw!' 'Mandelso!') He frolics in the park with Una Stubbs and unsuccessfully tries to dump a vacuum cleaner. Finally, wearying of his constant presence on the television screen ('I'm like a gold-fish in a bowl. I'm a poor squirming squingle under a microscope!') he begs the viewer to switch off the set and put him out of his misery.

The next few episodes were variations on the theme. Episode two in particular was a delightful romantic fantasy set on a disused airfield. Unfortunately it played out in front of an audience a good four million smaller than the opening show. ITV had a flop on their hands. Critics and punters, confused and bothered by this sullying of honest Saturday night fun with existential folderol, jeered as it all came crashing down. As one wag had it, 'Is your Gurney really necessary?'[68] Subsequent episodes were relegated to the depths of the night, where they could do less damage.

This turned out to be good timing, as things promptly became even stranger. Filmed well before the ratings nosedive, episode four swapped the bucolic exterior wanderings for the black-walled studio limbo of the avant-garde, presenting the trial of Gurney, before a Lewis Carroll kangaroo court, on the charge of having no sense of humour. ('I did a television show recently and they didn't think it was very funny.')

The fitful attempts of Gurney to win over the hostile opinions of the eternally perplexed Average-Viewer family, a jury of cloth-capped everymen and a dead-eyed manufacturer of countersunk screws, went about as well as the real world defence of the series. 'We have so much confidence in this progressive type of humour,' insisted ATV, 'that we are negotiating with Anthony Newley for another series in the new year. But not,' they judiciously added, 'necessarily *Gurney Slade*.'[69]

The sixth and final episode was further out still, being a formal deconstruction of the sitcom years before the concept made its academic debut. First a party of bowler-hatted bigwigs are shown the elements of a TV production, from cameras and microphones to The Performer ('it goes through various motions which are calculated to entertain or amuse the viewers'). Then assorted incidental characters from previous episodes reappear, and round on Gurney for giving them inadequately detailed backgrounds, leaving them in a hazily-defined state of limbo after their moment on screen. Finally Anthony Newley appears as Anthony Newley, Gurney Slade grotesquely turns into a ventriloquist's doll of himself, and Newley carries him off into the night.

At this point, the television sitcom was all of thirteen years old. When it was three, George Burns had given it the gift of self-consciousness. As it hit its teenage years, Newley granted it self-destruction. At the time it looked like just another odd little failed experiment; unlike *A Show Called Fred*, *Gurney Slade* had no Bernard Levin, no intellectual cheerleader, to trumpet its glory from the rooftops. It didn't entirely lack a legacy, though: young Newley fan David Bowie was transfixed by the programme, and started swanning about the streets of Bromley in a Gurney-esque off-white mackintosh.[70]

Green and Hills moved into firmer show business territory, helping to resurrect the television fortunes of floundering double act Morecambe and Wise. Newley carried on his own meandering course, majoring in high concept musicals, but returning to television to guest on everything from the Miss World pageant to *The Smothers Brothers Comedy Hour*. His later opinion of *Gurney Slade* was typically equivocal. 'I think it proved something,' he concluded, 'even if I'm not sure what.'[71]

# ARMCHAIR THEATRE: A NIGHT OUT (1960)

## ITV (ABC)

The theatrical revolution reaches the front room.

*I've read your bloody play and I haven't had a wink of sleep for four nights. Well, I suppose we'd better do it.*

Peter Willes commissions
Harold Pinter's *The Birthday Party*
for Associated-Rediffusion, 1959[72]

LEGEND HAS IT THAT John Osborne's *Look Back in Anger* transformed British theatre overnight from a staid world of French window farces and solemn verse epics into a fiercely committed force for social change. It didn't quite do that, but it did perform one useful service: getting the under-thirties into the stalls. This demographic shift was helped by the transmission of one of the play's cleaner passages as a BBC television 'Theatre Flash', alerting the chattering youth to the presence of something other than genteel matinees for scone-munching Aunt Ednas. A long and fruitful alliance between TV and the modern stage was born.

Another TV beneficiary was *The Birthday Party*, a drama of nameless persecution in a south coast bed and breakfast, written by jobbing actor Harold Pinter during a 1957 tour of *Doctor in the House*. Disastrous notices on its London debut threatened it with early closure until the *Sunday Times* praised it to the skies, but it took a production directed by Joan Kemp-Welch on peak-time ITV for it to reach ten million viewers. Many viewers took against its obscurity ('We are still wondering what it was all about and why we didn't switch it off').[73] Others had their eyes opened to 'a Picasso in words', something new and wonderfully different from the usual tea-table crosstalk. While many found it disturbing, one viewer reported 'loving every word . . . of the author's uproarious nonsense'.[74] After transmission, the ever-helpful press department of the Tyne-Tees region became so overwhelmed by inquiries it issued a fact-sheet offering a 'reason-able and interesting interpretation' of the play. Existential drama had joined the mainstream.

ITV's main dramatic showcase at the time was *Armchair Theatre*. Initially a ragbag of classics and light comedies, it was remoulded by incoming Canadian producer Sydney Newman in 1958 to reflect the new theatrical mood of contemporary social engage-ment. (Newman's archetypal idea of an armchair play involved a small-time grocer threatened by a new supermarket.)[75] Many new writing talents would be discovered or nurtured by Newman, and Pinter joined their ranks on 24 April 1960 with his first original television work, *A Night Out*.

The nocturnal jaunt is made by diffident office worker Albert Stokes (Tom Bell) escaping from the home of his pathetically possessive widowed mother. The works do he attends ends in disaster when he's mischievously accused of groping a secretary. He flees, ending up in a deeply uncomfortable encounter with a hooker (Pinter's then wife, Vivien Merchant), who affects a cartoon poshness. ('You've not got any cigarettes on you? I'm very fond of a smoke. After dinner with a glass of wine. Or *before* dinner . . . with sherry.') They almost start to bond over their shared tragic isolation, but when she asks him too many questions, in a manner too like his own mum, Stokes spectacularly falls apart. With nothing in his social armoury between taciturn gaucheness and inarticulate rage, Stokes proves himself completely incapable of starting a life outside the suffocating maternal evenings of gin rummy and shepherd's pie: not so much Angry Young Man as Awkward Old Boy. Osborne's threatened men ranted with theatrical garrulousness. More appropriately for the small screen, Pinter's Stokes agonises in silent close-up.

The mysterious, spectral characters that were Pinter's trademark were perhaps unsuited to *Armchair Theatre*'s bread-'n'-scrape naturalism. (Stokes certainly shows none of the buried redeeming features a social realist anti-hero usually possesses.) But his sheepishly combative dialogue fitted perfectly with Newman's mission statement, sketching a repressed lower-middle-class claustrophobia heightened by director Philip Saville's endlessly burrowing cameras. For extra realism, the coffee stall where Stokes meets his workmates was John Johnson's famous all-night concession, normally found outside the Old Vic but shifted to the studio for the occasion.[76]

Though it wasn't Pinter's greatest work, *A Night Out* was a solid hit, reaching 6.38 million. Three days after it aired, Pinter joined the theatrical aristocracy as *The Caretaker* opened to prodigious acclaim, but he calculated that the play would have to run at the Duchess Theatre until 1990 to get the exposure *A Night Out* caught in one go.[77] As well as plays, Pinter's subsequent TV work spanned everything from *The Dick Emery Show* to *Pinter People*, a collection of sketches animated by *Sesame Street* alumnus Gerald Potterton. This was for the psychedelic series *NBC Experiment in Television*, which gave US network time over to the imaginations of everyone from Tom Stoppard to Jim Henson.

By the end of 1960 the all-purpose avant-garde TV play had become such a part of the broadcasting landscape it was ripe for parody. The writer hero of Joan Morgan's *Square Dance* toiled away at a modishly obscure drama called *Ending's No End*, featuring a Greek chorus of Teddy boys and the cast turning radioactive in the final act.[78] The joke relied on every viewer having at one time switched off something by Pinter or his contemporaries in confusion and disgust. What it ignored was the significant portion who kept watching.

# HANCOCK: THE BEDSITTER (1961)
## BBC

One man, one room, twenty-five minutes – comedy stripped bare.

COMEDY HAS TWO POLES: far-out fantasy and close-up reality. Both have their problems and rewards, but only one almost guarantees critical esteem by its mere presence. Possibly because of its superficial kinship with drama, the realistic sitcom is often regarded as the superior comic format. No-one became more thoroughly wrapped up in this dogma than Tony Hancock.

On the radio, *Hancock's Half-Hour* distinguished itself by playing to Hancock's strengths as a reactive, deadpan performer, as opposed to the standard issue, wisecracking clown. Writers Ray Galton and Alan Simpson gradually moulded the programme to fit Hancock's sullen, defeated spirit, relying less on cohort Sid James's zany schemes and more on the mundane frustrations of real life. The less Hancock did, the funnier he got. The radio show's zenith was the episode *Sunday Afternoon at Home*: the dreariness of a wet, post-war Sabbath distilled into a litany of bored sighs, circular conversations and desperate inanities. The farce of a life going off the rails was replaced by the tragicomedy of a life waiting to start.

Hancock's television life was equally motionless. Ray Galton admitted the only concession they made to the visual was that 'instead of saying "pick up that bucket", we'd say "pick that up".'[79] What was new was Hancock's face. Framed by a heavy

Astrakhan collared coat and homburg hat, by turns boyishly jovial and froggishly depressed, its athletic malleability perfectly augmented Hancock's innate sense of comic timing. For once the weather-beaten putty features of Sid James were not the centre of attention.

For his seventh (and final) BBC television series, Hancock rationalised even further, dropping Sid and moving from East Cheam to an Earl's Court bedsitter. The new series, titled simply *Hancock*, was presented as a break with the old style. 'Ah yes, it's goodbye to all that black homburg and Astrakhan collar rubbish,' he confided to the *Radio Times*. 'Knowledge and self advancement are the things.'[80] The new Hancock was introduced with the creative bar set higher than ever.

The two-hander, an entire episode featuring just two characters confined to one set, is often seen as the hallmark of sophisticated character comedy, a rite of passage for 'quality' sitcoms. This tradition began on ITV in October 1960. *Bootsie and Snudge: A Day Off* by Marty Feldman and Barry Took saw the eponymous gentleman's club lackeys aimlessly passing the time on, again, a Sunday afternoon. (That pious ennui remains Christianity's lasting contribution to comedy.) Despite constantly making plans, they never left their shared dormitory, encountering no-one else save a rogue pigeon. Seven months later, *The Bedsitter* also centred on entertainment endlessly deferred, going one better, and one fewer.

The premise was simple: Hancock, gay bachelor in bedsit-land, idles his way through a wet afternoon (weekday unspecified), tries and fails to improve himself, accidentally secures then loses a hot date, and generally mucks about. Keeping a solo Hancock funny for 25 minutes was a tall order (aside from fleeting glimpses of Michael Aspel on Tone's dodgy telly, no-one else appears), but the mature Hancock persona was more than rich enough to fill the space – Galton and Simpson's first draft ran twenty minutes too long.[81]

The logistics of filming one man alone were intricately worked out by director Duncan Wood and designer Malcolm Goulding, ensuring the cameras could follow Hancock wherever he wandered.[82] Hancock himself became increasingly keen to exert his influence on the show beyond performance, and persuaded a grudging Wood to let him direct a handful of shots per show himself.[83] Rehearsals were rigorous, and by the time of recording Hancock was on rare word-perfect form. From Noel Coward impersonations to an elaborate TV reception ballet, he barely put a foot wrong.

At times in his frivolous soliloquy Hancock almost – but not quite – catches the camera's eye. There must have been a temptation to break the fourth wall in this episode, but the dedication to realism stopped it going down the *Burns and Allen* route (an episode of which followed *Hancock* at 9.25 p.m.). The early TV *Half-Hours* were awash with self-reference. In the very first, a couple watching Hancock's television debut annoy him so much with their snide comments he leaves the studio and enters their front room, smashing up their set, and finding himself doing the rest of the show live from a hospital bed. It wasn't a classic, and such gags were soon dumped.

A few episodes after *The Bedsitter*, a serious car accident started Hancock's well-documented decline. Galton and Simpson went on to take the two-hander to ever greater heights with *Steptoe and Son*, and the minimalist format remained a sitcom goal, attained by shows as diverse as *Porridge* and *Benson*. The solo feat has never been equalled, not even by the lad himself – ATV's lacklustre 1963 *Hancock* series tried to ape the formula in *The Early Call*, in which Hancock booked a wake-up call and fretted about it for the entire night. But the star was in the descendent and the script was second rate – in place of Tone's epic struggle with Bertrand Russell's *Human Knowledge: Its Scope and Limits*, we got some uninspired business with a chest expander. The closest contender is perhaps a 1973 episode of *All In the Family*, Norman Lear's reupholstering of Johnny Speight's *Till Death Us Do Part*, which locked central character Archie Bunker in the cellar for a night of drunken self-loathing, with only token appearances by other characters.

The cult of the one- and two-hander holds more weight with

writers than audiences, but its role in sitcom craft is considerable. The cult of realism is more problematic. Hancock's obsessive pursuit of it began with him shedding the unnecessary (trad jokes, wacky situations) and ended with him dropping the necessary (Galton, Simpson). He was not the last performer to lose his comic perspective chasing after a phantom seriousness – conversely, lesser talents have used ostentatious naturalism to bolster feeble scripts. A reviewer in 1960 observed, 'Mr Hancock teeters on the verge of tragedy: it is only his fine sense of the ridiculous that holds him . . . on the narrow path of sanity.'[84] In the quest for realism, that sense can be fatally neglected.

# KINGSLEY AMIS GOES POP (1962)
## ITV (Associated-Rediffusion)

### TV's introduces pop to high culture.

*I'm looking forward to doing this programme enormously. I'm going to have fun even if nobody else does.*

Kingsley Amis, *TV Times*, 14 October 1962

BY THE 1960s, TV had accepted the necessity of covering pop music, but remained confused as to exactly how to do it. Clueless but game, they tried everything. Ken Dodd flaunted his hip Liverpool connections in *Doddy's Music Box*, promising a 'psyche-diddylic' experience for all. BBC2 floated the unforgettably named *Gadzooks! It's All Happening!*, which became *Gadzooks! It's the In Crowd!* before sanity prevailed, and the title was rationalised to just plain *Gadzooks!* Producers were not so much going to the hop as caught on it.

In one grand misjudgement, BBC1 replaced its long-running *Juke Box Jury* with Alan 'Fluff' Freeman vehicle *All Systems Freeman*, which placed Fluff behind a gigantic space age console, sporting headphones (both to make the link with his radio DJ role, and to craftily relay producer's instructions in pre-earpiece days). 'I shall be sitting at a control panel,' he said, 'and not just for the glamour of it, either! If I press a button or throw a switch to bring in tape, film or disc, and nothing happens, I'm going to look a right idiot.'[85] It may have been a vestigial memory of Fluff fading in pop acts with his mighty right hand that influenced the world of Harry Enfield and Paul Whitehouse's Smashie and Nicey creations decades later.

These were sober affairs alongside Associated-Rediffusion's decision to hire a literary *enfant terrible* to cover the scene. *Kingsley Amis Goes Pop* ('a title which is still amusing him') was a fifteen-minute wheeze knocked out after the evening news in which the *Lucky Jim* author and fellow of Peterhouse College, Cambridge interrogated pop stars in a bewildered and mildly grumpy manner. Amis was no cultural snob – he would go on to write scripts for *Z-Cars* spin-off *Softly, Softly*, and in his later years described *Terminator 2: Judgment Day* as a 'flawless masterpiece'[86] – but rock 'n' roll was a blind spot. 'The pop music business is still pretty much a closed book to me,' Amis admitted. An accredited jazzer, he had little time for rock 'n' roll's 'vapid, monotonous, blaring'[87] asininity. ('Oh fuck the Beatles,' he once told Philip Larkin. 'I'd like to push my bum into John L[ennon]'s face for forty-eight hours or so.'[88])

Fortunately Amis had the help of his pop-loving teenage sons, Philip and Martin. 'Some of their records interest me and I have to ask, "Who's that?"' He also looked to his offspring for sartorial tips. On their advice, he hosted the show wearing the clothes he arrived in off the street – Terylene, head to toe. This brought a tie-in ad campaign. ('"My Terylene trousers are \*\*\*\* great!" says Kingsley Amis.') Thus clad, he began his pop quest in high spirits. 'Quite honestly, I welcome the chance of meeting these extraordinary pop-singer people.'[89]

The show started well enough. Cleo Laine was asked about the gulf between jazz and the hit parade, Bernard Cribbins dropped by to explain the craft of the comedy song, and dancehall tycoon Eric Morley explained how a dance craze could be promoted nationwide, before Amis flexed his Terylene slacks for a crack at Morley's latest fad, the New Madison.

All very amiable, but according to critic Peter Black, Amis the awkwardly groovy dad fell between two stools. 'Either you go along with pop, getting as much empty unquestioning fun from it as you can,' he reasoned, 'or you put up a critic and let him sink his teeth deeply into the rubbish. Mr Amis's teeth have apparently been drawn and he sits there like a vicar at an orgy.'[90] Maybe Amis took this to heart, or maybe he just became bored, but later shows were altogether more frosty affairs. 'Rubber Ball' singer Bobby Vee underwent a curmudgeonly grilling. A meeting with Rolf Harris found the 'Sun Arise' singer reveal his previously unseen prickly, sarcastic mode. '[Amis] must allow for everybody's taste,' complained one fan, 'not embarrass everybody concerned.'[91] By the final edition – a chat with Alan Freeman – the gloves were already off in the programme billing. ('Have DJs too much power in the pop world? Do they encourage "trash"?')

Television's first attempt to mix pop and high culture produced intellectual fireworks of the indoor variety. The series was broadcast to Londoners only, and only lasted eight editions of a planned twelve, shown at an ever-later hour of the day. Memoirs and biographies tactfully skirt its very existence. But it could easily have become a family tradition: as Frankie Goes to Hollywood's career stalled in the mid-1980s, their marketing strategist Paul Morley could have conceived a postmodern film as their swansong along the lines of *The Great Rock 'n' Roll Swindle* – to be scripted by Martin Amis.[92]

# THAT WAS THE WEEK THAT WAS (1962–3)
## BBC

### The establishment-shaking show that used the word 'bum' a lot.

*Come 6.30, four hours to go before the soft underbelly of society was to be obligingly exposed to the watching millions, and as yet nothing in the quiver save three outrageous puns and a joke about knickers.*

Alan Bennett on writing topical comedy,
5 October 1967

THE REVUE THAT HAD led Bennett to that quiet teatime desperation, *Beyond the Fringe*, is one of the landmarks of twentieth century comedy. As Bennett, Dudley Moore, Jonathan Miller and Peter Cook laid into Macmillan, Churchill and one-legged stuntmen in an apocalyptic basement set, the idea of comedy as a cleansing, angry, youthful force got its first British airing for decades. Many of the older generation hated it, but a surprising number applauded. Even staunch conservative T. S. Eliot gave praise. 'An amazingly vigorous quartet of young men: their show well produced and fast moving, a mixture of brilliance, juvenility and bad taste,' he wrote. In spite of reservations, 'it is pleasant to see this *type* of entertainment so successful.'[93]

Success piled on success. The show conquered the country, then the USA. Cook opened a nightclub, The Establishment, to show-case the best British and American insurgent entertainment in an atmosphere redolent of Weimar Germany. Scurrilous, bedroom-built magazine *Private Eye*, when it wasn't facing imminent legal destruction, thrived. The steady, apolitical 'progress' of the fifties transformed into urgent, questioning rebellion. Television, the medium of the hour, just had to be invaded.

And it was, on 25 October 1962. 'For the first time on television,' promised the publicity, 'a critical, funny, adult, non-singing, non-dancing show about current events.' This 'weekly dose of virulent, unrestrained satire' promised to take an unflinching look at 'people from a race-rioter to the PM, at subjects from the Common Market to the Space Race.' Its crack team of young Turks would 'be seeking pomposity – when they find it they will attack and deflate.'[94]

This crocodile of clichés described *What the Public Wants?*, a hastily assembled late-night sketch show from Associated-Rediffusion, which featured such incendiary concepts as Father Christmas's sleigh being mistaken for a UFO and shot down by the RAF. It was, said *The Times*, 'a feeble and irritating little show that suffers from the callow superciliousness of undergraduate revue'.[95] By the end of the year it was gone, with another, Granada's *Man Bites Dog*, scrapped in pre-production.

If the irresponsible commercial channel couldn't raise a decent satire, what chance the regulation-bound BBC? John Bird, a colleague of Cook, took the concept of 'Establishment TV' to young BBC producer Ned Sherrin, who moulded it into a hip end-of-the-week compendium of sketch, song, cartoon and political barb. The studio would be coolly stripped down, showing its busy internal workings and louche audience of wine-bibbing hangers-on. The pace would be relentless, the cast impeccable: improv singer Millicent Martin, *Private Eye* alumnus Willie Rushton, Joan Littlewood alumnus Roy Kinnear and 'calypsologist' Lance Percival among them. The host would be not Bird or Cook, but David Frost.

This decision raised eyebrows, and a few hackles. Regarded,

rather snobbishly, in his Cambridge years as a hyper-ambitious hack, Frost had already earned Cook's disapproval for performing highly derivative 'homages' to his material. His greatest television achievement to date was fronting Rediffusion's dance craze schedule filler *Let's Twist on the Riviera*. Sherrin ignored these concerns and launched one of television's most prodigious careers.

On 24 November, *That Was the Week That Was* played out in a welter of fluffed cues and missed cameras. The army, the police and composer Norrie Paramor were among the targets. Bernard Levin ('the most detestable smarty-boots on television') hosted an adversarial discussion with public relations workers in a debate disarmingly titled 'Invective'. The stand out sketch, a parody of ITV's shameless 'ad-mag' programme *Jim's Inn*, was a refugee from Cook's *Beyond the Fringe* days. 'Anyone who stayed up in the hope of enjoying some ripe topical savagery, continental-style, was doomed to disappointment,' wrote Peter Green in the *Listener*. 'I hope future editions will get some real bite in them, and shed that air of daring cosiness which bedevils British satire at its very roots.'[96]

Fortunately, *TW3* rapidly grew teeth. The third edition achieved Sherrin's dream of transition from the review pages to the headlines, thanks to comically edited footage of Macmillan talking cobblers and Levin putting the boot into hotel magnate Charles Forte. '*Private Eye* may lash out in all directions and provoke nothing more than a chorus of bland coo-ings,' observed *The Times*, 'but let the BBC do something similar . . . and they arouse the public to close on a thousand telephone calls and a threat of legal action.'[97] Anthony Burgess summed up its winning naivety: 'Its special virtue is its genuine innocence, a sort of schoolboy surprise that the adult world should behave as it does. A very nice little programme at which only a boor could take offence. Wholesome, high-spirited, unpretentious, humanly unbuttoned, often shrewd, amusing and – above all – totally lacking in malice.'[98] Even Peter Green was now sold. '[*TW3*] has acquired that *sine qua non* of satire, a firm moral stance. "We mustn't make fun of Mr Macmillan, we mustn't be rude about British catering" – the terrifying thing is that the views of these witless subtopian boot-lickers command attention. Why, in heaven's name?'[99]

Old and young, subtopian and cosmopolitan, reactionary and progressive – all went head to head last thing on a Saturday night, the latter always getting the final word. And what words they were, from a writers' roster that gathered illustrious names of the past, present and future: Dennis Potter, David Nobbs, Bill Oddie, Kenneth Tynan, John Betjeman, John Cleese, Roald Dahl and many more fed Frost and friends killer lines. For Green, and many others, *TW3* became unimpeachable, mainly because 'it carries a bigger moral punch than all of its critics combined, and the day it is bullied or snivelled out of existence will be a poor one for British television.'[100]

That day was close at hand. When a second series began in 1963, the blaze of triumphant pre-publicity soon faded into critical murmurings of a loss of purpose. 'There is less specific emphasis on politics, and a marked swing towards mildly risqué intimate revue.'[101] Sketches about open flies, and liberal sprinklings of outré words like 'bum' and 'poo', had a habit of taking over the more considered (and considerably harder to knock out) political material. This smutty path of least resistance would dog topical comedy shows ever after.

The heavyweight stuff did continue, though, and proved to be the show's undoing. When Macmillan was replaced by the questionable choice of Sir Alec Douglas-Home, *TW3* pounced, dressing Frost in Disraeli gear to deliver a politely damning 'in character' summary of Douglas-Home's unique attributes. What with this, a sketch mocking another Tory hero, Baden-Powell, and the continuing stream of 'racy' material, many formerly indulgent champions of the show reached their limits of tolerance, and called for cancellation.

The Director General, Hugh Carleton Greene, felt *TW3* was becoming an albatross for the Corporation, monopolising staff time and detracting from his achievements in the more serious departments of drama and current affairs. With a general election looming the following year, he curtailed its run at the end of 1963. *Private Eye*, the relatively low profile satirical survivor, summed up popular reaction to *TW3*'s sacrifice by having 'Greene' confess: 'What I really wanted was something reminiscent of Berlin in the 1930s; now that I've stopped it, I feel that I have at last recreated that atmosphere.'[102]

# THE SUNDAY-NIGHT PLAY: A SUITABLE CASE FOR TREATMENT (1962)

## BBC

### Drama drops out.

*Dear David Mercer, can you please explain why all your plays
are about David Mercer?*

A student writes to David Mercer, c. 1972

IN CINEMA, THE HIERARCHY was always plain. Stars first, then
director, and bringing up the rear, if they're even mentioned at all,
the writer. In the 1960s, television – smaller, more flexible and less
glamorous – had a more variable pecking order. Thanks to ever-
closer ties with the theatrical revolution, the writer could occasionally, and not always reluctantly, become the star of their own
show.

David Mercer was one of many post-war playwrights who had
risen from the provincial working class through state and self-
education. Born into a Wakefield mining family, he spent four
years with the Navy before moving to Paris to work as first a
struggling painter, then a struggling novelist. Realising the 'abstract
cul-de-sac'[103] he'd backed himself into, he turned to drama,

specifically the drama of his own experience. His first play, *Where the Difference Begins*, was intended for the stage but found a home on the BBC. It dealt with the culture gap between a working class artist and his suspicious kinfolk in an honest and very straightforward way. Mercer would later describe it as 'one of the dreariest plays ever written by me, or anyone else, for that matter.'[104] He seemed to be cultivating an oeuvre every bit as unforgiving as his resting expression of intense concern.

Then, in 1962, the usually methodical Mercer made a breakthrough, written 'in an absolute kind of trance for three weeks'.[105] When director Don Taylor, Mercer's main early creative collaborator, asked about it, he found his colleague's usual intense frown replaced by 'a large, round-faced Yorkshire grin'.[106] *A Suitable Case for Treatment* left the old straight track of social realism and hiked off into the unknown.

Morgan Delt, disillusioned thirtysomething man for whom 'life became baffling as soon as it became comprehensible', is in the process of being divorced from his wife Leonie. He sleeps in his car and spends his days railing against society like an Angry Brigade Hamlet, or palling around with Guy the Gorilla at London Zoo. Otherwise he keeps himself occupied by pestering his ex-wife, pinning offensive posters in her flat, shaving a hammer and sickle into her poodle's back, hanging her stuffed toys on a small portable gallows and blowing up her mother. A few years before the screen would fill with them, Morgan was its first drop-out hero.

Appropriately, the play didn't conform to the standard two act shape. Scenes fragmented and were interrupted by clips of films from *Battleship Potemkin* to *Tarzan*. Dream sequences were not the usual gauzy, slow motion affairs but stark skits in a black limbo with Morgan's mum in secret police uniform. Don Taylor somehow crammed it all into an hour – a pre-recorded and edited hour, the thing being far too complex to transmit live, as most drama still was.

These technical innovations would have meant nothing without Mercer's increasingly sharp dialogue. Morgan's cockney Trot mum, played to the hilt by Anna Wing, had some beautifully turned lines worthy of *Hancock*: 'Your dad wanted to shoot the royal family, abolish marriage and put everybody who'd been to public school in a chain gang. He was an idealist, was your dad.' But the main event was Ian Hendry's Morgan, manic in all emotional directions. 'I'm a bad son,' he mused. 'Is it the chromosomes, or is it England?' He castigated Leonie's suave new suitor, saying, 'He slid into our lives like a boa constrictor. You've never seen him with her – he undulates. Turned my back one day and he gulped her down like a rabbit.'

This unprecedented play left critics straining for parallels. The slapstick incursions and head-banging philosophy put many critics in mind of Spike Milligan. 'Like Milligan, Morgan Delt was either a thousand years ahead of his time or, more likely, probably an essential antidote *for* his time,' judged Derek Hill, approving what was 'less a play than a welcome disturbance of the peace.'[107] Michael Overton applauded what he saw as a long overdue BBC response to the dominance of *Armchair Theatre*. 'The BBC has been steadily playing safe and countering ABC-TV's adventurousness with dull doldrum plays unimaginatively directed and indifferently acted. David Mercer's play must have shaken the antimacassars in the most staid middle-class homes, and made the majority switch straight back to *Sunday Night at the London Palladium*.'[108]

Scheduled after Mercer was a repeat of Anthony Newley's *The Johnny Darling Show*, a pseudo-sequel to *Gurney Slade* in which the eponymous teen idol senses the end of the world and embarks on a philosophical fantasy journey of social and spiritual Armageddon, with songs by Leslie Bricusse. For some viewers, a whole evening of visual experiment and existential despair was too much, and in the following edition of *Points of View* many anti-macassars were shaken at the Beeb, and Mercer especially.

Mercer's protagonists were not so much off the beaten track as frolicking in the tall grass several fields away: a young man who takes an axe to a middle-class Sunday tea party; a leather-clad septuagenarian vicar biker; a childlike pair of zookeepers who fill a disused swimming pool with inflatable animals and trapezes. 'Mercer is not just a nonconformist,' reckoned Don Taylor, 'he is a nonconformist nonconformist, for whom a beard and a guitar are as square as a dark suit and rolled umbrella. He is his own strange self.'[109] *A Suitable Case* . . . became a film, *Morgan!*, in 1966, adapted by Mercer but sweetened, he felt, too much by director Karel Reisz into a poppy tale of swinging outsiderism. 'Dropping out' was now a cultural buzzword, on its way to becoming a mini-industry. Only conformist nonconformists need apply.

For a confirmed outsider, Mercer was gregarious to a fault. Joan Bakewell recalls the 'hotbed of neo-Marxism'[110] he presided over in Maida Vale, where she would dash after presenting *Late Night Line-Up* to hobnob with Pinter, Kenneth Tynan and company. He was the most visible of the new TV playwrights, interviewed by everyone from Melvyn Bragg to David Coleman. His goatee and polo neck became familiar enough for Michael Palin to impersonate him on *Monty Python*, chain-smoking behind a typewriter, captioned simply: 'A Very Good Playwright'.

Mercer's TV output declined in the seventies. Despite quirky successes like the half-hour *Me and You and Him* – a triumph of videotape editing in which three Peter Vaughans conduct a psychiatric slanging match – his style was sidelined in the push toward naturalism. Even the introduction of high-definition colour seemed set against him. In 1972's *The Bankrupt*, a crisis-hit Joss Ackland experiences the same kind of black limbo dreams as Morgan Delt, though where the original monochrome abyss sold the hallucination, the colour camera merely highlighted what Kenneth Tynan once dismissed as 'the platitudinous void, with its single message: "Background of evil, get it?"'[111]

And anyway, argued critics, TV had moved on from this sort of experimental tinkering, hadn't it? 'I'm afraid this kind of cross-word-puzzle drama may find a place in the so-called "intellectual" theatre,' opined John Russell Taylor, 'but it cannot make much sense to the average television viewer.'[112] Clive James thought *The Bankrupt* showed a writer losing his way: 'Mercer, like John

Hopkins, is likely to eke out a half-imagined idea by double-crossing his own talent and piling on precisely the undergrad-type tricksiness his sense of realism exists to discredit.'[113]

Mercer died in 1980, firmly out of step with the timid TV mainstream, which duly gave him a retrospective but otherwise continued to be suspicious of the risky and remarkable. Mercer set the template for the bold, confessional playwright who was as at home appearing on television as writing for it. His more concrete, if less eye-catching, quality was noted by Mervyn Johns: 'A television writer who cares, and is encouraged to care, about words is a rarity; without Mercer's example, that rarity may become an extinct species.'[114]

# THE TONIGHT SHOW STARRING JOHNNY CARSON (1962–92)

## NBC

**The king of chat show kings.**

*TV excels in two areas – sports and Carson.*
David Brenner, comedian
and frequent Carson guest, 1971

THE CULTURE OF THE United States tends to treat any new field of endeavour like the Wild West – a vast wilderness to be colonised and tamed. The TV schedules were no different – beyond the evening hours lay the call of the untamed daytime slots in one direction, and in the other the heart of late-night darkness. NBC launched a daytime expedition in 1952, beginning with early morning chat-in *Today*. Two years later came a companion trek into the late-night zone, which opened up a lucrative and fiercely contested new territory.

*Tonight!* was shaped by its first host, Steve Allen. A classic vaudevillian drifter who fell into TV comedy after a subversive stint on local radio, Allen turned what was planned as a fairly straight talk-show-plus-sketch format into a self-contained world – a club with its own rules and customs that made the viewers feel part of something wonderfully mad. He'd arrange complex one-shot gags such as being dunked into hot water wearing a suit festooned with teabags, but most of his comedy was cheaply improvised. Regular stunts included walking out into the New York streets in police uniform and stopping motorists for various bizarre reasons, or just pointing a camera at the passing street life and reeling off an impromptu commentary on its comings and goings. Late night was established as a freewheeling refuge from the daily schedule grind.

Allen moved on to Sunday prime time after an unsuccessful splitting of *Tonight!* duties with Ernie Kovacs. Reverting to the chat format, the show gained a new, more earnest host. Jack Paar gathered a round table of fellow wits (including token Brit Hermione Gingold), welcomed heavyweight guests from JFK to Castro, and put his own thin-skinned personality centre stage. A fragile star, Paar would fight the network on-screen, most famously calling out their censorship of a whimsical gag based on misinterpretation of the initials 'WC'.

Paar's successor couldn't have more temperamentally different. Johnny Carson boasted the ultimate down-home American background, having grown up in a backwater of Nebraska. His first TV success was the unpromising daytime game show *Who Do You Trust?* (formerly *Do You Trust Your Wife?*) where he built up the introductory banter with the contestants into a lengthy and often, for the time slot, bawdy art. He was also united with long-suffering *Tonight* second banana and announcer Ed McMahon.

Carson first appeared on *Tonight!* as a guest of Steve Allen, making a prank phone call to Jack Paar. (Paar rumbled the pair within seconds.) As host, he steered a steady course between the hyperactive pranking of Allen and Paar's earnest inquiry. Whether delivering the opening monologue in front of theatrical curtains or sat at his desk in front of a mural of imposing Midwest scenery, idly tossing cue cards full of failing gags over his shoulder, he exuded a comfortingly straight-up bonhomie in increasingly fractious times. The wit was bolstered by a platoon of star writers, and the lurid sports jackets were from his own line of dresswear, but the easy manner and genuine interest in what his subjects had to say were all Carson's own. The show soon became Carson's, incorporating his name into its title and eventually relocating with him from New York to beautiful downtown Burbank.

Teetotal and averse to showbiz parties, Carson was a reluctant off-duty celebrity, becoming a star only after he'd parted the stage curtains following McMahon's preparatory crescendo of 'Heeeeere's Johnny!' Under the lights, he could converse with the cream of Hollywood and hold his own with New York's literati. Long-standing tit-for-tat feuds, especially with actor and compulsive put-down merchant Don Rickles, escalated with each meeting into the realms of obsession; both men walking a fine line between the all-in-fun wink for the audience and all-too-convincing mutual animosity.

When the show ran out of stars, it made its own. Tiny Tim, a towering, baleful oddball who sang 'Tiptoe Through the Tulips' in an unearthly falsetto, was discovered by *Tonight* and became a regular, even marrying his beau in mock-Georgian splendour on a special edition of the programme, with McMahon as chief usher: 'We cordially request the pleasure of your company at the marriage of Tiny Tim and Miss Vicki right here on *The Tonight Show*. But right now here are some words of wisdom from Pepto-Bismol tablets.'[115]

Away from the star circuit, Carson invited 'ordinary folk with a story to tell', especially pensioners such as a 103-year-old woman who still drove regularly, whom he handled with warmth and a total absence of condescension. Folk with odd obsessions were another rich vein: Carson was the first to televise the subsequently worldwide craze for domino toppling, inviting Robert Speca into the studio to knock down 6,999 pieces. All civilians were treated the same as the stars: Carson gave them all their due, resorting to his trademark conspiratorial sidelong glance to camera only if the subject was really asking for it. A tangible link between celebrity and public decades before social media, Johnny Carson sat at the fulcrum of American popular culture.

His unaffected largesse prompted generosity in his guests. When Alex Haley appeared on the show to promote the mini-series *Roots*, he brought with him a leather-bound book entitled *Roots of Johnny Carson*, a 400-page, intensively researched trawl of the Carson family tree reaching back to sixteenth century Essex. It was, of course, the perfect all-American heritage, another piece of the Average Guy legend.

Other chat shows filed up alongside Carson. On ABC, Dick Cavett creamed off the intellectual crowd for whom Carson felt too safe. For CBS, Merv Griffin tackled Carson's populism head-on. From 1982, David Letterman followed Carson in the NBC schedules, triumphantly reactivating Steve Allen's intricate horse-play (including the teabag suit) in an hour produced, as part of Carson's uniquely favourable contract, by Carson's own people. Carson's stature was not so much presidential as kingly. Though Kermit the Frog was briefly mooted as a replacement in the late 1970s, the thought of Carson yielding his desk to anyone else remained taboo.

When Carson abdicated at the age of 66, the effect was of a long-peaceful kingdom plunged into civil war. Letterman, long seen as heir apparent, lost out to the less admired Jay Leno, and decamped to CBS, to be replaced by Conan O'Brien. Rivals, including Tom Snyder and Jimmy Kimmel, proliferated. Machinations behind the desks became as much a public spectacle as the encounters over them. The unholy viewing hour remained exceptionally popular, but it never regained the stature of the man whose one job was to introduce America to itself. Carson himself summed it up, when pausing for breath after an innocuous bit of business spun gloriously out of hand, climaxing in tearful laughter, trademark karate chops and cries of 'Hi-yooo!' 'That,' said the exhausted host, 'is what makes this job what it is.' 'What is it?' asked McMahon. Carson thought hard for a second, and eventually answered, 'I don't know.'[116]

# WORLD IN ACTION
# (1963–98)
## ITV (Granada)

### Current affairs go commando.

IN 1963 CURRENT AFFAIRS reached critical mass. In the summer, Britain's press enjoyed unprecedented levels of political influence when they published the indiscretions of John Profumo. The shaming of a British minister was followed by the death of a US President. For four days in November, from the first, breathless, interruption of an episode of soap opera *As the World Turns*, through the assassination of Oswald and the state funeral on the twenty-fifth, the USA turned to television for information and support, specifically to Walter Cronkite of *CBS News*. A programme that combined the fearlessness of an investigative tabloid with television's immediate visual impact had to be made, and it was.

The current affairs feature began with BBC's *Special Enquiry* in 1952 and, the following year, its flagship *Panorama*. ITV returned volley with *This Week* and *Searchlight*. The latter, edited by Australian ex-tabloid editor Tim Hewat, caused such regular controversy it devoted one edition to scrutinising itself. When the Television Act finally caught up with *Searchlight*'s insufficient impartiality, Hewat reassigned his men the banner of *World in Action*, a 'Northern *Panorama*' that would fundamentally change the look of TV documentary.

Hewat created *World in Action* to cover a single subject each week. On-screen reporters were replaced by voice-overs including that of James Burke, leaving the screen filled with the matter in hand. The matter was often visualised with shamelessly unsubtle tabloid stunts, such as staging a mass funeral in a Salford street to introduce a report on bronchitis. These were organised by the show's team of fixers, who also arranged everything from foreign currency to access to closed borders. Tactics like this helped *World in Action*'s audience rise to twice *Panorama*'s.[117]

*World in Action* also introduced the 16mm film camera. Several times less bulky than the usual 35mm Arriflex, the smaller gauge apparatus cut the size of a location crew from twelve to six, giving the team greater manoeuvrability. Where before events were brought in front of the camera, now the camera could dive straight into the situation. The consequent grainy smutch of those early guerilla reports was a badge of honour; Hewat upbraided one fastidious producer's suspiciously immaculate African footage as a screen full of 'bloody back-lit begging bowls!'[118]

When a huge story broke at an inconsiderately late point in the week, the leaner team could put an emergency programme together in under three days. All-nighters pulled to cover breaking scoops like the collapse of the John Bloom business empire were celebrated in hard-bitten Fleet Street tones. 'We have to do a week's work in two days. It's impossible, but sometimes it gets done,' editor Alex Valentine told *TV Times*, adding wistfully, 'I've never seen so many dawns in my life, I don't mind telling you.'[119]

Tabloid clichés in the publicity material were fine. Tabloid clichés in the content were signs of slackness. As the same subjects came round again each season, the show's style atrophied. Anything that worked, like the Salford stunt, was recycled when time and inspiration went. '*World in Action* is sometimes in danger of becoming a victim of its own form,' wrote Peter Hillmore, lamenting its use of picture postcard scene setting – canals to introduce Amsterdam, or a politician's view preceded by the Houses of Parliament from the Thames. 'I know the team has to fill thirty minutes with film, but it doesn't always have to look so desperate about it.'[120]

When all parts of the *World in Action* team pulled together, the results were unbeatable. Its many torture investigations of the early 1970s brought horrific news of every regime's actions from Zanzibar to Turkey to Ulster. It risked a great deal more than its reputation to demonstrate how simple it was to smuggle car parts into sanctioned Rhodesia, and arms to war-torn Biafra. It pioneered mass election debate with 'The Granada 500', a panel of pundits bussed in from bellwether constituency Preston East to grill the party leaders. The edition with perhaps the greatest impact, 'The Rise and Fall of John Poulson', didn't unearth much in the way of new material on the corrupt property developer, but did set out the available evidence in a clearer way than anyone had managed before, laying bare the dense web of connections. The film was still incendiary enough to be temporarily blocked by the IBA, which led to accusations of a conflict of interest among ITV grandees – T. Dan Smith, one of the main accused, had been until very recently a director of Tyne Tees Television. (Later, while in jail for corruption, Smith encouraged fellow inmate Leslie Grantham to take up professional acting, and a future star of *EastEnders* was born.)[121]

Occasionally the programme went too far. Covering anti-Sony factory protests in 1977, its team hunted America to film the rumoured gatherings of people in T-shirts claiming, 'Sony – from the people who gave you Pearl Harbor'. Not finding any such shirts, they printed a few off themselves.[122] 'Born Losers', shown in 1967, was a compassionate study of a nine-child family living on £16 a week; it got its message across to many viewers, but broadcasting the Walshes' intimate details came close to destroying the family itself.[123] From then the team were wary of putting members of the public quite so brazenly on show – a consideration regarded as optional by other programmes.

The emergent youth culture demanded coverage. Young producer John Birt's idea of helicoptering Mick Jagger into the grounds of a stately home to chat with the Bishop of Woolwich was a success, in publicity terms at least. ('We should aim to transmit at least one outrageous and improbable programme each year,' demanded long-serving editor Ray Fitzwalter.[124]) But most youth culture stories, from the Mod revival to acid house, tended towards prudishness. 'No speed party is complete without a joint of grass,' vouchsafed the authoritatively prurient narrator of Haight-Ashbury examination, 'Alas, Poor Hippies, Love is Dead'.

News technology progressed apace. Through the late 1970s, the old film crews were steadily replaced by 'creepy-peepies': lightweight video cameras far more convenient even than 16mm. A generation of cameramen were left feeling, in the words of one ACTT member, 'like wheeltappers at a hovercraft rally'.[125] Even the BBC's *Panorama* started to catch up with the times: a 1981 documentary on German rocket makers OTRAG used a blizzard of electronic effects to enliven the presentation of its great mountain of paper evidence. 'The days of pointing a camera at a newspaper cutting are threatened at last,' predicted Peter Fiddick. 'If you can't read it, they'll flash it, colour it and creep it across the screen . . . until you're blinded into literacy.'[126] The Richard Dimbleby generation of current affairs gave way to Hewat's boys across the board.

*World in Action* wasn't killed off by IBA ruling or legal challenge, but a soap opera. In 1994 *EastEnders* went thrice-weekly, ruining ITV's Monday night. The 1990 Broadcasting Act had already loosened the third channel's current affairs commitments. *World in Action*, now reaching as little as five million viewers,[127] was promptly shifted up against the soap as a sacrifice. It lasted a little over three years. Granada won the bid to replace its old show: 'Whether by performance, image, heritage or perception, all agree on the value of *World in Action*,'[128] it admitted in the tender, but 'we need to make current affairs less threatening to younger viewers.' Its solution, based on CBS's *60 Minutes* model, became *Tonight with Trevor McDonald*. Broadsheet pundits began making merry with the freshly imported phrase 'dumbing down'.

# PLAY SCHOOL
## (1964–88)
## BBC2

### The BBC loosens its old pre-school tie.

*Anyone can fill time with pap and the kids will watch it. It's*
*safe and it's easy. We are trying to break away from that.*
Joy Whitby, *Play School* executive producer, 1966

THE BBC'S EARLY CHILDREN'S television was a fortress of twee.
Amiable (if slightly grotesque) puppets would get into a jolly old
fix, patrician ladies would trill nursery rhymes in strident falsetto,
and improving fables would be slowly read out of leather-bound
books the size of shed roofs. When Doreen Stephens took charge
of the BBC's family programmes in 1963, this had been the case
for rather too long. She found a 'demoralised, miserable children's
department'[129] plodding along with the same *Andy Pandy* mindset
that harked back to before the Suez Crisis. Her initial desire to
scrap Andy, Bill and Ben outright was countermanded by an early
manifestation of popular nostalgia, but she did gradually phase
them out in favour of *The Magic Roundabout, Camberwick Green*
and a new daily morning programme for the under-fives.

Stephens employed Joy Whitby to edit *Play School*. With two
presenters, a tiny studio, a clock for telling the time and an initial
weekly budget of £120,[130] Whitby concocted a feast of ideas, songs,
rhymes and (very basic) documentary films designed to stimulate

toddlers' imaginations. The fustiness of old gave way to bold designs and plush soft toy companions (though Hamble, a grotesque china doll, was the one anomalous throwback to morbid Victoriana and suffered chronic abuse from presenters and technical staff as a result, before being replaced in 1986 by the marginally less creepy Poppy). In a reversal of the usual metrics, the programme was judged a success by its makers if children abandoned the show half way through to go outside and do a wobbly dance or search for round things.[131]

If this sounded like a tepid bath of liberal unction, the third woman involved in *Play School*'s inception, series producer Cynthia Felgate, added a tougher note. 'Talking down is really based on the assumption that you are being liked by the child,' she reasoned. 'But if you imagine a tough little boy of four looking in, you soon take the silly smile off your face.'[132] As a former actor with a theatrical troupe specialising in that toughest of gigs, the in-school educational performance, she knew whereof she spoke.

An experienced general, Felgate recruited troops from the ranks of repertory, with a sharp eye for nascent talent. *Play School* staff would take roles in countless other children's programmes after their toil at the clock-face. They included musicians, from the classically trained Jonathan Cohen to the folk-schooled Toni Arthur and the downright countercultural Rick Jones. The show also pioneered, in its own quiet way, the employment of non-white hosts, beginning in 1965 with Paul Danquah, fresh from filming *A Taste of Honey*. Humour played a huge part in proceedings, courtesy of Fred Harris (who graduated to adult comedy when radio producer Simon Brett chanced upon his work while, appropriately, off sick), Johnny Ball (soon to launch his own one-man science-and-puns initiative *Think of a Number*), Phyllida Law (sharing the arch eccentricity of her husband Eric Thompson, *Magic Roundabout* narrator and fellow *School* player), and virtuoso mime Derek Griffiths. Add to this a roster of guest storytellers from Roy Castle to Richard Baker, George Melly to Spike Milligan, and you had a clubhouse of wits in the front room daily: the Algonquin Round Window.

*Play School* was born with the BBC's second channel, the first scripted programme the morning after BBC Two's notoriously blackout-blighted launch. It became such a fixture that households equipped with sets new enough to receive the new UHF channel were often invaded by the children of less well-off neighbours round about eleven o'clock. Camera operators, who suffered previous *Watch with Mother* efforts under duress, actively fought over the chance to cover *Play School*.[133]

In 1971 there came a spin-off, the altogether less restrained *Play Away*. Eminent *Play School* old boy Brian Cant, 'merry as a stoned scoutmaster'[134] in one critic's memorable description, led cohorts including Jeremy Irons, Tony Robinson and Julie Covington through groansome puns, venerable slapstick routines and jolly songs which could, like the catalogue of gargantuan consumer goods 'Shopaway', become mildly satirical. This all-year panto became big enough to transfer to the Old Vic in 1976.

*Play Away*'s high standards drew high expectations from its audience. George Melly observed that while children never questioned the knocked-off likes of *Pinky and Perky* (rudimentary puppets jerking up and down to grating pitch-shifted covers of pop hits), when faced with the higher craft of *Play School* they 'become almost Leavisite in the severity of their criticism'.[135] The ability to spot quality among the dross was learned at an early age.

A few years in, the *School* started to expand. By 1970 it was playing, in recast local versions, everywhere from Switzerland to Australia, with the use of a specially assembled '*Play School* kit'. Most of the toys made the transition to other cultures more or less intact: Humpty, for instance, became 'Testa D'Uovo' – Egghead – in Italian. Unlike the conquering franchises of children's television to come, *Play School* established more of a commonwealth than an empire, importing songs from Israel and films of Roman ice cream factories as it exported Norwegian translations of *The Sun Has Got His Hat On*. (The Scandinavian connection, which culminated in a joint TV special between the UK and Norwegian *Play Away* franchises, highlighted an interesting difference in approaches to children's television. A 1973 Danish seminar on kids' TV produced a twelve-point list of good practice, a copy of which was pinned up in the BBC children's department in Television Centre's bleak East Tower. Alongside the expected exhortations to honesty and clarity was the suggestion: 'When you want to tell an exciting story, try to relate its conflict to the central conflict in society between labour and capital.'[136] If this particular directive was acted upon at the Beeb, it was well disguised.)

Like all timeless children's programmes, *Play School* became a slave to adult fashion. A much-publicised 'moving house' in 1983 altered the theme tune, redesigned the studio and replaced the magic windows with 'shapes', to the horror of many parents who'd grown up with the old show themselves. Five years after that the school was closed for good, replaced by *Playbus*, made by the newly independent Felgate Productions, which was 'more attuned to the needs of today's children' and featured children in the studio – one of the original *Play School*'s prime taboos. The intuition of a handful of creative producers was replaced by a squadron of educational advisers and child psychologists. No longer would British kids have their formative years soundtracked by vintage songs such as *Little Ted Bear From Nowhere in Particular* and *Ten Chimney Pots All In a Row (When Along Came a Fussy Old Crow)*. There's progress, and there's progress.

# CROSSROADS
# (1964–88)
## ITV (ATV/Central)

'Soap' becomes a four-letter word.

*Crossroads is not a programme, it is a vacuum. A hole in the air, abhorrent to nature.*

Nancy Banks-Smith, 1971

IF YOU WANT TO explore the fundamental differences between two cultures, take a look at how they handle their low entertainment. The soap opera, for instance. Its early American incarnation carried titles which were expansive, portentous, quasi-Biblical: *Days of Our Lives, The Bold and the Beautiful, The Guiding Light.* British afternoon serials, meanwhile, got the most humbly domestic of names: *Honey Lane, Castle Haven* and, most utilitarian of all, *Crossroads.*

An attempt by ATV to move into US-style daily serial territory, *Crossroads* was the culmination of Reg Watson's quest to find a solid vehicle for his daytime star Noele Gordon. Hazel Adair and Peter Ling were hired to fashion a genteel Midlands milieu set in the fictional Warwickshire village of King's Oak, paying special attention to the nearby Crossroads motel. Gordon was the motel's widowed owner Meg Richardson, the head of a tiny dynasty including her son Sandy and hapless daughter Jill, and assorted managerial staff. Beneath the matinee idol leads were the Dickensian comic foils, led by line-fluffing cleaner Amy Turtle, later joined by short order cook Shughie McFee and simpleton handyman Benny Hawkins. Cast regulars and intransigent guests conspired to commit adultery, grand theft, murder, suicide – just about every mis-demeanour aside from smoking, which was beyond the pale for a teatime slot.

Dispensing with ITV's standard twice-a-week soap model, *Crossroads* went daily, its production team ripping through five twenty-minute episodes a week. (From 1967 they got Mondays off.) With such a punishing itinerary, the scripts – production line affairs under the guidance of a supervising story editor – were of necessity thriftily furnished with off-the-peg dialogue. 'The sheer volume,' admitted producer Phillip Bowman, 'precludes excel-lence.'[137] The odd *Coronation Street*-style gag still managed to appear amid the expository tundra. ('What's that? "Goulash Budapest"? Looks like "Shepherd's Pie Walsall East" to me.')

Then there were the plywood sets and the under-rehearsed acting. Props were mislaid, eyelines unmet, extras (literally, on the first transmission) prodded into life with sticks. In Nancy Banks-Smith's opinion, 'The Acocks Green Wavy Line Drama Group could prob-ably put on a preferable performance.'[138] There was also Tony Hatch's strange theme tune, in which an electric guitar imperson-ates a doorbell, accompanied by a perfectly mismatched quartet of piano, harp, oboe and drums. And there was the odd inexplicable directorial flourish, such as the decision to open episodes with a prolonged close-up of a telephone, a half-eaten cucumber sandwich, or, on one Burns Night, a huge pile of sheep offal. This jumble of eccentricity gave the constant sense of a production obliviously strutting around with its flies undone.

The torrent of critical vitriol had no effect on *Crossroads'* march from regional curio to national mainstay. In 1972, the recalcitrant northern ITV regions finally took the soap. By 1974, it matched and occasionally outflanked *Coronation Street* in ratings terms, peaking at roughly fifteen million viewers, with the Queen Mother and Harold Wilson's wife Mary among its noted fans. It became a truly national programme on 1 April 1975, when the assorted regional stations synchronised their transmissions. ATV made special 'catch-up' programmes for the likes of Granada and Thames, who'd snootily let their screenings of the soap lag by the best part of a year.

With the entire country occupying the same time-zone, Meg Richardson and Hugh Mortimer had their marriage blessed in Birmingham Cathedral. This wasn't the normal soap wedding, with forgotten rings, catering panics and a ghost from the past interrupting the 'speak now's. This was a full mock ceremony, shot as an outside broadcast, not a million miles from Princess Anne's nuptial coverage a couple of years earlier. Soap royalty ruled for a day. A *TV Times* commemorative wedding brochure sold half a million copies.

Merchandise multiplied. In 1976, *Crossroads* became the first British TV show to have its own regular magazine: *Crossroads Monthly* was published by Felix Dennis of *OZ* infamy, with star profiles, a cookery column and a gatefold pin-up of Gordon. A roaring trade was also established around reproductions of a still life that hung on the wall of Meg's bedroom.

One spin-off had dire repercussions. Paul McCartney, another star fan, recorded a keening stadium rock version of the Tony Hatch theme. Jack Barton, then series producer, decided it was good enough to replace the original in the programme proper. Huge mistake. 'The *Crossroads* theme was bright and happy,' fumed Martyn Finch of Croydon to *TV Times*. 'Now it has plunged into insignificance. The rhythm has gone and the roll of the credits no longer fits the music.' This was perceptive; the famous crossover credit rollers did indeed come and go in reasonably good time with the old doorbell theme, and McCartney's theme upset the balance. After a few weeks of mass grievance, Hatch's original made a triumphant return, with Macca reserved, as Barton explained, 'for downbeat and dramatic, cliffhanging endings. I am hoping that Paul McCartney will write us another, more up-tempo, version of the *Crossroads* theme,' he added hopefully.

In 1981, the glory faded with the termination of Noele Gordon's contract: programme controller Charles Denton found the resulting correspondence 'ranged from abuse to lumps of foreign matter'.[139] On 11 November, after narrowly escaping death ('Oh, my God! The motel! It's on fire!'), Meg Richardson took her final bow in the *QEII*'s Queen Mary suite. Fans were beside themselves: 'The girls on the switchboard have been trying to sympathise,' reassured an ATV representative, 'and have been telling them not to give up hope.'[140]

*Crossroads* soldiered on for another six and a half years, but successive revamps and tinkerings with the theme tune couldn't stop its ultimate slide to an audience of a then paltry twelve million. It inspired few words but generated huge numbers. In a time before the posh papers found they could cheaply fill space by grabbing any piece of low culture that toddled along and hugging it to death in a giant set of inverted commas, *Crossroads* had a tremendous reach that was all but invisible to the media at large – the media still being dedicated, in Tom Stoppard's words, to 'preserving the distinction between serious work and carpentry.'[141] But as Stoppard would have admitted, there'll always be a market for stools.

# LE MANÈGE ENCHANTÉ (1964–1971)

# THE MAGIC ROUNDABOUT (1965–1977)

## ORTF/BBC One (Danot Films/BBC)

### The original cult children's programme.

ANIMATION IS THE MOST meticulously planned form of film-making in front of the camera. Behind the camera, it can be more chaotic than anything else. Serge Danot was a young technical assistant for French producers Cinéastes Associés, working on stop-motion animation for commercials and television effects under Leeds-born animator Ivor Wood. A keen and quick learner, Danot began regaling Wood with ideas for children's entertainments he'd come up with. One, based around the slapstick adventures of various people and animals who lived near an enchanted merry-go-round, was deemed strong enough to go into production in 1964.

Danot and Wood made the first thirteen five-minute films in a small back room in Danot's suburban Paris flat, which had to be periodically abandoned to allow the lighting equipment to cool off. A deal was made for French state television to broadcast them, due as much to the engaging character design and minimalist white scenery as the overt 'Frenchness' of the cast. Each character paid vocal homage to a different French region with the exception of Pollux – an initially incidental long-haired dog who, inspired by Wood, spoke broken French in an English accent.

Domestic success made the show a candidate for the international market, and the first thirty-nine films were bought by the BBC in 1965. Crucially, the means to translate the original dialogue from the French was not forthcoming, so it fell to Play School presenter Eric Thompson, hired to provide the English narration, to also provide the English translation. Unfortunately he hadn't a word of French, so he watched the silent episodes reel-by-reel and started scripting from scratch. Without even a character guide to hand, Thompson looked to his family and the pupils of nearby Ardentinny primary school in Strathclyde for personality types.

Azalea the cow became Ermintrude, Ambrose the snail became Brian, Father Peony became Mr Rusty, and Pollux the dog was rechristened Dougal. Zebulon's mystical incantation '*Tournicoti Tounicoton!*' was now Zebedee's thoroughly agreeable 'Time for bed!' Thompson's contributions are famous for turning the original knockabout cartoon into something subtler, even – in a very broad sense of the word – subversive. This stemmed from an attitude that would logically have debarred him from working on the show. 'I don't actually believe children exist,' he claimed, 'except as part of the adult imagination. When I started to write, I wrote for people, since I think that's what children are – people who haven't lived very long.'[142]

A professional children's writer would have diligently kept esoteric references to Ken Russell and trade unions well out of it. Thompson kept them in, like an inexperienced but eager dad reading a bedtime story and periodically drifting back into the workaday world, using 'long words, intricate phrases . . . if I could find a long word where a short one would do, I used it because children want the real thing.' Occasionally Thompson, by his own estimation, overdid the knowing asides. When Dylan the laid-back rabbit is introduced, Dougal remarks that for a rabbit he doesn't hop about much. Dylan's reply: 'We're re-thinking the image.' Thompson confessed, 'children couldn't really get hold of an idea like that'.[143]

The new narration had the side effect of quietening things down: the adversarial shouts of the French soundtrack were replaced with Thompson's more modulated table talk. This was easier on parental ears than the standard full-throated cartoon declamation, so child-minding adults were more predisposed to listen, catch Thompson's politely skewed monologue, and get hooked. Viewing figures leapt towards eight million, an extraordinary figure for an afternoon slot, equally split between adults and kids, united in their fervent love of Dougal. When the BBC moved it from 5.50 p.m. to 4.55 p.m. in 1966, as a spoiler against ITV's successful *Playtime*, the outcry was colossal. One letter to the *Guardian* complained that 'Mothers everywhere now clock-watch and switch from channel to channel in order not to miss the Roundabout and usually end up by spoiling both.'[144] It swiftly returned to its old slot just before the evening news. Further uproar occurred in February 1971, when it was decided the slot would be more profitably filled by currency aware-ness series *Decimal Five*. Once again, parents and children united in a national tantrum.

From Australia to Mozambique, *Magic Roundabout*'s staggering international success meant the programme was a perfect target for merchandising. A range of Pelham puppets were ready for Christmas 1967. The following December the *Roundabout* was the theme for Selfridges' window display. Along with the expected books and records, an unprecedented variety of trinkets rolled off production lines worldwide: Corgi cars, stationery, duvet covers, lampshades and wallpaper included. Anything with a printable surface or malle-able constitution became a facsimile of Danot and Wood's creation. Canny licensing deals made it all highly lucrative: when, say, a Canadian dog food manufacturer used Dougal on their packaging, Danot and the BBC received one per cent each of gross sales.[145]

From this point on, children's television animation was big business, and, inevitably, high risk. The fledgling London Weekend Television offered Danot £250,000 for UK rights to his follow-up *Les Poucetofs*, about a bunch of elves who live in a world reached via a hollow tree, to be screened in autumn 1969.[146] Unfortunately this coincided with LWT's near financial collapse, so British children thrilled instead to the more rough-hewn adventures of Dutch creation *Paulus the Wood Gnome*. Ivor Wood, meanwhile, set up on his own to animate a string of merchandisable hits for the BBC including *The Herbs*, *The Wombles* and *Paddington Bear*.

After around 500 episodes and a feature film, the original *Roundabout* stopped. Subsequent revivals have met with varied success, the most notable being 1992's affectionate update for breakfast show *The Channel Four Daily*, with Nigel Planer more than adequately filling the Thompson role. But there's never been a chance of recapturing the essential ingredient of the original adult/child TV cult: pure accident.

# WORLD OF SPORT (1965–85)

## ITV (ABC/LWT)

### The sports magazine that preached the three Rs: racing, wrestling, results.

TV SPORT RELIES UPON technology and scale. From 1937's momentous fifteen-minute spectacular *Football at the Arsenal* to the live worldwide televising of the 1964 Tokyo Olympics via the Syncom III satellite, early sports broadcasting went hand in hand with technical innovation and huge production armies: the broadcasters, like their subjects, pushing the limits of human endeavour each season. Just as sport is as much about skill as raw power, so its transmission isn't just a matter of throwing hardware and men at the pitch. Editorial cunning takes precedence over machinery and manpower, especially when the budget is tight.

The BBC, pioneers of the outside broadcast with a fast-growing national network at their disposal, took an early and seemingly unassailable lead. In 1958 it rolled out the Saturday afternoon miscellany *Grandstand*, which dipped into three or four sporting events from around the country, mixed in a bit of studio punditry and rounded things off with a frenzied dash to the football results – the dumpy, battleship grey teleprinter drowning out presenter David Coleman with its metallic clatter as the no-score draws piled up.

This simple format was immensely popular. By 1961 *Grandstand*'s four hour stretch was the only time the BBC outstripped the otherwise triumphant ITV in viewing figures.[147] It was also morally upstanding, refusing to show film of major boxing title fights as 'the programme audience includes many young viewers'.[148] The lack of time did rankle with fans – one viewer branded it a 'flibberti-gibbet lucky dip . . . which ensures that no sooner has the follower of one particular event got interested and involved than he or she is at once whisked away into something quite different, usually horse racing.'[149]

The independent channel, with no dedicated sports unit of its own, couldn't compete with that. For inspiration ABC, the weekend-only ITV company, looked to its state-side namesake. The third US network, still regarded as the runt of the TV litter, had since 1961 enjoyed modest success with its magazine show *Wide World of Sports*. While NBC had the money to snaffle the rights to major events, ABC looked outside the headlines – even outside the USA – at what else was going on in the name of sport. So instead of baseball and the NFL, it gave viewers pelota, lacrosse, sundry motorsports, competitive fire fighting, assorted kooky stunt chal-lenges and the ever-popular cliff diving from Acapulco. It even introduced America to something called the Wimbledon Tennis Championships.

Dropping the transatlantic plural, the British *World of Sport* made up for lack of coverage with urgent pizazz. *Grandstand*'s bare studio was replaced with a bustling typing pool. 'With a battery of tape machines, backed by a staff of Fleet Street sub-editors, *World of Sport* will bring all the glamour and thrills of Saturday afternoon sport right into your living room.'[150] Like *TW3*, *WoS* flaunted its workings, making the process of getting sport onto the screen part of the show itself. 'Film of outstanding sporting events of the day will be rushed onto waiting aircraft,' panted the publicity, cannily avoiding mention of what those events might actually be.

Sat in front of the typists was presenter Eamonn Andrews. A former boxing commentator, Andrews had been lured over from hosting *What's My Line?* on the Beeb with a rumoured £120,000 three-year contract. Viewers of his chat show often paused to wonder why. In 1968, as London Weekend gained control of *WoS*, he was replaced by infinitely more affable former cruise ship entertainer Richard 'Dickie' Davies, whose two-tone bouffant became as much a part of the show as the typists, the aeroplane banners bearing the programme titles, and the four sporting pillars of its afternoon line-up.

First, and in some ways least, was football. Even though *WoS*'s advent coincided with the deployment of the Ampex HS-100 video-disc recorder and the dawn of the action replay, full match coverage was beyond its remit. Instead the programme kicked off with 'On the Ball', in which Pete Lorenzo or Brian Moore rounded up the week's goals, knocked out a write-in postcard competition, and let LWT's Head of Sport, 'Jimmy Hill, the crusading ex-soccerman', pontificate at length on the state of the game. Similarly at large was champion cricketer Fred Trueman, who did pretty much whatever he fancied. 'Freddie has a roving commission with *World of Sport*. Might pop up at a rugby league match . . . or a gentle ladies' croquet meeting!'[151]

Next came racing. Weather permitting, *WoS* covered two meetings each week, the various races punctuating the programme as part of The ITV Seven, which for those of a betting disposition had a potentially lucrative accumulator attached to it. It was altogether more populist than the Beeb's blue-blooded coverage, though it was overseen by the gracious, trilby-sporting John Rickman. The Seven was 'a streamlined, more crisp, horse-racing service', in which hand-scrawled betting odds flashed on screen and 'an attractive girl' was nominated to give tips – a touch of ritzy glamour amongst the sheepskins and Woodbines.

'International Sports Special' usually followed, which was either the bought-in item from the US ABC show – truck racing, clown diving, bus jumping *et al* – or a useful boost for unsung pastimes like darts, bowls and table tennis, or the extraordinarily popular speedway. But the programme's main attraction was professional wrestling. ITV took the ancient art's modern equivalent to its bosom, helping it bloom into the loud and sweaty suspension of disbelief in leotards that drove eight and eighty-year-olds mad with pantomime rage. In drill halls across the land, slow-mo karate chops and well-rehearsed somersaults were executed by barrel-chested athletes with stage names steeped in bathos: 'Gentleman' Chris Adams, 'Mammoth' Ian Campbell, 'Cyanide' Sid Cooper, 'Gaylord' Steve Peacock. Everyone knew this wasn't a sport, but nobody gave two hoots.

Even this made-for-telly spectacle lost impact in translation – the wet slap of belly on canvas and the perspiration-drenched singlets fell, perhaps thankfully, outside the scope of UHF transmission. Atmosphere was replenished by commentator Kent Walton, host of ITV's earlier *Cavalcade of Sport* and the man who'd beaten Jack Good to the punch by hosting the UK's first rock 'n' roll TV show *Cool for Cats* in 1956 – thus knowing all about scream-worthy spectacle. 'You tell me where else a nice, demure young lady can scream or shout her head off,' demanded wrestling's star villain Mick McManus. 'It doesn't matter how sophisticated you are normally, you can become a fishwife for half an hour and then go home all relaxed.'[152] After that climax there was nothing for it but to read out the football results, 'presented in a slick, new, easy-to-follow method' with plenty of emphasis on the pools dividend forecast.

The sports magazine was a stopgap format, a compromise that had to do until there were sufficient channels to give sports of all kinds enough space – and the means to charge premium rates for the privilege. Good news for the major sports, but aside from darts, which *WoS* helped popularise, the also-rans faded from view. Without Uncle Dickie to guide them, generations grew up knowing nothing of the Wisconsin World Lumberjacking Championships.

# TALKING TO A STRANGER (1966)
## BBC Two

Television's 'first masterpiece'.

*It is wrong for all television programmes to be immediately understood . . . and forgotten. There must be some which nag the mind.*

John Hopkins, 29 October 1966

UNIVERSALLY FAMILIAR AND CHEAP to stage, packed with paranoia, resentment, barely concealed animosity and subtly devastating mind games – the family should be the most fruitful subject for the TV dramatist. For many years, however, the lid remained firmly on the familial study, and net-curtained nothings prevailed. Pull apart the family and you unnerve society, as Henrik Ibsen discovered when *Ghosts*, his destruction of Scandinavian moral hypocrisy, practically made him a theatrical pariah.

The respectable British stage recoiled from this dangerous filth and embraced what Kenneth Tynan called the 'Loamshire' play: the harmless, pointless minor mishaps of well-bred Home Counties model families. 'Loamshire is a glibly codified fairy tale world,' he wrote, 'of no more use to the student of life than a doll's house would be to a student of town planning . . . its inhabitants belong to a social class derived partly from romantic novels and partly from the playwright's vision of the leisured life he will lead after the play is a success.'[153] Loamshire is a resilient construction – turn on Radio Four of a weekday and you'll find it alive and well, dusted with a few contemporary references. Media spoof *On the Hour* perfectly captured its recycled angst with a twenty-four-hour rolling drama service, spewing an unbroken stream of over-emoted suburban boilerplate into the indifferent afternoon sky. ('She's my WIFE!' 'You OWE it to yourself, George!') Back in 1965, television drama was up to its aerial in Loamshire, and discerning observers prayed for a small screen Ibsen.

Despite working as a producer for BBC radio at the time, John Hopkins got his first written work televised, as so many first generation TV writers did, by Granada. The Beeb soon became his main source of work, largely via *Z-Cars*, Troy Kennedy Martin's northern police serial which startled audiences on its 1962 debut with a determinedly hard-edged realism that made Paddy Chayefsky look like Noel Coward. Sitting diligently down to work from nine thirty in the morning until the end of *Housewives' Choice*, Hopkins completed nearly twenty-four hours of *Z-Cars* material over two and a half years, which he came to regard not so much as a serial but 'the longest play anyone ever wrote'.[154] This regular grind contrasted with the drawn out creation of his magnum opus *Talking to a Stranger*, a four-part study of one fatal Sunday gathering of a fractious adult family.

The year 1966 was a peak one for bold British drama. In November *Cathy Come Home*, a docudrama dealing squarely with homelessness, stopped a good portion of the country in its tracks and set new standards for dramatic realism and journalistic fortitude. At the other extreme, Jonathan Miller served up his psychedelic, Orientalist *Alice in Wonderland* to a nation rendered powerless by the Christmas festivities. Hopkins, however, got in before both these milestones with what George Melly called 'the first authentic masterpiece written directly for television.'[155]

Melly credited Hopkins with being the first serious TV dramatist to read 'the cliché-ridden runes of the semi-detached petit-bourgeois.'[156] From these he created the Stevenses, an outwardly unremarkable lower-middle-class family: Ted and Sarah the ageing, unspeaking parents; Alan the son with a family and a business opportunity in Australia; Terry the headstrong, flippantly wayward daughter with a surprise baby on the way. Over six hours of television, Hopkins looked at their final get together from the perspective of each family member in turn, clarifying details and altering perspective as it unravelled. This was not just a TV novel, it was a modernist TV novel, shuffling time, juggling styles and occupying minds.

Psychologically speaking, the Stevenses had got the lot. This made the plays a slog in some ways but, as the lighter end of family television used to boast, there was something for everyone: a taciturn father, wanton teenage antagonism, unplanned pregnancy, miscegenation and parent-child relations that seemed to have stalled at the latter's twelfth birthday. Jam the lot into a now tiny-looking ancestral house and douse liberally with the pervading misery of an old school, full-fat Christian Sunday, and you have the modern British human condition in all its shameful ignominy – quietly having a nervous breakdown as it dodges into the kitchen and pretends to busy itself with the tea things.

It was tough going, starting off as suburban Ibsen and concluding, with the mother's tragic story, in the abyss-gazing manner of Eugene O'Neill. Like a good modernist, Hopkins incorporated phrases and words from pop culture into his script. 'Everything is relevant. I'm not in the market for polished sentences.'[157] The title of Ted's episode, 'No Skill or Special Knowledge is Required', came from an overheard ad on Radio Caroline.

It was heralded as Big Television, but reviews were thoroughly mixed. The scale of the piece baffled some. 'The dramatist, I am certain, could have expressed in sixty minutes all that was essential, and it would have been a much better, more compelling work.'[158] Some praised the restrained direction of Christopher Morahan, though many disliked what they saw as tricksy flashbacks indicated by 'meat safe mottling on the screen'.[159] Even those who longed for Loamshire gave the actors due credit, particularly Margery Mason as the mother and Judi Dench as Terry. J. C. Trewin, though no fan, captured its texture: 'a medley of half-sentences, choked emotions, sudden outbursts, hopeless realisations; in fact it was very much like life, in its drearier repetitions.'[160]

The BBC believed in the play, and gave it an unprecedented two repeats in eighteen months. It was granted a detailed, shot-by-shot analysis on arts programme *Late Night Line-Up*, the first in-depth technical criticism of TV on TV. Hopkins had cleared the way for complex, allusive, emotionally honest television drama.

He had also opened the doors to a flood of overwrought obscurity, with some of the most obscure stuff coming from his own typewriter. On two consecutive nights in 1972, the BBC screened *That Quiet Earth* and *Walk Into the Dark* – heavily symbolic studies of modern society and mental disturbance, directed by Hopkins himself and starring his wife Shirley Knight. They didn't go well. 'Drained of life-blood and injected up to the hilt with portent,' observed Clive James, 'each line is guaranteed to win from an actor the most face-wrenching trick in his book – abstract significance.'[161] Nancy Banks-Smith whittled her dismissal down to eight syllables: 'primeval mulligatawny'.[162] A wounded Hopkins bit back. 'Critics come to a play like a football match,' he complained, 'they are not prepared to work at it. It's almost like a conspiracy to stop me writing.'[163] TV gave Hopkins valuable early freedom, but as a mass medium it demanded in return a degree of artistic compromise. And as Ibsen said, 'the Devil is compromise'.

# THE SMOTHERS BROTHERS COMEDY HOUR (1967–9)

## CBS (Comedic Productions)

### Variety drops out.

*This is my electric cigar. I plug it in, smoke it . . . and it turns me on.*

George Burns guests on the third
*Smothers Brothers Comedy Hour*, 19 February 1967

THE COUNTERCULTURE HIT NETWORK TV like an ink dart in the back of a teacher's neck. While music could change its garb in a week and cinema created its own underground movements, TV was beholden to the conservative strictures of its sponsors and had the cultural flexibility and grace of an oil tanker. The television networks eyed up the long-haired dropouts, and vowed never to let their fragile offspring out to play with them. Until one day, when two nicely-barbered brothers came knocking.

Tom and Dick Smothers were a whimsical duo who rose through the US café scene during the early sixties folk revival. Not being virtuoso players of the guitar and double bass respectively, they gradually ramped up the sibling cross-talk in their act until their LPs were less a collection of toothsome ditties than one long tit-for-tat tantrum. Seeing TV potential, CBS snapped them up, and promptly wasted them on *The Smothers Brothers Show*, a cookie-cutter sitcom in the *I Dream of Jeannie* mould. It cast Tom as Dick's deceased brother, a bungling apprentice angel; appropriately, it stiffed.

The brothers were given creative control of their next show, a traditional comedy-variety hour. With a wacky toy town military band opening and Tiffany stage trappings, the early shows were safe, homely fare, and even admitted as much. ('We're going to present some pungent social comment on the pressing issues of the day.' 'Tommy, we're not going to do anything of the sort!') When George Burns and Jack Benny turned up to indulge in scripted horseplay, a coded marijuana gag delivered by Burns was as dangerous as things got. CBS were content with what they saw as a likeable, clean-cut duo gently but respectfully guying their star guests. It didn't hurt that they soon overtook NBC's behemoth *Bonanza* in the Sunday night ratings.

With Tom as the mainspring, the show evolved into something sharper than the networks had ever seen. The writing team, including Mason 'Classical Gas' Williams and, later, Steve Martin, began exploring the acceptable limits laid down by CBS's forbidding Department of Program Practices. These limits were tight indeed. Guest comedian Elaine May supplied a sketch about film censors which was itself censored for pivotal use of the word 'breast'. The brothers eventually got the sketch on TV – by holding up the pages to camera. While the Vietnam War and erosion of democracy on the home front became the show's main satirical targets, there was just as much risk in their taunting of CBS, its ultra-conservative affiliate stations and, most audaciously of all, the Nielsen ratings system. After several decades of uneasy coexistence, comedy had formally declared war on television.

Musical guests were initially as tame as the brothers themselves – the show introduced Glenn Campbell to the world. But the bookings became more esoteric, and so did the presentation. Jefferson Airplane were superimposed over the live psychedelic ink swirls of Glenn McKay. (For this and other videotape experiments, the show won the 3M company's inaugural award for 'Excellence in Electography'.) The Who overloaded a cannon in Keith Moon's bass drum, scaring the audience to death, singeing Pete Townshend's hair and, according to Roger Daltrey, causing guest star Bette Davis, watching in the wings dressed as Elizabeth I, to faint clean away.[164] But the greatest musical triumph was the reappearance, after seventeen years in the wilderness, of blacklisted folk pioneer Pete Seeger, performing an impassioned rendition of his anti-war song 'Waste Deep in the Big Muddy' to euphoric applause.

The show amassed a gallery of resident freaks. Leigh French appeared from the audience, seemingly unbidden, as flower-haired hippy child Goldie, firing off a dreamy stream of countercultural innuendo with wide-pupilled innocence. Writer Bob Einstein's Officer Judy, a motorcycle cop with a storm trooper's attitude to community policing, broke up sketches and threatened the hosts. Most of all, though, there was the numb and knackered Pat Paulsen, whose hapless disinterest and tenuous grasp of English made him the ideal candidate to run for the 1968 presidential elections. Following in the steps of Gracie Allen some twenty-eight years previously, Paulsen toured the country on a completely non-committal ticket. He laid into his opponents while getting their names wrong. He adopted a free jazz approach to policymaking. He conferred with Bobby Kennedy. He promised precisely nothing. He even defended the network censors. ('The Bill of Rights says nothing about freedom of hearing.') His vote collapsed, but he did much to dislodge presidential office from its lofty plateau. (His victorious rival Richard Nixon would soon finish the job for him.)

In 1968, the brothers lost their unique position in the affection of the youth audience as *Rowan & Martin's Laugh-In* debuted on NBC. *Laugh-In* was quick-fire, catchphrase-strewn and while superficially just as hip as the Smothers brothers, lacked their moral mission. Nixon kept close tabs on what the brothers said about him; *Laugh-In* welcomed him as guest star.

The third season of *Comedy Hour* opened with a statement of intent on the brothers' top lips. Moustaches, long considered a major viewer turn-off in the Midwest, were just the beginning. Guest Harry Belafonte sang a re-worded version of 'Don't Stop the Carnival', superimposed over footage of violent disorder at the recent, disastrous National Democratic Convention in Chicago. Program Practices snipped that out the instant they saw it. As compensation one sketch that did get through, parodying *Bonanza*, beat *Star Trek* to the first networked interracial kiss by a month – and this kiss was between Mama Cass and macramé-loving former LA Rams footballer Rosey Grier, both in drag.

These stunts riled the affiliates, who in turn riled Tom Smothers, creating an escalating atmosphere of mutual antipathy between show and network. It was made clear by CBS that the majority of Americans were not about to 'turn on' any time soon. 'In the Thirty Cities ratings the Smothers clan does well,' wrote Harlan Ellison, 'but in the outlying regions, where most of the soap-suds are bought, they die.'[165] Midway through the season, insurrection peaked. Joan Baez dedicated a song to her husband, in prison for protesting against the draft. Dan Rowan turned up to award a *Laugh-In* Flying Fickle Finger of Fate award to Smothers nemesis Senator John Pastore. David Steinberg delivered a comic sermon observing, with appropriate hand gestures, that Christian scholars 'literally grab the Jews by the Old Testament'. All three incidents were butchered in the edit.

Today, as Steinberg admits of his own bits, 'you look at these things and they're tame, they're just . . . *okay*.'[166] But at the time, combined with the crusading zeal of Tom Smothers, they created a national scandal and precipitated the firing of the duo. Adding inbreds to injury, *Comedy Hour* was replaced with *Hee Haw*, a backwoods *Laugh-In* clone that linked bluegrass numbers with cornball gags in a stream of Bible-belt-friendly inanity. This hayseed hooey would soon be swept away by incoming CBS vice president Fred Silverman, but for now it was a great stride backward for US TV. Still, the Smothers had unquestionably made their mark. Elvis Presley, who had recently used TV to great effect in NBC's stripped down comeback special *Elvis*, named the brothers in his 1970 meeting with the FBI as people who 'have a lot to answer for in the hereafter for the way they have poisoned young minds'.[167] After the Smothers brothers, television was no longer rock 'n' roll's square uncle. It was now its goofy younger cousin with a 1910 Fruitgum Company LP and subscription to *Tiger Beat*. Still, that was better than nothing.

# THE PRISONER: FALL OUT (1968)
## ITV (ITC/Everyman Films)

### TV collapses under the weight of its own splendid folly.

> *When The Prisoner finally got upstairs and tore off the mask in the end, who would Number One turn out to be? We knew it couldn't be an anti-climax and we knew on the other hand it couldn't be a climax . . . Well, one day I turned to Pat and said, 'I know! You pull the mask off . . . and it's Lew Grade.'*
>
> Alexis Kanner

THE RULE'S AS OLD as the medium itself: the more idiosyncratic the drama, the more rarefied the audience. Personal visions and big ratings don't mix. As an immutable law it only has one drawback: in 1968 it was not just flouted but comprehensively repealed by Patrick McGoohan.

When Lew Grade, ruler of the ITC production empire, offered McGoohan the lead in espionage thriller *Danger Man*, McGoohan did more than just turn up and read the lines: he made sweeping changes. He vetoed the 'contrived romantic liaisons and excessive violence . . . the corny show-business formula, the publicity machine grinding away,'[168] in favour of psychological complexity and character depth. Then, when he tired of the whole thing – the whole multi-million pound, salary of two grand a week, sold to over sixty countries thing – he quit. He was offered countless more action roles but turned them down flat, just as he'd refused James Bond a few years before.

In an early morning private meeting with Grade, McGoohan expounded an idea he'd been toying with since about the same time Anthony Newley – another leading man who couldn't abide the path of fame down which he was herded – came up with *Gurney Slade*. Grade couldn't make head nor tail of the pitch, but McGoohan's ambition, and the charming images of Portmeirion – his location of choice, previously used in an episode of *Danger Man* – sold it.

McGoohan's nameless hero was a high-ranking secret agent, similar to *Danger Man*'s John Drake, who quits his post on a point of principle, is subsequently abducted by forces unknown and sequestered in an inescapable 'village' of wedding cake architecture, English country manners and high-tech totalitarian surveillance. Re-designated 'Number Six', he first makes fruitless attempts to escape, then tries to break the security surrounding the Village authorities, never getting higher up the pecking order than the constantly changing 'Number Two'. Each self-contained adventure was also a baroque satire on modern concerns: technology, education, politics and defence were among the big topics allegorically served up at seven thirty on a Sunday evening.

*The Prisoner*'s look, masterminded by Jack Shampan, started from the same end of the Kings Road as *The Avengers*, before veering off into the films of Federico Fellini, with their incongruously costumed figures performing mysterious rites in remote landscapes. The plot similarly began with the standard ITC adventure serial, a rough and ready style known in the trade as 'kick, bollock and scramble', and added a dollop of colour supplement conspiracy from Hollywood paranoia trips like *Seconds* and *The President's Analyst*, where extravagantly sinister secret societies pursue our dauntless hero through a forest of sliding panels.

While *The Prisoner* operated in the familiar pulp world of sharp tailoring, bloodless gunfights and the single knockout punch to the head, there were hints at something more grown-up, perhaps even revelatory, behind it all, to do with society, identity and authoritarian control. Some found this blending of low- and high-brow hard to take. '[Is it] meant to be taken seriously,' asked T. C. Worsley, 'or is it a spoof? If the latter, it lacks edge; if the former, conviction.'[169]

It collected many respectable fans, including Anthony Burgess, who declared himself 'thoroughly hooked' on a series he likened to 'the old picaresque novel, [producing] characters and adventures of a Cervantes-like richness.'[170] A generation weaned on old-fashioned heroics, now maturing to the accompaniment of progressive pop, turned-on cinema and arch fashion, got McGoohan's creation instantly. Or at least, they were willing to go along for the ride without checking the destination first.

Lew Grade, while appreciative of the episodes he previewed, was enough of a traditional showman to voice concerns over where it was all leading. By now *The Prisoner*'s mix of High Englishness and international glamour had sold to the US, Canada, much of Europe, Australia, Latin America and Japan – no pressure. As the final episode approached, McGoohan finally came clean: he didn't have an ending. 'I thought it was very nice of him,' recalled Grade, reflecting in tranquillity some years later, 'to come straight out with me and admit it.'[171] But great things had come out of thin air before: the infamous Rover, a white, seemingly sentient balloon which menaced, chased and captured would-be Village defectors, was a last minute, desperate on-set replacement hurriedly deployed when the original prop robot failed. Grade gave McGoohan the benefit of a great deal of doubt.

In the final four episodes, the show's tics grew to excess: scripts that got bored with themselves before the ink was dry; the dressing-up-box approach to narrative continuity; the general atmosphere of a radicalised edition of *Play School*. The multifarious possibilities of Portmeirion having been exhausted, the show went on a metaphysical tour. A western episode was followed by a dialogue-free bedtime story that mixed *Mission: Impossible* and Roadrunner cartoons, with a crafty swipe at petty nationalism along the way. It went from a cricket match to Kenneth Griffith dressed as Napoleon in an exploding lighthouse without a pause – a parodic distillation of the camp action format the series had decisively outgrown.

The next episode, by contrast, was a minimalist fever dream. Locked for a week into a black-walled chamber, McGoohan and the final Number Two, Leo McKern, rounded on each other in a series of make-believe mental battles pitched somewhere between psychological torture and a fringe theatre party piece. Childhoods were relived, nursery rhymes chanted and brandy knocked back. Prop master Mickey O'Toole openly slagged off the abstruse script on set, unaware it was written, in one draft, by a pseudonymous McGoohan. The two-hander was so intense, it came close to killing McKern. The show was behaving like a cult before it was even broadcast.

McGoohan also wrote *Fall Out*, the anti-denouement: Number Six's enthronement in a Bond villain bunker, promising gobsmacking revelations to a Beatles soundtrack. Kenneth Griffith, in full-bottomed wig, presided over a court of symbolic, hooded and masked officials. (This was acute symbolism, the symbols being handily written down on nameplates, like a live action newspaper cartoon.) McKern was brought back from the (fictional) dead and given a shave. Alexis Kanner played a Revolting Youth, singing and capering like Anthony Newley. It was pompous, funny, insane, fascinating, boring: the most deranged thing ever to infiltrate peak time commercial television.

It was also, in conventional TV terms, cheating. The sets, speeches and mind games were like magician's props, patter and ceremony: an awesomely elaborate way of guarding an empty box. So Number One was . . . a *Morgan*-style gorilla? McGoohan himself? What kind of a punchline was that? Front rooms and pubs fell silent as the credits rolled, then erupted with the terrible rage of the insuf-ficiently entertained. 'The whole tumulus of the series rested on jelly; the crash was frightful,' wrote Anthony Burgess. 'I will never again hope [for] too much from television.'[172] McGoohan later admitted, 'I had to go and hide myself in case I got killed.' [173]

But among the mob, many appreciated this new way of doing serial business, seeing speculative possibilities in the untied loose ends. One viewer neatly killed two televisual birds with one stone: 'I have come to the conclusion that it was part two of the *Magical Mystery Tour*.'[174] (McGoohan was the Fab Four's prime candidate to direct a planned follow-up to that notorious Boxing Day indulgence.)

That promise of enlightenment, those unanswered questions, kept the show alive in many viewers' minds. The temptation to explore its self-contained world further than its creators had ever dared proved enormous. McGoohan, always coyly tight-lipped, refused to explain his 'allegorical conundrum', so amateur sleuths went to work.[175] A fan club formed in 1977, holding its first convention the year after, complete with screenings, seminars and home-made Village blazers. The hobby of filling in the show's many gaps became a vocation, at once knowingly frivolous and deadly earnest, giving *The Prisoner* an afterlife even more fruitful than its twelve-million-rating British heyday. Since then, cultdom has been the Holy Grail for the genre drama series, though few attain it and those that actively try to foster it often die an anonymous death. Almost half a century on, the formula for cult success remains as elusive as Number One.

# IF THERE WEREN'T ANY BLACKS, YOU'D HAVE TO INVENT THEM (1968, 1973)

## ITV (LWT)

### Alf Garnett's creator takes the race issue to its absurd conclusion.

> *JOHNNY SPEIGHT: I'm a Chekhov character, that's what I am*
> *– right out of* The Cherry Orchard . . . *I want to write a play.*
> *MRS SPEIGHT: I want to finish this ironing without a lot of*
> *aggro.*
>
> Dialogue in the Speight household, c. 1960[176]

JUDGING THE SOCIAL ATTITUDES of cultural artefacts from the past is always a fun sport, particularly if you get to feel smug about your own era in the process. Any TV programme of old that deals with race, sex or class is bound to look crass, bigoted or quaint to modern eyes. Something would be badly wrong if it didn't. The consensus is of a steady upward progression from antediluvian ignorance to modern inclusiveness, and this is often true. To complicate matters, however, many aspects of society and its entertainment have become more divisive. One notorious 1960s comedy play is an example of both cases.

A son of toil from Canning Town, Johnny Speight made his early fame writing comedy sketches for Arthur Haynes, whose gentleman tramp character achieved national recognition in the late 1950s. In 1962, the Arts Theatre Club launched a season of controversial, censor-baiting plays with *The Knacker's Yard*, Speight's tale of the sinister resident of a boarding house, a violent nihilist muttering 'Frozen peas and the H-bomb, that's the menu for this century.' Its combination of broad comedy and unrelentingly grim symbolism was tough on even the strongest critical stomachs.

Speight owed a debt to Pinter (who was no stranger to sketch comedy himself, writing spot pieces for Dick Emery in between 'legitimate' appointments), but overlaid the unease with a plethora of traditionally crafted one-liners. The end result was frightening and familiar at once: the continental Theatre of the Absurd passed several times through the music hall mangle. When Spike Milligan's post-holocaust phantasmagoria *The Bed-Sitting Room* arrived at the Mermaid Theatre the following year, the genre had acquired a reassuringly cosy name: British Rubbish. The nation's theatrical establishment was starting to give the avant-garde its due, but not if it was going to stoop to cracking jokes.

In 1964, Speight wrote *If There Weren't Any Blacks, You'd Have to Invent Them* – a knockabout *reductio ad absurdum* of racism, liberal guilt and entrenched bigotry for Sidney Newman's BBC Drama Unit. It was turned down in short order as being, in a typically vague description, 'unsuitable'. Speight put on a brave face by reflecting that he made more money by having it turned down, as he could then sell it to independent station Associated-Rediffusion. In the meantime the RSC performed a twenty-minute chunk on stage and Speight created his most enduring and problematic character: the East End bigot Alf Garnett. *Blacks* then sat on Rediffusion's shelf a while longer before finally becoming the first drama production of the new London Weekend Television.

The play takes place in a graveyard, presided over by an upright undertaker, two priests (Catholic and C of E, who squabble over particulars but back each other up in the face of secular threats) and a bolshie, salt-of-the-earth sexton. The latter tolls the bell and buries the dead till his joints give out and is the only character who manages the odd Brechtian aside to camera, rousing the workers and calling for 'council house bishops'.

Into this macabre plot stumbles a sickly young mother's boy with a morbid fear of 'postal diseases'. He falls foul of a bigoted blind man straight out of Beckett, who leads his constant companion everywhere, a *bien pensant* liberal who can see perfectly well but prefers to keep his eyes shut, and walk backwards. ('What the eye don't see the heart don't grieve over.') Between the two of them, they come to the conclusion that the young man must be black – or if he isn't, he ought to be. Gradually everyone else in the cemetery, including a doctor, military officer and judge, identify the boy as the weakest in the graveyard, and best done away with. ('Don't want your sort hanging round, lowering our land values, do we?') The gang swells via a mixture of unfocussed hate and circular logic, into a lynch mob. One more grave for the sexton to fill. Innit marvellous?

Speight's play may not add up to more than a selection of interlocking sketches, but he pinpoints origins of racism in social panic: 'they might be different, but you don't know until the damage is done, do you?' There are some grand acts of audience provocation, like the opening image after the commercial break of a 'Keep Heaven White' church poster in full close-up. Fine actors filled the cast, from Frank Thornton's stiff Undertaker to the rugged Leslie Sands's deeply sinister Blind Man and his cheerfully ignorant partner, played by Jimmy Hanley, best known to ITV viewers for hawking products in his pretend pub for advertising magazine *Jim's Inn*. The 1968 production, directed by Charles Jarrott with not too much gimmickry, was received with mixed critical enthusiasm. Tom Stoppard liked it, but felt its moment had passed: 'a bit too close to the post-*Bedsitting Room* period.'[177] Robert Pitman just let out a loud yawn: 'We were warned it would be oh, so controversial.'[178] Robin Thornber treated a stage revival a year later with more zeal – 'a Goon Show dictated by Alf Garnett to a drunken Ionesco.'[179]

Then in 1973 it received the rarest of all accolades for a television play: a revival. Big names were cast – Leonard Rossiter as the Blind Man, Richard Beckinsale as the young victim, Bob Hoskins as the sexton, now attired as a ragged ex-Teddy Boy. (Neither production cast any black actors, although that was at least partly the point.) The cemetery was now a stylised apocalyptic wreck of Cadillacs and Rita Hayworth hoardings, reminiscent of Fernando Arrabal's 1958 play *The Automobile Graveyard*. Directing, Bill Hays pushed the cast towards belly-laugh territory, and added rather intrusive comedy trombone interludes. Not so much the Theatre of the Absurd as the Plain Daft.

What had happened was that history had overtaken fiction. Enoch Powell had made his notorious 'Rivers of Blood' address while the original production was in progress, and in the intervening years had soared in public esteem to become pretty much the nation's most admired politician. In the meantime, *Love Thy Neighbour*, an ITV sitcom about a white bigot with black neighbours which treated the race issue in much the same way as Derek Nimmo's *All Gas and Gaiters* approached the deeper questions of theology, had become more popular than Speight ever dreamed. What had been a peripheral issue was now central to British politics, to a dangerous extent. LWT's answer was to camp the whole thing up. 'It is almost pantomime,' admitted producer Rex Firkin, 'although the underlying tone is still there.'[180]

Tastes would shortly change again, and not in ways of which Speight approved. 'Alternative comedy,' he mused, 'as far as I can see, sets out, not only not to attack our appalling prejudices and awful bigotry, but to assuage our prim national propriety by declining to notice them.'[181] An unfair generalisation maybe – Rik Mayall's congenitally hypocritical Rick the Poet alone refutes it – but a decade after *Blacks* was first broadcast, TV comedy increasingly segregated working class humour from its collegiate counterpart, and that gulf would only widen with time, leading to the marginalisation of the former and the distortion of both. The brief days when a factory worker, self-educated on volumes of Bernard Shaw at the local library, could get an absurdist satire on middle-class attitudes to race relations broadcast at peak time on a commercial channel on a Sunday night had gone for good.

# SESAME STREET (1969–)

## WNET/PBS (Children's Television Workshop)

### The awakening of public service broadcasting produces monsters.

PUBLIC SERVICE BROADCASTING, EDUCATIONAL television, non-commercial programming: in Britain, Canada and many European countries, TV funded by various means from the public purse with the sole intent of improving the cultural lot of the people was a familiar, sometimes dominant, part of the entertainment landscape. The USA, raised on a commercial system since the early days of radio, lacked a free, unsponsored national network.

One service, however, has somehow managed to keep going since 1952. Kick-started by a grant from the Ford Foundation and bearing several titles before settling on National Educational Television in 1963, it aimed to grow into a fourth network of intelligent, edifying material. In reality it had a job staying on air. Funding crises, government intervention and, in the late 1960s, fallout from controversial documentaries including *The Poor Pay More* and *Black Like Me,* threatened its very existence. In 1970, it was radically restructured into the Public Broadcasting Service (PBS), with over half its funding coming from private donations. A year before that, it inaugurated its greatest asset: the first global children's television programme.

*Sesame Street* was a colourful, inclusive, charming, laid-back and endlessly inventive jamboree, as far from the staid educational stereotype as anyone – and in particular Jim Henson – could imagine. Lloyd Morrisett, educational psychologist and vice president of philanthropic institute the Carnegie Corporation, concocted a pre-school programme with Joan Ganz Cooney, producer of some of those troubling NET documentaries. The show had to combine formal and social education, and be snappy enough to hold its own against the hit-and-run competition of the commercial channels' output, especially the commercials themselves, which Morrisett noticed had the knack of embedding themselves in the memories of small kids. The Children's Television Workshop was born, and two years of research and development, estimated at $8 million, went into honing a mixture of dramatised learning, puppetry and animation. The result was a programme that caught the attention of around ninety per cent of three-to-six-year-olds, as opposed to sixty-five per cent for traditional educational shows.[182]

These were forbidding figures, but in this case laboratory tested didn't mean sterile. Sesame Street itself – a partially idealised suburban set, complete with brownstone stoops and fire hydrants – was a more realistic take on another NET children's property, *Mr Rogers' Neighbourhood*. Initially, the street was populated by four adults – amiable musician Bob, married couple Gordon and Susan, and convenience store owner Mr Hooper – a rolling cast of children, and a repertory of monsters ranging from one to eight feet in height.

The monsters sold the show. Jim Henson had been plying his own style of puppetry – foam and fabric glove puppets with rod-operated marionette limbs – since the mid 1950s, on local Washington show *Sam and Friends* (featuring an embryonic Kermit the Frog) and a string of surreal commercials. Some puppets, like overstuffed greenhorn canary Big Bird, were overtly childlike, slightly cloying characters in the baby-talk tradition of children's entertainment. Others, most of them voiced and operated by Henson and master puppeteer Frank Oz, were a new breed: witty, sharp and gambolling on the borders of sanity.

There was Oscar the Grouch, a dyspeptic Diogenes who skulked in a trashcan and railed against such cissy activities as helping people and joining in. The Wheel Stealer, a boggle-eyed, shark-toothed monster who pilfered corn snack wheels in 1960s commercials, lost the teeth and became biscuit-revering buffoon the Cookie Monster. Ernie and Bert, a live-in couple with the personality dynamics of Henson and Oz allied to the crosstalk of Abbott and Costello, were the only good thing in the original pilot. Their touching co-dependence of wide-eyed wonder and obsessive worry become the show's internationally recognised backbone.

Two highly versatile puppets provided the best of the sketches. Henson's Kermit evolved into a crack roving reporter, covering historical events and fairy tales in an eager but increasingly bemused manner. He was on the spot when Don Music, precious composer of everything from 'Mary Had a Little Lamb' to 'Humpty Dumpty', stumbled over a crucial rhyme ('I'll never get it!') and slammed his face into the keyboard with artistic angst. ('You'll hurt yourself in the head there, Don.') Then there was Oz's Grover, an exhaustingly keen inhabitant of alter egos ranging from superhero to eccentric waiter at Charlie's Restaurant, where he forever wound up his fat, blue-headed customer by muddling orders ('Listen carefully . . . ' 'All right, speak carefully!') before promising a dramatic break-through in comprehension. ('Hold everything! Lock the doors, I've got it!') Through a mixture of breakneck scripting and grown-up (but never off-colour) ad-libbing, Kermit and Grover crammed basic life skills into young heads without a sniff of educational bromide.

As well as news reports, the team commandeered game shows, documentaries and dramas as clandestine vehicles of learning. Other PBS shows came in for parody, most notably the British heritage dramas shown under the umbrella title *Masterpiece Theatre*. Resplendent in velvet smoking jacket and pipe, 'Alistair Cookie' introduced 'Monsterpiece Theatre', 'home of classy drama' such as 'The Postman Always Rings Twice' ('famous drama of suspense and lots of waiting around'); 'Twin Beaks' (featuring David Finch) and 'Me, Claudius'. Truffaut's *The 400 Blows* became Grover's epic attempt to blow out the candles on his birthday cake. *One Flew Over the Cuckoo's Nest* was mistakenly translated as 'Two Flew Over the Chicken Coop'. ('Very beautiful, very moving . . . very silly.') Even Samuel Beckett appeared, with 'Waiting for Elmo'. ('A play so modern and so brilliant it makes absolutely no sense to anybody.')

Nobody at CTW was wringing their hands over how much of this would alienate your average Bronx toddler – meddling middle management was a luxury they couldn't afford – and kids accepted the fact that a blue monster could conduct a lightning verbal exchange one minute and be anxious about getting a haircut the next. The monsters were both kids and adults, bridging the gap between the two rather than seeking to preserve a sentimental innocence.

Less vaudevillian and more abstract were the musical cartoon interludes. The use of songs to drum in educational concepts was old news, but *Sesame Street* had no time for the traditional marching-on-the-spot with piano accompaniment. In the early years Joe Raposo composed the bulk of the songs, from the jaunty theme tune to esoterically specific numbers like 'Caterpillars Never Wear Brown Boots'. His speciality was pastiche: everything from country and western ballads about sharing to dirty funk workouts based around the number six sounded note perfect. A retouching of Talking Heads' 'And She Was' filled the viewer in on the Aristotelian concept of storytelling, while Otis Redding's '(Sittin' On) The Dock of the Bay' instructed children in the art of lake recognition. ('If you don't know by now, then you oughta/That a lake is a body of water.') Best of all, the Pointer Sisters sang a jazz-funk anthem counting groovily to twelve, accompanied by a psyche-delic animated pinball machine. While the visuals beguiled, the lyrics sank in as surely and as permanently as any frozen food ditty. Those pesky liberal do-gooders could out-Man the Man.

The *Street*'s decadent methods drew a wave of scholarly fire. The journal *Childhood Education* demanded to know why the Workshop thought it could 'debase the art form of teaching with phony pedagogy, vulgar sideshows, bad acting [and] animated cartoons, in rapid tachistoscopic style with an obbligato of juicy jingles.'[183] Britain was even more suspicious. The BBC turned it down flat, and some ITV regions only showed it sporadically, but it did precipitate a new style of home-grown pre-school programmes, from *Rainbow* to *Pipkins*, less schoolmarmish than *Watch With Mother*.

By the end of 1971, *Sesame Street* was showing in fifty countries, and would eventually reach over one hundred and twenty. '*Sesame Street* is an idea which has swept the world,' said Cooney. 'I liken it to a Tiffany jewel.'[184] Grand words for a kids' show, but they had shown that for children's TV to be taken seriously by its audience, it had to take its audience seriously, as minds to be entertained for their own benefit, not back doors to their parents' bank accounts.

# THE OWL SERVICE (1969)
## ITV (Granada)

### Children's drama reaches a whole new plane.

THERE ARE TWO WAYS to write for children. One is the self-conscious arm's-length approach, addressing the young audience with all the easy charm of a Tory minister kissing a baby in a covered market. The other is to forget the age gap and just write something that will entertain you and children alike. The latter being a rare skill, the former takes precedence in commercial entertainment, grasping nervously at tried and tested stories and formats, disgorging a parade of suspiciously uniform-looking product. Once you and your fearless dog have nabbed one gang of swarthy smugglers, you've nabbed them all.

Alan Garner, 'a cheerful egotist from Cheshire,'[185] had since the late 1950s been writing children's fiction – books that seemed to sell mainly to children, at any rate. Though they were steeped in historic fantasy and a soup of ancient mythology, Garner felt that his stories had to be anchored in actual places – 'everywhere I mentioned could be touched.'[186] The strange forces and mysteries were carefully tied to existing parts of the country, mainly Garner's childhood and adult home of Alderley Edge. For a fantasist, he kept it real.

Garner's profile broached the kids' ghetto with the publication in 1967 of *The Owl Service*, which put a fragile, re-married middle class couple and their new, combined family into rural Wales and at the mercy of ancient energy. Alison, the more sensitive of the two teenagers, takes refuge from family trauma in a weird owl patterned dinner service she finds in the attic of their inherited holiday cottage. Her tracing of the design was Garner's childhood method of creation – a sickly boy, he spent weeks on end confined to bed, with only a crazed, half-timbered ceiling for entertainment, which eventually became a whole obsessively imagined world.

Finding creativity by the back door, Garner dodged the clichés and hang-ups of mainstream juvenile fiction to make something unique and direct. As the poet Robert Nye put it, he 'starts up rhythms which haunt the memory'.[187] His publisher, William Collins and Sons, duly clad *The Owl Service* not in child-friendly watercolours, but 'a plain wrapper and no pictures because it mustn't be put too emphatically in the "children only" category.'[188]

Granada snapped up the TV rights, and set about adapting Garner's dense mass of allusions and apparitions into something that would fit into the children's drama landscape of rollicking adventure stories and lavender-scented period romps. The result, overseen by Garner and producer Peter Plummer, instead warped the habits of children's TV to fit its own landscape, the Welsh valleys. Garner had his own picture of the British countryside to paint, and bucolic didn't come into it.

There are no kindly adults in Garner's story. The father was haughty, the locals sinister and suspicious. Only Alison and house-keeper's son Gwyn started out remotely likeable, and they had their fractious side exposed soon and often enough. Old oppressed young, boys sulked from girls, common Celts squared up to silver spoon Anglo-Saxons – this was a farmhouse holiday without a drop of cold comfort. Shifting between petulant moping and baffled intrigue, the kids stumbled through a hormonally charged passion play, deftly played by the teen leads, especially Gillian Hills as Alison, taking a break between cavorting in *Blow-Up* and humping Malcolm McDowell Keystone Kops-style in *A Clockwork Orange* to work on some genuinely sensual material. When the fantasy arrived, it wasn't an escapist fairyland, but a dissonant, looming valley of patterns, objects and myths, half-glimpsed and semi-understood but totally mesmerising and utterly inescapable.

Plummer's camera lingered at the extremes too – either freakishly wide-angled to cram the landscapes and buildings into claustrophobic master shots or zooming in to patterns and photographs with a desperate curiosity. Topped with an impressionistic title sequence and theme 'tune' consisting of harp, creaking leather and an emptying bath, and you were looking at the most radical departure from the accepted way of doing things that children's entertainment could hold. There was no mistaking this for the standard frock-coated lark. Viewers lapped it up as they did the books; the children's department loosened its corset and youth drama came of age.

*The Owl Service* was shot on colour negative by cameraman David Wood, but only seen in black and white on its original transmission. After Wood's early death in 1978, it was given a Sunday repeat in colour as a tribute, along with some slightly grim publicity concerning a 'curse' on the series, referring to the murder of Michael Holden (Gwyn) in a Piccadilly pub the previous year, along with a few apocryphal stories of cursed editions of the real life crockery set on which Garner modelled the owl service in the book.[189] Tracing superstitious patterns could work in the publicity trade, too.

# NATIONWIDE
# (1969–83)
## BBC One

### Television news lightens up – and never quite comes back down again.

*A programme to be swallowed effortlessly between filling the children with beans and popping the old man's dinner in the oven.*

Richard North, *Listener*, 30 September 1976

IN 1957, THE BRITISH government relaxed the broadcasting restriction that shut down television entirely from 6 to 7 p.m., so that parents could pack young children off to bed with the minimum of distraction. The new slot gave the teenagers *Six-Five Special*. For the rest of the family there was *Tonight*, a stepping stone from the daily grind to the light entertainment pantomime, a removal of tight shoes via the medium of the whimsically extrapolated current affair. Cliff Michelmore linked quirky stories in the manner of an uncle extracting a shilling from behind the viewer's earlobe. *Tonight*'s reporters cultivated signature styles – Fyffe Robertson's arch confusion with the modern world, Alan Whicker with the levelled gaze and level drone of the man of experience running through that anecdote one more time – but the attitude was always gentleman amateur, and the humour agreeably hearty. This was a clubhouse of the air.

In 1969 Derrick Amoore, assistant head of current affairs, mixed *Tonight*'s spirit with the evening news proper. Tentatively titled *Britain at Six*, this truly national magazine would use telecommunications technology to link regional studios 'the length and breadth of the land' with Lime Grove mission control. Local representatives would fall in on a phalanx of monitors behind Amoore's chosen captain, Michael Barratt. A reporter of the sports jacket and sheepskin school, Barratt tempered his world-weary brashness with a raffish geniality, the embodiment of senior journalism in repose.

After several try-outs that rapidly fell apart while Barratt brushed up his apologetic twinkle to camera, *Nationwide* went live on 9 September 1969 with no major mishaps to report. Twenty minutes of regional news gave way to the national confab without a hiccup. Items including an investigation into Belfast's sectarian schools were capably carried off. 'Technically it was a good, clean, professional job,' thought Peter Black. 'In content it was dullish. Amoore's chief difficulty will be to inject some fun into it.'[190]

All was set fair for the second edition. Barratt began the national section with confidence, following on from one regional story – the end of a brewery strike in Glasgow – with a light item starring their first guest eccentric, 'Mr George MacRae of Hackney, who drinks twenty-one pints a night!' The camera cut, not to MacRae, but a confused-looking chief constable in charge of security at Heathrow Airport. Back in the studio, a now flustered Barratt suggested we instead go over to David Coleman in Belfast, to see 'if they're at half-time'. But Coleman came there none. Barratt picked up the phone on his desk and began one of those achingly long conversations with the production gallery. 'I'm sorry about that mix-up. We're lucky it didn't happen on the first night!' The rest of the show, now firmly jinxed, stumbled through its main item ('Gypsies') in the same haphazard manner, before ending with the now located MacRae downing pints over the closing credits as the crew chanted 'Drink! Drink! Drink!'

From such misfortunes are reputations made. 'The Michael Barratt *Nationwide* comedy show is off to a grand start!'[191] chuckled the *Daily Express*. 'The danger with technical gimmicks,' wrote William Hardcastle, 'is that the news is bent out of shape to fit them.' The glitches that dogged *Nationwide*'s first year were gradually tamed, but the damage had been done. The laughter would always be as much at the programme as with it.

Calamity notwithstanding, *Nationwide* established itself both as family viewing and as a family in itself. Barratt was head of the clan. Eldest son was Bob Wellings, the South East's linkman promoted to national status, a move that seemed to puzzle him more than anyone else. ('Wellings breaks the gloss barrier. His manner is of inspired muddle, a sort of highly-tuned bewilderment.'[192]) Under the editorship of Michael Bunce, Wellings was joined in 1972 by Sue Lawley ('drips competence and breeding'[193]), Esther Rantzen and the cheerfully reassuring Frank Bough, sports department graduate and natural heir to Barratt's comfy, reclining throne.

December 1972 also saw the founding of the Consumer Unit. Just as the increasing polarisation of mainstream politics was putting fresh heat into studio debates, so the inflation-stoked national preoccupation with 'prices' gave this normally dreary form of television crusade a sudden urgency. Nearly two years before Shirley Williams was made Minister of Prices to enshrine the obsession in government, Valerie Singleton was created 'high street ombudswoman', rescuing the realm from stagflation, dodgy retailers and lipstick made out of 'soot, chalk, whales' innards and civets' naughty bits'.

Consumer Unit producer David Graham understood that consumer affairs were never going to be Pulitzer material and so let the unit wear its investigative muscle lightly. The detective theme was played for laughs: an anonymous local authority informant was dubbed, Watergate-style, 'Shallow Larynx'. Richard Stilgoe turned viewers' consumptive woes into droll musical routines. Composing elegantly witty squibs about the Supply of Goods (Implied Terms) Act was an esoteric skill, and Stilgoe was its singular master. His finest three-and-a-half minutes came on New Year's Eve, 1974. Tasked with detailing the various professions possessing a statutory right of entry to your home, he recorded a full explanatory song and dance number, performed by seven electronic duplications of himself. With just forty-five minutes in a blue screen studio to tape the various elements, Stilgoe over-fulfilled his brief by a mile, crossing in front of and manoeuvring around 'himselves' in a technical *tour de force* that was reprised by popular demand several times. It was froth, but precision-tooled froth.

By 1975 *Nationwide* was a genre in itself. New editor John Gau helped it become a law unto itself. The tone lightened and the coffers expanded. Barratt's hub was shifted for a week from London to Newcastle in the first of several stabs at increasing regional appeal. Likewise, local mainstays did duty in the capital. ('Mike Neville did get quite larky.'[194]) After an item on package holidays featuring the music from *Colditz* led to a tour firm successfully suing the Consumer Unit for 'unjust ridicule', Stilgoe was moved to the lighter 'Pigeonhole'. His mission, to 'reflect ideas from the *Nationwide* postbag', started as it meant to go on with a man who'd spent sixty-five consecutive summers in a tent. *Nationwide* was the country's showroom for harmlessly aberrant behaviour: if you'd taught a duck to skateboard, could impersonate a Trimphone or hatched an adder's egg in your late husband's trilby, an audience of ten million was a phone call away.

There was a great deal of serious reportage as well, like 'Inside Parliament', 'On the Mersey Beat' and Tom Hodgkinson's famous retread of Orwell's footsteps through London's hostels in 'Down and Out'. But the show's image was formed by the daft stuff. Rival current affairs producers like *This Week*'s David Elstein jeered at the Corporation flagship's pedalo trimmings. But one man's inanity is another child's stepping stone into the forbidding world of grown-up affairs. *Nationwide*'s large youthful following showed they were giving plenty of otherwise uninterested kids a taste for keeping up with the news.

The programme slowly became more self-indulgent. During Silver Jubilee year, television went nuts by royal appointment. *Nationwide* expanded accordingly, beginning at nine forty-five on the morning of the big day with the entire studio dancing a commemorative Jubilee Rumba. This was nothing compared to the self-regard of July's *Nationwide InterCity*. To mark Barratt's retirement, the BBC chartered British Rail's conference train, fitted it with an OB studio and sent it to towns with 'special emotional resonance' for Barratt. Here he would meet old faces, greet local nutters, and generally reminisce to his Boswell, Valerie Singleton ('who looks only slightly sickened by it all'[195]).

In Bournemouth, Barratt enjoyed community singing led by Arthur Askey while a man threw himself off a sixty-foot building. In Leeds, he discovered his birthplace was now an NCP car park. The tour wound up at Saltburn-by-the-Sea in a hubbub of vintage cars, Denis Healey, and regional presenters towing a tractor with their teeth. 'If there is a lesson here,' wrote John Naughton, 'it is that media planners should be more sceptical about the myth of their omnipotence.'[196] With Frank Bough now presiding over the family, this year of indulgence culminated in the *Nationwide* pantomime, one of those end-of-term shows of compulsory jollity with which the humourless let down their hair. Hence, perhaps, the willing involvement of Healey, Norman St John Stevas and several trade union bosses, all paid the standard appearance fee of ten pounds.

Things were never the same after that. A 1982 reshuffle made Roger Bolton editor, David Dimbleby anchorman, and gravity the new watchword. ('Light Entertainment is not my job,' said Bolton. 'I'm not interested in custard pies.'[197]) Inevitably, fans protested ('return the chubby chap to "Miserama" and give us back Frank and Sue!') but points were scored. In a 1983 'On the Spot' election interview, schoolteacher Diana Gould cornered Margaret Thatcher on the sinking of the *Belgrano*, affording a rare glimpse of sheer panic in the PM's eyes. But it was both too little too late and too much too soon. For the final edition in 1983 Bough was restored to the throne and presented with a cake 'passed' from presenter to presenter across the regional studios. *Nationwide*, like all British institutions, retained its pomp and ceremony to the bitterly jolly end.

# THE MARY TYLER MOORE SHOW (1970–7)

## CBS (MTM Enterprises)

### Women liberate the sitcom – a bit.

LAUGHTER IS A REACTION, and comedy naturally tends toward the reactionary. Television's first female comedy star embodied this dilemma. While the off-screen Lucille Ball was one of the most powerful people in the 1950s television landscape, co-owning what became a giant production company, the on-screen Lucy Ricardo was as flaky as they came – a wide-eyed, wide-mouthed grasper of the wrong end of the weekly stick, deferring to the men in her life to sort out her many self-authored disasters. Nevertheless, Ball's achievements changed the comedy game, clearing the ground for the next woman to make significant inroads.

Mary Tyler Moore had certainly risen through the pecking order. Her first regular gig was as David Janssen's receptionist in 1959 detective drama *Richard Diamond*, taking no screen credit and being mainly shot from the shoulders down. It was a slow slog from there to her star-making role. *The Dick Van Dyke Show* had been a rare gem in the 1960s, a far from vintage decade for American sitcoms. Moore's character, Laura Petrie, was significantly truer than the doting waifs in floral prints who rose from the Midwest's collective psyche to sigh with affectionate tolerance at their quarrelsome broods. More active by far, and smarter too, Laura was often the one explaining the world to her Milquetoast husband (though more often still, she burst into tears or got her toe stuck in the bath tap).

By the end of the 1960s, Moore was treading water on Broadway. CBS offered her a series of her own after reunion variety special *Dick Van Dyke and the Other Woman* reminded both the public and Moore what they'd been missing. With husband Grant Tinker, then head of 20th Century Fox Television, she formed MTM Enterprises and hired an unlikely duo to produce the as-yet nebulous show: James L. Brooks had a background in documentary; Allan Burns cut his writing teeth at Jay Ward's cartoon studio, and was half the brains behind archetypal dumb sixties sitcom *My Mother the Car*. Together they'd made *Room 222*, the story of an African-American high school teacher that took situation comedy closer to serious drama than was previously thought sane or decent. Somewhere between those two poles, reckoned Tinker, was Mary's show.

In Brooks and Burns's concept, Moore's character Mary Richards was a thirty-something divorcee, moving to Minneapolis to start a new life and job at the local TV newsroom. CBS had a problem with that, their audience research team protesting that divorce was one of America's great viewer turn-offs, just behind 'moustaches, New Yorkers and Jews'.[198] They eventually downgraded Richards to just single. If the premise was tamed, the scripts themselves would be more progressive, with Brooks and Burns hiring women writers (most notably Treva Silverman) in an acutely male field.

Despite the star's name in the title, this was an ensemble piece. 'At one time in television Jackie Gleason could sit out there and practically do it all by himself,' explained Tinker. 'But by the 1970s the attention spans of viewers had shortened . . . you had to come at them in all directions.'[199] Mary Richards may have shambled through the days in a jumble of berets, scarves and assorted floor-length static generators, but her life took on a sharp symmetry. In her one-room, split-level, shag-pile-and-distressed-brickwork home, she was suspended between kvetching single neighbour

Rhoda Morgenstern and antsy family woman Phyllis Lindstrom. At work Mary clashed with a full spectrum of male personality disorders, from writer Murray Slaughter's lofty sarcasm, through newsreader Ted Knight's idiot dignity to editor Lou Grant's defensive machismo. Though the cast wasn't intended as a diagram, this bunch of arrogant stumblebums were a shorthand for society.

The show inaugurated or developed a range of modern sitcom techniques. Mary and Rhoda were the prototype single girl survival pact, equal parts heart-on-sleeve emotional support and two-fingered defiance to the world at large. The newsroom milieu launched the modern workplace comedy that James Brooks's *Taxi* would make into a thriving sub genre with its web of alliances, rivalries, insults and in-jokes. Crucially, the show wasn't afraid to cut through a life-affirming resolution or heart-warming bonding session with an acerbic aside. Later the comedy of sexual one-upmanship arrived in the form of waspish, horny 'Happy Homemaker' Sue Ann Nivens, played by Betty White, who judged her character 'a very lonely, frightened lady'.[200]

The show's advances in character development were, on the face of it, absurdly elementary, but hardly anyone had applied them before. Simple addition of basic traits multiplied depth and possibility. In a typical 1960s sitcom, Lou Grant would distrust Mary simply because she was a woman in his rightful domain and all plots involving them would flow from there. Here, Lou actually distrusted Mary because her mixture of cocksureness and honest empathy both mocked his aggression and teased out his insecurities, meaning he was often in her debt, which he hated more than anything. There was almost no limit to where you could go with that.

There was texture in the cast as well. Straight actor Ed Asner gave Lou Grant more of an edge to his rage than broad tradition dictated, which meant he could crumple into a desperate, vulnerable heap that bit more credibly. As Bronx Jewish Rhoda, Valerie Harper avoided the obvious burlesque delivery, perfecting instead the fine art of throwing away prize zingers, and doubling the laughter in the process. Cloris Leachman, meanwhile, inhabited the restless Phyllis with Method levels of status-mad tetchiness. All three would eventually get their own shows.

The first series gathered less than stratospheric audiences. If it had arrived a year or so earlier, it might have been swiftly dumped, but in the meantime Nielsen, the TV rating yardstick of choice, had added demographic information to their equations. Suddenly a show needn't pull in huge numbers if it was doing especially well with young, educated urbanites with income to burn – the people who bought a disproportionately large amount of the luxury goods advertisers hawked in and around the action. From now on, TV in America (and, slightly later and to a lesser extent, elsewhere) would follow their tastes. This wouldn't always be to TV's benefit, but for now CBS knew these folk liked their sitcoms enlightened and classy. Talking cars were out, head-scarfed professional women in.

*The Mary Tyler Moore Show* was the first of a series of intelligent, honest sitcoms that placed adult life centre stage. The following year saw Norman Lear and Bud Yorkin's Alf Garnett-inspired *All in the Family*, with film spin-off *M\*A\*S\*H* the year after that. Of these three, Mary Richards's world was the most reserved, and these days provokes little beyond a marshmallow feeling of nostalgia, but it was an entirely original creation, and deserves immortality for its impact behind the cameras.

Moore herself tried several unsuccessful further combinations of comedy and variety, many referring back to her previous sitcom roles with increasing archness, one featuring David Letterman in full dance. The blow-out came with *Mary's Incredible Dream*, an all-singing, all-dancing trawl through the Bible, with Jack Good at the controls. This $900,000 affair soon became known as *Mary's Indelible Nightmare*. MTM the star had peaked. MTM the production house was just getting started.

# MISS WORLD (1970)
## BBC One

**The year the beauty contest fell apart as the world watched.**

MANY OLD TELEVISION CUSTOMS are unfathomable to the modern viewer. American hosts suddenly breaking character to recite short eulogies to orange juice and Spam without missing a beat hail from a world simultaneously more innocent and cynical than our own. The Great British closedown, with its spiritual poem, blast of national anthem and screaming point of light, could only be the last broadcast of a dying alien civilisation two billion light years away. And what uncharted Dark Age could have produced the annual contest in which women from all over the world, aged seventeen to twenty-five, were lined up in glittery formality and judged on the condition of their teeth, hair, legs and torso measurements, the possessor of the best being crowned by the owners of a ballroom and bingo empire?

*Miss World*'s formula was set in stone from the start. All the girls paraded before the audience in 'national dress' (lace bonnets and frumpy frocks for northern Europe, bare midriffs and/or neck-straining head ornaments for most territories south of the equator). Then a classy judging panel whittled the numbers down, and the remainder paraded once more in evening gowns. More whittling, and the final group trooped out once more in swimwear, and were engaged in famously fragmentary chat by the host.

This gesture towards intellectual appreciation was swiftly undercut by the final humiliation, in which the finalists lined up and, at the organiser's shout of 'Turn!', made a military about-face. ('And there they are,' wrote Ian Hamilton, 'for Everyman, a screen full of silken bums to choose from.'[201]) Then a stretched out snatch of hushed tension before the part where, as Nancy Banks-Smith described it, 'Reg handed up the results and Thingy was It.'[202] In a final flourish of ersatz pomp, the newly-crowned Miss World ascended to a golden throne and was helped into a silk cape by two periwigged footmen.

The contest was inaugurated in 1951, and the BBC first televised it in 1955, with a short after-ceremony meet-and-greet for the winner and runners-up. The following year they lavished half an hour of peak time on the ceremony's final half-hour, 'organised by Mecca Dancing in association with the *Sunday Dispatch*'. It pulled the crowds, but some were already noting how the 'far from flawless presentation arrangements made it sometimes hard to suppress the ribald mood, especially when the chosen beauty's crown slipped down over her right ear.'[203]

It wasn't to everyone's taste. The poet Hilary Corke (Mr) was confused as to the judging criteria. On what grounds, he demanded in 1954, were the hopefuls whittled? 'Of abstract beauty? Of charm? Of "personality"? . . . Or what was presumably in all our male minds but the promoters agreed to pretend wasn't?'[204] He also noted all non-white contestants 'were eliminated without question on the first sitting . . . on the next, out went all the non-Teutonics.'[205] But wilful detachment from the real world was exactly what its audience wanted. Whether commentators thought it a 'human Smithfield' or 'as meaningless as a beautiful baby contest at a West Hartlepool church fête,' by 1962 *Miss World* was ensnaring a reasonably healthy seventeen million viewers globally.

Dissent became serious in 1969, with feminist protests outside the Albert Hall and a telephoned bomb threat during the ceremony. But this was just a practice drill. At 9.20 p.m. on 20 November 1970, as the Lionel Blair Dancers ran through a desultory opening routine, it looked like business as usual, with the biggest upset of the evening likely to be Miss Yugoslavia almost toppling down the stairs in the evening wear round. While in London, Miss Brazil professed her desire to 'get to know the manifestations and faces of one of the basic civilisations of the world,' while Miss Hong Kong wanted to meet Cliff Richard. Among the expected tide of models and mannequins (a seemingly important distinction), the Gibraltarian contestant presented the local franchise of children's programme *Romper Room*, while Miss Malaysia was 'a colour consultant'.

The set combined classical kitsch with modernist glitz: Corinthian columns and polystyrene Venuses de Milo populated a disco causeway of glitter-encrusted hexagons. The judges represented the cheesily lavish realm where show business meets diplomacy, as Joan Collins and Glen Campbell shared a joke with The Maharajah of Baroda. The hosts poured forth a stream of calcified patter. 'Sweet and petite, Miss Japan!' chortled Michael Aspel. 'Quite a character, is Miss Tunisia!' vouchsafed 'second lucky man' Keith Fordyce, tantalisingly declining to elaborate further.

At the halfway mark came the star turn, a languorous Bob Hope, unashamedly reading third-string gags from idiot boards. ('I'm very happy to be at this cattle market tonight . . . I've been back there checking calves!') After a few minutes, he was interrupted by a squall of whistles and rattles, as members of the Women's Liberation Workshop stormed the hexagons with flour bags, stink bombs, rotten tomatoes and a water pistol filled with blue ink, chanting, 'We're not beautiful, we're not ugly, we're angry!'

Though the activists never came into shot, viewers were treated to the heady spectacle of live television completely breaking down. The Albert Hall swam and shook on the screen. A halting voice-over tried to hold the fort: 'Not entirely unexpected . . . the security here has been extremely tight . . .' After about five minutes of pictures of the floor and backs of bewildered men's heads, a visibly shaken Hope remounted the causeway: 'For a minute there I thought I was back in vaudeville!' Last year's winner was bustled on for a stilted time-filling chat. 'Sooner or later, these people have to get paid off,' Hope muttered conspiratorially to a nonplussed

Miss Ruber-Staier. 'There's someone upstairs who takes care of that.'

Slowly things got back on track. Places were found ('Can you just stand on where that cross used to be?' asked Aspel of one contestant). Cameras resumed pointing in purposeful directions. Men in headphones stopped darting in and out of holes in the set like meerkats at war. On went the swimming costume round, introduced by Aspel as 'lock-the-husband-in-the-coal-house time', and then the meet-and-greet: 'the part where I say "Is this your first time in London?" and they answer "Steve McQueen".' Protesters were still in the building – one was just stopped from letting off a smoke bomb during the crowning – but aside from a residual unease, ceremonial normality was restored. Miss Grenada won, and came out, unsurprisingly, against the militants. 'I do not think women should ever achieve complete equal rights . . . I still like a gentleman to hold my chair back for me.'[206]

Five protesters were arrested, and turned their magistrate's court appearance into an interrogation of witnesses on their attitudes to women's rights, with some success. Their actions became a media chattering point for months. Many censured, some supported. Germaine Greer reckoned they got it all wrong. 'Women should buy tickets,' she suggested, 'and just take off all their clothes, so that all these extraordinary dolls were surrounded by real people, and you could suddenly see what kind of fantasy the whole thing was, and the bottom would drop out of it.'[207]

As it was, the bottom remained in place for a long time. The next year protesters were kept firmly outside the Hall, staging their own 'Miss Used' mock contest. Thames Television snatched the rights in 1980 and retained them until its dissolution in 1988. It remains a big deal in many countries, but in its nation of origin it can now only be watched via a corner of the Internet, a genteel flash of thigh in a liberated hardcore supermarket, a relic of times more innocent – or at least differently guilty – than our own.

# COLUMBO
## (1971–8/1989–2003)
### NBC/ABC

### A shabby revolution in crime.

LIKE SOLAR SYSTEMS LIGHT years distant, TV action series
sometimes need sensitive probing to discern signs of intelligent
life. While many have exploited the infinite possibilities of the
format for thrilling, ingenious plotting and gleeful absurdity, many
more are mere snap-together schedule fillers with the sole ambition
of detaining a few million teenagers in the living room long enough
to clock the sponsor's merchandise. When John Boorman described
filmmaking as the process of turning money into light, he meant
to invoke the mysterious art of creative alchemy. The average
network drama series preferred to just pump in the coins and pull
the lever.

The action production line couldn't expunge wit entirely. In 1957
producer Roy Huggins, tasked with lashing together a western
series for Warner Television, created *Maverick*, an inveterate
gambler played by James Garner, who cut a louche, non-heroic
figure in a land full to brimming with noble white hats. A show
already retreating at speed from sombre tradition was tipped into
outright comedy when Huggins's collaborator Marion Hargrove
caught herself typing the cornball line, 'MAVERICK LOOKS AT
HIM WITH HIS BEADY LITTLE EYES'.[208] Like a painted
desert backdrop, the façade slipped to the floor. Neither writers,
producer or star could look at a stagecoach or saloon pianola with

a straight face again. *Maverick* was TV's first self-aware outlaw, and the American action series developed a sly wink to go with its right hook.

Despite this playfulness, dumb sincerity largely prevailed. Nothing was more sincere than a Quinn Martin production. Beginning with melodramatic prohibition procedural *The Untouchables*, Martin set the standard for breathlessly serious tales of high drama. With title and cast formally announced by an urgent, authoritarian voice, and the hour divided into three 'acts', plus an 'epilog'[sic], Martin took the structural divisions imposed by commercial breaks and fashioned them into the stone-tablet gravitas of hard literature. *The Fugitive, Cannon* and *The Streets of San Francisco* were but three series that shook to Martin's thunderous end-of-days treatment.

Martin made solidly popular shows, but there was something about the totally solemn adventure that paradoxically made it less of a serious dramatic proposition. With their brass-driven theme tunes, off-the-peg plots, actors gamely frowning their way down endless corridors of explanatory dialogue and flop falls from fire escapes onto concealed mattresses, the mid-evening dramas of the sixties and seventies became increasingly hard to tell apart.

NBC, who'd resisted Martin, changed the emphasis of the action slot with *Mystery Movie*, a rotating bill of (initially) three maverick detective stories rich in humour and personality. Dennis Weaver, when he wasn't taking advantage of a gap in the shooting schedule to star in Spielberg's *Duel,* was *McCloud,* a New Mexico sheriff at large in the Big Apple using frontier methods to round up dope dealers. The premise was a straight rehash of Clint Eastwood film *Coogan's Bluff,* and the second *Mystery Movie* strand was similarly derivative. *McMillan and Wife* cast Rock Hudson and Susan Saint James as a sophisticated crime-solving couple very much in the mould of the *Thin Man* films of the 1930s. Not so much 'mystery movies' as 'mystery re-sprays', but at least they weren't stiff.

The third story was far less blatantly derivative. Lieutenant Frank Columbo, the brilliant detective in the dull mackintosh, was one of TV's enduring cops, even holding his own against megastar confectionery addict *Kojak*. The creation of William Link and Richard Levinson, he first appeared in *The Chevy Mystery Show* in 1960, played by the thick set Bert Freed. This decrepit gumshoe, extracting a confession by sheer dogged pestering alone, stood out from the identikit mob. A dedicated Columbo special, *Prescription: Murder,* was commissioned as a vehicle for Bing Crosby. It was probably fortunate that the casting changed. Peter Falk, the eventual occupant of the celebrated raincoat, had previously appeared in *The Trials of O'Brien*, the comic adventures of a down-at-heel lawyer with a trash-strewn office and a wily way with an argument. He shifted those low qualities onto *Columbo*, along with an array of brow-clutching mannerisms and a casual slyness to his delivery of the dreaded, arrest-heralding phrase, 'just one more thing . . .'

*Columbo* was fresh because Levinson and Link looked beyond detective shows for inspiration. A major inspiration was Porfiry Petrovich, the sly, unassuming magistrate in Dostoyevsky's *Crime and Punishment* who interrogates the suspect Raskolnikov in unorthodox but effective style. When we first meet him, he's 'wearing a dressing-gown . . . and trodden-down slippers . . . His soft, round, rather snub-nosed face was of a sickly yellowish colour, but had a vigorous and rather ironical expression. It would have been good-natured except for a look in the eyes, which shone with watery, mawkish light.'[209] These could almost be *Columbo* stage directions. They certainly beat 'beady little eyes'.

Columbo's raincoat was the nearest thing in mainstream American TV to a class signifier, allowing him to slip under security cordons, get mistaken for night-watchmen and worse by haughty suspects, and produce hard-boiled eggs miraculously from the pockets *à la* Harpo Marx. A constantly amused outsider of low birth, he brought down well-connected killers as a flea might make a bear collapse in ticklish agony. Action had been stripped out, replaced with a series of intense one-to-one conversations as Columbo slowly homed in on the suspect's motive and method. These were punctuated by moments of high-octane excitement where Columbo would bend down to inspect a discarded tie clip. It was talk, talk, talk – but what talk!

The programme's quality reputation established, talent beat a path to *Columbo*'s door. From Faye Dunaway to Janet Leigh, John Cassavetes to Johnny Cash, special guest villains gladly submitted to sweaty inquisition. Patrick McGoohan was a serial guest murderer, often directing his episodes himself. The scruffy upstart hassled the best in the business.

*Columbo* didn't take the business of murder too seriously. The killings could get ridiculously convoluted, involving subliminal advertising and Heath Robinson contraptions wired up to record players, but all that was deposited in the opening reel to make way for the good stuff: Falk and defendant facing off in lush locations. Falk would freshen up long production runs by ad-libbing around the script in an attempt to catch his co-stars off-guard. There was a spirit about the show, beginning with Falk and spreading in all directions, that Quinn Martin would never achieve with all the concerned frowns in Christendom. The sincere-but-stupid crime series had been on the case too long; in all senses but the sartorial, *Columbo* smartened it up.

# THE LARGEST THEATRE IN THE WORLD: THE RAINBIRDS (1971)

## BBC One

### Drama goes off the rails.

*I have not been impressed by BBC One's* Play for Today *series
– there have been too many weirdies, too much self-indulgence
by the producers.*

James Thomas, *Daily Express*, 11 February 1971

WEIRDNESS IS IN THE eye of the reviewer. Some of the 'weirdies'
in BBC One's flagship single drama slot had recently included a
study of teenage existentialism with added pot smoking and
underage gay sex, an everyday tale of ritual human sacrifice in a
Black Country village, and a mid-life crisis told through the
medium of the saucy seaside postcard. But James Thomas hoped
that night's offering, in which a young man throws himself out of
a window, goes into a coma and hallucinates nightmarish visions
of his oppressive family, wouldn't fall into the weird basket. It was
by Clive Exton, whose 'name on the titles usually spells an interesting piece'.

Exton was one of the most lauded of early TV dramatists.
Turning from acting to writing in his twenties, he made his name
at Granada with *No Fixed Abode*, a terse encounter between various

reprobates in a lodging house. Hard-bitten realism gave way to something headier in 1962 with *The Big Eat*, a satire on consumerism in which a food company organises a television eating contest, complete with smarmy compère (Peter Sallis), rock 'n' roll interludes and gluttonous contestants (including Arthur Mullard) sat in high chairs suspended on giant scales. The results are loud, crass, and fatal. Exton wrote it for ABC, but the commercial channel found a satire of commercialism too hot to handle, and it went to the BBC. On the night, thirty-six viewers phoned Television Centre in outrage.

*The Trial of Dr Fancy* depicted a court case which uncovers a conspiracy between a psychiatrist, a surgeon and a gent's outfitter to induce a complex in tall men about their height, leading them to seek amputation of their legs. It was made by ABC in 1962 and then sat on for two years for fear of offence. A fortnight after *Dr Fancy* finally went out, the BBC were to show Exton's *The Bone Yard*, about a slightly dim police constable who thinks he can talk to Christ, though he may just be being set up by his randy, tap-dancing chief inspector who's having it away with his wife ('as nice a piece of knitting as I've laid eyes on!') while he hangs around graveyards at night. Unfortunately it coincided with the trial of Harold Challenor, a delusional flying squad detective prone to fitting up suspects in the most blatant manner, and was pulled for fifteen months.

Understandably nonplussed by this treatment, Exton moved into films, writing screenplays for *10 Rillington Place* and Joe Orton's *Entertaining Mr Sloane*. The BBC tempted him back in 1970 with the most prestigious slot they could muster. In 1962, the European Broadcasting Union decided to augment their already ridiculed annual Song Contest with a regular exchange of new drama between its thirteen member states. *The Largest Theatre in the World* employed big names like Terence Rattigan and Ingmar Bergman to write a play which each country's public service station would then produce as they saw fit. The attractions were obvious: a vast potential audience, strewn across the cradle of western culture, the prestige of the art-house with the scope of a blockbuster.

Exton gave Europe the mother of all satires. The family, the military, the medical profession, Christianity, television, the monarchy and any class you cared to mention were thrown up as distorted vignettes within the comatose brain of John Rainbird. His parents, oddly demoted half a class from genteel reality, become monsters obsessed with 'testing' him in combat. He's signed up to the army, strung up in an abattoir, and repeatedly finds himself in a white limo that keeps crashing. In the real world, his mother is encouraged to accept a dangerous operation which will bring him out of his coma while knocking his IQ down a hundred points. With the prickly young man reduced to a mooing infant, the fractious family unit is saved.

Who could direct this heady brew? Exton had reservations about the way *The Bone Yard* was played up for panto laughs by James MacTaggart. *The Rainbirds* was given to Philip Saville. His portfolio veering between a sombre *Hamlet* shot on location at Elsinore and a comedy about Victorian prostitution written by Denis Norden, Saville had come a long way since the days of *Armchair Theatre*'s kitchen sink. The kitchen sink is what he threw into this already well-stuffed play. Observing theatre's total liberation with the arrival of the anarchic 'Happenings' in the late 1960s, Peter Brook observed, 'give a child a paintbox, and if he mixes all the colours together the result is always the same muddy browny grey.'[210] With TV drama hitting similar all-bets-off territory, the evening schedules were daubed in many shades of experimental taupe.

Shooting colour film entirely on location, Saville was given *carte blanche*. With no chance of executives idly patching into the closed circuit to see what he was up to – the bane of directors working in studios – he was free to augment Exton's already baroque script with cigar-smoking male nuns, S&M nurses, inflatable fish and yards of graphic Vietnam footage. This last had become a radical TV mainstay since Tony Palmer stuck clips of napalm victims in between scenes of The Who and Hendrix in concert for his 1968 pop documentary *All My Loving*. The TV director was starting to catch the writer up in the production pecking order, with Saville as frontrunner. Exton's hopes for a sober treatment went out of the window.

The critics didn't know where to begin, but generally agreed on where to end. 'Surely it would be churlish to be disappointed,' pre-empted *The Times*. 'It was a virtuoso piece, using all the tricks of the medium.'[211] There were plenty of churls about, though. *The Observer* reckoned the dream sequences suggested John Rainbird 'had spent far too much time watching fashionable television plays,' adding that 'they do these things much more amusingly (and imaginatively) on *Monty Python*.'[212] In the *FT*, the venerable T. C. Worsley had trouble believing this was the work of men in their forties: 'Surely the mature Exton wouldn't be naïve enough to expend such a waste of spirit on the simple psychological truism that over-mothered boys risk emasculation? If it was therapy for him, it was a pain in the psyche for us, and I still cannot imagine how it ever got on.'[213] Neither could the *Daily Mail*: 'I imagine very few viewers will have stayed longer than ten minutes . . . nothing but the worst was good enough.'[214] Nancy Banks-Smith in the *Guardian* just exclaimed, 'I feel rather as if I had been run over by a bus.'[215]

After the fallout subsided, Exton quietly switched to lighter fare like *The Crezz*, a valiant attempt to create a middle-class soap opera set in west London. After a fruitless dalliance with Hollywood in the early 1980s, tinkering with stillborn dreck like *Red Sonja*, he scored a solid hit with Granada's Fry and Laurie period caper *Jeeves and Wooster*. His deft translation of P. G. Wodehouse's comic rhythms to the screen might seem the antithesis of the crazed sprawl of *The Rainbirds*, but a keen ear for snappy lunacy had always been in his work. (Even his contributions to dour apocalypse adventure *Survivors* were made under the pseudonym M. K. Jeeves, as previously used by W. C. Fields.) Exton's last big project was 'gardening detective' series *Rosemary & Thyme*, a distillation of the British Sunday evening tea-and-crumpet murder mystery that took cosiness to new heights. It's tempting to see his leap from extreme bad to extreme good taste as symbolic of TV drama's rapid retreat from the avant garde, but Exton was no hack. He just appreciated that the highly regulated televisual climate where ambitious TV writers could make a living from their esoteric visions alone was devolving into a much less forgiving environment. The 'weirdies' would have to pay their way.

# DUEL (1971)
## ABC (Universal Television)

### The TV movie beats the big screen.

'TV MOVIE' IS THE perfect oxymoron. The words don't just repel each other, as in 'rock opera', they actively cancel each other out. It's a zero-sum phrase, holding no promise and reeking of shame, like 'government initiative'.

Despite their similarities, the two media work in completely different ways. Most cinema films make a loss, but the potential is there for amassing a fortune, hence the fevered speculation and constantly inflating budgets. Television operates on limited stakes – the best you can hope for is to fill the full complement of advertising slots, with the promise of syndication a distant incentive. The life-blood of television is the series, the franchise, the rolling cash generator. Stuffing a one-shot TV movie with millions of dollars makes no sense – it's a sure way to turn a king's ransom into a tramp's pension. TV movie directors have to add ingenious thrift to their armoury. They often treat it as a means to get noticed by Hollywood, but in the process they can learn a great deal.

One of the better TV movie slots in the early 1970s was the *ABC Movie of the Week*, an anthology of seventy-five-minute dramas ranging from series pilots like *Alias Smith and Jones* to continuations of the cutesy 1960s *Gidget* franchise, wrapped up in a title sequence that was half *2001*, half Pearl & Dean. Some were fine, some were lousy, but their artistic ambition generally lay no higher than tempting a significant chunk of Tuesday night's audience away from the charms of *Hawaii Five-0* on CBS.

Universal Television had started the made-for-TV game with 1964's kids-and-criminals adventure *See How They Run*, for NBC. By 1971 their allegiance had switched to ABC and staff writer Steven Bochco was engaged in turning up material for *Movie of the Week* when he found *Duel*, a Richard Matheson story, in an issue of *Playboy*. The minimalist tale of an average guy in the Californian desert menaced, for no reason, by a battered articulated tanker with an unseen driver gripped Bochco. Matheson, whose novels *I Am Legend* and *The Shrinking Man* had been filmed with varying results, and had written the odd TV script himself (most significantly classic *Twilight Zone* story 'Nightmare at 20,000 Feet'), tried to sell *Duel* as a TV episode idea, but was told it lacked enough meat for a whole hour's drama. When Universal accepted it as *Movie of the Week* fodder, he was understandably sceptical, especially when he got wind of the appointed director.

Awarded a seven-year contract by Universal head Sid Sheinberg on the strength of a twenty-minute home movie project, Steven Spielberg was warily regarded by his colleagues. He was wet behind the ears, he was self-important, he couldn't handle actors, he wasted time setting up tricksy shots – he was every inch the irksome tyro. He'd steered some decent TV through production, though, most notably the Bochco-written *Columbo* episode 'Murder By the Book'. He had big ideas for *Duel*.

Spielberg imposed his will on the producers from the start. A less committed director would have caved in to the studio's insistence on filming most of the in-car close-ups indoors, with back-projected desert. Spielberg knew how cheap this would look, and insisted on a full location shoot. He also demanded as little speech as possible. The studio wanted chunks of the protagonist's explanatory interior monologue in voice-over. Spielberg cut them down as far as he could. But he couldn't do much about the budget and schedule: $750,000 and two weeks' shooting in the San Fernando valley would test his creative generalship to the limit.[216]

TV production schedules militate against creativity. A good director is one who can shoot the most footage in the shortest time. Spielberg put in the cost-cutting work, varying camera angles to help the same car travelling round the same bend work in a dozen separate scenes.[217] Everything else from the TV directing rulebook he ignored. Hating the preponderance of close-ups on TV – a hangover from its low-definition origins – Spielberg favoured the wide angle, deep focus shot. An anxious interlude in which Dennis Weaver's petrified hero stumbles, dazed, through a remote diner was shot in one three-minute, hand-held take. The final collision between Weaver's car and the truck, due to good planning, great stunt work and a massive dose of luck, similarly came in one long, slow motion chunk.

Spielberg's balance of compromise and vision was perfectly judged. Marshalling his limited resources to the best possible end, he and his team injected a hitherto routine format with atmosphere and visual excitement. *Duel* was an instant hit, attracted lustrous reviews, and got the most out of its mayfly spell in the limelight. An extended cinema version was released theatrically in Europe. Its central conceit was blatantly ripped off by third string efforts like *Killdozer* and *The Car*. Finally, its many gorgeous vehicle shots were recycled as stock footage in cheap action series like *The Incredible Hulk*.[218] The odd late night rerun aside, such is the legacy of the made-for-TV masterpiece.

Small wonder, then, that Spielberg, after a couple more TV pictures, including rakishly shot paranormal oddity *Something Evil*, ran off to the cinema and rarely looked back. The TV movie, once more starved of hungry geniuses, slipped back into its cycle of cop show try-outs, bleary alcoholics and 'Disease of the Week' tear-jerkers, begging for the more financially viable format of the mini-series to come along and put it out of its misery. Spielberg, though, had proved this most workmanlike of formats could be dragged in the direction of art. Even cultural deserts can harbour the odd breathtaking explosion.

# THE SPECIAL LONDON BRIDGE SPECIAL (1972)

## NBC/BBC One
## (Winters Hollywood)

### Big time variety makes a
### transatlantic trip – by bus.

SMALL AS IT WAS and shoved in a corner, television always struggled with the spectacular. Fuzzy pictures of the moon landing had
the weight of history behind them, but live coverage of a circus just
made an immersive experience tiny and distant. This didn't stop the
late 1960s wave of international variety spectaculars: latter day Busby
Berkeley musicals shrunk to a square foot of phosphor. The hidden
motive was to make the squinting viewer upgrade their set, but a
twenty-four-inch colour screen was still a dream for most. They
thrived nonetheless, simultaneously monolithically self-assured and
gawkily ingratiating: visually a knockout, verbally a coma.

One of its chief architects was steeped in television. David
Winters began as a dancer on Jack Good's *Shindig!*, then graduated
through choreography (mentoring Toni Basil among others) to
produce the sort of jet-setting musical TV specials that were the
inevitable result of the perennial network demand: 'We need something for our very expensive talent to do, and fast.' First came *Lucy
in London*, CBS's contract-renewal sweetener for Lucille Ball in
1966, sending the red-haired ditz on a breakneck trip through the
swinging capital in a motorcycle-sidecar combination driven by

Anthony Newley. The formula was simple: a bare bones storyline, camped up and semi-acted by the star, is unceremoniously stuffed with musical guests (in this case the Dave Clark Five) and character actors (James Robertson Justice). What it lacked in art it more than made up for in sheer all-singing, all-dancing, all-Rolodex-consulting effort.

In 1970, Winters took full creative control of *Raquel!*, a gossamer-thin vehicle for Raquel Welch to hop across the globe in assorted tiny outfits of scalloped Bacofoil. She sang numbers from *Hair!* on the slopes of an Aztec pyramid accompanied by twelve dancers in costumes half Zodiac sign, half genetically engineered football mascot. She teamed up with Bob Hope to sing – and, in a cack-handed way, act out – the Beatles' 'Rocky Raccoon'. With some judicious manipulation of microphone levels, she duetted with Tom Jones on a medley of rock 'n' roll standards. Welch's indeterminate song-and-dance skills were ameliorated by Winters's production, a high camp jamboree in which Broadway reached out to Haight-Ashbury in entirely the wrong direction, settling somewhere between Cairo and Cape Canaveral.

Jones the Voice acquitted himself well enough to earn the Winters treatment two years later. Tom, being a more heavyweight talent than Raquel, was going to require a more substantial vehicle: less your standard featherweight rump-shaker, more a modern opera. 'Tom has a proper acting role in *London Bridge*,' insisted Winters. 'He has seven songs, but they arise from the story.'[219] He was suitably vague on what this story involved.

On transmission, all became clear. Tom, having toured the capital's overcast tourist spots while singing an ode to 'cockney champagne' called, indisputably, *London Is London*, boards a bus conducted by Hermione Gingold. Gingold is in full Grand Dame mode, with, in Philip Hope-Wallace's phrase, 'her voice swooping campingly through a whole two octaves of sneer.'[220] Tom is gobsmacked when the bus is spirited to the Arizona tourist resort where the original London Bridge has been relocated piece by piece, thus conveniently aligning him with a galaxy of Hollywood stars and sealing a lucrative sponsorship deal with the resort's proprietors in the process. This was screened the night before the Queen opened the relocated bridge for real, with live coverage of the snip to a Tom Mangold commentary.

Having retrospectively funded his own TV special by magic, Tom finds no showbiz feat beyond him, and demonstrates his new acting chops by reciting lines of the script while a) smiling, and b) not looking into the camera. There's almost a plot in which Jones has a desultory romance with Jennifer O'Neill, which consists mainly of longingly reciting chunks of the Lake Havasu City guidebook at each other. The resort's non-bridge attractions are highlighted by having The Carpenters sing on top of them, Charlton Heston play tennis in them, and Kirk Douglas shoot Lorne Greene off their roofs.

The weird US/UK hybrid theme is kept up at all times: 'Consider Yourself' becomes a hoedown. For the connoisseur, art is provided by a gratuitous ballet interlude with Rudolf Nureyev. It comes as a relief when Tom finds the whole thing's been a dream, and Terry-Thomas sticks his head into shot to deny that he's Terry-Thomas, presumably for tax purposes. As with all these specials, there's some solid musical talent at the root of it – here co-ordinated by Marvin Hamlisch – but what defines the genre, for better or worse, is the half-ton of ludicrous icing under which it's buried.

Such chaotic exorbitance suggests the variety spectacular was in rude health, but a long decline was just beginning. The insane amount of money required to hire, co-ordinate and film all that talent, let alone fly it round the world, was running out. The feeble gags which held the numbers together were never fresh, but in an increasingly sophisticated comedy environment they began to look less like an indulgent groan and more like an insult. Most devastatingly of all, music itself was moving on, and decisively away from the shiny studio floor. Showcases for Doris Day and Cilla Black were the rearguard of an entertainment force that had flattened the competition when Perry Como first stretched his lungs on behalf of Chesterfield Cigarettes in the early 1950s.

The name-in-title series slowly thinned out, replaced by the once-in-a-blue-moon special. In the US the genre went right back to its roots, with Perry Como shepherding holiday audiences through songs and sketches into the late 1980s. Its British cousin tended instead toward the humble environs of the holiday camp. *Hi Summer!* and *Summertime Special* toured the country's holiday destinations for tunes, jokes and – weather permitting – displays of formation dancing to increasingly inappropriate current hits. Out of time they certainly were, but only a cynic wouldn't regret the loss of the most audacious TV confections ever baked.

# UN, DOS, TRES . . .
## (1972–2004)
## TVE1

TV's first political allegory with cash prizes.

URUGUAYAN WRITER-DIRECTOR NARCISO IBÁÑEZ Serrador holds a singular place in the history of Spanish – and through one programme, world – television. A pioneer of dramatic anthologies, he made the horror story a crucial part of Spain's early television drama with series like *Historias Para No Dormir* (Stories to Keep You Awake), which ran from 1965 to 1982. His major legacy, however, was in an entirely different field.

On 24 April 1972, Serrador's game show *Un, Dos, Tres . . . Responda Otra Vez* (One, Two, Three . . . Answer Again) opened its doors with cartoon ceremony, making as colourful an entry as Spain's monochrome state television service permitted. Sprawling over ninety minutes of Monday evening television, the contest was interspersed with musical, comedy and variety guest turns, a game show version of the mammoth variety spectaculars that filled entire evenings of European television.

Each edition had a broad theme: horror, the circus, ancient Greece, and so forth. It was formed of three stages, corresponding to Serrador's theory of the three basic types of contest: a test of knowledge, a challenge of skill and good old fashioned gambling. In the first round, four pairs of contestants competed to name as many things in a given category as possible. They had forty-five seconds to itemise 'famous Greeks', say, 'parts of a rocket' or 'reasons for a car accident'. There followed an elimination round based around party-game physical challenges like walking a tightrope or passing eggs around without using the hands. The remaining pair of contestants had the long final round, the auction, all to themselves. Assorted variety turns appeared, leaving cryptic clues to one of the prizes. The contestants had to eliminate the inferior prizes, ideally retaining the star prize – a car, a holiday, 100,000 pesetas – and avoiding the duff booby traps.

Serrador the game show deviser had created an original, if unspectacular, format. Serrador the writer added the crucial twist. Looking at the quiz as a dramatic situation, he reasoned that everyone on set needed a role – either for or against the contestants. Support came from the genial host (initially Peruvian actor Kiko Ledgard) and six 'secretaries' in outsize glasses who chaperoned the contestants and wheeled prizes on and off-stage. Against them were the 'Downside': three ashen-faced, long-bearded men dressed like Victorian undertakers in frock coats and stove-pipe hats, led by one 'Don Cicuta' ('Hemlock'). These miseries held the purse strings, operated the stopwatches and generally radiated bad vibes from the sidelines, heckling successful contestants and relishing wrong answers.

The Don was more than just a pantomime novelty. He was, according to Serrador, 'an image of the Censor', symbolic of the spooks of Franco's late-period dictatorship who repressed anything lively and progressive, enforcing the resentful austerity of 'black conservatism'.[221] This Franklin Mint Franco stalked a Spain-in-miniature, the fictional community of Tacañón del Todo (roughly: 'misers of everything'), a society crushed by puritanical bureaucracy.

When *Un, Dos, Tres . . .* launched, Spain was preoccupied with what would happen after its ailing dictator finally passed on. With various factions of the ruling elite jockeying for position, and ETA's bombing campaign on the rise, the heartening prospect of an end to decades of repression was tempered with fear and uncertainty. This wasn't, of course, the kind of thing that could be openly aired while Franco still drew breath, but under cover of a harmless game show, a little of that unease could be relieved. Kiko and his Secretaries were performing a unique public service.

After Franco, *Un, Dos, Tres . . .* evolved elaborate new features. When Valentín Tornos, the veteran actor playing Don Cicuta, retired in 1976 through ill health, his role was split three ways, creating the Tacañones: Don Slacker, Don Strait and Professor Pencil; a miser, a prude and a pedant respectively. In the eighties, three distaff Tacañonas took over: Mary Immaculate, Mari-Puri and the Little Widow, as cheerless and sombre as ever. Over the next two decades more changes were made to the show's burgeoning mythology, including the introduction of two-faced Secretaries who could suddenly turn against contestants. The original bold anti-fascist statement faded from the collective memory, but the simpler advocacy of hedonism over inhibition remained. For once, the epithet 'national institution' seems genuinely deserved.

The format was adapted all over Europe, most notably in the UK as Yorkshire Television's *3-2-1*, commissioned as a rival to the BBC's big couples contest *The Generation Game* (itself an import from the Netherlands). Despite Britain picking up the show just as it was entering its own long period of political repression, the allegorical elements were the first to be dropped. Ted Rogers compèred a simple variety quiz, half the length of the original, with two new ingredients: Rogers's high speed hand jive illustrating the show's title (which was later re-assimilated into the Spanish show), and Dusty Bin, a remote-controlled ash-can clown acting as programme mascot and booby prize signifier (which wasn't). It didn't give any Catholic military autocrats a metaphorical poke in the eye, but it did send a young married couple back to Gateshead with a forty-four-piece canteen of sterling silver cutlery.

# INIGO PIPKIN/PIPKINS
# (1973–81)
## ITV (ATV)

### The puppet show that pulled strings but no punches.

PUPPET SHOWS ARE POPULAR with children's programme makers of a subversive bent, being great decoys for smuggling all types of mischievous business onto the screen. They're equally popular with TV stations being, as they are, phenomenally cheap to make. Children, naturally, can't get enough of them. With such universal appeal, puppetry has enjoyed a long and lunatic tenure on television. The odd professionally outraged moral guardian aside, everyone's happy.

Hand-operated sedition featured in one of the first regular children's shows, *Time for Beany*. Broadcast on America's short-lived Paramount Network from 1949, it was the brainchild of Bob Clampett, the most energetic and surreal of Warner Brothers' golden age cartoon directors. In the few years before the intro-duction of the Television Code in 1951, *Time for Beany* frequently pushed the boundaries – and its luck – with randy puppet wolves chasing after nubile blonde actresses, and demented puppet sea serpents singing jazz standards accompanied by President Truman on the piano.

In Britain, puppetry could be relied upon for teatime smut (Basil Brush's not-so-cryptic monologues about 'Dirty Gertie at number thirty') and afternoon terror (the nightmarish marionettes of *Rupert the Bear* and *Paulus the Woodgnome*). One puppet show, however, stuck its stubby plush paws into more subtle areas.

*Inigo Pipkin* was one of several children's programmes (*Rainbow* was another) that arrived on ITV in the wake of two major changes. The first was the permission given to TV companies to disport themselves on the previously protected weekday afternoons by the Minister of Posts and Telecommunications, who offered a vague hope the extra hours could provide 'more time for experimental programmes ... perhaps'.[222] The other was the shadow cast over British children's programmes by *Sesame Street*, which generated earnest pedagogic debate by the yard. Parents and kids loved it, while many educationalists 'abhor it for possibly corrupting educational objectives'.[223] *Sesame Street* was for several years only shown in small pockets of the UK, but the new home-grown pre-school programmes carried its influence nationwide.

*Inigo Pipkin* was instigated by Michael Jeans, who had curated some potent schools programmes for ITV. Graphic social justice primer *Law and Order* was denounced by Mary Whitehouse as 'brutal, despicable and a very bad example to children'.[224] *Rules That Are Not to Be Accepted* imagined an Orwellian future Britain where smoking is a prison offence, leading to bursting jails, overrun police and the rise of lighting up in public as the ultimate rebellious act. This new programme, about a lovable old puppet maker whose creations come to life, with a catchy theme sung by Jackie Lee of *Rupert* and *White Horses* fame, was going to be altogether more wholesome, though, wasn't it?

Up to a point. Jeans was keen to escape from the restrictive pre-school template of the time, where a responsible, omniscient adult leads a group of inquisitive child-surrogates on a journey to discover where biscuits come from. He still had the responsible adult (George Woodbridge, veteran comic actor and rare survivor of John Gielgud's ill-fated production of *Macbeth*) and the child-surrogates (expertly manipulated by Heather Tobias and Nigel Plaskitt), but their concerns went beyond the genesis of baked goods.

Though they were full of life, Hartley Hare (fey, mischievous), Topov the monkey (childlike, curious), Pig (sarky, omnivorous) and Tortoise (mature, avaricious) were manifestly puppets. Their manufactured nature was emphasised by showing Pipkin making new companions in early episodes, to the confusion and concern of Hartley. This was existentialism with stabilisers, but it all related to real life – main writer Susan Pleat, a *Coronation Street* graduate, treated the show as 'a soap opera for the under-fives' that aimed to 'take small children seriously'.[225] Hence Hartley's ignoble reaction to the creation of new puppets: he was only reacting as many viewers would to a new baby in the family. Tackling the issue indirectly, the script achieved honesty and avoided sentimentality. It was metaphor, not euphemism.

A more head-on approach was adopted after Woodbridge died. Jeans made the decision to address the actor's death in the series (now called simply *Pipkins*), having Pipkin die, and the puppet shop carry on under his assistant Johnny. Suddenly children's lunchtimes were awash with grief, confusion and insecurity (Johnny, being a novice craftsman, was unlikely to keep the gang solvent). Despite complaints (usually from adults acting unilaterally on the children's behalf) Jeans and co. stuck to their guns, confronting eternity once more when a pet goldfish died. This episode, written by former *Siege of Golden Hill* star Billy Hamon, captured the frightened, shapeless worry of the underage mind, as Topov asked Johnny if they were going to die too, and Johnny admitted that yes, they were. This was strong medicine, outpacing even *Sesame Street*, which wouldn't tackle death until 1983, after cast member Will Lee passed on.

In terms of content, *Pipkins* was audacious. (It only rarely capitulated to censorship, such as when a Johnny Morris story about a cow trying to achieve herd domination by braving an electric fence was nixed by the British Safety Council.) Visually, *Pipkins* was no kaleidoscopic sugar dream. The gang's headquarters was located at ATV's Elstree studios, adjacent to *The Muppet Show* (which had a habit of pulling rank over its neighbour, often commandeering the platforms which raised the human actors above the puppeteers),[226] but had the fly-blown, cluttered look of a genuine backstreet emporium. The puppets were similarly ragged, though expertly made by Jane Tyson, who went right back to the BBC's *Andy Pandy*. *Pipkins*'s dilapidation was precisely crafted.

Jeans's pensive innovations and flea-bitten aesthetics didn't make a great impact. As *Pipkins* ended, a new ethos emerged in children's programming, filled with dreams of international markets, easily merchandised designs, primary colours and relentless exuberance. There was no place for questions of mortality in the new, heavily monetised, no-risk set-up – it was back to happy songs and biscuit nativities. The moral of today's story: mindful melancholy may help a child's development, but it's crap at shifting pencil cases.

# THE INDOOR LEAGUE (1973–8)
## ITV (Yorkshire)

### TV sport in its cups.

*It is a rather pathetic idea to think of people, in the sort of ghastly modern pubs which have television, standing there watching traditional olde worlde pub games on television.*
Stanley Reynolds, *The Times*, 6 April 1973

FOR THE BETTER PART of half a century, British independent television was a cluster of cantons. The larger ones provided output for the nation: London's timesharing duo, Granada's titan of arts and current affairs, and Lew Grade's entertainment palace ATV, based in the Midlands but prone to 'nip up' to the capital on frequent away days.

Regions too thinly populated to raise enough cash for regular national programming found their niches. Rural Anglia and Southern brought their rolling acres to metropolitan viewers via nature documentaries such as *Survival* and hymns to country crafts like Jack Hargreaves' *Out of Town*. Welsh and Scottish stations promoted their native culture and language. But it took Yorkshire to curate a sporting tournament that was the very essence of the locale, distilled into twenty-five minutes of parsimonious broadcasting.

*The Indoor League* was a simple knockout pub games tournament, brought to the nation from Leeds's Queens Hotel (later upgrading to the more spacious Irish Centre) by illustrious England cricket captain Fred Trueman. Pint in one hand and pipe in the other, Fiery Fred burst onto the afternoon schedules to open jaded eyes to the pseudo-athletic prodigies loitering by the pickled eggs.

With the action on such a small scale, the commentary obligingly thickened to compensate. Fred, mindful of his sport's tradition of sumptuous prose embodied by the likes of C. L. R. James and Neville Cardus, waxed lyrical over the Old Peculier. 'We openly and humbly salute the wizards of the taproom,' he intoned, anticipating 'the biggest bonanza of sporting skill I've ever clapped eyes on.'

Initially, five games were covered: bar billiards ('snooker with bunkers'), table skittles ('the Devil among the tailors'), table football ('very popular in the technical colleges'), shove ha'penny and darts. ('That's real darts on a Yorkshire board, with no trebles and no flukey shots.') Further series added pool and, notably, arm wrestling, precipitating a national revival of the contest supposedly invented by Genghis Khan, thanks to the runaway success of a southerner, Don 'Buster' Whitney, Kent's Ace of Armlock.

Darts would prove to be the show's big draw. In the past decade it had grown from pub game to spectator sport, but while tabloids sponsored well-attended tournaments, TV coverage remained sporadic. Three weeks after its *League* debut, the game was televised in earnest as the *News of the World* Championship took up residence on *World of Sport*. For now, though, the arrows lined up among the other tavern pastimes for a top prize of £100. 'Let's see how they go on with the smell of money up their nostrils!' said Fred. 'Just how tense are these lads when the money's on their arrows? Are they cocky, or quivering? Who's your money on? I'm saying nowt.'

Much of this sonorous hyperbole was the work of producer Sid Waddell who, on his way from the mines of Northumberland to a history degree at Cambridge, had picked up a few tips for embellishing introductory speeches. Shove ha'penny players became 'stars of the sliding small change,' exhibiting a flair to 'match the delicateness and the dexterity of the miniature portrait painter'. Leaning on the skittles table like Dr Bronowski on a lectern, rolling every 'r' within reach, Fred eulogised, 'what's probably the oldest pub game in England. I hear Henry VIII used to knock the old shove ha'pennies about a bit – when he weren't bashing t'missus. Well, I don't know how Barry Stones or Alan Brown of Durham treat their missuses, but they certainly can nudge a crafty ha'penny!'

Aside from the sport's 'wild characters' like 'Buffalo Bill' of Scunthorpe (who shoved ha'pennies while wearing a ten-gallon hat), Fred drew tantalising sketches of the contestants, giving each one an intriguing *nom de guerre*: 'Charles Ellis, the Dark Horse . . . he's got five kids, and he takes his arrows seriously and all'; 'Dennis Jones, the Lad Who Crouches to Swing, owns a chip shop, and is going a bit thin on top.' These portentous vignettes were often brutally undercut when he interviewed the man in question, with thoroughly prosaic results. 'You weren't as consistent as you usually are today.' 'No Fred, I forgot me darts. I left them in the pub and had to borrow some.' Occasionally the programme unearthed a snug bar Muhammad Ali, like 'King Ben' Bootham of Keighley, who proudly declared, 'I can ride a unicycle after downing ten pints!' Supermen all.

The commentators varied in style as much as the players. Neil Cleminson filled the layman in on arcane technical matters. 'He knocks off that chalk in the bay, but still has two required in the first bay. So this means he has six to get in the top, and two in the bottom, so it's twenty chalks already in, seven to get, and the break ends.' Dave Lanning, meanwhile, hyped them up for all they were worth. 'Ooh, shiver me timbers! The drama! The stark naked drama of table skittles! He got two successive floppers . . . Now, can he get all twenty-seven? No, he can't.'

*The Indoor League* is one of those programmes that gets dragged out today as an example of the screamingly parochial – a room-size remnant of a fag-packet world long since gentrified to oblivion. Such easy mockery conveniently ignores the fun Fred and company had at their own expense. It's not immediately obvious – it is, admittedly, a very Yorkshire kind of fun – but it's there.

The 2012 Olympic Games, legend goes, saw the UK shed its entrenched mardiness and become a nation of grudgeless, classless joiners-in. But *The Indoor League*'s combination of domesticated superlatives and floor-gazing trophy exchanges points to a more nuanced form of support. Pulling in two directions at once, local pride is elegantly cantilevered; like a Playtex bra, it lifts as it deprecates. *The Indoor League* was a monument to human endeavour that never got too peas-above-sticks, a tongue-in-cheek thumbs-up, a lavishly tooled tin medal. It hailed its saloon bar heroes with a beautifully muted fanfare that seemed all the more genuine for its sardonic undercurrent. In Dave Lanning's immortally moderate words, 'The hundred pounds is in his back pocket and the beer will be flowing tonight I am sure!'

# WHATEVER HAPPENED TO THE LIKELY LADS? (1973–4)

## BBC One

### The sitcom sequel that outdid its original.

COMEDY HISTORY IS LITTERED with legends of executives bumping into canteen staff and commissioning six episodes of a national institution from them on the spot. Such stories are often romanticised – John Sullivan was less a scene shifter who happened to have written *Citizen Smith* than a sitcom writer who happened to realise the best way to collar producers was to get a job on the studio floor – but many great comedies have had the most ad hoc conceptions.

At the start of the 1960s in Notting Hill's Uxbridge Arms[227] Dick Clement, a young radio producer for the BBC's African service, and drinking pal Ian La Frenais wrote 'Double Date', a conversation between two idle, sarky and randy lads, for the off-duty amusement of the BBC staff drama society.[228] When Clement took a TV directing course and was given one day, £100 and the Corporation's tiniest studio with which to make broadcastable television, the trenchant two-hander seemed obvious material. The result was deemed good enough for the consideration of Head of Comedy Frank Muir, who was advised, 'it won't do anything, but at least it's cheap'.[229]

*The Likely Lads* debuted on the fledgling BBC Two in 1964,

with twenty-something Tyneside mates Bob Ferris (Rodney Bewes) and Terry Collier (James Bolam) returning from holiday to their mundane world of dominoes, electrical repairs and largely fruitless wooing of the local talent. You couldn't hope for a less remarkable premise, but from this barren plot grew some of television's ripest comedy.

Naturally funny dialogue had already been cultivated by Ray Galton and Alan Simpson in *Hancock* and *Steptoe and Son*, but these shows retained an element of the grotesque, be it Hancock's surreal delusions of adequacy or Steptoe's operatic filial resentment. Bob and Terry weren't oddballs or outcasts. Their ordinariness was absolute; it was the writers' genius to locate the rich comic seams in the workaday landscape. The lads transferred to the BBC's main channel via a sketch on 1964's *Christmas Night with the Stars*, in which dewy reminiscence over old Rupert Bear annuals turned into a full-blown duel of competitive nostalgia. The most prosaic subject matter became comic poetry.

The duo's regrouping a decade on was something else entirely. Bob and Terry have grown from their original broad types into those rare birds – fully-rounded sitcom characters. Bob, once meek, naïve and apologetically gauche, has thrown in his lot with the newly rampant middle class. With one foot in the badminton club and an eye on the Rotary, he clings to the suburban greasy pole for all he's worth – not because he relishes its rituals, but more out of sheer relief that others are prepared to do the hard work of ordering his life for him.

Terry, once brash, ignorant and unrepentantly rude, has been hardened by a dud marriage and a singularly humdrum tour of duty into a shambling, shiftless professional prole, half Orwellian autodidact (thanks to such crucial texts as the Open University's *Metamorphosis of the Frog*), and half northern Nietzsche, foretelling imminent doom for those above him on the social ladder, and an imminent thick ear for those in front of him in the bus queue. The small things that differentiated the pair in youth have grown into an unbridgeable social chasm. Naturally, this makes them closer than ever. Apart, they're the two poles of male hopelessness incarnate. Together they're a complete fool.

Wedged disconsolately between them is Bob's fiancée Thelma Chambers (Brigit Forsyth), chief architect of the Ferris renaissance and congenitally deaf to the Collier repartee. While Terry stews in his ancestral back-to-back, Bob and Thelma are snug in their Arcadian bolt-hole on the Elm Lodge Estate. Inside it's all melamine serving hatches, heliotrope cookware and pottery owls in self-assembly nooks. Outside the anaemic brick terraces are fringed with a front garden of blasted tundra and the milkman does double duty as a John Pilger of inter-mews gossip. When Terry tells Bob he'll need to give his house a name otherwise he'd never be able to find it again his words have weight, or at least they would if he wasn't kipping on Bob's sofa-bed at the time.

If *Whatever* . . . were a drama series, it would be renowned for the way it compresses the grit of quotidian domestic experience and working class male angst into crystal-clear speech. Sadly for posterity's sake, the writers had to go and make it funny as well. Drama is the minutes of life's meeting taken down in exquisite copperplate. Sitcom is the conversation in the pub afterwards copied in Teeline shorthand onto a fag packet. *Whatever* . . . is a parade of observations so deadly accurate as to give the illusion of a fully-fitted history. Characters like Lugless Douglas and the infamous Sylvia Braithwaite, legendary hang-outs like the Go-Go Rock Club ('the north's premier music Mecca') exist only as a few lines of bitty recollection, but are all the more vivid for it. Each word has a job to do, and every word counts.

Clement and La Frenais give all their characters due sympathy. Even Thelma, who initially lived up to her Medusan reputation in the lads' Park Junior School mythology ('We tried not to make her a monster,' said Clement, 'but I'm afraid we failed'[230]) was gradually rounded out as Bob's true other half: equally neurotic, but emotionally practical (unlike Terry, who's free of neuroses but cooks chops in the toaster). This was partly due to Forsyth's skill in humanising the authors' rough model, just as Bolam and Bewes's on-set back-and-forth enriched the original scripts to create, in less than fourteen hours of television, three of the most solid, believable characters of any genre.

It sounds odd to describe such a downbeat show as revolutionary, but *Whatever . . .*'s realism made a great impression on the brightest of its successors. Sitcom talk dropped the last vestiges of the old punchline set-ups for the rattle and roll of real speech. Characters occupied the same readily recognisable world as their viewers. The dialogue was littered with cultural ephemera. Once established, all these traits, especially the last one, could be grossly overused by writers looking for a shortcut to 'quality' comedy. They forgot to purloin the trick *Whatever . . .* didn't invent, but helped to perfect: a script which, by judicious craftsmanship, is perfectly balanced, even – especially – when the situation goes haywire. Towards the end of the last series, various confusions lead Terry and Thelma to charge into the kitchen and pull Bob out from what looks like a gas oven suicide attempt. The concluding tableau, straight out of stock melodrama, with the three of them sprawled tearfully on the kitchen floor, is capped by Bob's plaintive cry to a distraught Thelma: 'You'll get Ovenstick all over your blouse!' Advantage: sitcom.

# THRILLER (1973–6)
## ITV/ABC (ATV)

### The deluxe crime anthology.

*The perfect murder, like the perpetual motion machine, has often engaged the attention of the whimsical. And, as parlour games go, both are better than snakes and ladders. It is as harmless as a bug in boiling water. Even the corpses appear to wink!*

Dennis Potter, *Daily Herald*, 12 May 1964

THE CRIME DRAMA IS as much sport as art. While a football match only has so many different outcomes, there are infinite ways to reach a no-score draw, some more thrilling than others. A murder yarn also sets its field at kick-off – playing the young married couple freshly moved into an old cottage up front, putting the stranger who may not be all he seems on the wing, keeping the recently escaped serial killer on the subs bench. The joy's in the journey, the masterly variations and wrong-footings wrought from these familiar scenarios.

By the early 1970s Brian Clemens was one of British television's most successful scriptwriters, with a hand in creating many of the big Golden Age action hits, from *The Avengers* to *The Persuaders*. He learnt his craft in the distinctly un-flashy B-movie trade of the 1950s. Quota producers like the Danziger Brothers inherited some random sets from major films and Clemens ran up a script that somehow tied together the Old Bailey, a Georgian street and the bridge of a nuclear submarine. It was this artisan dexterity that he most prized. 'Any fool can do a good job given £10 million and a hired army to stage the Battle of Waterloo,' Clemens reasoned. 'But it takes real ingenuity to do it with two soldiers.'[231] Lew Grade gave him the ideal opportunity to showcase his prudent knack when he commissioned one of Clemens's long-cherished ideas: a thriller anthology.

The anthology series was a familiar feature of the 1970s schedule. Ratings-conscious channel controllers saw how conveniently they combined the benefits of the long-running series (which made the money, but caused a lot of damage when they crashed) and the single play (which won the accolades, but was already lost to posterity as the end credits rolled). All the stories had in common was a loose theme or genre, but add in a snappy theme and stylish introduction, and a bunch of light dramas became a scheduling fixture. *The Wednesday Play* and the *Philco-Goodyear Playhouse* reclined at the posh end of the form, while peak time mustered Rod Serling's *The Twilight Zone* and Roald Dahl's *Tales of the Unexpected*. (The anthology was just about the only TV format in which a writer could get his name billed above the title.)

*Thriller* wasn't monogrammed with Clemens's name, but his fingerprints were all over it. Out of forty-three episodes, he wrote over thirty and provided detailed story outlines for the rest. His building blocks were life's mundane panics: the front door creaking after midnight, the shifty stalker in the crowd, the boarding house full of ominously frosty tenants. His narrative tools were unabashed cliché. Characters entered living rooms refracted in crystal decanters placed just so on an occasional table in the foreground. Anonymous black-gloved hands picked up telephone receivers and slowly dialled very long numbers. Flashy TR7s would gravel-crunch up driveways of well-appointed country houses, arousing the mutton-chopped gardener's suspicion. Blonde Americans in trouser suits merrily announced they were 'new in town' to public bars full of ruddy and watchful character actors.

The budgets were boosted by a deal with US network ABC, who insisted on two alterations in return. First, they wanted each episode to cover ninety minutes of American evening, which worked out at seventy-two minutes of programme content. This turned out to be a boon for Clemens, who could use those extra twelve minutes over the hour to build suspense in long, largely silent takes, helped immensely by the bespoke incidental music of Laurie Johnston (standard procedure at the time was to slap on a slice of 'Eerie Oboe' from the music library every time the killer wandered on set). Second, a high proportion of the tales had to include, somewhere near the top of the billing, either an American actress with a first name for a surname, or an American actor with a surname for a first name.

Research was not Clemens's bag. He wrote a police procedural or court case as he imagined it, only running a cursory check against the facts on completion. He claimed that ninety-nine per cent of the time he didn't have to alter anything, although one notable feature of the series is the high incidence of walk-on desk sergeants who comment darkly on the 'highly irregular' methods of the detective in charge. The production schedule was tight: ten days' rehearsal in a draughty Masonic hall, a four-day shoot in ATV's Elstree studios (plus a few exterior shots, often just a silent trudge from front door to Ford Granada) and three days for editing.[232]

All this suggests the worst kind of slapdash stab-'n'-scream fare: Primark Hitchcock shot by the yard. Clemens's writing raised the game. While characterisation never rose above broad types and the dialogue largely stuck to unvarnished exposition, Clemens marshalled the familiar, the expected and the done-to-death into flamboyant new combinations. Twists were second-guessed, undercut and double-crossed. The rug was pulled out from under the viewer, often taking several square feet of parquet flooring with it. The giddy feeling of a murder case folding in on itself like deadly origami enhanced the already giddy feeling of sumptuous 1970s interiors peopled with famous murder suspects clad in vibrant artificial fibres. Sometimes the detective schlepped more satin than the kidnapped heiress. Everything on screen was arch contrivance. Subtlety got you nowhere.

Take 1975 episode, 'The Double Kill'. Ingredients: one desperate, psychopathic cat burglar; one loud-mouth Yank hubby of a wealthy heiress; and one suavely unorthodox detective played by a pinstriped Peter Bowles. The three men confront, dodge and bluff each other as clues and events pile up. A botched burglary, a murder contract, a giveaway pair of blood-stained kid gloves – championship games of Cluedo have unfolded in less ceremonial fashion. Blackmail leads to counter-blackmail, murder weapons appear and vanish, a Wodehousian dipsomaniac stumbles in with crucial evidence, and copper and suspect size each other up via protracted sidelong glances across the crime scene. But while the screen overflows with old chestnuts, the plot keeps throwing curveballs up until the closing lines, and the players visibly relish every minute.

This is after-dinner crime: murder as party piece. Future generations would delight in this florid overkill, but it was considered outrageously camp even at the time. It was TV's equivalent of Victorian melodrama, and like that much derided genre its job, according to Eric Bentley, was 'not to tumble into absurdity by accident but to revel in it on purpose'.[233] Unspeakable evil and outrageous coincidence reigned supreme. Sir Arthur Conan Doyle, priding himself on the insoluble nature of his Sherlock Holmes plots, 'positively bet his wife a shilling that she would not guess the true solution of it until she got to the end of the chapter'.[234] *Thriller* pushed the limits of credulity in all directions. Its closest thing to a recurring character, private detective Matthew Earp, played with Noel Coward levels of fanciful abandon by Dinsdale Landen, was prone to prefacing revelations with 'fasten your seatbelts!' Writer, director, cast and even the characters they played were having a lark. The game show was afoot.

When a TV format accumulates this much froufrou garnish, diagnosis of decadence is never far away. *Thriller* and its contemporaries engendered a backlash and a thirst for realism. Crime in the cinema was starting to get very bloody. TV couldn't be that explicit, but its locations slowly became back alleys rather than front parlours, and murders shattered whole families instead of just altering wills. The detective was just as likely to be an amoral thug himself rather than an omniscient savant with a passion for real tennis. But this messier, less reassuring thriller wasn't always more real. Take *The Professionals* – top-level criminal intelligence operations performed by a Ford Capri-skidding, semi-automatic firing pair of dolly boys with an eye for the birds and a morbid fear of car door handles. Bodie and Doyle set new standards for unflinching depiction of mob violence and terrorism, but with all the documentary realism of a school playground reconstruction of *Diamonds Are Forever*. For this, they could thank their creator: Brian Clemens.

# TISWAS (1974–82)
## ITV (ATV)

### Television gets the kids right.

*Surrealism is an almost impossibly demanding aesthetic, since only a genius can be free without restrictions.* Tiswas *is a surrealist television programme. It ought to be a flop. Happily it is quite the opposite.*

Clive James, 'The True Artists',
*Observer*, 18 February 1979

SOME GREAT TELEVISION PROGRAMMES are painstakingly constructed. Others achieve success through trial and error. A tiny few are the product of one brief flash of inspiration. Perhaps the rarest category of all, though, is the kind of programme which spontaneously crops up, often unplanned and beneath the radar of both executive and critic, in the gaps between other programmes: televisual weeds.

Saturday mornings in the early seventies remained one of British television's many uncultivated waste grounds. If ITV bothered to stir at all before *World of Sport*, it was for a hotchpotch of children's reruns like *Thunderbirds* and adult education series on DIY or bridge playing. Gradually the kids' stuff won out, and the couple of hours before noon became the new teatime.

On 5 January 1974, in the tiny presentation studio at ATV's Birmingham headquarters, the regional links between the old shows were billed as an umbrella programme, tentatively titled *Today is*

*Saturday*, or the *Tis-Was Show*. Gags, competitions and 'fun facts' festooned the spaces between old episodes of *Tarzan*, providing a bit of conceptual glue and cutting drastically down on costs. In charge, at least nominally, were the '*Tiswas* Twins', John Asher and Chris 'Strawhead' Tarrant, administering ad-hoc bits of business that were half written in the pub the night before, half pulled out of thin air before your very eyes.

It was, as the *TV Times* quietly allowed, 'informal and experimental in a modest way,'[235] but nobody, the Twins included, realised how big it would become in its first eleven-week run. Producer Peter 'Poochie' Tomlinson and sports presenter 'Me, Myself, Yours Truly' Trevor East were enlisted to make up the show's original back-seat-of-the-coach crew. Gradually the inter-programme chaos began to take over from the pre-recorded stuff it was supposed to be linking. Confidence grew, and with it, chaos. It moved into the significantly larger Studio Three, where an important discovery was made: water and other substances could be thrown around without fear of electrocution. The plot thickened.

Week by week, almost imperceptibly, a new show formed, concerned less with back-announcing the exploits of *Arthur, King of the Britons* and illustrated lectures on the life cycle of the moth, and more with ramshackle, off-the-cuff parodies of current films, TV shows and celebrities, which began with a chorus of barely suppressed giggles and rapidly descended (or rather ascended) into a maelstrom of airborne fluorescent treacle. Then, as the typhoon wore itself out, Tarrant, gasping for breath as the last empty bucket careened off the woodwork behind him, hastily looked for the working camera and panted the introduction to an ancient Roadrunner cartoon; after which, the fury would start up all over again. Veteran supervisors of Tartrazine-fuelled children's parties recognised the pattern.

*Tiswas*'s most significant contemporary, *Saturday Scene*, grew out of programme links in the same way, moulded by London Weekend's head of presentation Warren Breach around repeats of *The Bionic Woman*. Its most popular segment was a quarter-hour pop slot, in which David Essex and the Bay City Rollers were interviewed by actress Sally James. By early 1977 *Tiswas* had become big enough to poach Sal from the metropolis to conduct her patent Almost Legendary Pop Interviews. Genuine star guests were augmented by Tarrant and East impersonating names too big to hit the Midlands, donning outsize cardboard grins as Donny and Marie Osmond. In the days when pop music was still presented with wooden mock enthusiasm across the board, this implicit mickey-taking was a welcome corrective to the 'teenybop' ritual, earning the respect of many post-punk acts. The Clash boycotted *Top of the Pops* outright, but had no objections to a quick chat with Sal.

For the rest of the decade the show retained its rough format, though personnel changed around it. Out went Tomlinson and East. In came ex-Scaffold member John Gorman (specialities: tramps, military types, high-concept mucking about); Bob Carolgees (dim escapologists, phlegmatic pets) and Lenny Henry (moustachioed newsreaders, bearded botanists, reggae artistes with exacting dietary requirements). And in all directions, the constant chorus of kids, often holding up jokes on placards like a cracker factory picket line, alternately cheering and jeering the adults, sometimes both simultaneously.

The show slowly smothered the country in its Wunda-Gloo. First Wales, then the North West and Scotland fell. By 1979 only the Southern and Tyne-Tees areas held out with their own brave but inferior stabs at a rival, leading geographically deprived youngsters to hit the black-and-white portable set in an attempt to catch some fuzzily fading remnants of the Midlands signal. By 1980, it was finally a true national programme, and a considerable threat to the BBC. Edward Barnes, head of the BBC children's department, labelled it 'indigestible candyfloss with no intellectual grit',[236] as opposed to his own stately rival, *Multi-Coloured Swap Shop*, with mugs of tea, a cosy club atmosphere and an initial theme of diligent collecting (admittedly soon abandoned in favour of pop guests). Everyone had a preference, but the idea of the rival shows dividing the nation's youth along tribal lines was largely a myth: both had peaks and lulls, and many kids energetically switched between the two.

This made ratings very difficult to measure, but relatively modest estimates of between two and three million for turn-of-the-decade *Tiswas* still constituted a solid achievement for those who remembered when this part of the schedule was all farming bulletins. The ATV mailbags were gargantuan. The show got through fifty cans of custard pie foam a week, supplied by local joke shop proprietor David Lynex. Tarrant, James, Carolgees and Gorman formed the Four Bucketeers, had a hit record and did a national tour of rock venues.

National glory latest barely a year. Tarrant, Carolgees and Henry left the show in mid-1981 to found *OTT*, Tarrant's vision of an 'adult' *Tiswas* at the other end of the Saturday schedule, which introduced the comedy of Alexei Sayle, and stirred up plenty of froth in the press, but never quite got its round in. Under the quieter reign of Gordon Astley and Den Hegarty from doo-wop revivalists Darts, *Tiswas* carried on until Central Television, new holders of the Midlands ITV franchise, put it to bed.

Central's replacement, *The Saturday Show*, showed how much work really did go into keeping *Tiswas* running, by letting the chaos overwhelm the hosts. Cues were fluffed, cameras lost, and microphones flooded with crowd chatter, resulting in a blob of grey un-television with all the party ambience of a fire assembly point. They really did just throw that show together, and it showed. Later Saturday morning affairs were better than that, but rarely touched *Tiswas* for spontaneity that sparked.

*Tiswas*'s greatest innovation took time to become apparent. The adults allowed themselves to be witty in a way which belonged to the world at large rather than the imagined world of children, giving the kids the benefit of the doubt. By not giving two hoots about responsibly preparing its young charges for adult life, *Tiswas* gave kids perhaps the most appealing and honest advice about what lay ahead for them: it's all just a big, ridiculous mess anyway, so get stuck in.

# DON'T ASK ME
# (1974–8)
## ITV (Yorkshire)

TV science goes populist in a big way.

*In this state of unselfconsciousness, it seemed that, to emphasise what I was saying, I made certain characteristic gestures.*

Magnus Pyke

FOR DECADES, SCIENCE ON television commanded reverential restraint. Straight dissemination of the known facts with a bare minimum of visual garnish gave broadcasts plenty of sombre purposefulness, but minimal entertainment value. When heavyweight presenters were replaced by laymen things relaxed slightly, though critics often bridled. *Meet Mr Marvel*, co-hosted by Muriel Young, was dismissed in 1956 as 'an extraordinary farrago of pseudo-scientific demonstrations at nursery level and facetious backchat.'[237] But it took one of the country's top nutritional biochemists to turn science into full-blown cabaret.

Dr Magnus Pyke began his unique broadcasting career at the age of sixty-three, when a graphic lecture on synthetic foodstuffs he delivered to the Royal Society led Yorkshire Television to employ him for *Magnus and the Beansteak*, a premonition of the imminent future of texturised vegetable protein with everything. Pyke's gambolling analysis caught the eye of producer Duncan Dallas, who hired him for the new popular science show he was putting together. Pyke joined lisping, booming, bearded botanist David Bellamy and personable pharmaceutical magnate Miriam Stoppard, both equally new to the cameras. 'We decided that authority and enthusiasm were more important than slick television technique,' explained Dallas.[238]

The chasm between the scientists and lay public was bridged by a down-to-earth interlocutor, initially actress Adrienne Posta, latterly future MP Austin Mitchell, *Play School*'s Derek Griffiths and ex-wrestler Brian Glover. With friendly in-the-round presentation, a firm focus on science's place in the everyday world, and a bevy of decorative young women in *Don't Ask Me* T-shirts, the show was unashamedly targeted at what Pyke called 'the great, multitudinous *Sun*-reading backbone of the nation'.[239]

Pyke stole the first show with a demonstration of the Coriolis effect: the old saw that bathwater drains in opposite directions on each side of the equator. To this end he pulled the plug from a bath in the studio, while acrobatically referring to a six-foot model globe and simultaneously holding long-distance telephone conversations with bath-watching scientists in New York and Sydney, as well as cueing in some film of a similar set up bang on the equator in Kenya. After a tenuous moment when it looked like the props department's little balsa wood raft would turn obstinately in the wrong direction, it miraculously corrected itself, and the yelp of joy emanating from Magnus's direction sealed his fate as the nation's favourite hysterical boffin. The fact that the Earth's rotation actually has little or no effect on bathwater direction was neither here nor there – a star was born.

Pyke's windmilling gestural ballet, swooping here, grasping there and ducking behind his own shoulders as if he was trying to capture the Higgs Boson with his bare hands, was eminently imitable. In a decade where impressionists sat at the peak of light entertainment, his rise to fame was almost instant. Dallas instructed his cameramen to always hold Pyke in a wide shot, lest he bound out of frame. With all this energy directed to the extremities, sometimes the words went awry: reference to rump steak came out as 'ox bum';

'My Uncle Harry,' he once found himself expounding, 'is older than I am, because he is dead – though that doesn't necessarily follow . . .'

Fame didn't lead Pyke to give up his day job as chairman of the British Association, so the inevitable flood of showbiz opportunities had to be managed with a discerning eye. Offers of Penguin biscuit ads and panto in Norwich were regretfully turned down, as was the suggestion made by the *Parkinson* chat show that he team up with Bellamy and the BBC's own crazed boffin Patrick Moore for a full drag rendition of 'Three Little Maids from School'. He did, however, join Moore in a full dance rendition of 'Tiptoe Through the Tulips' for *The Lennie and Jerry Show*, and accepted invitations from nightclubs to stand on a podium and answer the kids' hastily scribbled scientific posers between records. His attitude to all this was somewhere between modestly grateful and loftily ambivalent – he reflected that his turn on *Celebrity Squares* 'was, I suppose, of some sociological significance, if nothing else.'[240]

As *Don't Ask Me* continued, the stunts got bigger and bolder, and so did the cock-ups. In 1978, new recruit Rob Buckman presided over the firing of a nineteen-year-old woman from a circus cannon, to answer the vexed question of whether human cannon-balls lose height during the flight. Sadly she fell short of the safety net and suffered injuries serious enough for that particular theory to remain untested.[241] The following year, with Pyke and Bellamy now familiar enough to television for the 'common man' presenter to be made redundant, it relaunched as the equally frenetic *Don't Just Sit There!* Subsequent science shows would clone the approachable question-and-answer formula, but none managed to dig up a host that could match Pyke in what he daintily identified as 'the element of unselfconscious loquacity in my make-up'.

# SUPERSONIC (1975–7)
## ITV (Thames)

### The glitter-strewn apotheosis of pop TV.

*Don't stare at the monitors and say, 'We're on now, Sylvia, ooh,' that's a terrible drag. And do watch the cameras . . . they go zooming around and if one hits you you'll know all about it. Make some sort of motion to the record, don't stand gawping, or chewing or nattering. If I catch anyone hanging round the side there'll be a quick one up the backside.*

Assistant producer to audience, *Top of the Pops* recording,
Lime Grove studios, 27 October 1966

THE STORY OF *Top of the Pops* is long, well-rehearsed and in places deeply disturbing. Though it had longevity and star power on its side, as television it was tame. In the mid 1970s its production values were still making Jack Good seem radical. '*TOTP* mummifies rock in a middle-aged, pop casket,' wrote Bart Mills. "'All right, kiddies," says the BBC, holding its nose. "Unfortunately, you exist, and I'm told there are millions of you. We must give you something. Here, take this. I think I'm going to be sick.'"[242] The pop audience was getting younger every year. *TOTP*'s core constituency became pre-teen, though it still provided thrills for older kids when the right acts were on, but usually in spite of the surrounding show.

There was a more dynamic pop TV producer at large. Mike Mansfield was an ambitious, technically adept gallery controller who cut a distinctive figure in Southern Television's Southampton studios in the late 1960s with his coiffured hair, Aztec-patterned knitwear and huge 'M'-shaped medallion. His early works included *As You Like It*, a lavish pop request show in which Adam Faith solicited viewers' requests from a different novelty location each week, and *Time For Blackburn*, a spoiler scheduled against the BBC's *All Systems Freeman*. Tony Blackburn was an affable host, but the real star was up in the gallery.

Denied Fluff's lavish gimmickry, Mansfield got creative in the control room, getting the most out of the studio basics – three cameras and a vision mixer. When The Who turned up to perform a tumultuous version of 'Magic Bus', Mansfield instructed his mixer to switch cameras with psychedelic abandon, practically on every beat, resulting in a blizzard of images of Daltrey and Moon flashing before the unwary audience as they had their Saturday tea, and doubtless playing hell with a few poorly-adjusted vertical holds. Southern's viewers blinked, and so did the Beeb. *All Systems Freeman* was off the air within two months.

Mansfield moved to London Weekend Television, and seizing two exciting new developments – colour and glam rock – instigated *Supersonic*, his own musical attempt 'to beat the Depression'. Gurning presenters were out; silver-maned producers were in. From the gallery, Mansfield himself linked acts with manic techno-chat. 'Lights, standby studio, going to you, three . . . and cue Gilbert O'Sullivan!' The studio proper was worlds away from *Top of the Pops*. The audience, though seated, was visibly enthusiastic. Cameras glided shamelessly into shot, often with flashing police lights on top. The glam rock acts of the day performed on an appropriately glittering set – a multi-level glass and steel construction which seemed only just capable of supporting the full weight of the Rubettes. Mansfield deployed a battery of technology: fish-eye lenses, mole cranes ploughing into swarms of descending balloons and drum kits going up and down on the pallet of a fork lift truck.

'I was sick of seeing groups who seemed rooted in concrete,'

Mansfield explained. 'Any director can shoot that standing on his eyelashes. I wanted to contribute something visually . . . People love our machinery and our ironmongery. The success of the show is that it proves pop is fun.'[243] Such was *Supersonic*'s level of innovation that even the *Listener* grudgingly approved. '*Supersonic* does, at least, present its rubbish with panache,' it mused. 'The cameras swoop and soar. The props glitter and flicker. The audience seems wakeful. There is no Jimmy Savile. At one point, I thought Mike Mansfield was going to direct one of his cameras into a fifty-foot dive through a hoop of fire. Maybe, next week, this bricks-without-straw craftsman will find a way to do that.'[244]

Mansfield didn't have independent pop TV to himself. Muriel Young shared the channel with him, offering her more conventional takes on underage rock, *Lift Off with Ayshea* and *45*, the latter hosted by ex-Radio Luxembourg DJ David 'Kid' Jensen from the Hardrock Disco, Manchester. Young's attitude to pop was perhaps less wholehearted than Mansfield's. 'My work fills a gap between baby and adult music,' she said, adding hopefully, 'pop music brings them to progressive jazz.' Visually, she had predictably firm views. Mentioning no names, she railed against the 'mind-battering camera antics and lightning changes of shot' of other producers. 'It's not fair to the artists and children don't specially like it.' Smoke machines were also out: 'it makes the singers cough.' Instead, she favoured 'lighting effects and abstract graphics' which 'take a week to do and last eight seconds on the screen.' Both Mansfield's and Young's gimmicks were quietly co-opted by *Top of the Pops* over the years.

The unsettling phenomenon of the Bay City Rollers proved a strong enough force to unite Young and Mansfield for scarf-waving scream-in *Shang-A-Lang*, with Young producing and Mansfield calling the shots. Though the show came from a tiny studio, it generated mass hysteria. Fans hid in bins and smashed windows in attempts to broach Granada's hastily erected ring of steel and touch the hems of the Rollers' sainted tartan 'trews'. Inside, the mania was beyond even Auntie Mu's control. 'I once screamed

"Shut up or I'll kill you all!" at them,' she admitted. 'I think they were quiet for about six seconds that time.'[245]

The Rollers were big time, but *Shang-A-Lang*'s budget was small beans. This frustrated Mansfield, who soon left the programme. 'There's a prejudice against pop,' he complained. 'Whenever they put pop on TV they do it on a shoestring.' Young was more sanguine. 'I work on minimums and imagination . . . I think I'd be embarrassed if someone gave me an enormous budget. I wouldn't know how to behave.'[246] *Supersonic* came to an end in 1977, and after an abortive attempt at a more 'adult' sequel, *Blast Off!*, presented by Michael Aspel, Mansfield moved into pop promos.

In 1983, he made a return to broadcast television with a *Supersonic* special for Channel Four, keeping the original format, with some new-fangled Quantel visual effects on top. His other work for the channel was more controversial. In the summer of 1982, nationwide auditions were held at theatres, schools and youth clubs for a pre-teen musical talent show. As the tots gamely trilled to an accompanying pianist, all seemed innocuous enough. The programme was the creation of Martin Wyatt, who'd had a success with an LP of kids performing popular songs in a winsome manner. 'Don't forget,' he reassured the *Mirror*, 'they're all twelve and under. When they get older than that I have to say, that's it.'[247]

When the *Minipops* arrived on screen, togged up in appropriate (or perhaps inappropriate) costumes, given the full-on glamour treatment by Mansfield and mouthing lyrics with, albeit fairly mild, sexual content, the press grabbed at the stick Channel Four had lovingly crafted to beat them with. The confusion and unease this 'shop window of junior jailbait' engendered was best summarised by Julian Barnes. 'Is it merely priggish to feel queasy at the sight of primary school minxes with rouged cheeks?' he pondered. 'Does the show thrust premature sexual awareness onto its wide-eyed performers? I don't know.'[248] To which a waggish reader responded, 'Since paedophiles are a minority in this country, it's only right they should get their own show on Channel Four.'[249] Rock 'n' roll's wilful blurring of the age of consent had by now become an established tradition, but misgivings were starting to be voiced – albeit mainly directed at the less coolly aloof, old-school showbiz end of operations. It would take another few decades for the activities of certain *Top of the Pops* presenters to really get out. Which is, unfortunately, where we came in.

# THE THRILLA IN MANILA (1974)
## HBO (United Artists-Columbia)

### The dawn of pay-per-view sport.

TELEVISION WAS MADE FOR boxing. In the years after the war, the USA's fledgling networks would fill whole evenings with an extended programme of prizefighting live from New York's Madison Square Garden or Jamaica Arena. Viewers gathered round sets in bars, just as they did for the big variety specials, and created their own crowds in miniature. Through the '50s and '60s however, boxing's network popularity dwindled. An over-reliance on the sport and increasingly blatant match fixing played their part, but the writing was on the wall after the 1962 bout in which Emile Griffith pounded Benny 'The Kid' Paret into a coma from which he would die ten days later. ABC carried the scenes live to the nation's living rooms. This was not the kind of event television they wanted on their books.

Fights became increasingly scarce on the networks after that, but a different way of viewing was on the rise: the closed circuit show. Theatres, sports halls, and even real boxing venues like Madison Square Garden were fitted out with a huge projection screen and had distant fights cabled in to hundreds, maybe thousands of paying punters. The coverage was a fraction of what the network would bring, but with customers willing to pay as much as five dollars per fight, business boomed once more. But there was a third television technology, then still in its early days, that would slowly gain momentum over the next couple of decades to become the default televising method for big name prizefights. It was pay-per-view cable, and it appeared on the scene during one of the most famous and mythologised boxing matches of all time.

No single sportsman has ever revitalised the fortunes of his game as much as Muhammad Ali. In the 1960s as Cassius Clay, he had perfected something rare in the sports world, a magnetic personality, by turns witty and pugnacious, charismatic and belligerent. His garrulous confidence took some getting used to on the part of his interviewers – he walked out on a live edition of the BBC's *Sportsview* after David Coleman complained that he 'talked too much'[250] – but they quickly realised that an articulate, funny champion was the best asset a sport could possess, and played along. His name-changing affiliation with the Nation of Islam made things difficult all over again, especially when he came out against American involvement in Vietnam. His refusal to fight the Viet Cong earned him, with no small irony, a three-year suspension from fighting in the ring.

Ali's eventual return marked the beginning of a new phase of both his career and the sport in general. While Ali was kicking his heels, Smokin' Joe Frazier had risen to prominence. With Ali back in action, their first bout in 1971, nicknamed 'The Fight of the Century', ended in a win on points for Frazier and a ratings triumph for ABC. A disappointing rematch followed in 1974 which Ali won, but the most memorable punches were thrown outside the ring, when the pair, invited to talk over the fight on ABC's *Wide World of Sports*, came to blows in the studio after Ali taunted Frazier for being 'ignorant'. As the two suited heavyweights sprawled on the floor surrounded by their respective entourages, the familiar nasal tones of presenter Howard Cosell chimed in. 'Well, we're having a scene, as you can see,' he observed. 'It's hard to tell whether it's clowning or for real.' At that moment Frazier really let fly, and Cosell changed tack. 'It's a bad and an ugly scene, and it's unfortunate I think that it's happened.' It also happened to set the stage beautifully for a third fight.

The next development was the arrival of promoter Don King. Relatively new to high-end boxing but with a canny eye for the main chance, King raised a $5 million prize purse for a fight between Ali and undefeated champion George Foreman by staging it in Kinshasa, capital city of the then African dictatorship of Zaire (now the Democratic Republic of the Congo). The bombastically titled 'Rumble in the Jungle' of 1974 set new standards for big name fight promotion. The controversial 'rope-a-dope' methods Ali employed to seal his victory were of a piece with the intensely theatrical nature of the bout and its build-up. King immediately set about planning a similarly grandiose match between Ali and Frazier. For this he picked another third world country keen for good publicity – this time Ferdinand Marcos's Philippines, then under martial law – and ran up another memorable rhyming title: 'The Thrilla in Manila'.

The fight was scheduled for 10 a.m. local time to maximise American ratings, but unlike previous fights, it was not to be networked. Many viewers watched it in the old closed circuit style, in 276 locations across the USA.[251] Some viewers had another option, courtesy of the struggling early cable provider Home Box Office. One of the cable pioneers, HBO had been around since the mid-1950s when, as Box Office Television, it organised closed circuit broadcasts of sport and Broadway plays, with financial backing from comedian Sid Caesar, among others. Two decades on, cable was steadfastly refusing to take off, but it retained a foothold in rural parts where conventional TV signals were weak. Vice president Bob Rosencrans took the plunge and bought the rights to transmit the fight on a pay-per-view basis.

The gamble paid off. The satellite broadcast, even after a transfer from ground station to cable, was crisp and clear. 'When you looked at the close-ups,' claimed Rosencrans, 'the fighters looked like they were in the next room, the picture quality was that extraordinary.'[252] The threats of closure HBO had been facing receded, and the painfully slow progress of cable television in the USA turned into a gold rush, propelled mainly by big sporting events. A fully-fledged cable service delivering satellite-transmitted events from around the world, the Madison Square Garden-affiliated MSG Sports Network, launched in 1977; many more would follow. The decisive step from television being a mass, communally viewed medium to a fragmented cornucopia of entertainment options had been taken. Oh, and Ali won, of course.

# THE NORMAN GUNSTON SHOW (1975–9)

## ABC/ Seven/ BBC Two

### The spoof interviewer arrives in the form of a little Aussie bleeder.

> *'Let's get on with the in depth questions and get out of here real quick.'*
>
> Norman Gunston interviews Sally Struthers, 1975

ONE OF THE DEFINING moments in Australian culture was Gough Whitlam's brief but busy reign as Labour prime minister in the early 1970s. Before then, national culture was safeguarded by men like Adelaide's Detective Inspector Vogelsang, who impounded poetry books for containing the word 'incestuous' while freely admitting he didn't know what it meant.[253] Once the cultural shackles were loosened, there was a lot of ground to make up.

Those impounded poems turned out to be spoofs, and parody thrived in the newly permissive environment. Barry Humphries was the foremost exponent, already long adept at skewering Melbourne's suburbanites through characters like time-stopping convalescent Sandy Stone and as-yet-untitled denizen of Moonee Ponds, Edna Everage. Edna's nephew Barry MacKenzie epitomised a whole sub-genre of Akubra hat-sporting, Fosters-chugging,

Technicolor yawning 'ocker' humour, which was founded back under the old regime on *TW3* clone *The Mavis Bramston Show*, and moulded into a global industry by Paul Hogan. Elsewhere there was untrammelled sauce, in the form of Graham Blundell's *Alvin Purple*, close relative of the *Confessions* films' Timothy Lea who brought full frontal nudity to network television screens. 'Making *Alvin Purple* without frontal nudity,' claimed ABC's Head of Light Entertainment, Maurice Murphy, 'is as ludicrous as it would have been to ask Edward G. Robinson to play Shirley Temple.'[254]

Another of Murphy's commissions was *The Aunty Jack Show*, a knockabout pantomime with overtones of *The Goodies* that racked up a healthy tally of complaints for swearing and violence. One of the *Aunty Jack* troupe, Garry McDonald, featured in a recurring sketch called 'What's on Wollongong'. In the guise of anaemic reporter Norman Gunston, he covered local events from a grotty bedsit in the eponymous Sydney suburb, or promoted sophisticated new perfume 'Après-Midi in Port Kembla'.

The hopeless but keen would-be star had been a comedy staple since Horace Kenney toured British music halls in the 1930s as a whey-faced weakling, nervously dragging himself through a singing fireman act by the power of totally misplaced self-belief.[255] McDonald, who shared Kenney's sickly appearance, shaped Gunston into a similarly overconfident 'feeb': nervous and mal-adroit, but with a mile wide narcissistic streak, convinced of his destiny as a star of titanic renown.

Gunston's showbiz origins lay in the interminable evening chat shows Australian TV would put on in the late 1960s to fill space on the cheap, and have McDonald and his mates 'falling about laughing at them'. Their deadly combination of tenacity and inepti-tude was poured into Gunston, who was recast as a walking cultural cringe, forcing his crass ignorance on assorted visiting stars, begin-ning with Joe Frazier, preparing for the Thrilla in Manila and snared by Gunston for ABC's *Sports Scene*. Gunston's intrusion into the 'real' world brought him alive. Mock interviews were nothing new – San Franciscan duo Coyle and Sharpe were bamboo-zling the man in the street with questions about hockey puck shortages in the early 1960s – but here they were part of a frontal assault on the showbiz system itself.

With a gigantic 'Press' badge on the lapel of his shop-worn jacket, thinning strands of hair slicked over his shiny pate, chin festooned with shaving wounds and clutching a Qantas holdall for dear life, Gunston crouched at the feet of the showbiz elite, showering them with backhanded compliments and befuddled platitudes. Crashing press conferences guerilla-style, he left touring stars including Burt Reynolds ('How's your mum, Debbie?'), Warren Beatty ('Did Carly Simon write that song about you, "The Impossible Dream?"') and Kiss ('Which one of you is the construction worker?') bewildered. Tame stuff by modern standards perhaps, but the po-faced ceremony of the showbiz press conference had never before been subjected to such mongrel disrespect.

Through two series for ABC, Gunston, guided by the show's chief writer Bill Harding, developed from basket case to perversely dominant personality, fronting 'half an hour of packed entertainment with the slow learner in mind'.[256] His technique even filtered into the legitimate chat circuit, as hosts like Paul Makin began playing the innocent to spice up otherwise deadly dull interviews with low wattage celebs like Leif Garrett. In retaliation, Gunston took to introducing himself as 'the thinking man's Paul Makin'. The second series took him to the UK, where he requested the pleasure of an interview with the Queen, Edward Heath and Harold Wilson, though after their respective offices found out the nature of the man from Australia House, they wisely backed out.

After years of pining for a Gold Logie – the greatest prize in Australian television – Gunston was finally awarded one, and accepted in character. 'When you do an excellent programme like mine, it's not just you up there on the screen – there are many other people behind the scenes that you have to carry as well.' Flipping between parochial naivety and grandiose gracelessness in a second, Gunston laid out the form for every fake interlocutor thereafter.

In November 1975, Gough Whitlam was controversially dismissed from office by the Governor-General. Appropriately enough, Gunston was in Canberra, soliciting views, congratulating incoming PM Malcolm Fraser on being nominated 'Father of the Year', and all but upstaging Whitlam himself as he addressed the crowds outside parliament, many cheering 'Gunston for Governor-General!' One bystander added, 'Norman, you're the only true Australian!' A sobering thought.

# PLAY FOR TODAY: DOUBLE DARE (1976)
## BBC One

### Dennis Potter writes himself into a corner.

BY 1976, DENNIS POTTER was ready to quit television. In just over a decade, he'd graduated from co-writing quick squibs for *TW3* to being television's most prominent, and certainly most identifiable, playwright. But censorship, executive timidity and the sheer frustration of pushing ideas through the production mill became wearying. 'I think the days of the television play are numbered,' he told the nation in the publicity for his valedictory work, 'but before it ends I want to make a few defiant noises.'[257]

Before his dramatic career, Potter spent the early sixties as chief TV critic at the *Daily Herald*, cataloguing his television likes and dislikes. Into the 'hate' pile went ecclesiastical sitcoms ('as predictable as the epilogue, but considerably less amusing'[258]) and humorous panel games ('this rather coy, ponderous, often excruciatingly twee sort of comedy is as depressingly English as fried eggs and thumb-thick chips'[259]). Conversely, he was a champion of 'the rather shrill, often overblown journalism of *World in Action*,'[260] shed a nostalgic tear for *Children's Hour* ('the thing [the BBC] has slaughtered so wantonly'[261]), and declared a fondness for the weird, semi-abstract animation then colonising British TV from Canada and Eastern Europe, with its 'tipsy triangles and pompous oblongs, depressed squares and bad-tempered rectangles . . . an exuberant delight.'[262]

On the one hand, he wanted sexual frankness on the box: 'A lot of prigs seem to get very hot under the collar when contemplating something as harmless and pleasant as an unclad breast.'[263] On the other, his squeamish inner censor occasionally showed its head, most often when confronted with bloody operation footage on programmes like *Your Life in Their Hands*. 'I was left wondering whether the BBC . . . had gone too far in permitting pictures of the kind we saw.'[264]

His opinions on drama were naturally forthright. He had a sharp eye, spotting even in 1964 a fall-off in the quality of revolutionary police serial *Z-Cars*. ('The mannerisms of the actors have replaced characterisation. The tiny bursts of automatic dialogue squirt onto the screen without producing truth.'[265]) While not a massive fan of American crowd-pleasers like *Dr Kildare* and *77 Sunset Strip*, he admired their energy, lamenting 'I've always wished this compelling know-how could be transferred to our so-called "serious" TV.'[266] It was 'serious' drama he craved the most, the sort of stuff that exposed 'something rotting and horrible beneath even the most placid surface,'[267] and got under its characters' skin. ('Plays that prowl around inside the head can be even more exciting than those which deal only with external actions.'[268]) After he left the *Herald* in 1964, he put this manifesto into action.

Some plays betrayed his critical origins. *Paper Roses*, set in a flea-bitten Fleet Street tabloid office, was periodically interrupted by a cantankerous TV critic moaning to himself about the play's shortcomings – an arch, self-exonerating gag. *Follow the Yellow Brick Road* gave Denholm Elliott's cuckolded misogynist actor a paranoid suspicion that his whole life was a television play – a cheap, badly-scripted one, at that. *Double Dare* was a further inversion: creatively exhausted playwright Martin Ellis (Alan Dobie) organises a 'date' with an actress (Kika Markham) in a London hotel to kick-start inspiration for what, he says, will be his last ever television play. Nearby, a seedy businessman has a baleful meeting with a hooker (Markham again) which eerily starts to resemble Ellis's work in progress. Either his characters are becoming real people, or he is turning into a fiction himself. The writer's conflicting senses of power and helplessness, stirred up by his fear and mistrust of women, intensify as the evening progresses, and it's clear the actress – both of her – will be the victim.

Often the phrase 'fiction becomes fact' is a warning sign of writerly indulgence ahead, a respectable version of the lazy child's 'it was all a dream' essay, but *Double Dare* is no soft play fantasy. Potter prepared for the play by . . . meeting Kika Markham at a hotel. Markham has claimed whole chunks of the conversation they had there are quoted, almost verbatim, in the finished work. Discussing acting and writing, the actress muses 'we both fall headlong into other people's dreams,' a sentence Ellis had written on the back of an envelope that morning. Unsure if he's psychic or delusional, Ellis is gripped by a morbid apprehension: 'Someone's going to get hurt.'

Ellis is bitterly misogynist, but his attempts at verbal connection with Markham's character are painfully universal examples of male hopelessness: awkward and aggressive, nervously choking back sentences for fear of offence, then ploughing ahead in another, equally obnoxious, direction. Likewise, Markham's actress has increasing trouble keeping up the headstrong assurance she feels obliged to project to stay one step ahead of her 'puppet-master', and bristles when her work on a blatantly pornographic ad for 'Fraggie' chocolate bars is brought up. Potter denies the viewer any moral high ground, even when events turn monstrous. The vile businessman and the cheap whore are caricatured Aunt Sallys to help excuse our own flaws. *Double Dare* shows the dangers of this sort of detachment.

The middle-market hotel, fully recreated on an Ealing sound stage, is a sumptuously artificial, Muzak-backed and air-conditioned pocket of potted palm unreality – just the place for fact and fiction to lose their distinction. The world claustrophobically closes in on Ellis as Klaus Wunderlich performs a jaunty rendition of 'Magic Moments' on the Hammond organ. John Mackenzie directs the ensuing collapse with an adept deployment of uncomfortable close-ups and vignettes of tacky detail. It's the visual equivalent of a clammy handshake that won't let go.

Predictably, breast-fearing prigs got hot under the collar. 'Some authors,' wrote Mrs Joan M. Cutts admonishingly to the *Radio Times*, 'seem to have as little sense of responsibility as the peculiar, unreal people they write about,' suggesting some elements of the play had completely escaped her.[269] Professional critics also felt stung. Richard North thought Potter's plays were 'a propaganda exercise in a private crusade . . . that I wish was either more out in the open, or which he would grow beyond. I'm beginning to feel got at.'[270] This was Potter's main distinction from other writers – he was so overwhelmingly present in his work, in many ways, that the viewer felt they weren't so much being entertained, or even lectured, as entering a personal confrontation. Critics were always calling for greater intimacy in TV drama, but Potter got too close for comfort.

# PAULINE'S QUIRKES (1976)

## ITV (Thames)

**The foul-mouthed teatime scandal that pre-dated the Sex Pistols.**

*I'm sorry if I offended anyone. I believe I did say 'get 'em off'
several times.*

Pauline Quirke, 1 December 1976

CHILDREN'S COMEDY WAS, FOR much of television's early life, one long pantomime. Variety stars delivered knowingly corny gags and well-aimed custard pies with a mannered 'kindly leave the stage' flourish as an audience of cub scouts groaned theatrically. When pop was allowed to intrude on this hermetic world, it didn't quite fit. The prime example was *Crackerjack*, which featured a long, rambling sketch performed by the show's regulars, ending in a maladroit segue into a rendition of a hit parade tune. As the programme got further from its 1950s roots, the discrepancy between the songs and the ability of ageing entertainers Peter Glaze and Don McLean to get a handle on them increased to absurd proportions. The comedy/rock generation gap was perfectly illustrated.

Enter Roger Price, a children's producer at Thames Television who, in 1973, had been the driving force behind *The Tomorrow People*, a science fiction serial that melded the tribulations of adolescence with the Nietzschean concept – brought into pop culture by David Bowie – of the *homo superior*. Price treated the kids and their concerns in an honest, unpatronising way which sealed the programme's popularity. Two years later he turned his attention to comedy, assembling a group of child actors, including brassy London teenage chums Pauline Quirke and Linda Robson, for *You Must Be Joking!*, a raucous sketch show featuring material sourced partly from the juvenile cast. Unsurprisingly, the results were rather less innocent than the adult-administered groaners of *Crackerjack*. As the theme tune put it: 'Even Mary Whitehouse can't touch you for it!'

The following year, Price gave Quirke the starring role in an even more outlandish comedy. *Pauline's Quirkes* cast the seventeen-year-old as bolshie mistress of ceremonies, obsessed with Flintlock, the house band featuring Mike Holloway, who also starred in *The Tomorrow People*. Modelled on the Bay City Rollers, Flintlock inspired similar levels of randy delirium in young girls, as the *TV Times* discovered when their reporter trailed a gang of stalkers camping outside their houses. ('I think I can safely say that is Mike Holloway's underwear hanging on the clothes line.') Price, amused and concerned by the slavish adoration such ordinary lads could command, mined the fandom for subversive giggles.

Sketches included Quirke and Robson buying and selling Flintlock members as slaves, complete with chains and leather accessories ('I'll 'ave 'im!'), and an odd gender reversal number wherein the girls tried to look up the skirt of a cross-dressing Flintlocker climbing a ladder in a library. Then there was Quirke's continuing quest to get hold of a rumoured nude poster of the boys, whipping the under-sixteen female studio audience into a lustful frenzy with the rallying cry 'Get 'em off!' Eventually, Flintlock appeared nude – albeit with their groins rendered completely transparent by Chroma keyed swimming trunks, leaving Quirke crestfallen that they literally had 'nothing down there'.

The kids might have gotten away with it, if it hadn't been for Alan Coren. The normally unflappable humorist, then TV critic of *The Times*, happened to see the second edition, and felt duty bound to inform his readers of the filth their children were imbibing while they were hard at work. It was 'the endorsement of ignorance, the celebration of vulgarity, the apotheosis of trash,' he fumed. 'I really do not know which I most hate: the ruining of the language, the pandering to the lowest levels of intelligence . . . or the smut. All I know is, I hate.'[271] The tabloids picked up the story, eliciting a sheepish apology from Quirke at her Stoke Newington home, while mum looked disapprovingly on. Anglia became the first ITV region to drop the show, replacing it with the more wholesome *Spiderman*.

Two days later, the Sex Pistols were invited to fill up the very tail end of Thames TV's teatime magazine *Today*, as an 'if wet' replacement for Queen, and promptly outed host Bill Grundy as a 'rotter'. Only Londoners who'd knocked off work early actually saw the offending item compared to Pauline's national audience, but a slew of press coverage followed, some stories linking Johnny Rotten and Pauline Quirke as twin figureheads of feral youth.

Price defended the programme's satirical content. 'The programme was made exclusively for partially-literate teenage girls, the sort you see hanging around pop groups, prostrating themselves in blind worship,' he explained. 'We want to show them that they don't need to behave in that sort of way.' He also impishly suggested that Coren 'was giving vent to suppressed male chauvinism.'[272] These remarks cut little ice with the offended, who took exception more than anything else to the autonomous nature of the unchaperoned revels, with Quirke as *de facto* Lady, in all senses, of the Flies. It's precisely this quality that seems winning today. In a world where teenagers are given ludicrously airbrushed sexual ideals to live up to, these sketches have an authentic ring of panicky teenage curiosity about the opposite gender, with awkward eye contact and sarcastic jibes deployed to deflate the sexual tension. The show had one adult champion in the *Guardian*'s Nancy Banks-Smith, who judged it a 'cheap, cheerful pop show,' lavishing special praise on Quirke as 'a Janet Street-Porter whose line-hold has gone.'[273]

*Pauline's Quirkes* continued, in most regions, to the end of the year, introducing Pauline's all-girl rival group, The Flintarts, throwing themselves at then Radio 210 DJs Mike Read and Steve Wright, and forewarning viewers with mischievous 'clarifications' in the *TV Times*. ('All the times Derek wears dresses or cuddles up to Bill in a sketch, they're not doing it because they're kinky, but because it's in the script. Who is the kinky scriptwriter?') Dodgy moments aside, *Pauline's Quirkes* still comes across as a genuine, if often slightly corny, attempt to get modern adolescence onto the small screen, with a minimum of adult prudery. Even Coren's heart would have melted in the final edition, as Flintlock presented Pauline with end-of-series gifts, prompting a bit of *X Factor*-style emotional journeying: 'I expect now I'll be able to move me, me mum and me little brother Shaun into a flat with a bathroom!'

# I, CLAUDIUS (1976)
## BBC Two (BBC/London Films)

### The imperial phase of period drama.

FOR ALL SOCIETY HAS progressed in the past couple of millennia, superstition seems as rife as ever. People still fall for a good curse. In 1937 cinematic potentate Alexander Korda began film production at his brand new Denham studio complex. *I, Claudius* was adapted from Robert Graves's two bestselling volumes of mock autobiography detailing the accidental rise and largely benevolent rule of the third emperor of ancient Rome. The books had everything: epic sweep, carnality, and the fairy-tale transformation of a lame stammerer into – however briefly – a deity on Earth.

Korda's *Claudius,* directed by Josef von Sternberg in riding breeches and Javanese turban, was colossal, and modishly with-it; the *Daily Mirror* discovered the makers had 'psycho-analysed the character of Messalina to find out why she was such a lurid lass'.[274] The actress in that role, Merle Oberon, was put out of action in a serious car accident. With no replacement found, the £100,000 picture was abandoned. The curse had descended.

Nearly four decades later, the BBC had a go. A painful rights deal was extracted from Korda's London Films and the budget was set at £750,000 – a big investment for such a 'cursed' project, but comparisons with Korda were briskly warded off. 'Allowing for inflation, it won't cost anywhere near as much,' said producer Martin Lisemore, 'but we do intend to finish it.'[275] Jack Pulman, capable adaptor of Dickens, Tolstoy and Henry James, prepared the screenplay for Herbert Wise, a director with twenty years' experience in the studio.

In front of the cameras, Derek Jacobi's Claudius avoided speech-impaired sentimentality with a performance of confusion, slyness and desperation. Brian Blessed's Augustan thunder was succeeded by John Hurt's pathologically twee, demented Caligula; while Livia, wife of the former and great-grandmother to the latter, was given conniving life by Siân Phillips. There was more group sex, murder, incest and infanticide per square inch than anything previously screened. In one irate viewer's opinion, it was 'far more damaging' to potential teenage viewers than even the dreaded *Pauline's Quirkes*.[276]

The casting of Graves's multitudes summoned actors from the four corners of *Spotlight*. Patrick Stewart commanded the Praetorian Guard. Bernard Hill identified Jacobi as the new emperor. Ian Ogilvy fell off his horse. Peter Bowles was an unusual choice for an ancient British chieftain; Christopher Biggins – soon to appear as Mother Goose at Darlington's Civic Theatre – a surprisingly appropriate Nero. There was even a mini *Z-Cars* reunion as Inspector Barlow (Stratford Johns, aka Gnaeus Calpurnius Piso) was put on trial for treason against the stepson of PC Fancy Smith (Brian Blessed, the Emperor Augustus). Quentin Crisp was assassinated by George and Mildred's uppity next-door neighbour, who in turn was grandson of the Emperor Inspector Wexford. Television's version of the MGM 'cast of thousands' helped audiences follow the story's labyrinthine, genealogical body swerves.

It wasn't an instant hit. In fact, early critical impressions were poor. The chief stumbling block was creating a believable yet intelligible antiquity. Modern parallels helped the makers get a handle on the distant times: Pulman visualised the Empire as a branch of the Mafia; Siân Phillips played scenes as Jewish family comedy.[277] Graves' books described great and lurid events in the flatly chatty, rambling style of the often boring Claudius, but some critics had trouble with Pulman's version of this ironic effect: modern phrases delivered in togas. The *Guardian* complained that 'a Roman lady turning to her threatened husband in the moment of crisis and crying "They're bluffing!" evokes not so much the shades of Plancina, wife of Piso, as of Olivia de Havilland, wife of Stewart Granger.'[278] The reviewer also thought Wise had dished up 'the worst lighting and camera angles since 1925.' (In fact Wise and cameraman Jim Atkinson achieved wonders with intricately choreographed cameras and little more than a dozen extras.)

This initial dismissal was understandable given the Roman pageant's reputation for cinematic lavishness. The Hollywood epics scored zero for historical accuracy, but the sheer bombast of the production values and costumes, combined with the distancing sheen of film, made television's harsh lighting and self-assembly villas look cheap and very recent indeed. Unfair perhaps, but it would soon lead to the abandonment of videotape for period drama, then gradually all drama outside of soap opera. When Simon Langton was preparing to direct Andrew Davies's 1990s version of *Pride and Prejudice* – the one which would finally demolish television's historical inferiority complex – he watched a copy of the BBC's previous version from 1981. As the videotape unspooled, 'my partner's daughter, who was about thirteen or fourteen at the time, just sort of walked through the room and glanced at it and just went, "Ugh!" and I said, "Well, why did you go like that?" and she said, "It's all artificial" – and that's all I got. Then she went out.'[279] Sporting lush 35mm from head to toe, *Pride and Prejudice* would re-conquer the world in the name of British drama.

For those who could look past the lack of sumptuous super-ficialities *I, Claudius* brimmed with restive psychodrama and sharp observation. Clive James noted that, contrary to the videotape gripers, 'the differentness and long-ago-ness were maintained throughout the series, less by trying to prove that the ancient Romans were unlike us than by assuming they were just like us but living under different laws.'[280] That perfectly summed up Pulman's masterstroke, although, James noted, some of the old period vices remained. 'There were numberless Flanagan and Allen routines where pairs of subsidiary characters in tightly gripped togas met behind a convenient column to tell each other what they already knew and so update us on the plot.'[281]

Critical misgivings had little effect on the saga's popularity. *I, Claudius* came to a triumphant end in December after twelve episodes. Like its protagonist, it had proved all those who grossly underestimated its worth hopelessly wrong, although within months of transmission, Lisemore and Pulman both died far too soon, and the press had its 'curse' restored. In 1977, it was show-cased in the USA on Brit-heritage strand *Masterpiece Theatre*, with each episode introduced by Alistair Cooke surrounded by grapes, scrolls and statuary. The critical drubbing started all over again: the *New York Post* called it a 'masterpiece of a bore'[282] and the *Christian Science Monitor* alluded to a '*Monty Python* Royal Academy of Overacting'.[283] Once again, opinions had to be reversed as ratings took hold. *I, Claudius* made popular, quality drama from one of history's most alien, barbaric periods. For boldness and grandiosity, nothing before or since in the pantheon of TV drama can touch it.

# THE FALL AND RISE OF REGINALD PERRIN (1976–9)

## BBC One

### The sitcom's nervous breakdown.

THERE'S SOMETHING ABOUT THE transparent etymology of the word 'sitcom' that encourages waggish critics to pick it apart as they take down one of its less triumphant examples: 'LWT's latest Saturday night offering was all sit and very little com', and so forth. Something about the word suggests a crude sketch of life, with gags bolted on willy-nilly. Only the poorest sitcoms are actually like this, but the inglorious label is hard to shift. One sitcom asked the opposite – what if life was a crass imitation of a sitcom?

*The Fall and Rise of Reginald Perrin* only became a sitcom by degrees. It began as a contribution David Nobbs made to BBC Pebble Mill's *Second City Firsts* strand of half-hour plays, which would give early breaks to artists as diverse as Mike Leigh and Toyah Willcox. Nobbs had graduated from *TW3* to various sketch shows and sitcoms with writing partner Peter Vincent, including one set in the ultimate minimalist sitcom location, a lighthouse. He gave Pebble Mill the tale of a businessman sent mad by the frantic emptiness of the commercial world. Their curt rejection was, he claimed, the best news he ever received.[284]

Nobbs radically reworked the half-hour play into a comic novel that did pretty well. Ronnie Barker enthused about it on book programmes and it started doing very well. Granada wanted to turn it into a two-part prestige drama with Barker in the title role, but the Beeb weighed in with an offer of a seven-part sitcom starring Leonard Rossiter. Sitcoms and novels were still regarded as mutually incompatible arts. Nobbs's friend Peter Tinniswood was just starting to break the mould with *I Didn't Know You Cared*, based on his mordant Yorkshire family saga *A Touch of Daniel*, but many still nursed memories of the BBC's ill-starred attempt to adapt Evelyn Waugh's *Scoop!* into a vehicle for Harry Worth. Despite the weight of history, Rossiter it was.

*Perrin* was born from banal fragments: a colour supplement feature on jam marketing, fatuously cosy building society ads, all the asinine trappings of modern life which nobody ever asked for, but were presented as indispensable. The more examples Nobbs amassed of this emetic hokum, the more he wondered who could stand to live and work amongst it. The vision came of a hapless middle-aged dessert pedlar, bored with his job, failing to have a torrid affair with his secretary, suddenly realising he's been sleep-walking his life away, busting out of his confined little world and faking his own suicide on a beach at night. (Soon after Nobbs completed the novel, MP John Stonehouse was coincidentally arrested for turning the same trick.)

In later and more affected times, this plot would be called 'dark'. But *Perrin* was quite the opposite – it was sitcom with the brightness and contrast turned right up. The umbrella-swinging, whisky-swilling, British-Railing repetition of middle class middle age became a gaudy diagram via high-key performances, a litany of catchphrases and Ronnie Hazlehurst's chirpily melancholic incidental music. Elizabeth the patient wife, CJ the pompous boss, the saucy secretary, the drop-out son, the woolly liberal and the pseudo-American go-getter lined up like a demographic identity parade. Boring dinner party followed soul-sapping meeting followed nightmarish in-law visitation with exhausting relentlessness. It was a close thing as to whose nerves would snap first – the viewer's or Reggie's. As only a few dramatists like David Mercer understood, comedy proves a sharper tool than straight drama for conveying the depths of a crack-up.

Creating a sitcom that pulled the clichés of the genre apart as it piled them up was not, of course, Nobbs's intention – he was too smart for all that. When a close reader over-interpreted Sunshine Desserts' corporate tyrant CJ's initials (CJ – JC – Jesus in reverse – the Messiah of Mammon, etc.) Nobbs politely acknowledged the coincidence, but said that if he'd consciously come up with something like that, he'd have nixed it immediately.[285]

He did have serious intentions, though. Reggie's drunken address to the Fruit Association is both funny ('You show me a hero who makes fondue tongs and I'll show you happy man who earns his living perforating lavatory paper') and a sincere anti-capitalist rant ('Man's the only species neurotic enough to need a purpose in life'). It would sit well on *Play for Today*, one of the prime liberal targets on Reggie's brother-in-law Jimmy's famous hit-list. And for emotionally fraught drama, it's hard to beat the scene where Reggie, having faked his suicide and disguised as a buck-toothed plumber, revisits his 'widow', finds she's remarrying, fails to pluck up courage to reveal himself and politely leaves the house as an agonised scream echoes through his skull. *Perrin* drastically pushed the limits of what you could do in front of a studio audience.

In an eminent cast Rossiter excels, maintaining the shrill authority of a man who knows he's the fixed centre of a capering universe. He addresses professional superiors and family members alike as if they were slow children or *Generation Game* contestants. Impatient to hear their dull conversations, he fills in their replies before they can get them out, reacts to them, and hammers out another half dozen lines before they can muster an 'erm' of protest. Surrounding him is a range of sitcom types, or – different thing – people who've acquiesced into sitcom types, from Geoffrey Palmer's bewildered former major to John Barron's childish sociopath CJ. That Perrin's path to happiness was obstructed by the greatest concentration of loveable berks ever gathered together gave his struggle a redeeming warmth.

The perfection of *Perrin* and its full-circle ending made further series a heavy task, which Nobbs deftly tackled by making the sequel a straight inversion of its predecessor. While the resurrected Reggie alternates between the dole and the piggery, Elizabeth (Pauline Yates, given much more to do this time round) joins Sunshine Desserts, fails to have a torrid affair with CJ at Sunshine Desserts and is sacked from Sunshine Desserts. Together they decide to play one last joke on the world and open Grot, a shop selling all the useless junk made by their berkish friends and relatives. True to form, the parody company becomes a real international success, and Reggie this time is trapped in the unfulfilling drudgery of an ironic millionaire lifestyle. Happiness is thus proved impossible. A third series, concerning a suburban drop-out community, was less successful, merely retreading this theme.

It was still way above average, and several leagues ahead of American adaptation *Reggie*, with *Soap*'s Richard Mulligan in the lead and a mawkish theme song bathetically conflating *Perrin*'s desperate rebellion with the USA's burgeoning self-help industry. A Rossiter-free UK sequel in 1996 and a full remake thirteen years after that were less gruesome, but still little more than footnotes to the original, which generated a very rare and special experience: that giddy feeling of space being warped in the name of laughter. *Perrin* was properly serious comedy, a psychic spring clean that wasn't afraid to rearrange the furniture while it was in there. After *Perrin*, only the most obtuse snobs still considered 'sitcom' a dirty word, however they sliced it.

# BBC NINE O'CLOCK NEWS (1976)
## BBC One

The year when information went showbiz.

*Like the electricity bill and the income tax demand, the revamped*
BBC Nine O'Clock News *is a nasty shock in a tasteful, plain*
*beige envelope.*

Nancy Banks-Smith, *Guardian,* 9 March 1976

NEWS IN PRINT OR speech is a thing of direct simplicity. When visuals enter the mix, newsmakers can find their attention drifting away from hard reportage and towards the more superficial matters that occupy less serious forms of television. For a long time, the BBC refused to have their television newsreaders appear in front of the camera. If a disembodied voice was good enough for radio, it would do for the cathode upstart. (Having said that, radio news-readers were still obliged to perform for the microphone in full evening dress. The Corporation's sense of protocol overruled its austere logic.)

When the independent channel launched its rival news service, the bare bones ethos was, if anything, amplified. Producer Robert Tyrrell recalled the dummy bulletins staged in ITN's brand new, sawdust-strewn Aldwych headquarters before cameras or lights were installed. The newsreader, lit by an overhead projector, peered 'through a rough wooden frame rather like a gallows, which was supposed to represent the screen of a television set.'[286] Describing the early years of television news, the last word you'd reach for would be 'glamorous'.

Newsreaders did become household faces, though. American anchormen like Walter Cronkite and Ed Murrow had, in the rough times after JFK's assassination, become sturdy father figures on a national scale, and there was much excited talk of US network bulletins shaping the self-image of the States. British newsreaders, by tradition as well as temperament, settled for a more modest form of fame. 'We're terribly well known to people,' admitted Kenneth Kendall, 'being part of their daily deliveries, along with the milk and bread.' On the other hand, Leonard Parkin observed, 'there's a feeling that it's no job for a grown man.'[287]

Things changed when a woman joined the men's club. A reporter for BBC South West since the sixties, Angela Rippon's sober style and Waterford Crystal diction helped her broach the news's hyper-masculine domain. When she got a regular gig behind the desk on BBC One during 1975, it was promoted as an equality breakthrough, even though she was still referred to as 'the BBC's cover girl'.

She wasn't the first: Nan Winton had a brief stint at the Beeb in 1960, but the country wasn't ready. Inevitably, a female newsreader was watched as much for how she looked as what she was saying. Rippon's sartorial decisions for each bulletin were scrutinised in a way Richard Baker's choice of blazer had never been. When, on 12 January 1976, her earring fell off just after she announced the death of Agatha Christie, the country gasped as one, twice.

Angela enthralled the nation and pundits spent a great many words trying to sum up her often contradictory qualities ('a plucked arch of the eyebrow and a sense of steel in the bones' – Peter Fiddick). These descriptions were often physical (Dennis Potter compared the baleful eyes of Rod Hull's Emu to those which Rippon 'keeps for news of the pound'), occasionally patronising ('stern and delicious' – Barry Norman), but always affectionate. Unless you counted the disgruntled newsroom assistant who complained that Rippon, to maintain her stately, unflustered manner, read the news at twenty words per minute slower than her male colleagues, thus providing less news per bulletin.[288]

On 8 March 1976, the *Nine O'Clock News* was completely overhauled with less clutter, the retirement of the bank manager nameplates on the desk, and a return to a solo newsreader instead of the double act that had prevailed in recent years. Angela would be first on air. She more than rose to the occasion, but that still didn't stop the press concentrating on her clothes. In a surprisingly twenty-first-century-style 'open letter to TV's first lady,' the *Daily Mirror*'s fashion editor implored Rippon, thirty-one, to dress her age and less like a maiden aunt: even though 'we know you get a clothes allowance of only £70 a year.'[289] The 'letter' was accompanied by a month's worth of 'telesnaps' (the old money equivalent of screen grabs) detailing the frosty sartorial parade. ('March 19: paisley blouse, cream jacket.')

Angela wasn't the only source of aesthetic concern. The *Nine*'s new title sequence was a matter of great press interest. To modern eyes it was so basic as to hardly be noticeable at all, but in the days before no self-respecting news source would release so much as a travel alert without a good ten seconds of bombastically somersaulting CGI globes, the very idea of the news having animated titles could still prompt sniggers. 'The trumpeted titivations will come into vision,' wrote Peter Fiddick with mock awe, 'a new opening map of the world, with two hemispheres moving into one before our very eyes.'[290] Another critic reckoned the programme was 'in need of more than a pair of sliding soup plates for starters.'[291]

Then came the set. Incoming news editor Andy Todd had, for the first time, devoted serious thought and research to the question of what Rippon and company should deliver their reports in front of, and the result was . . . beige. Or, to be completely accurate, gamboge. Creating a comforting, warm environment to offset the discomfiting content of economic and foreign bulletins, gamboge was 'a sort of pale yellow, but done on a weave-textured backcloth which replaces the more assertive geometric reliefs we have been used to.'[292] The newsreader's domain was no longer an abstracted military bunker – or if it was, it had been given a lick of paint and a few rolls of hessian wall-weave left over from doing up a nearby unisex hair salon.

Rippon was also at the forefront of the newsreaders' crossover into light entertainment. They'd been popping up in comedy programmes ever since wartime radio announcer Stuart Hibberd was lightly roasted by Arthur Askey, but only started fannying about themselves after Robin Day cracked a public joke about his ITN cohort Reginald Bosanquet, with the result, according to ITN editor Nigel Ryan, that 'people suddenly realised you could be light-hearted without losing authority.'[293] Despite this, comedy and news remained separate TV disciplines, and attempts to generate fun at the end of bulletins often looked woefully misplaced. 'The Newsreader's Joke,' said Jeremy Bulger, 'stands in the dunce's corner of humour.'[294]

Wisely, Angela Rippon's comic debut was largely wordless: a comedy song-and-dance routine on the *Morecambe and Wise Christmas Special*. Unlike Michael Barratt's in-depth interview with Sooty for *The Goodies*, or Richard Baker's appearance on *Monty Python* earnestly enquiring, 'Lemon curry?', this was a media event of the very top rank, garnering acres of jokey pre-publicity. The intended surprise was spoilt by one George Harris, former editor of Rippon's *alma mater* the *South Devon Times*, who obtained some on-set stills of the threesome in mid-prance and promptly flogged them to the *Daily Mirror*. With the floodgates opened, Rippon's male counterparts signed up *en masse* for a *South Pacific* pastiche the following year.

After her Christmas triumph, Rippon became a fully articled celebrity. In 1977 she presented everything from the *Eurovision Song Contest* ('I think we're having a bit of trouble with our scoreboard again!') to fledgling motoring magazine *Top Gear*, becoming the first British newsreader to employ a personal PR consultant on the way. Margaret Thatcher prepared for government by adapting her hairstyle into a pointedly Ripponesque form. On a purely presentational level, the new News had won over the population.

From now on, visuals and personality would compete with reporting and analysis for the news editor's attention. This was fine, but, as the *Listener* pointed out, BBC news had far more serious problems, namely 'the radical ills of an overgrown and impoverished bureaucracy, whose money troubles at once bind it to cheap coverage of home affairs, and make it particularly sensitive to political pressures on the home front.'[295] It would take more than a new pair of earrings and some gamboge wall-weave to fix that.

# BATTLE OF THE NETWORK STARS (1976–88)

# STAR GAMES (1978–80)

## ABC/ITV (Trans World International)

**Celebrities start to be celebrated for what they can't do as much as for what they can.**

CELEBRITY IS A STRANGE and confusing state for a human being to inhabit. In the majority of cases (contrary to popular cynicism) a celeb achieves fame via the mastery of a particular skill (singing, cooking, talking and walking simultaneously) to at least a basic level of competence. When their star status exceeds a certain level, though, the system demands they start spreading themselves thinner, branching out from singing to acting, say, or from grilling sardines to descending a staircase while giving a potted history of the fish finger. Perform these new tasks badly, and the brand is irreparably damaged. Unless, that is, the cocking up can be wrangled to show the celeb to be, hey, human just like us after all.

One of the first manifestations of this kind of second-tier

celebrity came via a televised end-of-term sports day. Trans World International was a grand-sounding US media company that began in the late sixties staging exhibition golf tournaments for British TV before landing a hit with *Superstars*, an all-comers gala in which sportsmen at the top of one particular field of physical endeavour gamely fell straight to the bottom of half a dozen others. Then Trans World kingpin Jay Michaels struck on an idea so shamelessly opportunist that its place in television history is assured. Translating the *Superstars* format to the world of TV, Michaels envisioned a grand athletic face-off between the star rosters of the three US network stations. In order to get them to co-operate, he sold a variation on the format to each of them. CBS had *Us Against the World*, in which a US celeb team competed against the rest of the world's stars. NBC were given the self-explanatory *Celebrities Challenge of the Sexes*. ABC, the sportiest, most downmarket and, at the time, most successful network, got the most successful format: *Battle of the Network Stars*.

As befitted a self-confessed 'trash sport', *Battle* was presented with maximum pomp and energy. The three teams were pictured arriving in separate fleets of limos. Esteemed *Monday Night Football* frontman Howard Cosell was MC and commentator, giving earnest appraisals of Loretta Swit's chances in the tug-of-war or Lynda Carter's form in the swimming relay. (If the activities sometimes seemed devised to maximise the exposure of young, tanned celebrity flesh, that's because they were – Michaels himself categorised the tournaments as 'underwear shows'.[296] *Battles* were staged twice a year, give or take, for over a decade.

Two years in, it spawned a British variant, necessitating a certain amount of adaptation to the local climate and customs. Actors, comedians, newsreaders and continuity sundries from 'both sides' divided into teams by occupation to compete at sprinting, swimming, motorcycling, ten-pin bowling and a climactic obstacle relay race direct from Jesus Green, Cambridge. Michael Aspel, the presenter's presenter with an unmatched ability to meet with gravity and trivia, and treat those two impostors just the same, provided what Martin Amis identified as '*Jackanory*-style unctuousness'.[297] Punters slavered at the spectacle of Roy Kinnear sweating through a round of clock golf, Blakey from *On the Buses* floundering in a canoe, and a short-trousered Bonnie Langford and Sandy Gall colliding on the six-a-side pitch. The winning team garnered £15,000 for charity. Boxing Day specials were scheduled. This was event TV.

It wasn't all sweat and grunt. Stars being stars, theatricality and swanning about were never absent for long. Reggie Bosanquet swaggered the length of the mud-churned sports field, resplendent in leather cowboy boots and a tracksuit with 'REGGIE BOSANQUET' emblazoned on the back. Each team was granted a 'non-playing coach', a whimsical ruse which allowed the likes of Magnus Pyke and Frankie Howerd to sling towels round their necks and excitedly organise pep-talks and strategic huddles as the drizzle set in.

The first series was such a hit that two more followed, keeping the formula the same but downgrading the location slightly: first to a Finsbury Park leisure centre and then to a field near High Wycombe. This did not, however, lessen the momentousness of the occasion. The 1979 tournament saw prize signing Captain Mark Phillips called off with flu, to be replaced, somewhat anticlimactically, with Jess Conrad. Princess Anne phoned Mark's team-mates to apologise, but failed to comfort Robin Askwith. ('Our spies told us he was hot stuff in the swimming pool!') Then, when Conrad was put in goal for the six-a-side, rival captain Patrick Mower stormed off the pitch, protesting that Conrad was a ringer, a seasoned custodian of the onion bag. The whole tournament was thrown into chaos. It made the papers. Interesting times.

# ROCK FOLLIES (1976–7)
## ITV (Thames)

### A depression musical for the 1970s.

LIKE ANY OTHER BRANCH of entertainment, television progresses not through the smoothly executed plans of creative masters, but an endless stumble of fudge, calamity and betrayal. Brooklyn-born and Berkeley educated, Howard Schuman spent his youth on New York's off-Broadway circuit, devising experimental musical happenings of varying failure before emigrating to Britain in 1968. Deciding that television was the thing in the UK, he pitched two ideas to Joan Kemp-Welch, now head of drama at Thames Television. *Censored Scenes from King Kong* concerned a frazzled journalist obsessed with the idea of tracking down a missing scene from the 1939 movie featuring graphic ape-Wray congress. This didn't go down too well with the former devotee of *Little Women*.

A second idea, about a marital therapy clinic that used video cameras as tools, enthused Kemp-Welch with the potential of visual tomfoolery, and *Captain Video's Story* was commissioned for the late night half-hour *Armchair 30* series. In addition to that, an hour's worth of *Armchair Theatre* proper had suddenly been freed up, which was promptly filled with another Schuman play, *Verité*. This story of a quiet, middle-class North London couple's life invaded by underground filmmaker Tim Curry and unstoppable tap-dancing Brooklynite Beth Porter went a mile over the top but put Schuman on the map.

Then *Censored Scenes* was picked up for a BBC series of topical plays, which was drastically cut after the 1974 miner's strike necessitated the closedown of all television by 10.30 p.m. It was shot using what power was available, in a budget-beating bare studio plus blue screen inserts, with Beth Porter joined in the cast by Julie Covington as an intellectual cabaret act billed as a cross between John Stuart Mill, Nietzsche and the Andrews Sisters. The production beat the blackout, but failed to get past Head of Plays Christopher Morahan, who took against Schuman's trash aesthetic and canned it indefinitely.

The central idea of smart women being turned into a dumb show business act resurfaced when Schuman and producer Andrew Brown concocted a version of Hollywood's 1930s *Gold Diggers* movies for the new depression of the mid-seventies. The rock music scene was to be the backdrop, or rather the homogenised branch of show business Schuman saw rock as becoming by the middle of the decade. Hapless group the Little Ladies comprised three dissimilar aspiring actresses: Nancy Cunard 'Q' de Longchamps (Rula Lenska), a laid-back Sloane Ranger with a dim-witted surfer boyfriend who dreams of being a 1920s-style 'topping girl'; Anna Ward (Charlotte Cornwell), juggling a thin career on the serious stage with a decaying marriage to a nihilist Eng. Lit. teacher; and Devonia 'Dee' Rhodes (Covington), magician's assistant and increasingly reluctant member of a radical commune that's a tad heavy on the group hugs. It's an obvious cross-section of British class, but Schuman fills out the diagram with living details.

The three meet as auditionees for *Broadway Annie*, a foredoomed 'let's do the show right here' revue of the pre-*TW3* variety. 'A bum script, a nowhere score and a squiffy director,' notes Q. 'All the hallmarks of success.' It crashes in short order, and musical director Derek Huggins promises he can 'mould' the girls into an all-female rock group – reluctantly they agree. 'If I don't have a mystical experience, at least we might get a new boiler out of it.' Cue a dilapidated switchback ride of manipulation, penury, paranoia and appending the definite article to every noun, coming to a desultory end with the Little Ladies, powerless and utterly spent, cynically refitted as a wartime cabaret nostalgia turn.

The fully rehearsed, fully scored, multi-set six part musical drama was made on a swift six-month turnaround in late 1975. It had to be fully written too, which put the free-forming Schuman under intense pressure, leavened only slightly by two timely strikes. Roxy Music's Andy Mackay created the musical numbers, while Rod Stratford and Alex Clarke got round the panic-inducing number of set changes with a spare, stylised look which would serve pop video makers well throughout the following decade. Its 'indoorsy' nature was pointed up in the opening shot, when a panning shot over a tranquil English landscape turns out to be a picture on the wall of a grotty Soho office. It was all, of course, shot on crisp, bright videotape, praised by Schuman as 'a bolder medium which conveys an immediate "presence" that is, paradoxically, far more unreal than film'.[298] The video sheen that some thought cheap-looking in *I, Claudius* was a perfect match for this lurid adventure. Its relative low cost led Thames to agree.

*Rock Follies'* appeal was broad. The music and the citric burn of the visuals brought in a younger crowd who normally eschewed the worthy, taupe-hued drama of the time. The all-female focus was a refreshing change too, evoking fond memories of the BBC's swinging series *Take Three Girls*. The risqué dialogue – 'As far as I'm concerned, the straight sex brigade are a load of wankers' – sent the press into spasm. A soundtrack album was released and spawned a few minor hits, even though the songs sounded slightly ludicrous away from the cartoonish context of the show itself. Huge audiences and a BAFTA for best drama sealed the triumph.

A sequel quickly followed. *Rock Follies of '77* promised more of the same ('Do you get the feeling that we've only changed the date?' asked one number, knowingly). Finally, tangible success was within reach for the group, moving from grubby digs and flyblown back offices to the pile-carpeted, chrome-trimmed world of the record business proper. They gained a new manager: Beth Porter stealing every scene as the rapacious Kitty Schreiber, 'cray-ZEE' about everyone and everything. A new recruit, Rox (Sue Jones-Davies, late of the Bowles Brothers Band who'd recently shared a studio with the Sex Pistols' TV debut), ruffled group relations, Bob Hoskins played a John Bullish club owner and Tim Curry cameoed as Stevie Streeter, a Kwik Save Springsteen. It was twice as mad and loud as its ancestor, but no less despondent about the moribund state of the business. The shooting schedule was as enervating as before for all concerned, not helped when a strike by female production assistants over pay increases caused a break in transmission of several months.

By 1977, Schuman was convinced society had already moved into the eighties. When the eighties did arrive, so did a nasty shock. Rock Bottom, an all-girl vocal trio formed in the early 1970s under the aegis of composer Don Fraser, claimed they had approached Schuman and Brown with the concept of a series based on their tribulations, starring the three members as themselves.[299] Though the basic idea was nowhere near as refined, the group's stories were eerily familiar: Annabel Leventon had toured her Desdemona around France, just as Anna had 'given her Ophelia' at Preston. Schuman, Brown and Thames were judged in breach of confidence, and settled out of court for a sum reportedly reaching £500,000.[300]

Drama soon moved decisively away from Schuman's kitsch video techniques. One of his last efforts in this mode, 1987's *Up Line*, another semi-musical about desperate ambition with pyramid selling replacing show business, made little impact. '[Schuman's] apparent love for ... the low-rent side of "the show business",' wrote David Housham, 'rubs uncomfortably against the tougher, satirical edge of his writing, giving it an overall camp, throwaway gloss that makes *Up Line* ... seem unconvincing and dated.'[301] One minute you're up ...

# TRANS AMERICA ULTRA QUIZ (1977–92)

# ULTRA QUIZ (1983–5)

## NTV/ ITV (TVS)

### The West laughs at those crazy masochistic Japs, then has a go itself.

WHEN DOES A GAME show become a reality show? The simple answer is when it gets beyond a certain size. The longer each edition lasts, the more it has to bring the contestants' personality into the foreground far beyond the usual hurried courtesies exchanged over the buzzer. ('Now Adrian, a little bird tells me you're something of a whiz on the old Rubik's Cube?') The more money a show costs, the more it tends to blot out every other programme on the channel, a monolithic skyscraper leaving well-mannered Neo-Georgian dramas cowering in its mighty shadow. *Ultra Quiz* was one such competitive carbuncle.

For decades, British game shows were held back by the scale of prizes. Remuneration was heavily restricted to avoid the unedifying scenes of naked greed witnessed in America. The Yanks even had a soppy-ugly word for the phenomenon: these weren't quiz shows, they were 'desire' shows. Foreign language, foreign concept. We're made of sterner stuff.

If American techniques were off the menu, what chance had British channels of buying *Trans America Ultra Quiz*, a gargantuan Japanese trivia trail which began with 5,000 contestants and slowly whittled them down in a variety of increasingly cruel ways while touring the beauty spots of the States over many weeks, before packing off the eventual winner with a 'life-changing' lump sum? Even the Americans themselves couldn't stomach their own version, *All-American Ultra Quiz*, hosted by *Laugh-In*'s Dan Rowan and Dick Martin, for more than one season. Such obstacles didn't stop both BBC and ITV representatives sizing up the format when Nippon Television put it up for grabs at the Monte Carlo Festival in 1982. Calculators and napkins were employed to determine the likelihood of bringing an affordable version to our shores. 'Maybe we could run an in-flight quiz to Jersey or the Isle of Man,' mused a BBC buyer. 'I wonder if we could interest Cross-Channel Ferries?'

The show was finally sold to brand new ITV franchise TVS. Keen to distance itself from its regional predecessor, the rural-traditional Southern, TVS aligned itself with the sort of south coast viewer who was more likely to own a yacht than a potting shed, and *Ultra Quiz* was just the sort of big, loud, network-frightening entity which could help propel them into the national consciousness. A few judicious tweaks of the maximum prize fund ruling allowed for a top bounty of £10,000. (Soon afterwards, *The Price is Right* would similarly break the agreed limit, but they used a different tactic: they just didn't tell the IBA.) Glamorous locations were sussed out: planes and boats were chartered; Michael Aspel, Sally James and Jonathan King were hired.

On the morning of Saturday 16 April, 2,000 contestants assembled on Brighton beach for the first round, a mass 'yes or no' marathon to sort the wheat from the chaff. The wheat would then board a ferry to France, answering more questions en route, with only the winners allowed to disembark at the other end. To provide a bit of variety, Eddie Kidd performed impressive stunts, astrologer Russell Grant competed with a 'computer boffin' to predict who would make it to the next stage, Sally James wore a jumpsuit accessorised with a Panama hat, and Jonathan King shouted encouraging things like 'He's got brain power packed in his head!'

Even Aspel's capable hands couldn't mould that into light entertainment. As the quiz ambled from exotic location to exotic location (and, for the final, back home to Southampton), viewers dropped out faster than the contestants, and derision multiplied by the week. Even TVS controller Michael Blakstad had to admit the programme had been 'quite awful'. Stuck with a costly dodo, TVS had a choice: silently bin it in favour of something nice and cheap with Fred Dinenage, or fiddle with the details and launch a second series. Stubbornly determined to prove themselves the equals of Granada and Thames, they went for the latter option.

The 1984 series of *Ultra Quiz* is the one most people tend to remember. Fronted by David Frost ('Hello, good evening, and a thousand welcomes!') and assisted by his *TW3* compadre Willie Rushton, it held together slightly more convincingly than the first incarnation, helped in no small measure by Frost's legendary connections: when the owners of Leeds Castle refused to host the final there, fearing the large-scale silliness might dent its image, Frost secured the use of Arundel Castle instead, by dint of being the son-in-law of its owner.

Despite Frost's mollifying assurance that the UK *Ultra Quiz* was 'as different from the Japanese as karate is from cricket', similarities with the cruel daftness of the original remained. On the beach at Deauville, twenty-eight contestants were buried up to their necks in sand, with balloons attached to strings held between their teeth, the release of which would constitute their answers to questions. Rushton, perhaps not the best choice for a programme that relied on taking stupidity seriously, observed that the losing contestants, when they were dug out of their pit, looked glad to be out of the running.

In Paris, with a characteristic mix of jet-set glamour and party game tomfoolery, the remaining hopefuls were ushered into a high class perfumery, blindfolded, and asked to identify a series of increasingly rancid smells, under the watchful eye of TV production legend (and, appropriately, *It's a Knockout* instigator) Major Barney Colehan. Then came Bruges, a tour of California, and back to Arundel. Ratings this time held up pretty well, but then they had to. With a budget of over £600,000, TVS had a lot more than their fledgling reputation riding on *Ultra Quiz*. So when questions of decency arose, they were ready to tackle them.

Matters came to a head in a debate at the 1984 Edinburgh Television Festival, chaired by one D. Frost. Putting the case that ITV's mania for game shows lowered standards was Jim Moir, BBC Head of Light Entertainment. *Price is Right* producer William G. Stewart put the case for the defence, cannily pointing out that ITV's ratio of quizzes to LE shows was the same in 1984 as it had been in the 'golden age' of 1968. More vocal still was LWT director of programmes John Birt, who unsettled the audience by insisting the anti-game show agenda was a case of middle class snobbery. 'Is the BBC interested in entertaining the working class?' he demanded.[302] The names may have changed, but today's arguments over 'reality' shows run on exactly the same lines as the 'desire' show debate.

*Ultra Quiz*, meanwhile, plugged away for another year. *Ultra Quiz '85* saw yet another clear-out of personnel. This time the master of ceremonies was Stu Francis, and locations were very much restricted to the UK, a tour of grey beaches and crumbling pier heads more reminiscent of the Radio One Roadshow than a slick globetrotting mental tournament. Gyles Brandreth, roped in to devise puzzles, wondered in his diary what he was doing with his life.

The modern reality juggernaut is run on much tighter lines than *Ultra Quiz* ever was but there's a similar weakness at their heart. The sheer scale of the programmes is forever in danger of being undercut by their inherent absurdity. It takes a great force of will to keep the ship afloat, hence the overbearing seriousness that often pervades the likes of *X Factor*. By treating a random MOR singing contest as if it were a war crimes tribunal, buoyancy is achieved, but only as long as the audience are willing to provide the necessary hot air. Lose them, as *Ultra Quiz* quickly did, and the enterprise comes crashing down under the weight of its own triviality. Today's craft may be capable of longer flights than *Ultra Quiz*, but there's no guarantee they won't end in the same undignified way.

# SOAP (1977–81)
## ABC (Witt/Thomas/Harris)

**The troughs of drama become peaks of comedy.**

*TV is a business, and you're not allowed to be as adult as I wish you could be and you're not allowed to do things as adult as I wish you were.*

Susan Harris,
*Toronto Globe and Mail*, 8 January 1983

THEY ONLY EXISTED TO sell soap powder. They purveyed dumb stimulation to bored housewives in the days before Quaaludes and Valium. They habitually featured at least one murder, abduction, divorce, suicide attempt, conversion to the priesthood or fatal act of God per episode. They were, according to James Thurber, twelve minutes of dialogue spread between thick slices of advertising.[303] The list of cultural charges against the American daytime soap opera is long and damning.

By the late 1970s, the network soaps were among the last relics of TV's post-war gold rush. *As the World Turns, Search for Tomorrow, The Guiding Light* and their ilk had been around for a quarter of a century. Some were even older, having begun as radio soaps before the war. They drew flak from the beginning, the wireless pioneers accused of hobbling the war effort by unnecessarily adding to their audience's neuroses.[304]

Yet soaps had social purpose. In the early days, they took a strong, moralistic stand on their characters' antics. Bad deeds were punished, familial loyalty and civic duty espoused. They later became a platform for promoting health and psychological issues. The problem was that they did it so crassly. A 1963 episode of *The Guiding Light* illustrated a traumatic birth with a shot from the unborn child's point of view: a leg on each side of the frame and a concerned obstetrician thrusting a giant pair of forceps toward the camera. The cast of *As the World Turns* were menaced by a giant Venus flytrap. This was *Grand Guignol* with pelmets, positively begging for parody.

Susan Harris began her TV career writing drama, but 'it came out funny,'[305] so she joined Norman Lear's new wave of sitcom outrage. For *All in the Family* spin-off *Maude*, she wrote 'Maude's Dilemma', the celebrated two-parter in which Bea Arthur's eponymous middle-aged liberal gets an abortion. Transmitted two months before the Supreme Court's Roe v. Wade decision legalised abortion nationwide, the story was a turning point for Harris. 'It became impossible,' she decided, 'for me to write something that didn't have a point of view, that wasn't about something, that couldn't touch you in some way.'[306]

Harris began creating her own series in partnership with producers Paul Junger Witt and Tony Thomas. Their first effort, divorcee study *Fay*, came and went in short order, so they started again. Instead of reining in *Fay*'s controversial aspects, they cranked them up. The new scenario was deliberately off the daytime peg: sisters Jessica Tate and Mary Campbell married adulterous, wealthy and disturbed, poor men respectively. Affairs, murders, personality disorders and aliens appeared weekly.

Initially, *Soap* wasn't so much a satire of daytime drama as an experiment in form. Harris's main reason for adopting the serial format was liberation from the need to wrap up a tight twenty-three-minute plot each week, freeing more space for 'scenes that were just good talk'.[307] That 'good talk' was the Susan Harris formula, nailed by Martin Cropper as 'social embarrassment punctuated by daggered one-liners'.[308] *Soap* the comedy was soap grown up.

Harris broke the daytime style down into its constituent parts, supersized each one, and crammed them willy-nilly back into the box. The base note was absurd, melodramatic exposition. On top of this came a steady stream of minted witticisms ('What use is algebra? I have never once, in all these years, had to find x'), with a top note of out-of-character meta-commentary. ('I always over-react when the person I love more than anyone else in the world drops dead. I'm sorry.') By bending realism, *Soap* could have its dramatic cake, eat it, and make sarcastic comments about its own rotten table manners all at once.

Trouble began in June 1977 when *Soap* was screened as part of ABC's new season première for critics in San Diego. *Newsweek* wrote of an opening episode packed with filth, including ecclesiastical sex scenes on consecrated ground, prompting a loose coalition of church leaders and right-wing pressure groups to call for a ban, sight unseen. Atlanta's Baptist minister Bob Spencer echoed the sentiments of censors down the ages. 'We don't have to see the show to know it's indecent . . . I believe in the Bible and I don't have to see certain things to know they are wrong.' Nineteen panicking ABC affiliates cancelled *Soap* and twenty more shunted it to the late night slot of doom. It was, claimed Harris, 'the first fatality of the moral majority'.[309]

Why did ABC stick with it? One reason was the tenacity of Fred Silverman, now ABC's head of entertainment after revitalising CBS's comedy roster with *The Mary Tyler Moore Show*, *All in the Family* and *M\*A\*S\*H*. There was another factor more appropriate to the spirit of the show. Beverlee Dean had been hired as 'creative consultant' by network president Fred S. Pierce. She was previously a consultant psychic to Hollywood stars. With stakes so perilously high, a network will rule out nothing to get in front. Dean predicted hit status for both *Soap* and *Taxi*. She even got a visit from a sceptical Harris. 'As a writer, I'll try almost anything once. She told me *Soap* would become a hit, but then my grandmother said that too.'[310]

In the studio Jay Sandrich, director of *The Mary Tyler Moore Show*'s early years, was in charge, swapping the former's orange-and-brown film of hugs and resolutions for a non-stop nightmare on acid-hued videotape – a striking change of tone and pace. With no pausing for breath, or even sitting down, acting in *Soap* was an equally tough assignment. Moore's sitcom offered lovably flawed role models. *Soap* was a parade of clinical case histories.

The cast, bouncing in and out of melodrama and panto with the odd heavy thump on the fourth wall and the occasional oasis of genuinely touching sentiment, had a gruelling task. As the otherworldly Jessica Tate, Katherine Helmond turned blanket ignorance into a state of grace, like Katharine Hepburn channelling Lamb Chop. At the other end of the scale, Richard Mulligan's Burt Campbell was a full-blown dyspraxic fidget: a startled dinosaur with a separate brain for each limb. Somewhere between, Robert Guillaume made the Tates' butler Benson into a Greek chorus of narrow-eyed, scattergun contempt. Billy Crystal's Jodie Dallas wasn't the first gay sitcom character – ABC's 1972 summer filler *The Corner Bar* was first with rococo set designer Peter Panama – but he did develop from the predictably stereotyped early sex change and suicide storylines into one of the show's few points of relative normality.

Risking her own sanity, Harris wrote the entire first season by herself. The inevitable collapse convinced her to collaborate on the remaining seasons and restrict her future comedy work to creating shows, rather than day-to-day scripting. After *Benson*, a conventional sitcom spin-off relocating Guillaume in governmental service, she tried to repeat the serial pastiche with *Hail to the Chief*, a misfire starring Patti Duke as the first female US president. The shock ante was upped, but by now pensioners contracting herpes and eight-year-old boys complaining of enlarged prostate glands seemed somehow stale. Harris finally reached the top of the sitcom pyramid with *The Golden Girls*, an altogether more empathetic comedy with fully rounded characters and family appeal. A sell-out to respectability in situation terms perhaps, but a quick survey of the Miami quartet's back-chat showed Harris's daggered one-liners had, if anything, been comprehensively sharpened.

# ROOTS: THE SAGA OF AN AMERICAN FAMILY (1977)

## ABC (David L. Wolper)

### Network television's black history week.

*You've probably noticed that I was a little late in arriving. I met Alex Haley outside, and I made the mistake of saying, 'Alex, how's your family?'*
Jimmy Carter addresses the Congressional Black Caucus
annual dinner, 24 September 1977

WHILE IT WAS YEARS ahead of other countries, early American television struggled to present non-white characters, particularly African-Americans, in a balanced and unpatronising light. Sitcoms led the charge in the 1960s, with Bill Cosby's equal top billing in *I-Spy* and Diahann Carroll's positive lead role in MTM's *Julia* helping banish painful memories of The Kingfish, the eye-rolling get-rich-quick schemer from cartoonish radio and TV coon turn *Amos 'N' Andy*. By comparison drama held back for an unconscionably long time, but when it did broach the subject it was at top volume.

*Roots* the book was the result of twelve years' genealogical research by Tennessee journalist Alex Haley, sparked by the story his grandmother told of Kunta Kinte, a Gambian youth who was captured by colonialists and put to work on a plantation. The TV rights were bought by producer David L. Wolper, who'd been trying to get a pan-generational saga on screen for years, pitching native American family sagas, police family sagas, blue collar car worker sagas and the like to little network interest.[311] *Roots*, however, already had momentum. It was taken up by ABC, who had pioneered the mini-series format by taking big novels and splitting them into multiple hour-long chunks, beginning with Leon Uris's *QBVII* in 1974 and finding mass success two years later with *Rich Man, Poor Man* by Irwin Shaw. Audience attention spans had been tested by the new format, and passed. *Roots* would assess their stamina in a few more areas.

Its scope was epic, from the Mandinka village of Jufareh in The Gambia in 1750 to Tennessee shortly after the Civil War. Kunta Kinte (played by eighteen-year-old student LeVar Burton) is uprooted from the village and shipped to a Tennessee plantation. His tribulations are followed by those of his daughter Kizzy (Leslie Uggams), who is sold down the river to an even harsher planter. He rapes her, leaving her with a son who becomes skilled in the art of training fighting cocks, earning him the name Chicken George (Ben Vereen) and a sojourn in England breeding birds for his new English owner. Back in Tennessee, George's son Tom Harvey, a plantation blacksmith, faces the Civil War and the rise of the Ku Klux Klan.

Four generations of bondage, rape, violence, poverty, starvation, stillbirth and murder at 9 p.m. was a massive risk. The all-important Midwestern (and predominantly white, conservative) audience was mollified by a raft of big name white stars – Lorne Greene, Lloyd Bridges, Chuck Connors and Ed Asner among them – alongside an encyclopedia of black talent (Scatman Crothers, O. J. Simpson, James Earl Jones, Maya Angelou). They pitched *Roots* as a saga about a family that happened to be black, rather than a black story *per se*, with much talk of Kunta Kinte being a 'universal symbol'. Finally ABC president Fred Silverman decided to strip the show across eight consecutive days in late January. If it flopped hard, it would at least flop fast.

Within a couple of episodes the impact of ABC's strategy was obvious; the country stopped as one when *Roots* aired. Audiences started at nearly twenty-nine million and rose to over thirty-six by day eight. The idea of a huge, diverse nation coming together over a simple story of suffering and injustice was not the whole truth: when Kunta Kinte was hobbled after an attempted escape in episode three, a rise in racially based fights was reported in schools. But it was an education for many in the reality of the West's ignoble past, and chimed with the new, compassionate mood which had got Jimmy Carter into the White House just three days before transmission. It was showered with Emmys and a special Pulitzer, and merely watching the show counted towards academic credit in universities across the States. No television programme had made anything like this impact before, especially with such a short run-up.

*Roots* was as expansive, solemn and simple as the watercolour montage that opened each episode, straight out of your illustrated family Bible. Some had reservations about the broadbrush approach adopted by Wolper's team. Much of Haley's 700-page book had necessarily been trimmed away and the straightforward, populist style of the series was open to accusations of trivialising slavery by adopting a personal, 'soapy' approach. Richard Schickel in *Time* magazine famously derided it as a 'middlebrow *Mandingo*'.[312] The simple answer to that was that the show's remit was to reach the maximum audience, and you didn't do that by wedging huge tracts of socio-historical analysis into a compelling yarn. Haley was transmitting history 'gut-to-gut' and television was the ideal medium. Others quibbled in the margins over anachronisms. 'It was painful,' wrote Anthony Burgess, 'to watch natives of West Africa who had never been in contact with white society indulge in facial gestures they could have learnt only in sophisticated Manhattan.'[313]

Most damningly, Mark Ottaway of the *Sunday Times* claimed the whole justification of Haley's story was unsound: the Gambian storyteller who told Haley of Kunta Kinte's entrapment being 'a man of notorious unreliability'[314] and telling him what he wanted to hear. Now it was political. Haley dismissed the criticisms. 'For years we've been offered a Tarzan and Jane view of Africa and there was no quarrel with it . . . there are basic vested interests in maintaining the old social order.'[315] Black academics piled on this attempt by the British establishment to distract from the show's central message. 'The English know better than anyone else what black research will lead to,' claimed Professor John Henrik Clarke. 'It will expose that the English were the leaders in slave trade and that they made the greatest profit from it and built an empire on those profits.'[316]

*Roots* affected the American populace in many ways. Radical African Americans disavowed their 'slave names' in the greatest numbers since the late 1960s, while babies were named Kunta and Kizzy by the score. A craze for genealogical research in general took off, which proved big business for the Mormon Church, owners of a mammoth vault of historical records. Historical tales of family turmoil appeared everywhere, the strongest being NBC's *Holocaust* with Meryl Streep.

*Roots* established the mini-series above the derided TV movie in the pecking order of American drama for the best part of the next two decades. It wasn't a fail-safe format though, as Wolper found when he finally broadcast his 1984 native American *Roots* series, Sioux saga *The Mystic Warrior*, to mass indifference. Even in the diverse USA, some stories were still a touch too niche.

# LEAPFROG (1978–9)
## ITV (ATV)

### Educational programming goes in at the avant-garde deep end.

MENTION SCHOOLS' TELEVISION AND a dull, half-baked world is evoked of pencils pointing at litmus papers in huge close-up and jobbing actors fluffing lacklustre speeches while dressed unconvincingly as Victorian industrialists. But creativity touched even this arid broadcasting sector, in some very unusual ways.

The BBC made the first broadcasts in 1952 to a handful of London schools equipped with special aerials, but America saw the first regular service two years later, as WQED sent out four hours of educational fodder a week to the folk of West Philadelphia in a pre-breakfast 'sunrise semester'.

The first closed-circuit BBC programme – Leslie Woolf of Hemel Hempstead Grammar doing the old 'electric current through the frog's legs' biology crowd-pleaser – was, like many early programmes, a no-frills lecture.[317] In 1965 ITV explored new areas, techniques and frontmen. In *One World* the young Peter Snow explained contemporary geopolitics. English language lesson *English and Life* was introduced, strangely, by 'Come Outside' singer Mike Sarne.[318] On the wilder shores, *Picture Box* sought to stimulate children's creativity through a range of usually wordless and often psychedelic internationally-sourced short films of the type that could lead to much thoughtful 'topic work'.

ITV was also the first to televise sex education in 1970 with *Living and Growing.* Sex-ed films for cinema distribution caused controversy at the time for their graphic approach, as the director of one, *Growing Up*, explained: 'if you were making a film about cooking, you would photograph an egg.'[319] ITV's effort was an orgy of soft-focus diagrams and deliberately non-Anglo-Saxon terminology, carefully preceded by a late night discussion for anxious parents, chaired by Ludovic Kennedy. This diligent decorum didn't stop Mary Whitehouse lodging a complaint against Granada Television over a mid-morning broadcast of *The Facts Are These: Venereal Disease*.

By now TV was steadily becoming a fixture of school life. Most schools still had one set apiece, usually pushed from class to class on a sturdy trolley. In primary schools children would ritually gather cross-legged on the floor to bask in its instructive glow. This led to spurious health warnings, with one orthopaedic surgeon claiming children's feet could be permanently deformed by the 'TV squat'. But the medium became a scholastic fixture, thanks to the combined attractions of pupils getting to pursue one of their favourite pastimes during school hours and teachers having to do little more than turn the thing on and run a few fact-sheets through the duplicator.

Drama prepared teenagers for life in the real world. Thames's *Viewpoint* encouraged kids to question their elders and betters in the media. (When this list of elders was shown to include several ITV companies, the IBA stepped in and quietly put it to sleep.) Andrew Davies, dramatic champion of the 1980s and 1990s, got an early break chronicling the trials of a working class school leaver in ATV's *The Time of Your Life* (sample episode title: 'I Don't Like Them Hippies'). Even experimental author B. S. Johnson was drafted to create an entire class of 'C-stream' sixteen-year-olds for Thames's *You and the World*. (His original script featured the suicide of the class's old teacher, which was tactfully removed after he took his own life and the show was completed by other hands.[320])

Programmes for primaries reborn as 'active learning' became the new orthodoxy, shifting the emphasis from learning by heart to finding out for yourself, and swapping regimented lines of desks for tables set at jaunty angles and womb-like walls of maroon sugar paper. It arrived on screen in the shape of BBC literacy fantasy *Sam on Boffs' Island*. An innovative bit of whimsy which saw Tony Robinson transported over his morning cereal to a world of phonetically challenged puppets, it combined artwork from Oliver Postgate and Peter Firmin with a script from Michael Rosen. Sadly Rosen was soon politely asked to leave the BBC (allegedly due to his troublesome far-left political sympathies), and the Corporation's schools' output returned to more conventional styles soon afterwards.

It was left to ITV to pick up the creative slack, which they did while wrestling with the thorny problem of interesting the average seven-year-old in maths. *Figure It Out*, a previously mundane numbers-and-shapes affair, was refitted in 1974 with a 'magazine' format comprising characters, sketches and achingly bad puns, delivered by actor and maths graduate Fred Harris. Harris ('a relaxed and dashing presenter using a variety of household objects' – the *Listener* [321]) combined knowledge with kid-friendly charisma in ideal proportions to engage the short-trousered masses.

This was revolutionary enough, but *Figure It Out*'s replacement, *Leapfrog*, took the most abstruse of primary school subjects into the outer realms. The Leapfrogs Group were a band of radical educators led by Dick Tahta, a maths evangelist cited as a great inspiration by Stephen Hawking. They adapted Egyptian peda-gogue Caleb Gattegno's intuitive teaching methods into a quarter-hour jamboree of graphics, mime, abstract film and hypnotic geometrical animations set to the eerie synth-blues of Pink Floyd collaborator Ron Geesin. Fred remained as a friendly face to guide the kids through this disjointed, occasionally disturbing fantasia, helped by others including, appropriately, *Vision On*'s Sylvester 'Sylveste' McCoy.

Not everyone approved of this kind of trendy flimflam. Teachers who thought innovations like 'circle time' were the work of a dungaree-clad devil abandoned the series mid-way, and many chil-dren proved less receptive than Tahta hoped. Sequels such as *Basic Maths* slowly added more explanatory chat and moved back towards the conventional middle ground. Eventually technology would make mainstream educational TV redundant, but for a brief while its ingenuity ranked it among the medium's weirdest and best.

# THE BBC TELEVISION SHAKESPEARE (1978–85)

## BBC Two/PBS (BBC/WNET/Time-Life)

### The last hurrah of prestige single plays.

'O for a highbrow play, that would ascend
The brightest heaven of syndication,
All channels for a stage, big names to act
And billionaires to fund the swelling scene!'
So went the dreams of certain drama chiefs
In times when brows soared high, but funds ran low.
What if the nation's broadcaster took on
The work of history's greatest dramatist?
It couldn't lose! Esteem! Fame! Merchandise!
A credible and creditworthy scheme.
The Bard, the Beeb: a dish fit for the gods
That some called, 'gloriously BBC!'[322]
Cedric Messina, of *Play of the Month*,
Was ministering angel to the plan.
Fond of the grand gesture, he came up with
The idea to produce Shakespeare complete –
No skipping out the likes of *Pericles*,
Nor all those Henrys, nor the one which has

The daft, bathetic cry 'Where is thy head?'
There was to be no short shrift, no foul play,
Just every Bardic drama, soup to nuts.
The single play, though still a 'prestige' form,
Had shed its old contemporary grit
As period pomp brought better sales returns
From overseas. (Despite the sorry sight
Of duds like *Churchill's People*, ill-conceived
Dramatic squibs adapted from the book
That won the ex-PM the Nobel Prize
But on the screen looked stiff, cheap and absurd,
And soon were dashed to pieces by the press.)
The raw, unflinching modern single play
Remained a tricky sell to foreigners,
But antique stuff sold like hot cakes and ale
To lands with anorexic history books.
The Beeb had knocked out Shakespeares all its life,
But thirty-seven plays in just six years
Went way beyond its public-funded means.
The budget shortfall led Messina to
Acquaint himself with strange bedfellows for
Such highbrow entertainment. Even then
The idea of a drama series backed
By Exxon Oil, a huge investment bank
And an insurance company seemed mad,
But there they were, each chipping in a third
Of the outstanding million-and-a-half
Required to get Messina off the ground.
There were conditions that came with the cash,
The main one being, 'Please don't muck about.
Don't do the plays in ersatz modern dress
To make some vague point about Vietnam
Or Ulster, or some made-up fascist state,
And don't go mad with kooky abstract sets
Or kinky costumes. Stay traditional.

Doublet and hose, crossed garters, and the rest.'
The money-men demanded heritage,
And 'maximum acceptability'.[323]
The series was to start with *Much Ado*,
That most agreeable romance of wits
With Penelope Keith and Michael York,
But someone, somewhere, called Messina out
For past injustices (no-one knows what)
And, in the row, the play was quickly binned,
Abandoned as a sacrificial goat
To BBC internal subterfuge.
To kick things off instead, they played it safe
With *Romeo and Juliet*. The leads
Were two unknowns, but big names dwelt
Within the lower body of the cast.
The look of it, though, was another thing.
By taping in the studio, the costs
Were kept down, continuity maintained
And dialogue kept mostly audible.
The problem was that Zeffirelli's film,
Though ten years old, was still definitive
To public taste. The poor old BBC,
With no backlighting, no heavenly beams
And, worst of all, no lush location shots,
Was naff enough to set your teeth on edge.
The old Verona square looked oddly flat,
And Alan Rickman's tights from Woolies bought.
The critics, sniffing mediocrity,
Were minded to dismiss the thing outright,
And household words were tossed Messina's way.
He had successes too, but two years in
He quit, and in his place the station hired
Jonathan Miller, a Renaissance man
In both the modern and Renaissance sense.
A polymath, exceedingly well read,

He looked at Exxon's strict proscriptive list
And, rather than lie low, fought fire with fire.
Taking the period trappings to extremes,
He laid on references with a trowel
To Veronese, Dutch masters and the like,
By recreating their work on the screen
As knowing *cinquecento* allusions.
The budget, just two hundred grand an hour,
Was made to work in new and lateral ways.
The castle walls were still of plywood hewn,
But now, instead of corny painted stones,
The plywood remained plywood, unadorned,
For Miller knew the trick with stylised sets
Was not to ape materials, just the shape.
Though still on tape, it broke the studio curse,
And grew an atmosphere all to itself
For actors to breathe in – that is, when they
Weren't trying bits of business Miller cribbed
From Erving Goffman's books on social gaffes.
(The best examples came when Miller cast
John Cleese as lead in *Taming of the Shrew*.)
It wasn't all about the Miller way.
The new directors whom he took aboard
Had striking visions of their own to stage.
Elijah Moshinsky, an opera man,
Turned off the studio's usual million watts
And lit whole scenes, it seemed, with just one bulb,
Suffusing actors with gold candlelight.
Then, later on, Jane Howell went for broke
With cones and wedges in *The Winter's Tale*,
Creating just the sort of abstract set
The Exxon boys specifically ruled out.
She also organised *Henry VI*,
As three gargantuan games of soldiers, in
A vast, decaying adventure playground.

This wouldn't have done on Messina's watch.
If these were gimmicks, no-one could complain
In light of their success. As Miller said,
'They're only "monkey tricks" if they don't work;
When they come off, they're "strokes of genius".'[324]
The educational cherry on the cake
Was *Shakespeare in Perspective*: lecture films
Presented by big names to warm things up
For each play that was broadcast. So you got
Frank Kermode on *Lear*. *The Winter's Tale*
By Stephen Spender. Clive James did *Hamlet*
In witty fashion, and the *Merry Wives*
They gave to Jilly Cooper – quite a range.
One week Roy Hudd explained *The Comedy
Of Errors* from a music hall in Leeds,
Then Donald Sinden appraised Anne Boleyn
As (his words) 'eminently beddable',
And Dennis Potter savaged *Cymbeline*
While trudging through the dark Forest of Dean.
Something, as linkmen say, for everyone.
The *Shakespeare* was originally pitched
In 1975, when single plays
On BBC TV, across the year,
Filled a hundred and twenty slots, against
A figure less than one-third that when Howell's
Vastly delayed *Titus Andronicus*
(All severed hands and Toyah Willcox Goths)
Stood hairs on end in 1985,
And brought the project to a bloody close.
(By now Shaun Sutton, veteran of the Beeb
Who had directed *Z-Cars* episodes
Some twenty years ago, was at the helm,
Producing the last fourteen of the plays.)
The studio-bound drama, on its own,
Would scarcely make it to the next decade

As TV plays contrived to look like films,
And took their style cues from the cinema.
The long and fruitful exchange of ideas
Between theatre and television was
Cut by the former's slide into a niche
As musicals became its staple fare,
And by the shift of TV's self-image
From national stage to pseudo-Hollywood.
It's bleakly fitting that the Shakespeare plays
Became the curtain call for the old style
Of making drama. While its look and style
And methods swiftly died out, other things
Such as the corporate funding, worldwide sales
And wrangles over star names, would increase
And dominate productions from then on.
Since films cost more than plays, they had to make
More money back, which meant that any risks
Had to be minimised, and 'Play it safe!'
Became the rule. To innovate is to die.
The game was up, and drama on the box,
After this business-related sea change,
Became a lot more rich, but much less strange.

# CONNECTIONS (1978)

## BBC One/PBS
## (BBC/Time Life Films)

The blockbuster science documentary grows too
rich for many people's blood.

*Morecambe and Wise on ITV, James Burke on BBC One – who*
*says the autumn schedules have given us nothing to laugh at?*
David Wheeler, *Listener*, 26 October 1978

WHEN EDUCATION IS DISCUSSED, the relative merit of a scientific versus a literary schooling is guaranteed to bring out the priggish schoolboy that lurks within even the greatest thinkers. In the nineteenth century the botanist T. H. Huxley had it out with poet Matthew Arnold in a relatively civilised duel of words. The quality of debate went down a notch in 1959 when C. P. Snow, scientist turned novelist, delivered a lecture lamenting the widening gulf between the 'two cultures'. F. R. Leavis, self-appointed guardian of the grand literary tradition, mocked Snow's thesis as biased, vulgarly written, and told him his novels were rubbish to boot. Since then, the borderland between the humanities and science has been a minefield for well-meaning pundits. James Burke stepped boldly into it with the world watching.

An English graduate, Burke started out as a language teacher in Bologna before getting into broadcasting almost by accident, when Granada Television cast about the locality for resident reporters. Moving to the BBC he fell, equally serendipitously, into science with *Tomorrow's World* and a central role in round-the-clock coverage of the Apollo space launches. With his boundless, electric enthusiasm and his penchant for eye-catching visual aids, including scale models of orbiting craft into which he gleefully clambered, he became TV's technological figurehead.

For Burke, though, space-shots became increasingly monotonous. He dismissed the 1975 Apollo-Soyuz link-up, a political stunt with little technological benefit, as 'crucifyingly boring'. Burke the humanities man was only interested in technology that affected society, and to this end he fashioned *The Burke Special*. Clothed head to toe in black, he dashed through an audience seated in a set decked out in chrome and nylon shag-pile, reeling off informal lectures-cum-demonstrations of everything from body language to biological terrorism. His mission was to explain without being dull or appearing elitist. The presenter, he said, must keep things accessible: 'if you're bored stiff by the man, you won't listen to what he says.'[325] One critic compared his performance to 'a finely honed conjuring act'.[326] Another, less enthusiastically, lamented his tendency 'to dash around from spot to spot, shaking trinkets in people's faces so that they wouldn't notice the nonsense that was being babbled.'[327]

Burke wasn't confined to a studio for long. The US bicentennial celebrations prompted NBC to hook up with the Beeb for *The Inventing of America*, in which every major technological breakthrough made on American soil was recreated by Raymond Burr while Burke explained what connected them in animated fashion. Dramatic skits, song and dance numbers choreographed by Arlene Phillips, gags and TV parodies crowded into two frenetic hours. Critics reeled from the overload. 'The show's script was so bent on finding ways to say things,' complained Clive James, 'that it hardly got anything said.'[328]

The dissenters couldn't stop him. Burke's next series, tentatively titled *Changes*, was a juggernaut. Ten hours to give an 'alternative view' of technology, taking Burke, now clad in an off-white safari suit, to 150 locations around the globe. The task, as laid out on a mammoth wall chart in Burke's office, was to trace the history of eight key inventions, brought about by accident as much as design. A change of name to *Connections*, a lavish transatlantic budget and the skills of *Ascent of Man* producers David Kennard and Mick Jackson gave Burke an impressive setting from which to ask probing questions like: 'What has the recipe for Chicken Marengo got to do with air conditioning?'

Here, for many, was the problem. The production values suggested seriousness, authority and weight. But Burke's skittish script was never far from a flippant aside: 'When Queen Elizabeth took over the place in 1558, it was national disaster week!'; 'Meanwhile, at the King's palace, it was lead balloon time'; 'Who knows what somebody's doing with a toilet roll right now?' Combine this with a puckish tendency to start a sentence in downtown New York and finish it on a rocky promontory in the Mediterranean, and a certain omniscient smugness was palpable. It grated with Clive James, who diagnosed 'Burke's Smirk – a twitching grin of self-approval at being in on secrets.'[329] For Julian Barnes, 'everything is terribly, terribly clear to Mr Burke, which is a major reason for being suspicious of him'.[330] Brian Winston demanded: 'If he is a reporter, why does he never let anyone else get a word in edgeways? If he is an authority, what exactly is he an authority on, other than talking to the camera?'[331]

Conversely many viewers, mainly the young, were riveted by the gee-whiz visual rhetoric and inspired to discover more for themselves, which was Burke's main goal from the outset. The style wasn't an issue to them then, and the controversy seems distant today, when even world leaders habitually remove ties and preface each obloquy with a chummy, Burkean 'Look . . .'

*Connections* broke public TV ratings records in the US and was exported to over ninety countries. Two sequels followed: *The Real Thing*, concerning human perception; and *The Day The Universe Changed*, on philosophical perspectives, which ended with Burke delivering an impassioned and prescient speech arguing that a global network of computers might one day democratise all knowledge, encourage true freedom of ideas and challenge centuries-old systems of repressive government. He did this from the top of a mountain in the Himalayas, of course.

# BLANKETY BLANK
## (1979-90)
## BBC One

### The little game show that couldn't.

IN THE EARLY DAYS of American television, the quiz show ruled. The Federal Communications Commission had cracked down on network radio's proliferation of phone-in giveaways in 1949, and the celebrity panel show expanded to fill the gap. Five years later the ban was lifted, and television decided anything radio could do, they could do a thousand times bigger. Never mind *The $64,000 Question*, US quizzes offered prizes all the way up to $250,000 (which was never won) and a genuine Scottish island (before the British government waded in to stop them).[332] The real winners were the networks, as the national press became captivated by the progress of punters up the prize ladder, moving coverage of the shows from the TV section at the back to the headlines at the front.

Producers' desire to control those headlines became the format's undoing. Addicted to front page exposure, they replaced the disappointing, know-little members of the public with ringers groomed to romp to victory week after week. In August 1958 they were called out, when a contestant was found in possession of a book of answers on the set of NBC's *Dotto*, precipitating a federal inquiry which soon became a scandal when the fixing of *Twenty One* came to light. Contestant Herb Stempel revealed how he'd been coerced into crashing his winning streak (pretending not to know *Marty* had won the Best Picture Oscar in 1955) to clear the decks for suave WASP ringer Charles Van Doren. The producers started appearing in the headlines rather than writing them. By the end of the year the big quizzes had been cancelled in favour of comedy and westerns. They would slowly reappear over the next few years, but only as also-rans in the margins, never the day's main draw.

One of the schedule fillers was CBS's *Match Game*, a two-handed word quiz with celebrity trimmings devised by Frank Wayne of 'telepuzzle' behemoths Goodson-Todman Productions. Contestants completed the blank space in host Gene Rayburn's statement with a word or phrase, which was tested against the written guesses of a panel of assorted celebrities. If they matched, points were won. It lasted nearly twenty-two years in its original form, during which American screens captured the rise of the natural born game show contestant, as brash and slick as the compère, miming theatrical concentration when asked the question and gleefully applauding themselves when they got the answer right. Competing on afternoon TV quizzes was the USA's true national sport.

As with all game shows of even moderate fame, the format was sold overseas. Australia's Network Ten, well on the way to becoming a Rupert Murdoch majority interest, took it up in 1977 as *Blankety Blanks*. The host this time was Graham 'Gra-Gra' Kennedy, who'd become one of Australia's first bona fide TV stars via the thirteen-year Johnny Carson-style chat show *In Melbourne Tonight*. Filling the star stalls with his pals from the rather restricted pool of home-grown celebrity, Kennedy made the show less formal, funnier, more relaxed and less and less about the contestants and their tedious task of filling in the blanks. In-jokes proliferated: the hapless stagehand who uncovered the clues from behind a screen was dubbed 'Peter the Phantom Puller', and every drop of potential innuendo arising from the missing words was milked. If all else failed, he just shouted 'bum!' The wholesome *Match Game* had a feeling it wasn't on KOAM-TV Kansas any more.

The British adaptation of Kennedy's adaptation, subtly renamed *Blankety Blank*, was launched by the BBC on 18 January 1979

– the very bottom of the year. The UK was already up to speed with the 'wall of quipping celebs' format, with ITV having adapted *The Hollywood Squares* – a US format that post-dated *Match Game* – into the slick Bob Monkhouse vehicle *Celebrity Squares*. That show stacked its stars in a three-by-three formation, while *Blankety Blank* went for two rows of three. Otherwise there was only one fundamental difference between the two shows, but what a difference it was.

The son of a Limerick grocer, Terry Wogan made his name in Irish radio in the 1960s as a disc jockey and on television replacing Gay Byrne as host of Ireland's first game show, *Jackpot*. When the BBC assimilated elements of the offshore pirate broadcasters into its national radio line-up, Wogan was also inducted, and soon forged a dreamy, chatty manner, heavy on the whimsical non-sequiturs. He amassed over seven and a half million regular listeners to his Radio Two breakfast show, and his commentaries for the Eurovision Song Contest added a welcome layer of homely scepticism to the international MOR tournament. If anyone could make a go of this inane format it was him.

From the opening theme music, the show was seemingly designed to sour the sherry of the BBC governors. Ronnie Hazlehurst, the number one light entertainment composer, turned in a four-note motif that sounded like a cashpoint's nervous breakdown. Wogan, light-suited and brandishing a slim silver microphone (a copy of Gene Rayburn's original) was the only mobile figure on stage. Contestants from central suburban casting (here's Nigel Creffield, who works in the plywood business) came and went via a turntable, not even trusted to negotiate a flight of illuminated stairs. From the first, the tone was one of resigned stoicism: 'You've already met the creatures from the black lagoon . . . let's meet the plain but honest people of England'; 'Lennie Bennett, what are you doing these days, as if anybody cared?' Not for Tel the one-man party atmosphere of the US hosting regime.

Nothing was talked up, least of all the micro-achievement of thinking of the same word as Gary Davies. Even commiserations were barbed: 'It's hard to think in these circumstances, particularly when you're surrounded by eejits.' The hollowness of the enterprise was out there in the open. The American aspirational dream had its wings clipped with a stout pair of British garden shears (which is roughly what a score of fifty blanks would win you). At no point did anyone concerned forget the reality of the situation: nine grown-ups in a television studio doing something inescapably stupid. Only a change of host in 1984 modified the Soviet bread queue vibe. With Les Dawson presenting, it became a wet whist drive in purgatory.

Yet *Blankety Blank* was insanely popular. From a tentative debut it shot up the ratings to third place, just behind *Coronation Street* and *This Is Your Life*.[333] This caused some embarrassment to BBC bosses, keen to paint their channel as the home of quality acts like *Life on Earth* and *The Voyage of Charles Darwin*. 'They regard it as a bit silly,' admitted an insider, 'more the kind of quiz show that ITV puts on.'[334] Reluctantly, 'the most imbecilic programme in the history of the world'[335] was renewed for the autumn season, where it promptly started pulling in nearly twenty-three million viewers, making headlines through the power of pure crapulence.[336] With woks, croquet sets and self-assembly greenhouses as the ultimate reward, any accusations of contest rigging would have been laughed out of court.

Set among the serious entertainment of the 1979 schedule, *Blankety Blank* provided a corrective to the main diet of gut-punching drama and showbiz ostentation. Years later, when plummeting budgets led to a more widespread adoption of its apologetic shrug, the effect was lost. Twenty-first century evenings burst at the seams with cookery contests and celebrity jousts decked out in the knowingly guilty fashion that says 'Yes, we *know* we're better than this, but come on, so are you, and here we both are, eh?' When ironic underachievement becomes the rule rather than the exception, when everything's a guilty pleasure and no-one makes the effort, you're in trouble. 'The only consolation to be derived from this ongoing débâcle,' wrote John Naughton of *Blankety Blank*, 'is the thought that a TV programme can never be worse than its viewers; for the more stupid it is, the more stupid they are to watch it.'[337]

# LIFE ON EARTH (1979)

## BBC Two (BBC/Warner Brothers/ Reiner Moritz)

### The apex of the educational blockbuster.

WHEN TELEVISION STARTED TO educate the people, it looked to the universities for interlocutors. Some made a notably better fist of it than others. An early success, Professor Alan Taylor gave historical lectures which may seem staid by modern standards but at the time were praised as 'mischievous, and his satirical remarks about history have the authentic dig of the irreverent, independent mind.'[338] Charisma was the quality that would sort television's men of intellect from the mumbling, donnish boys.

In the late 1960s, BBC Two controller David Attenborough commissioned Sir Kenneth Clark to produce a history of Western art, with no location too exotic. *Civilisation*, the first of the authored blockbuster documentary series known in the trade as 'sledgehammers', was born. Jacob Bronowski's *Ascent of Man*, also greenlit by Attenborough, concentrated on scientific advancement. The genre soon attracted dissidents, with John Berger's *Ways of Seeing* and James Burke's *Connections* arguing across Clark and Bronowski respectively – all on BBC Two. When he retired from executive office, the man who'd introduced the sledgehammer took charge of one of his own.

The natural history TV film evolved from the basic chimp-on-a-table exhibitions of George Canston's *All About Animals* into two distinct species. The lecture, usually consisting of wildlife footage strung together over a voice track, was simple and respectable. Less so was the explorer's diary, in which flamboyant experts toting pith helmets and snorkels – Armand and Michaela Denis in Africa, Hans and Lotte Hass or Jacques Cousteau in the sea – chronicled their fearless sojourns to the outer reaches, often usurping their zoological quarry as their own central subject.

Attenborough had a foot in both camps, having produced straight lectures like Sir Julian Huxley's *The Pattern of Animals* and hopped into khaki shorts himself to front the massively popular *Zoo Quest*. He built a new type of programme that fused the best of the lecture and the explorer's diary formats, taking the authority of the former and the showmanship of the latter. David Bellamy was already taking the world of botany for an enthusiastic, cactus-hugging ride on ITV. For zoology, Attenborough went much further.

Each of *Life on Earth*'s thirteen editions would deal with one evolutionary step along the archaeological timeline. More than thirty cameramen brought back footage from exploratory South American treks – lugging heavy and fragile equipment deep into rainforests and up to the rims of volcanic craters – to microscopic laboratory work, patiently waiting for a dragonfly to shed its skin or a breeding pair of deadly spiders to start going steady.

Each programme started, in all senses, with a wide view. Attenborough set the scene in aeons past, walking through a prehistoric landscape (often Yellowstone National Park), lifeless rock and sulphurous seas up to the horizon. The landscape presented an evolutionary challenge. The camera zoomed in to a hand-held fossil, mixing into micro-photography from the programme's many laboratory set-ups. (Only rarely did the footage need help from that cop-out of TV nature shows past, the watercolour artist's impression.)

Time was just as easily manipulated: a fern could show a month's worth of growth in ten seconds, and the exquisite mechanics of a beetle's wings were decelerated a hundredfold. A lot of scientific ground was covered, but it never felt like hard work keeping up. The specific case having illustrated the general point, the camera refocused on Attenborough, succinctly wrapping up with a tantalising glimpse of next week's treasures. The grim prospect of waiting a whole seven days was offset by a mid-week repeat, often devoured by eager viewers as a second helping. This wasn't TV made to be casually glanced at – by constantly outdoing itself visually, it challenged you to take your eyes off the screen from one moment to the next. You couldn't miss a frame.

The Pre-Cambrian oddness of the early shows made the series a hard sell internationally. American executives were not overjoyed about the series kicking off with what they anticipated as an hour of green slime.[339] In the end PBS was *Life on Earth*'s only American outlet, with network suggestions of an American alternative narrator – Robert Redford was a favourite candidate – calmly but firmly batted back.

Attenborough somehow managed to flit through time and space, laying down the origins of everything alive while remaining humble. He wore his knowledge lightly, and his enthusiasm like an old sweater over the shoulders. In Attenborough's eyes, if a peacock was a miracle, so was a hagfish. He hymned them all in gentle tones, letting the cameramen do the majority of the work.

Over the next thirty-five years, *Life . . .* became an accidental franchise with ever bigger, more technically advanced, more visually spectacular sequels. It's true that the visuals, more than anything else, have helped this strain of the sledgehammer series to survive in the harsh wastelands of the twenty-first century schedule. There's always a sense of more to be shown. Blue whales look progressively more imposing with every leap in camera technology, while a Caravaggio remains the same Caravaggio. The nature documentary looks like lasting as long as its subject – although as Attenborough's more recent programmes point out, how long that might be is anyone's guess.

# MINDER (1979–94)
## ITV (Euston Films)

The comedy drama becomes a nice little earner.

THE FIRST FOUR DECADES of British television had little use for the entrepreneur. Between the state-funded BBC monolith and the old-style entertainment palaces of the independent channel, there was little room for the sort of seat-of-the-pants backroom set-up on which much of the nation's cinematic glory had rested. Programmes were made, by and large, by the channels that ran them, and were seldom expected to be seen anywhere else. The chief exception was ITC, Lew Grade's transatlantic action-fantasy partnership, but that always seemed at the mercy of American money and tastes. In the late sixties executives at Thames, a new and forward-thinking independent station, took the plunge and inaugurated a fully home-grown filmed drama unit. Euston Films was born.

Euston eschewed standard TV practice. With no large permanent studio at their disposal, production was entirely location-based. When a major series got underway, London would be scoured for a 'base' – an abandoned public building or disused warehouse – which would serve as production HQ, rehearsal space and home for any regularly occurring sets. Everything else was shot on location, with as slender a crew as possible and maximum efficiency.

The first production, *ITV Playhouse* entry *Suspect*, achieved an authentically dilapidated look thanks to the new method and the experience of its director: *World in Action* graduate Mike Hodges used hand-held cameras for a style later christened 'wobblyscope'.[340]

Directors were valued at Euston – American conveyor belt productions often mutilated a director's intentions in the editing room, but Euston gave Hodges and his cohorts final cut, getting better quality results and attracting greater talent. These aesthetic achievements produced commercial success through two block-buster police series, the violent *Special Branch* and the more sophisticated *The Sweeney*, creating a crime sub-genre of their own: two-fisted, foul-mouthed and bleary-eyed, with every trace of American cop show glamour ruthlessly expunged. Its unofficial title was 'kick, bollock and scramble'.

Leon Griffiths was a writer with a solid and wide-ranging portfolio stretching back to *The Adventures of Robin Hood*. One of his most notable works was 1965 sitcom *A Slight Case Of . . .*, which starred Roy Kinnear as a shady operator professing to work very high up in a different profession each week – out-manoeuvring, swindling and generally one-upping his competitors with high-flying patter and low moral standards. Another was *Dinner at the Sporting Club*, a downbeat *Play for Today* set in the sleazy world of small-time prize-fighting, where dreams were ground into the canvas and the best anyone could hope for was being slipped a fur coat as a backhander or saving enough for 'a down-payment on a bungalow out in Ongar'. When Thames were looking for a replacement flagship series for the freshly decommissioned *Sweeney*, Griffiths gave them a combination of these two shows, placing the comic wide boy into real, inescapable dramatic situations.

*Minder* was conceived as '*The Magnificent Seven* minus six,'[341] the misadventures of a professional minder operating in the grey area between legitimate business and organised crime. It followed the pattern of *Budgie*, Keith Waterhouse and Willis Hall's under-world sleaze-com from the other end of the decade, with the awkward corners knocked off and less salubrious values thrown into storage. Terry McCann is an ex-boxer who fell into violent crime and now works through a kind of East End purgatory as a hired heavy to various physically vulnerable clients. Griffiths stressed from the outset that Tel was the strong, silent type, more likely to use his nous to prevent a situation flaring up than to wade in with fists flying. The aim was to instil a sense of menace without the 'shattered balsa-wood bannisters' of *The Sweeney*. And lest ITV's moral guardians quail at making heroes of ne'er-do-wells, a simple, transcendent morality ran through the series. 'Although Terry sometimes finds it hard to distinguish between legal right and wrong he is always certain about good and bad.'[342]

Dennis Waterman, junior partner in *The Sweeney*, did the part of Tel justice, neither overplaying the lovable rogue or acting dim for laughs. But for many the real star was Tel's sole agent and confidant Arthur Daley, a borderline respectable conman who knew everyone from East End thugs to Mayfair socialites, yet always had a consignment of gentlemen's literature in his lock-up awaiting shipping. George Cole, former protégé of the great Alastair Sim, was Arfur incarnate from brogues to trilby. A fully certified comic actor, he knew how to turn down the jokey business many straight actors would have wrongly piled on. With a mantle of streetwise confidence sitting on his shoulders as snugly as his camel hair coat, Arfur introduced young Terence to the denizens of the underworld with the wise wit of a Castella-sucking Virgil: 'She caught the old man in bed with the au pair and took him for the national debt'; 'He's got a degree in sociology. He still does the thieving but now he knows why.' Guest star villains were drawn from the cream of the character-acting crop: Kenneth Griffith, Alfie Bass, Max Wall. Script, actors and locale were perfectly matched.

The show took a while to establish itself. The first episode transmitted shortly after the end of a three-month ITV strike, so publicity was practically non-existent – but it soon outstripped expectations. After a couple of series the reason for this success was unearthed: *Minder*, though firmly tucked in after the 9 p.m. watershed, was playing to a family audience. Not the traditional notional family audience, settling down to a Sunday evening period romp with crumpets on the trolley, but an organically grown one of kids allowed to stay up late. One 1983 survey estimated nearly half of Britain's twelve to fifteen-year-olds were at least semi-regular watchers, fluent in the ways of the Winchester Club.[343]

ITV turned an entirely appropriate blind eye to this transgression, and marketed the programme to kids as much as adults: Waterman and Cole started turning up in character on children's programmes; there was a novelty Christmas single 'What Are We Gonna Get for 'Er Indoors?' and a spin-off computer game enabling kids to trade ballcocks and dirty books for a tidy bundle in their own bedrooms. Eventually this appeal began to affect the quality, as off-the-peg swindling capers swamped the well-observed character work, but most of the time *Minder* was a trans-generational joy, a crafty shandy in the beer garden of TV drama.

# NOW GET OUT OF THAT (1981–5)
## BBC One

Personal incompetence becomes a spectator sport.

THE HIGH CONCEPT, PRODUCER-LED programmes that form the core of terrestrial broadcasting in the twenty-first century are painted as something new and utterly modern. Their Year Zero was 1999, when *Big Brother* was first transmitted on Dutch TV station Veronica on 16 September. But however achingly fresh the show, it doesn't take much work to dig up some vintage ancestors.

Take the millennial incarnation of *Top Gear*. Did any twentieth century show shamelessly take a blokey, suburban hobby out of the garden shed, pump it full of testosterone, set fire to it and push it into a canyon for laughs? Well, there was BBC Two's 1976 squib *The Fishing Race*, a raucous, semi-scripted pseudo-competition devised by sports writer Ian Wooldridge, pitting three teams against each other for a sixty-hour dash across the UK in specially tooled-up Range Rovers to catch as many species of fish as possible, including stingray in the Thames and piranhas in Essex, slagging and sabotaging their rivals all the while. It was silly, offbeat and over the top, condemned by the National Angling Council for not treating the sport with 'due solemnity'.[344] Unrepentant, the team took to Sweden for a second series, augmented the four-wheeled transport with speedboats and helicopters, and the cast with rugby star Gareth Edwards and a naked woman in a canoe. Though fuelled by Watney's rather than Stella, laddish abandon was present and incorrect.

Channel Four pre-empted their own recent success story *Gogglebox* by nearly thirty years with *Open the Box*, which invited Oxford psychologists to install cameras in the nation's front rooms to observe the public watching television. As with the twenty-first century incarnation, choice epigrams flowed like fine wine. 'She's a lot of use, isn't she,' muttered one Mrs Brown, watching *Dallas*'s Pam Ewing emoting helplessly as husband Bobby was gunned down, 'fucking around like that. Get a bloody ambulance!' In a further twist, the subjects were shown the recordings of themselves watching TV, which they then watched on TV, their reactions in turn recorded for posterity. 'So much self consciousness,' lamented Julian Barnes, 'so little insight.'[345]

Then there's another modern format, which lumps together two teams of self-regarding dimwits, lumbers them with some fiddly task which we can see is plainly beyond their meagre abilities (though they of course must never realise that), and films them bickering, backstabbing and falling on their collective arse while a hired smart Alec rolls his eyes theatrically in the background. This clan is headed by business-oriented sneer-along *The Apprentice*, but it can trace its lineage back to *Now Get Out of That*, BBC One's outdoor puzzle-solving romp launched in the dog days of 1981.

Described by its deviser Derek Smith as an 'open-air action crossword', *Now Get Out of That* sent two teams (initially Oxford vs. Cambridge, latterly Brits against the Yanks) stumbling across overcast hillsides, surviving on badly-cooked rabbit and applying logical brainstorming to such tasks as retrieving a Land Rover from a swamp with nine yards of rope, a milk bottle and a house brick. All rather wholesome, really.

Fortunately, there was Bernard Falk. Blessed with a raised eyebrow of a voice, Falk sat snugly in a presentation studio, watching and reprimanding the contestants' windswept fumblings with all the sarcastic devices of the TV viewer at his disposal. There was the sarcastic riposte. ('Why am I standing in the middle of a river in my swimming costume?' 'You might well ask!') The sarcastic reversal. ('Here's Tony, showing all those qualities of leadership

271

that inspire others to follow without question.' Cue Tony being shouted at while squatting miserably in a stream.) The sarcastic benefit-of-the-doubt. ('Either they like the extra work, or this lot can't measure eight feet properly.')

Stripped across a week of teatimes – then a novel scheduling approach, hitherto restricted to Scottish soap operas and embassy sieges – the show thrived in the only niche it could have hoped to occupy, the frivolous teatime filler slot. It served its humble station perfectly. The *Guardian* called *Now Get Out of That* 'hypnotic viewing, truly terrible but unmissable once you get stuck in. This is as moronic as you could hope for.'[346] Over eight million viewers agreed.

It was all based on army survival games of the type which had lately been adapted by some wily entrepreneurs and flogged to corporations as staff 'team building' exercises. In this way, it was a consummately eighties programme, and more vocational frolics would follow. Various ITV regions aired their own knockout competitions for businesses, typified by Granada's *Flying Start*, though these tended to be the driest game shows imaginable. ('Who's likely to create most jobs – the canvas bag maker from Chester, the Runcorn firm which makes healthy Middle Eastern snacks, or the welders from Winsford?')

What distinguishes *Now Get Out of That*, *The Fishing Race* and countless other proto-reality programmes from their modern descendants is their modest nature. Made on a shoestring for the scheduling wilderness, these shows were never intended as anything more than a bit of close-season tomfoolery to mark time while entertainment's big guns were stripped and reloaded. The idea that they might ever be the main draw, or even come to represent the station in the mind's eye of the nation, would have been laughed out of the boardroom. Whimsical, impromptu fun, yes, but flagship material? What a load of old toot.

# ARTEMIS 81 (1981)
## BBC One

### Christmas holiday viewing doesn't get tougher than this.

IT WAS NO DOUBT near the bottom of their list of priorities, but the incoming Conservative government of 1979 had it in for state subsidised drama, especially the sort that attracted the epithet 'pretentious'. Pretension is a slippery word, one that often says more about the person employing it than their target. It becomes a catch-all synonym for 'ambitious', 'solemn', 'confusing' – anything the critic finds a chore. As hard-headed populism swamped the corridors of power, the P-word was heard more than ever.

From May 1979, the word started appearing a lot more in discussions of subsidised theatre, and especially the BBC. Licence payers' money, it was decreed, shouldn't be frittered away on the impenetrable, obscene outpourings of the beard-and-polo-neck militia. One of the first casualties of the new regime was *Solid Geometry*, Ian McEwan's complex trawl through mathematics and sexuality. Two days before shooting began, the play was summarily canned by Head of Network Production Phil Sidey, who explained his reasoning in concrete terms to David Hare. 'How do you think it would look,' he confided, 'if, just as Margaret Thatcher was about to be elected, we were stupid enough to record a play which featured a twelve-inch penis in a fucking bottle?'[347]

David Rudkin was another prime candidate for the priggish chop. His stage debut *Afore Night Come*, a tense tableau of ritual slaughter among volunteer apple pickers in his native Worcestershire, took its place alongside works by Pinter and Beckett in the early 1960s 'dirty plays' controversy, which precipitated the abolition of stage censorship by the Lord Chamberlain. Given a few drama slots on TV, he emerged as 'a playwright of strange powers, with a capacity to illuminate the dark crannies of the soul'.[348] Despite swimming directly against the mainstream, he scored a big hit in 1974 with *Penda's Fen*, the emotional awakening of a repressed vicar's son in a riot of ancient legends, homoerotic wet dreams, government conspiracies, severed hands and Elgar symphonies.

Summarised, Rudkin sounds distant and humourless, but this wasn't the case. *The Sons of Light*, a sprawling, solemn and portentous epic staged by the RSC in 1977, featured a scene in which the saturnine Dr Nebewohl, overseer of a post-apocalyptic underground mine staffed by zombified slave children, whips off his dark glasses – to reveal another pair of dark glasses underneath. This same gag would turn up – presumably coincidentally – in the comedy film *Airplane!* three years later.

But despite such moments, *The Sons of Light* was heavy going. 'It's as if he had taken a plot from *Doctor Who*,' wrote Michael Billington, 'and rewritten it in the language of the Authorised Version.'[349] A later, even darker stage play, *The Triumph of Death*, was likened by Michael Coveney to 'watching a dramatist topple over the edge then clamber up to the summit only to leap joyously once more into the abyss.'[350]

Rudkin operated from the centre of an impenetrably dense personal mythology. So naturally the BBC, at the word of commissioning editor David Rose, spent half a million pounds[351] on bringing it to the nation's front rooms over the 1981 Christmas holidays.

The result was three hours long and enigmatically titled *Artemis 81*. Director Alastair Reid described it as 'a television Rubik's Cube.'[352] No two plot summaries were the same, and it definitely looked like tough going for those torpid evenings between Boxing Day and New Year's Eve, but the British media were still receptive to ambitious television. Even the red tops offered good will. 'Don't worry about understanding it,' reassured the *Daily Mirror*, 'just relax and enjoy it.'[353]

This was easier said than done. From nine till midnight on Tuesday 29 December, BBC One broadcast one of the most densely symbolic, allusive and obscure pieces of television ever made. (The commercial channel were showing – what else? – Trevor Nunn's production of Chekhov's *Three Sisters*.) Flitting from a North Sea Ferry to Liverpool Cathedral to a laser-festooned slave camp buried under a Welsh mountain to an alien planet with two suns, *Artemis 81* was a thicket of classical Gods, fragmented relics, Hitchcock blondes, dry ice, master organists, trolleybuses full of consumptive Danes, abused jellyfish and mass clinical torture with muzak accompaniment. Low on explanatory dialogue and rich in meditative atmospherics, it was, even by Rudkin's own standards, extraordinary.

Hywel Bennett was the nominal protagonist, a fantasy author who stumbles from one weird piece of the puzzle to the next, sporting an expression of quizzical determination throughout. The name that got the papers excited, though, was Sting. This was a time when rock stars and heavyweight TV drama were in alignment – Sting would next star in the cinema version of Dennis Potter's banned *Brimstone and Treacle*, while David Bowie turned up a couple of months into 1982 playing the title role in Bertolt Brecht's *Baal*. In *Artemis 81*, Sting didn't exactly do much apart from drift moodily across the landscape in a cowl and dangle from a helicopter, but his teen appeal put him top of the publicity pecking order.

As a whole, *Artemis 81* struck a chord with the same thoughtful teenagers who'd fallen for *Penda's Fen* – many of them still shell-shocked from the traumatic finale of space opera *Blake's Seven* the previous week – but adults were less entranced. The reviews weren't nearly as forgiving as the previews. The *Listener*, admirably reluctant to wheel out the P-word, found it 'absorbing, bounteously over-stuffed,'[354] but the general impression was of a large egg painfully laid. 'The tail-end turkey of the year,' snorted the *Express*, 'turned out to be three hours of codswallop.'[355]

It wasn't that, but it was no flawless classic. Half a million quid was extravagant for the time, but it wasn't nearly enough to illustrate the apocalyptic cities, swarms of ravens and mythic alien worlds Rudkin's script demanded, despite some resourceful production shortcuts. Rudkin's preference for long, portentous speeches instead of naturalistic dialogue was another problem, making comparisons with the cheesier end of science fiction inevitable, though Bennett's character's girlfriend got a good speech tearing into the cheap end of the fantasy genre. 'In your stories . . . man is a moral child, because you who tell them are yourself a moral child. Those who so love your books are moral children, too. For them the world's too much.'

For the 1980s, Rudkin was too much. David Rose jumped ship to the new Channel Four, and Rudkin made only two more TV appearances for the rest of the decade. Fearful of getting its fingers burned on such a scale again, the Beeb wound in their commitment to dramatic experiment. Many argued they were throwing out the ambitious baby with the pretentious bathwater, lamenting the loss of 'the right to fail' – a noble mantra that unfortunately just served to drive home that final, four-letter word in the ears of executives who heard it. As time went by, though, even they came to agree that something special had been lost: the sort of television Nancy Banks-Smith once described as 'made with great skill, devotion, beauty . . . and no mercy.'[356]

# HILL STREET BLUES (1981–7)
## NBC (MTM)

### The cop show disintegrates, and reassembles.

*No matter how well intentioned you are when you go out to do a cop show, it's almost impossible not to end up with a bag of shit afterward.*

Michael Kozoll, co-creator, *Hill Street Blues*

THE GREAT BREAKTHROUGH IN police drama, the one that separates the old world of wisecracking maverick gumshoes from the new world of fallible folk desperately holding the fort, is often depicted as instantaneous. One minute Kojak is inhaling kids' lollipops and shouting for Crocker, the next Captain Frank Furillo is contending with an officer down, a rogue lawyer and pressure from his ambitious junior staff to take early retirement all at once. The gulf between crime on the screen and on the street decisively narrowed overnight. Things were more gradual than that.

Upon his appointment as President of NBC in 1978, Fred Silverman began shopping around for a police programme with grit. Cinematic portrayals of crime-fighting had taken a dive into the seedy and morally dubious over the past few years. Silverman felt this should be reflected with something a few degrees tougher than recent hits like *The Rockford Files* and *Police Woman*. At MTM Productions, Steven Bochco and Michael Kozoll, veteran writers of *Quincy, Columbo* and *Ironside*, envisioned a cop show that worked like a soap opera: one that didn't reset at the end of each episode; where the characters remembered, evolved, became worn down and grew before the viewer's eyes.

In Britain this was nothing new – Troy Kennedy Martin's *Z-Cars* had turned this trick on the BBC nearly twenty years ago – but the American crime drama was firmly cast in self-contained, heroic mode. Bochco and Kozoll looked to other genres. Workplace banter and social unease were there in sitcoms like *M\*A\*S\*H* and *Barney Miller*, which also had an ethnically mixed cast that avoided stereotype, with its liberal ex-Marine and African-American sergeant who wrote memoirs on the side.

To this soft soap they added harsh abrasives. Their previous collaboration, *Delvecchio*, was a routinely episodic story where Judd Hirsch had the guilty banged up by the epilogue. But Delvecchio had compassion. Not the 'tough love' one-liners of the old school 'tecs', staring into the middle distance and musing tritely on the bad hand life had dealt the scum they'd apprehended, before grabbing a Danish and wiping the moral slate clean. This was full-blown liberalism: a constant burden on the conscience of the law, bullishly masked with streetwise gags and worldly cross-talk. In *Hill Street Blues*, this wit was distributed among everyone: cops, gangsters, hookers and Puerto Rican kids alike drew crystal clear epigrams from deep wells of bitter experience. Then, just when it looked like the cast were going to collapse under the weight of their own lay wisdom, they started playing infantile pranks against each other with candy cockroaches and butcher's offal. The creators themselves exhibited an unquenchable thirst for toilet humour, getting scatology into the script as often as Program Practices would allow. This was an indulgence, but it still contributed to reality – the gents' toilet became an unofficial secondary briefing room, much like in a real station.

Much like a real captain, Frank Furillo (Daniel J. Travanti) was besieged on all fronts, taking it from his own men, his superiors and the press as much as from the criminal element. He didn't make things any easier for himself by conducting a dangerous affair with the station's resident public defender. Joyce Davenport (Veronica Hamel) was a new type, the tough but glamorous high-flying professional woman, a role so enticingly fresh it just had to be trodden into cliché by the end of the decade. At the other end of just about every scale, Lt. Howard Hunter was a special weapons zealot who made John Wayne look like Jimmy Carter. A character who could so easily have become a *Police Academy* punchline was redeemed by a writers' campaign of strategic humiliation, from losing an assault tank to impotence and a cancer scare, and an Emmy-nominated performance from James B. Sikking. Even walk-on parts were carefully considered. It was a living, breathing, farting, swearing world.

The most immediately striking thing about *Hill Street Blues* was the way it looked. Much of this was down to line producer Greg Hoblit and director Robert Butler. The network's model for the series was recent Paul Newman vehicle *Fort Apache: The Bronx*, a popular but unspectacular slice of ghetto sleaze that used industrial no man's land locations to good effect, but suffered from banal direction. Butler had a hatred for the traditional visual syntax of establishing shot followed by cuts back and forth between two characters who politely took it in turns to do the talking. It was unreal, lethargic and deadly dull.

Butler's visual bible was *The Police Tapes*, a 1977 PBS documentary covering the same locale as *Fort Apache*, but shot on a smudgy portable video camera, giving a frustratingly messy, chaotic view of street confrontation. To ape this look as closely as possible, Butler suggested black-and-white 16mm film stock full of bobbing and weaving camera moves.[357] The network insisted on full colour 35mm like every other show, but allowed the hand-held work to remain. Like *World in Action*'s Tim Hewat, Butler abhorred polish as the enemy of realism. 'Don't use the stuff once the shot has settled down,' he told his editors. 'Use the bad stuff. It's terrific.'[358] The result was an atmospheric cacophony of muted colour, woozy motion and competitive yammering, plunging the viewer into the urban maelstrom right from the opening moments of Sgt Esterhaus's quick-fire morning roll call. It took more mental effort than *Kojak* demanded, but the rewards were far greater.

*Hill Street Blues* had a troublesome birth. The first season thrilled the critics and surfed a tidal wave of Emmy nominations, but ratings were dire. It took network goodwill, and not a little creative bartering, to ensure a second run of thirteen episodes. Hoblit reckoned it was 'the lowest-rated renewed show in the history of television.'[359] Even after it became a fixture, things remained dicey. A Writers' Guild strike in 1982 took its toll on the quality of the scripts, as did network insistence that more story strands come to a satisfactory conclusion by the end of each episode. Quality began to decline, and stunts covered the cracks. The seventh and final season didn't even figure in the Emmy nominations for outstanding drama – a flop by the show's lofty standards. But its bold synthesis of difficult elements lasted as long as could be reasonably expected against television's glide into blandness.

The show established a new direction for mainstream drama. Its influence remains tangible, though not all its imitators flatter. Butler's camerawork is probably the most obvious legacy, its ubiquity bordering on infamy. Some time in the late 1990s, hand-held camera became the default visual aesthetic for TV drama. It wasn't restricted to street locations: before long even period drama was dripping with shaky telephoto takes. A generation of hacks discovered a way to add visual interest, even a sense of urgency, with minimal expense and creative effort. The style seeped into sitcoms, game shows, even cheery commercials for bingo websites. A bold directorial risk had grown into a cheap, context-free add-on, as much a part of the optical furniture as the use of close-ups or colour. What began as an augmentation of already highly advanced realism became, at worst, a lazy substitute for it.

*Hill Street Blues* also pioneered, in its own modest way, another twenty-first century mainstay: online audience interaction. The producers hooked up with *The Source*, a primitive information exchange service used by roughly 17,000 computer users, inviting them to share and discuss their opinions on the series as it played out over the season.[360] *The Source*'s effect on the show might have been minimal, but the willingness to listen to and cater for a discerning, educated and – hopefully – loyal band of fans would, thirty years on, become a priority for TV dramas faced with shrinking budgets and multiplying competitors, finding it all the more important to heed Sgt Esterhaus's motto: 'Let's be careful out there.'

# THE OXFORD ROAD SHOW (1981–5)

## BBC Two

### When 'youth' TV tried far too hard.

FOLLOWING PUNK'S EXPLOSION OF discord and nasal haberdashery, questions were asked of television's predilection to douse the kids with non-stop rhythmic licentiousness. *Broadcasting and Youth*, a 1979 report commissioned by various organisations including the BBC and IBA, concluded that 'the 14-21 age group does have needs distinct from the totality of the adult population' not adequately served by TV, which was 'offering "circuses" when what they need is "bread".' For the next decade, the video toaster went into overdrive.

The first specimen, Chris Tarrant's *Kidsworld,* was a magazine programme which aimed to serve the kids' needs by putting them in charge. In a phrase that was to become wearyingly familiar, it was 'a magazine for young people, presented by young people'. *The London Weekend Show* was a spin-off from LWT's Friday news magazine *The Six O'Clock Show*, masterminded by Janet Street-Porter. 'London's fast-moving programme for young people' covered everything from pirate radio to Barry Sheene to 'why more and more children are burning down their schools'.

BBC One's *Something Else* opened with a timely montage of Damned posters and venereal disease leaflets. Its content was decided by a hundred-strong teenage panel, from which its presenters were drawn. A typical edition featured collectively written and performed sketches interspersed with public information films on what you could legally get up to at the age of fifteen, and music from Sad Café and Secret Affair (the choice of bands was also rigorously put to the vote).

Such a doggedly democratic programme could justly claim to be 'by teenagers for teenagers'. 'What the kids on *Something Else* have got that TV producers obviously lack,' said the *NME*'s Phill McNeill, 'is *empathy*. I mean, suppose you forget about technical wizardry, fancy dress audiences and pristine studios, and just put a band in a conducive situation in front of a small, genuinely responsive audience and then *concentrate on getting the best out of the group!* Y'know, it might just work . . .'[361]

Janet Street-Porter's next LWT venture, *20th Century Box*, was a programme 'for and about young people' made, in modish black-and-white, in association with the London Minorities Unit. The first series tackled an uneven mixture of hobbies and 'issues' from dog grooming to incest. It stood out in two ways: it boasted a slick graphical title sequence to the music of John Foxx, and a genuinely smart and personable presenter, Danny Baker.

The high spot was a look at 'the growth of gang fights in the towns and villages around Watford and Aylesbury,' which, in its hilariously bathetic scenes of bored rural skinheads telephoning desperately around to try and organise a regional rumpus for the cameras, said more about teenagers' lives than any number of hard-hitting urban exposés. The *Observer* predicted Baker, with presumably laudatory intent, would be 'a cockney Parkinson for the 1990s'.

The mutual suspicion between television and youth was crippling. Nevertheless, 1981 saw the advent of the longest-lived, and most reviled, of the right-on youth magazines. Again, The Kids were consulted at every step. After punk, TV's relationship to youth culture had gone beyond anthropology and was now in the realm of quantum experimentation: the very act of observation skewed the results. When the BBC's *Arena* arts strand made a study of earnest New Wavers Sham 69, the small hand-held camera they deployed to cover a gig (operated by Philip Bonham-Carter, brother of Helena) spurred some skinheads to comprehensively break up the place, and helped the band itself implode.

Broadcast from the BBC's Manchester studios on Oxford Road, 'opposite Amigo's Café and just past the faulty traffic lights,' *The Oxford Road Show* promised to be 'a live and lucid look at the week.' Its main presenters were a trifle doddery: Rob Rohrer, ex-*Sunday Times* Insight journalist, and former Cambridge Footlights performer Martin Bergman ('the thinking man's David Frost') lacked Baker's street cred, but were soon joined by the more youthful Jackie Spreckley and Paula Yates.

After a quiet try-out, a rejigged second series, this time with Spreckley and Robert Elms as main presenters, was trumpeted abroad. 'Every Friday there will be 150 people on the set sounding off, questioning, caring and generally carrying on in a way that's bound to upset some older viewers,' reported John Craven. 'Because involvement is what the show is all about, the Manchester switchboard will be open until 9 p.m. after the programme for reactions,' he explained, 'and if they choose to ignore it in their millions they can, in the words of the production team, "belt up about the fact that TV doesn't cater for them or provide a platform for their views".'[362]

This effort to silence derision was doomed, with the hapless enthusiasm of the presenters provoking the worst brickbats. 'Robert Elms poses as the representative for happy vacuity,' sniped Ian Penman. 'When he smiles one fears that his whole face shall disappear between his teeth.'[363] One correspondent attacked the general patronising youth tone in spookily modern terms, bemoaning 'the great levelling-down fever that grips much of the communication industry today'.[364] Clive James identified youth presenters' propensity 'to talk a strenuously classless language from which all consonants have been removed.'[365] All identified a condescending insincerity – a trendy vicar in a studded dog collar.

It wasn't just critics who mocked. In an attempt to leaven the earnest debate, the *Road Show* booked alternative comics including

Ben Elton, Adrian Edmondson and Rik Mayall. They exacted their revenge the following year in the pilot episode of student sitcom *The Young Ones*, creating *Nozin' Aroun'*, a painfully hip programme 'for YOUNG ADULTS, by YOUNG ADULTS'. ('I'm standing up here on this scaffolding because that's what this programme is all about: shock!') After that, the show had a drastic clear-out, putting Radio One veteran Peter Powell in charge of 'TV's electronic magazine', now chummily abbreviated to *ORS*. The final 1985 run went for broke with different celebrity hosts each week and a phone-in Megaquiz captained by Timmy Mallett.

Youth TV soldiered on. BBC2's *Sixteen Up* air-dropped the likes of lawyer Paul Boateng into regional coffee bars with modish names like The Negative Café and Action Space for some heartfelt civil rights chit-chat, 'with interruptions from John Cooper Clarke,' a sort of apocalyptic Ollie Beak. The *Observer* judged it 'remorselessly glum'. Channel Four contributed *Whatever You Want*, the most radical show of all, which lured the kids with the promise of Wham!, and hit them with lengthy political discussions chaired by Keith Allen. Some small infamy was achieved when a vicar stormed out as fringe actors simulated sex on stage. Then Allen made history when, in protest at the butchering of a film on trade unions, he stormed out of his own show.

Such transgressions were the exception for a format that, much as it denied it, had more in common with a church youth club than street-level insurrection. In the late eighties it retreated into precisely that pious mantle, as ex-choirboy Aled Jones interviewed reformed glue sniffers for HTV's *Chatterbox*. When Jonathan Meades visited the set, he discovered a sinister green room containing 'more orange squash than I've ever seen.'[366] Maybe this was what the kids wanted all along.

# JANE (1982–4)
## BBC Two

### The apotheosis of television's flagship special effect.

THE STORY IS TOLD of Andrew Gosling, young and enthusiastic television director with a keen interest in technology, on the set of 1978 Christmas fantasy special *The Light Princess*. His task for the day was to initiate Irene Handl, veteran actress of stage and screen, scion of European aristocracy and obsessive Elvis Presley fan, into the mysteries of Colour Separation Overlay.

'You see,' he began, 'I shall be filming you against this blue screen. Now, at the editing stage, a special electronic device will remove the blue from the picture and replace it with all the wonderful phantasmagoria our animators can dream up, so it will look as if you're standing in the middle of this fantastical realm. All you have to do is . . .'

'I'm sorry, dear,' interrupted Irene, 'you're confusing me . . .'

'Ah. OK, look at it this way, then. The television picture is made up of hundreds of lines . . .'

'No, no,' came the reply. 'I mean, you're confusing me with an actress who gives a fuck.'

So it ever was. CSO (or, for those operating outside the wilfully idiosyncratic BBC's nomenclature, Chroma Key) defined the look of television, be it in dense scientific lectures, experimental dramas or slapstick sketch shows, for a generation. Whenever TV felt the desire to explain the workings of this omnipresent process, however – and it happened a lot, especially on children's programmes – fidgety incomprehension and glazed eyes were the result. But even if they weren't aware of the skill involved, everyone came to know the harsh, acidic fizz which took hold of the screen whenever it was employed.

Technology improved all the time. As well as advances in the 'box of tricks' itself, lights and cameras became ever more powerful and sensitive. Even so, certain problems would always arise. Most noticeably, the electronic gate separating foreground from background was very strict – each pixel was judged to be either one or the other. Hence anything blurred or rough on the outline of your foreground subject – diaphanous clothing, hair, shadows, spectacle lenses, a physics lecturer's beard – had a tendency to fox the electronics, which would allocate it foreground status one instant, and relegate it to the background the next. You had to work hard to avoid the subject breaking up into a feverish swarm of electronic midges.

Other shortcomings required meticulous planning. Unless you had days to spend in the studio lining up sets, actors and background artwork (and you didn't), errors of scale crept in, angles became contorted, and perspective went for a Burton. Despite your best efforts, colours and lighting angles were doomed to clash, giving the effect of a moving collage of random cut-out photographs from colour supplements. To get that blue screen nice and clear, lighting tended toward the over-bright and the flat, limiting dramatic possibilities. And any camera movement was right out.

These issues combined to give the 'Chroma look' to vast swathes of television. Fantasy serials and weather forecasts took on a visual kinship that wasn't necessarily flattering to either. Nevertheless, in the early days of colour television it was the number one new toy, and prone to pop up everywhere. As John Beveridge, videotape editor for *Nationwide* and consequently no stranger to the process, cautioned in 1975, 'it is just a tool of our time. It should be put in a drawer and only used where there is good reason.'

In the view of James MacTaggart, a producer with a strong antipathy to naturalism, drama provided many good reasons. His 1973 adaptation of Voltaire's *Candide* used CSO in every shot, founding the short-lived genre of the blue screen epic. Ian Ogilvy's eponymous delusional optimist tripped gaily from one hand-drawn set-piece to another while Frank Finlay, as Voltaire himself, took charge of the paper environment, at one point literally drawing a discreet veil over a bedroom scene. It was praised as 'the work that took the medium a step nearer its future,'[367] though not everyone was convinced by the technique. 'Maybe irony isn't televisable,' mused John Carey, 'but a firmer substitute for it than these doll's house droolings could surely have been managed.' For him the cartoon backgrounds overwhelmed the foreground, and had an adverse effect on the cast. 'Actors seemed to have been left over from when they cast *Whoops Baghdad*, and to imagine that the same sort of effect would be welcome here.'[368]

The tendency of these dramas towards pantomime was perhaps inevitable – outlandish scenery (which the actors couldn't see anyway) encouraged gigantic performances. MacTaggart's second bite at the blue screen cherry was *Alice in Wonderland*, a more fittingly over the top subject. Piers Haggard picked another appropriate source with his *Chester Mystery Plays*, placing his mumming actors, including Michael Hordern as God, into the warped anti-perspectives of medieval religious paintings (which handily got round the perennial scale problem).

After that, the technique was largely relegated to children's fantasy fare. (Although it remained strong in the gaudier reaches of Italian television, where all-dancing extravaganzas like *Tilt* and *Chromakey Follies* were awash with electrical fizz.) Andrew Gosling did give it one last 'adult' hurrah, however, when the curious decision was made to adapt *Jane* for television. The original wartime *Daily Mirror* comic strip chronicled the misadventures of an accident-prone blonde who habitually found herself behind enemy lines with no clothes on. Simultaneously quaint and creepy, it was such a relic of its time that any revival could only take place under a thick crust of irony. Which is where the blue screen came in.

Gosling and designer Graham McCallum took the comic strip

element literally, boxing Paul Birkbeck's elegant art deco illustrations in tight areas of the screen, and draining the colour from the live action elements (mainly Glynis Barber in assorted camisoles) just enough to mute the usual retina-scorching electronic palate to a more restful wartime sepia. As a ten-minute frippery it more than fulfilled its remit, 'a sprightly bit of nonsense told more delicately than one could have expected.'[369]

Shortly after the sequel, *Jane in the Desert*, digital effects superseded the bare-bones Chroma Key set-up, and the visual aspect of TV moved inexorably closer to unmitigated realism. More recently, though, the coloured screens have made a comeback, as effects overtake location shooting in terms of value for money. Directors are ever more required to brush up their technical chops, and actors can no longer exercise the Handl Defence. The possibilities are endless once more, though only the skill of the writer can decide whether digitally augmented drama will be a flight into the imaginative wilderness or just a flashier heap of doll's house droolings.

# BOYS FROM THE BLACKSTUFF (1982)

## BBC One

### The North rises, again.

'TELEVISION DRAMATIST' MAY BE a legitimate career these days, studied in universities and taught in creative writing courses, but until recently it was more something for writers to fall into on the way to and from other things.

Alan Bleasdale stumbled into drama via the stories he wrote, after sifting through uninspiring published alternatives for the slow learners he taught at a Huyton secondary modern. Franny Scully, the hero of the tales, was a disenfranchised but smart, put-upon yet indefatigable amalgam of his pupils and the near-legendary exploits they relayed to him in class. Bleasdale soon picked up a voice for Scully, a breathing, scheming entity rooted in life, who graduated from hosting his own radio show to infiltrating otherwise misbegotten Saturday morning kids' jamboree *The Mersey Pirate*. Bleasdale would later reflect that latching onto Scully's personality at the start of his career stopped him becoming 'sub-Beckett, sub-Pinter for the rest of my life.'[370]

His voice matured with *The Black Stuff*, the tale of five lads in the building trade whose decision to do a 'foreigner' – a crafty cash-in-hand extra job using their firm's 'borrowed' time and equipment – ends in calamity. The series that grew from there, exploring the subsequent struggles of each of them in the tanking labour market, was depressingly timely. In the decade to 1982 employment in Liverpool fell by nearly a third. Tapping directly into a national fear via a regional crisis, *Boys from the Blackstuff* outgrew its Sunday night slot on BBC Two and was repeated in full fig on the main channel for an audience of up to eight million. Kids who'd developed a palate for this sort of drama via the likes of *Minder* lapped up at least some of its expansive imagery, though its physical manifestation, the playground Yosser Hughes head butt, did little for its educational rep.

The apolitical Bleasdale dropped the baggage of northern drama and struck out on a more personal, simultaneously more and less real, course which perfectly matched the awful absurdity of the state of Merseyside, seemingly abandoned by the rest of the country. Two of the sharpest ears in the business gathered anecdotes, attitudes and patterns of speech fresh from the front, and with plenty of input from the actors, five solid characters emerged from behind the DHSS grilles, from Michael Angelis's slowly drowning Chrissie Todd to Bernard Hill's bricklaying Titanic Yosser Hughes.

The production was almost as strapped for cash as its subjects. Still the default medium for quality drama, film was out of the question for all five shows, with video – the sharp and tacky stuff of soap opera – the only viable alternative. Only Yosser, the most lost of them all, was granted the mythical soft light and grain of film, a fitting atmosphere for his quixotic bouts of violent self-assertion. His cohorts, denied the luxury of full mental breakdown, were stuck on unforgiving videotape.

Philip Saville, a TV director with an apprenticeship stretching back to the dawn of ITV, was a keen experimenter who adored the lurid sheen of video. His 1964 *Hamlet at Elsinore* set the Dane on his home turf in moonlit chiaroscuro, and he was the first of the drama department to start fiddling with the new 'pick-a-back' electronic news gathering kit in 1974's *The Actual Woman*. For *Blackstuff*, he was given the BBC's latest acquisition to play with – a fully-fitted multi-camera mobile location unit which could capture the performances with the pin-sharp, wide-angle, bleached-out accuracy of sports coverage. Using tape rather than film preserved the sense of immediacy viewers knew from sport and, increasingly, current affairs reports. Saville could stretch and distort his shots with Grand Guignol flourishes and the thing was still visually locked somewhere between a riot and a second division match. Life on the social was a dismal sport, happening now.

'What were you doing during the Toxteth riots?' 'Well, I was down the supermarket quite a lot.' The Boys aren't comic types, they're semi-pro comedians. Deftly avoiding the rarefied pity-from-on-high of the earnest poverty play, Bleasdale shows the man first, and gets the social comment from his mouth, not over his head. He never slips into sentimental editorialising, even when the symbolism is spelt out, as when Snowy the proud Marxist artisan plasterer is literally killed by mass-produced shoddiness. Bleasdale knows the dramatist gets nowhere by battering stoic ciphers about, so his Liverpool becomes a music hall approached via the sewers. These are boys you could get on with in the pub.

But not the Green Man, where they repair after giving old socialist George the final send-off – an inferno full of sacked bouncers and faded speciality acts reduced to inebriated self-parodies by lunchtime, with the occasional frenzied redundancy party turning the ambience from Breughel to Bosch. This maelstrom of menace, psychosis and bird impressions was broadcast as the rest of the country's media either tossed off platitudinous editorials on the 'Liverpool situation' – treating Liverpudlians literally as boys, like teachers muttering about a problem child – or washed their hands of the matter entirely. 'They should build a fence around it and charge admission,'[371] as the *Daily Mirror* notoriously put it. *Boys from the Blackstuff* was a more humane alternative to that sort of brutal instruction. If you took the right cues, you *could* make it up.

# ST ELSEWHERE (1982–8)
## NBC (MTM Enterprises)
### The chance encounter of realism and whimsy on an operating table.

THE PRODUCTION COMPANY FOUNDED in 1969 by Mary Tyler Moore and Grant Tinker gave American comedy and drama new texture: intricate, realistic, innovative; but also, to some, overly playful and indulgent. No series of theirs embodied this double-edged quality better than hospital drama *St Elsewhere*. The show began as, to all intents and purposes, Hill Street Wards. The *Hill Street Blues* formula was first tried out in 1979 pilot *Operating Room*, following the intertwining travails of three doctors in an LA hospital. NBC and MTM mulled over where to take this odd but promising concept, with Fred Silverman, as ever, having the final word. 'Let's try it as a cop show first, and if it works we'll do it with doctors.'[372]

They didn't even wait to see if it worked. With *Hill Street Blues* still bouncing along the bottom of the ratings charts after its first season, NBC gave producer Bruce Paltrow the go-ahead to make the medical version, now relocated to St Eligius: a crumbling, cash-starved teaching hospital on the wrong side of the Boston tracks. The three senior medics were kitted out with stories that, in précis, looked like pure cliché: Dr Westphall (Ed Flanders) was a widower with a severely autistic son; Dr Auschlander (Norman Lloyd) a liver specialist with incurable liver cancer. Then there was

Dr Craig (William Daniels), the most brilliant heart surgeon of his generation who, naturally, found the hearts of healthy people, his family and colleagues especially, an unfathomable mystery. It sounded like sub-*Kildare* soap, but Paltrow's writers, especially story kingpins John Falsey, Joshua Brand and John Masius, were adept at spinning gold from corn.

The many hospital dramas television had minted so far all featured the same elements: heroic senior doctors, awe-struck nurses, surgical races against time and an all-round setting of finely-chiselled profiles against the encroachment of death. Any viewer who'd spent time in a hospital knew this was nothing like the reality. Heroism was absent. Treatments didn't so much race to a nail-biting conclusion as involve hours of aimless hanging about. And never mind the ailment you came in with: shonky equipment, staff shortages and lack of funding were equally prevalent threats to existence. Drama, of the brow-mopping, double-door-crashing, defibrillator-clearing strain, was in short supply. Real hospitals exuded a weird, shapeless melancholy atmosphere that nobody, perhaps quite sensibly, had tried to condense into an hour of television before.

The pilot swarmed with exhausted medics, graphic descriptions of acute dysentery, low-level racism, doctors passing off patients on others, snatched romantic interludes in the morgue and general non-stop intra-staff bickering. Doctors were lazy, lustful, jealous, prejudiced and – the biggest taboo – variously incompetent. The assorted students presented as jokily frivolous (Dr Fiscus, played by stand-up Howie Mandel); bumblingly privileged (Dr Ehrlich, Ed Begley Jr.) right down to the resident pill-popping rapist (Dr White, Terence Knox). Taking its lead from Paddy Chayefsky's cynical 1971 film *The Hospital*, *St Elsewhere* established a new benchmark for realism in medical drama – *M\*A\*S\*H* notwithstanding – from the beginning.

Almost immediately, it set about breaking that realism up. While the subject matter became ever more daring – including the first appearance of an AIDS storyline in late 1983 – the playful house style of MTM Productions began to assert itself with ever more extreme results. The usual trickle of in-jokes became a flood. Characters would appear or be paged with names familiar from a host of other TV shows, past and present, or (often suffering from embarrassing ailments) the names of network executives. Lines which seemed like plain non-sequiturs to most would, to the TV adept, be revealed as arcane references to old sitcoms, films or, as the show built up its own mythology after a few seasons, old episodes of *St Elsewhere* itself. Mandel reckoned this play-along aspect created a new hybrid genre, the 'drama game-show'.[373]

Occasionally the references threatened to take over. In one episode an amnesiac becomes convinced he's Mary Tyler Moore, and casts his fellow patients as Rhoda, Phyllis *et al*. In another, the three senior doctors repair to a bar across town, which happens to be Cheers. There they chat with Norm, Cliff and Carla from the NBC sitcom, in dialogue that drips with that show's expected wisecracks, although shorn of audience laughter and shot in *St Elsewhere*'s relentlessly grim visual style; America's favourite bar for a moment looks like a stagnant purgatory full of losers. On other occasions the conceit swamped the story. An episode where Fiscus, hovering between life and death, hallucinates a whimsical *Divine Comedy* populated by deceased characters from the series, ended with its flighty protagonist vowing to stick more closely to the straight and narrow in future. Some viewers were left wishing the writers would make the same pledge. The small art of deconstruction and the greater art of character development came together perfectly in 'Time Heals', a virtuoso two-parter in which fiftieth anniversary celebrations for the hospital trigger a series of personal memories for various characters going back through the decades to the opening of the place in the thirties. Past traumas shed light on well-known characters as they're relived (Dr Westphall's wife's death, Dr Craig's disastrous first operation) and social points are deftly made (the hospital is revealed to have been falling apart almost as soon as it went up). The dexterous use of visual cues to trigger flashbacks and the neat circular structure satisfy without shouldering the story into the background. Like the hospital itself, *St Elsewhere* somehow survived six seasons of dire ratings, relying on award nominations and the good favour of executives for a stay of execution. After a standoff over budgets in 1987, the end finally loomed, which raised the problem of exactly what that would look like. Finishing a continuing series is never satisfactory. Either the whole thing goes over the top to outdo the combined effect of what's gone before, or things peter out in an overly sentimental dimming of the lights. After toying with ideas ranging from Westphall confessing to the Kennedy assassination and a full-on nuclear holocaust,[374] the producers decided that the show that lived by self-reference should die by self-reference.

After a (relatively) sober parting of the ways for the staff, a strange coda was tacked on, recasting Auschlander, Westphall and Westphall's autistic son Tommy as a blue-collar family worrying over Tommy's constant fixation with a toy snow globe. The final shot of the series revealed the globe to contain a tiny model of St Eligius, implying the entire six series had been the boy's crazily elaborate daydream. Even more so than the end of *The Prisoner*, which nobody truly hoped to see neatly tied up, it was a masterclass in burning artistic bridges, undercutting years of accumulated drama with one last table-upsetting caprice.

It was also the kind of ending that could only be conceived in the days when TV drama was still ephemeral – syndication aside, everything was bet on the first transmission of every episode, after which all concerned simply moved on to something new. As cable channels became a low(er) pressure proving ground for drama, and the box set recast it as a permanent work of art, producers would have a little more control over when and how their creations came to an end, and bewildering reversals like *St Elsewhere*'s would fall decisively out of fashion (although the last few minutes of *The Sopranos* came close to bringing them back). The end of a long-running series will always sound a note of compromise and self-indulgence, and sabotaging everything you've created at the final hurdle is just another form of conceit. It's also part of a long artistic tradition: as Max Beerbohm observed when Ibsen summarily killed off an artist in his final play, 'It is but another instance of his egoism that he has reserved his most vicious kick for himself.'[375]

# THE TUBE (1982–7)

## Channel Four
## (Tyne Tees Television)

### The music show that talked itself off the air.

Producers of youth programmes were used to being mocked for their 'groovy teacher' attitudes. In one case, such criticism had a point. At Ryhope School near Sunderland, Mr Malcolm Gerrie, 'Fuzzy' to his pupils, was a drama teacher with ambitions for the annual school play above and beyond the usual plywood-backed run-through of *Oliver!* His mammoth 1974 production of *Tommy* garnered the attention of the *NME*. The following year he topped it with a gargantuan version of the David Essex rock parable *Stardust*. Russell Harty of ITV's *Aquarius* arts programme marvelled at his effortless stewardship of a hundred-strong cast, baths full of dry ice and a revolving stage holding three different sets.

Having exhausted the possibilities of academic show business, Gerrie handed in his elbow patches and decamped to Tyne Tees, working on the production teams of youth-oriented shows such as *Check It Out* ('issues and news for the under-twenties') and *Alright Now* ('Big Den Hegarty hosts a happy half-hour of rock, pop, punk and funk'). In 1981 he gave children's ITV its most successful pop format since *Supersonic*. *Razzamatazz* was billed as 'a *Ready Steady Go!* for the teenyboppers of the eighties,' though Gerrie's description was more accurate: 'a rock 'n' roll party in a Rupert Bear environment.'

On a set decorated with clouds and rainbows, presenters Alastair

Pirrie and Lyn Spencer (later joined by a young Lisa Stansfield) introduced Kate Bush and Kiki Dee, items on roller discos and electronic T-shirts, Popscotch (a hopscotch-based competition involving kids jumping on images of pop stars' faces) and the Human Jukebox Man, who claimed to sing any song if you stuffed ten pence in his mouth. With the inky warhorses of the music press fast losing circulation to the shiny, knowingly naive *Smash Hits*, Gerrie's bubbly confection chimed perfectly with the times.

*Razzamatazz* impressed enough for Channel Four's Jeremy Isaacs to approach Fuzzy about making something a little more fifth-form. The commission was broad, and Gerrie broadened it further still: what began as a brief for eight half-hour magazine programmes ended up as twenty compendiums of live music and features running 105 minutes each. 'You've got the freedom to fail,' Isaacs told Gerrie. 'Just make sure you make it lively and give it some balls.' Gerrie, with fond *Ready, Steady, Go!* memories still fresh in his mind after two decades, knew what he wanted.

Scaffolding was erected, presenters were cast: dapper ex-Squeeze keyboardist Jools Holland, who struck just the right mock-formal tone and exuded a singular kind of laid-back anxiety; and Paula Yates, whose pop credentials included a long-running *Record Mirror* column, but who was still best known for her relationship with Bob Geldof and best-selling book *Rock Stars in Their Underpants*. They were assisted, in time-honoured fashion, by a rotating line-up of five 'rookies' recruited from over 3,000 applications. First, and longest lasting, was museum assistant Muriel Gray, who'd answered Tyne Tees's classified ad in the *NME*.

The inaugural edition of *The Tube* set out its stall with films on the LA music scene and African dance, alternating with valiantly uncool comedy monologues from Mark MiWurdz (né Hurst) and the latest video from Duran Duran. Holland interviewed Pete Townshend, Gray interviewed Paul Weller, and Yates 'chatted up' Sting on a double bed. The second half was devoted to live performances from The Jam and Heaven 17, whose keyboardist Martyn Ware neatly summed up proceedings: '[Tyne Tees] might lack a bit technically, but they more than make up for that with their enthusiasm.'

The normally sniffy music press were enthusiastic too. *The Tube*'s launch made the *NME* cover and inside, the verdict was one of mildly qualified praise. 'If the presentation can be given more pace and punch,' mused Adrian Thrills, '*The Tube* will be on the point of becoming the first pop show really worth watching in years.'[376] A note of dissent came, ineluctably, from Julie Burchill. 'The presenters are no Cathy McGowans, or even Aysheas,' she sniped, before exclusively revealing, 'I personally have turned down THREE OFFERS to present TV teen shows for the simple reason that at twenty-two I am simply TOO OLD to tell teenagers what's what. *The Tube* – the weekend stops here.'[377]

The show's temperament largely matched the post-punk scepticism of the record business. Holland, for instance, abandoned industry etiquette when he introduced Tears for Fears with: 'Here's a bunch of posers. If you want a cup of tea, now's the time to go and make it.' On the other hand, the lasting achievement of the show's first series was the kick-starting of Paul Young's solo career.

As *The Tube* grew in stature, so did the list of complaints. Paula Yates, linking the programme from the studio roof, blurted 'it's fucking freezing up here,' unaware she was on air. Holland surprised goth act Lords of the New Church by taking a camera unannounced into their dressing room, only to find singer Stiv Bators stark naked. Rik Mayall opened one edition by voiding a mouthful of vomit. Robbie Coltrane was doused with paraffin. Mel Smith complained the studio catering was 'worse than the fucking Beeb'. The phrase 'hamster turds' was uttered. Barely a week went by without the IBA having to deal with something on the show that caused outrage.

With its only other competition coming from Jonathan King's BBC2 vehicles *Entertainment USA* and *No Limits*, the latter sending 'its well-scrubbed teen hosts to sundry British towns accompanied for no fathomable reason by a soundtrack of bland stadium rock,'[378] *The Tube* was out on its own, but not everything was going well.

Andy Allan, Tyne Tees MD and the show's most influential champion, left for Central Television at the end of 1984. A wave of budget tightening followed, meaning cutbacks on trips to the States and the loss of annual late-night knees-up *A Midsummer Night's Tube*.

Then came 1986 spin-off *Come Dancing with Jools Holland*, a New Year's Eve hootenanny with a celebrity audience, featuring comedy from Mayall and Edmonson's Dangerous Brothers and the *Who Dares Wins* team, involving evocations of a woman pissing into a wok and sexual relations between newsreader Alastair Burnet and Prince Charles. Home Secretary Leon Brittan, in the audience with his wife, was apoplectic. Foreign Secretary Geoffrey Howe, watching at home, made a formal complaint to the IBA, resulting in instant sackings for producers Royston Mayoh and Peter McHugh under charges, later rescinded, of gross misconduct. It was made clear to Holland that he would have to watch his step from now on.

This he conspicuously failed to do on 16 January. Just before half past five, in between the Gold Runs of *Blockbusters*, Holland fronted the show's usual cheeky live trailer reminding the cooler viewers of ITV's sixth form quiz to switch channels immediately. After announcing The Mission, Michelle Shocked and Timbuk 3, he improvised a sign-off line. 'I said, "Be there . . ." then I thought I'm not going to say ". . . or be square" so I said "or be a completely ungroovy fucker!"' he later recounted. 'It just slipped out. I nearly said "Oh shit" directly afterwards which would really have clinched it.'[379] Tabloid consternation followed, bringing a six-week suspension for Holland and the second reprimand in a month from the IBA. One more and Tyne Tees's licence to broadcast would be 'seriously reconsidered'.

With its every move now subject to crippling restrictions, *The Tube* was mortally wounded. Everything was examined for potential offence. The band Stump were made to alter their lyrics on the show, to remove the words 'Tupperware' and 'gonads'. Gerrie handed in his resignation in February, but stayed to the end of what would be the final series, disgusted at 'a cold wave of puritanism blowing through the industry.' *The Tube*'s very final link summed up the once joyous programme's late-period frostiness. Paula hailed closing act Duran Duran as 'possibly the greatest band' they'd ever had on, prompting a grimace from Gray. 'Don't get any closer, Muriel,' retorted Yates. 'This isn't hot lesbo action time.' She was quite right – that was on Sundays after the racing.

# M*A*S*H: 'GOODBYE, FAREWELL AND AMEN' (1983)

## CBS (20th Century Fox Television)

### The sitcom takes its final bow seriously.

THE TELEVISION SERIES, BOTH comic and dramatic, told its story at two paces. The first was the obvious, episode-long tale, an hour or twenty-five minutes in length, which set out its stall with characters already familiar to the audience, developed the action and brought things to an amusing or satisfactory conclusion before the end credits. The second pace covered more ground. Smarter series didn't just reset everything at the start of the episode – characters and situations developed over the thirteen or twenty-odd episodes of the season. This wasn't a full-blown serial, where a missed or out of order episode could lead to utter confusion, but it did endow its characters (and credit the audience) with memories slightly longer than that of a goldfish. The 'story arc' had arrived.

In sitcoms, this was kept firmly in the background – nice to have that extra layer, but a casual viewer needed to be able to stumble across a random episode for the first time and not feel hopelessly confused. In the 1970s, when demographic targeting led to increasingly sophisticated sitcoms with more dramatic qualities and complex characters, the successful ones could afford to make more of their own history. A viewer who began watching *The Mary Tyler Moore Show* with 'The Last Show' might have got a chuckle out of the clumsy group hug, but the emotional impact would have eluded them. Shows can fall into a pit of their own indulgence: *Friends* dissolved into a chorus of mawkishly quivering goodbyes, while *St Elsewhere* double-crossed its entire existence. Generally the temptation to coast along on the store of sentimental goodwill accumulated over the years proves too good for the creatively exhausted makers to resist. One sitcom, which had been straining at the boundaries of its genre for over a decade, broke into pure psychological drama.

Robert Altman's 1970 film *MASH* was a loose – very loose – adaptation of *MASH: A Novel About Three Army Doctors*, a fictionalised memoir of a military surgeon's chaotic tenure in the US army's 4077th Mobile Army Surgical Hospital during the Korean War, reworked to comment on the then ongoing conflict in Vietnam. Altman's fluid camera and editing combined with Ring Lardner Jr's transcendentally caustic screenplay and some ultra-naturalistic acting to create a new type of Hollywood film comedy, grossing over $20 million. Distributor Twentieth Century Fox offered CBS the series rights, but network executives initially worried it might be 'too hip for television'.[380]

Military sitcoms were surprisingly common in the sixties, but they tended to omit one crucial aspect: death. *McHale's Navy*, *Gomer Pyle USMC* and especially PoW pantomime *Hogan's Heroes* didn't so much draw black humour from the horrors of war as turn the whole thing into one big, silly game between stuffy top brass and klutzes in the ranks. If there was to be any point to a *MASH* sitcom, this taboo would have to be skilfully broken.

Gene Reynolds, producer of the re-punctuated *M\*A\*S\*H*, enlisted writer Larry Gelbart, a TV veteran who started out on Sid Caesar's gag-writing team, to find a workable way to adapt Altman's bitter creation. The pair spent several weeks gathering situation and character ideas with a real MASH (this time the 8055th). The result was decidedly warmer than the film, though no less honest about the terror of the situation: medics larked about to keep themselves sane in between mortar attacks and waves of incoming wounded. All agreed the new template worked, but CBS still didn't know where to put it, initially scheduling it at 8 p.m. on Sunday opposite NBC's *Wonderful World of Disney*.

Sitcom conventions almost derailed the show. Creators were aghast at network insistence on a laugh track, and fought hard for it to be removed. Eventually a tepid compromise was reached, with CBS supplying an attenuated 'chuckle track' instead of the regulation torrent of hooting, which was respectfully switched off entirely during the operating theatre scenes. (A version with no laughter at all was shown by the BBC.) *M*A*S*H* soon became a national, then an international, favourite.

Gelbart left after the fourth season. His valedictory episode took every liberty with prime time comic practice. 'The Interview', patterned after a grim documentary made by Ed Murrow, was a semi-improvised affair based on 'in character' interviews conducted by an intern during free moments on set while filming the 'proper' episodes.[381] The result, complete with Father Mulcahy's unforgettable story of surgeons warming their hands in the steam from open wounds (a line directly taken from life), went out with no laugh track and in black and white.

After Gelbart departed, Alan Alda, established as the show's biggest star in the role of Lieutenant Benjamin Franklin 'Hawkeye' Pierce, became the driving creative force, directing and writing an increasing number of episodes himself. (Cast members Harry Morgan, Jamie Farr and Mike Farrell also got behind the camera.) The final episode, at the end of eleven seasons, was predominantly his work, and it was like no sitcom finale before or since.

Clocking in at over two hours minus commercials, 'Goodbye, Farewell and Amen' matched the original film for length and scope. For the most part, it was an emotionally charged tying up of loose ends and character stories in the manner of every sitcom finale before it. The haughty Charles Winchester finally engaged with the people whose country he was fighting to liberate. Cross-dressing discharge chaser Klinger married a local and stayed in Korea. After lasting three times the span of its real life counterpart, the TV Korean War came to an end, and several latrines were destroyed. All sound stuff, if unremarkable by the show's usual high standards.

Hawkeye's final story set it apart. He spends the first half of the programme in a mental hospital, as a psychiatrist homes in on the events of an ambushed charabanc outing to Inchon and what a civilian, overreacting to Hawkeye's desperate demand for silence, may or may not have done to what may or may not have been a chicken. All the small comforts of comedy were struck out of the frame in seconds: no small feat for a show that had made its name by giving and rescinding the reassurance of the sitcom, like a play-fully malicious parent proffering and suddenly withdrawing a dummy to a frustrated baby. No other sitcom, and few enough dramas, spent every episode in the shadow of death. Viewers may have thought they'd developed immunity after eleven seasons, but seeing the indestructible Hawkeye, previously always a cross between Superman and Groucho Marx by dint of his defiantly flippant worldview, brought to his knees was one last, magnificent, slap in the face.

The most widely publicised sitcom episode thus far received acres of pre-transmission press coverage and speculation on its tightly guarded contents. *M*A*S*H* had always bucked the American trend by combining fearless innovation with sky high ratings, but the last episode took things to a new level, reaching well over a hundred million viewers on transmission – three quarters of that night's audience – squarely beating previous record holder *Roots*.[382] That the top end of American TV popularity had such serious fare in it – with, of course, plenty of fluff like the shooting of J.R. as well – should have given the lie to US TV's dumbass international reputation but prejudices, as well as habits, died hard.

# SATURDAY NIGHT AFFAIRS (1984)
## BBC One

In which television is made by sticking some stars in a room, and then doing nothing.

From the moment George Orwell conceived the two-way telescreen, the thought of electronic voyeurism was tempting and terrifying. In 1956 maverick columnist Maurice Richardson, musing on the sort of programmes Britain's mooted third TV channel might show, decided the usual diet of drama and quizzes was old hat, and suggested 'a combination of concealed microphone and electronic eye, so that people could be televised without their knowledge, could be fascinating; but it is scarcely practicable; memories of Big Brother are too painful.'[383]

When Michael Parkinson vacated his beige swivel-throne in 1982, pundits predicted the end of the chat show. Said pundits can't have been paying much attention. From under Parky's dinosaur shadow scurried countless chattering mammals. Harty, Wogan and Aspel fought to unite their soft furnishings with the most exclusive showbiz bottoms. Breakfast television set commuters up for the day with nutritious anecdotes by the ton. Richardson had a phrase for chat show viewers, too: 'embarrassment perverts'.

With the market full of identikit mug-'n'-plug outlets, the BBC cast about for a celeb vehicle that could be called 'distinctive'. Its answer was 'a completely different new-style entertainment,' a star-studded mock party thrown at its Pebble Mill studios in honour of a distinguished guest, with a hundred other faces from their life paying tribute – some famous, some not; some aware of the cameras, some not. *Saturday Night Affairs* aimed to 'sidestep the set piece chat show and get natural entertaining conversation and music – just like you might get at a famous star's party.' Vidal Sassoon was lined up as the first guest of honour, with plenty of waspish indiscretion promised. 'There are no rules and no rehearsals,' said producer John King. 'There were times when I blushed to hear what they were saying.'[384]

At this point the fatal flaw of the enterprise became clear. King, Sassoon and pals were free to hear the juicy gossip and catty banter, as were the operators of the concealed cameras and mics. The forty-five minutes of each affair that made it to the screen, however, were of legal necessity the low calorie version. Beyond a minor spat between former *Generation Game* hosts Bruce Forsyth and Larry Grayson ('Oh, you're kidding,' groaned Brucie as the pair met at the studio doors. 'We're not walking on together!') and some digs at Richard Harris's prowess in the bedroom, the only distinction between this new-style chat and the school of Parky was its longueur-festooned aimlessness. Annie Ross asks Vidal if he knows Toyah Willcox. Vidal says no, he doesn't. The convivial ice remains stubbornly intact.

Next week was the turn of Dave Lee Travis. The public fled in droves, ignoring some encouraging critical notices. ('There has never been anything more gloriously awful in the history of television' – the *Guardian*.) The top brass hastily decided the party was over, leaving six editions untransmitted. We never got to see Pamela Stephenson's bash, which seemed the most likely to live up to the series' saucy ambitions, despite the Corporation vetoing her request for a drugs budget. (It was replaced with an emergency late film, *The Honkers*.) Or the party thrown by Spike Milligan, who wanted to invite people he hated, offer them bread and water and ignore them all evening. Or an entire forty-five minute celebration of the life and work of Lennie Bennett. It was the viewer's loss.

In hindsight, it's easy to see what *Saturday Night Affairs* lacked. Not the firm guiding hand of a seasoned chat show host, or some tighter editing to remove those shoe-gazing conversational cul-de-sacs – modern reality television is all but held together by awkward pauses and shifty coughs. What the new breed of all-star showcases have that *Affairs* didn't is the small but essential democratic element of *schadenfreude*.

'Presumably the champagne and prawns-the-size-of-lobsters, with which they were stuffing their faces,' inquired one disgruntled viewer, 'were paid for by millionaire Mr Sassoon himself and not by our licence fee?'[385] If only the stars had to sing, or do something much more demeaning, for their supper. 'There is a case for exhibiting people like Bruce Forsyth,' averred John Naughton, 'but *Affairs* provides the wrong kind of zoo for the job, not least because it insists on feeding its inmates.'[386] It would have been so much easier to stomach DLT fooling about with a set of bagpipes if the viewer had the knowledge that he could exact vengeance at a stroke, for the price of a premium rate phone call. But that quantum leap would have to wait.

# THREADS (1984)

## BBC Two

### The bleakest television programme ever made.

> *I want some of you to stumble, and some of you actually to keel over and give up . . . it's not a very pleasant scene. And please, don't forget to shiver.*
>
> Mick Jackson directs nuclear holocaust survivors, Cumbar Edge, Peak District, February 1984

THE SECOND HALF OF the twentieth century unfolded in the shadow of a potential disaster everyone over the age of seven knew about, but nobody could fully comprehend. Peter Watkins, recalcitrant producer of perfectly observed mock documentaries, delivered *The War Game* to the BBC in the wake of the Cuban Missile Crisis. Lucidly detailing the effects of nuclear attack on Britain, and the inevitably inadequate response the authorities could be expected to supply, it was refused transmission by the Director General Hugh Carleton Greene (with guidance from Harold Wilson's cabinet). It was, of course, suppressed in the name of children – in an unfortunate turn of phrase, Mary Whitehouse claimed it would 'blow their minds'.[387] For the next fifteen years, while ITV produced bomb programmes both avowedly anti-nuclear (John Pilger's *The Truth Game*) and unrepentantly hawkish (Max Hastings's *The War About Peace*), the BBC made *Nuclear Nightmares*, offering four plausible Armageddon scenarios rendered slightly more palatable by some turns from Peter Ustinov.

With Soviet aggression in Afghanistan sparking panic, the BBC acquired a new urgency. *QED: A Guide to Armageddon* detailed the effects of a one megaton warhead detonated a mile above St Paul's cathedral. Produced by James Burke's prime collaborator Mick Jackson, it used a variety of deadpan techniques – most effectively the deployment of ripe fruit and cuts of meat to demonstrate the effects of flying glass and intense heat on the populace – to give a sane, honest and horrific glimpse of the apocalypse that felt, at the time, like a racing certainty.

In 1984, Jackson took charge of a much grander apocalyptic affair – a two-hour drama showing the effects of an all-out superpower confrontation on the people of Sheffield. *Threads* was written by Barry Hines, unsentimental chronicler of the northern working classes best known for his study of disaffected youth and wistful escapism, *Kes*. It was a fortuitous pairing: Jackson dedicated to factual accuracy, Hines attuned to social bonds and human grief. They carefully avoided taking any overt political stance, Hines claiming 'it was my duty to be as even-handed as possible'. Besides, it wasn't as if the bare scientific facts needed any partisan garnish.

Their research took in a Home Office training course at Easingwold for the civil servants expected to try and maintain some semblance of civilisation, during which they encountered gallows humour among the delegates so dark it bordered on pathological denial. The futility of that exercise impressed on Hines the problem with dramatising the Big One: the enormousness and enormity of the statistics reduce individual lives to motes in a desert. In *Threads*, human scale is provided by the story of engaged couple Jimmy and Ruth (Reece Dinsdale and Karen Meagher), he an apprentice joiner and – in an echo of *Kes* – parakeet fancier, she a teacher heavily pregnant with their first child, who experience 'the suffering without the understanding'.[388]

The programme itself had to make some attempt at understanding. To this end Paul Vaughan, authoritative voice of *Horizon* documentaries, provided a minute-by-minute commentary, turning a melodrama into a public information film. Actual information films concerning survival measures – made by the Home Office but never transmitted – punctuate the days before the attack with their chillingly deadpan instructions on shelter and improvised burial.

There's black humour – or rather fearful irony – in abundance. The first warhead is notable for its effects on various characters' bladders. In a more subtle physical gag, a young man rendered speechless on sight of the first mushroom cloud instinctively brings hand up to mouth in a thumb-sucking gesture. Human nature asserts itself in ways more varied than the expected chorus of despair. Kids take to the flimsy homemade fallout shelters with giddy excitement. Sealed in their bunker under the town hall, councillors retain their political tribal instincts and buck-passing games, despite knowing full well there's little above ground to administrate. Spike Milligan's 1963 play *The Bed-Sitting Room* played the nuclear aftermath as surreal farce, and, despite being its polar opposite in tone, *Threads* sometimes looks weirdly similar in its depictions of normal life vainly continuing in the face of Armageddon: jolly test card muzak heralds the arrival of emergency TV broadcasts, and a fleeing family are advised: 'Make sure you turn the gas off. Don't want the whole street going up!'

Jackson evoked a city's destruction on a tiny budget. Model shots are whisked off the screen just before the viewer's eye starts to get suspicious, and memorably small details like melting milk bottles take the place of fiery panoramas. Tightly framed locations and reaction shots do the majority of the work special effects can't manage, and only a select few of those well-worn nuclear test images – the shockwave ripping through a barn, the row of trees mown down – are wheeled out. It's an impressionism born of economic necessity and Jackson's solid documentary training.

So far there's nothing here that wasn't already covered by the programme's American precursor, ABC's *The Day After*. What sets *Threads* apart from its peers is the second act, where we're taken through a decade of nuclear winter. Cameras track through an interminable wilderness of the dead and dying, mountains of rubble and charred bodies, both still and twitching. The style turns from kitchen sink science fiction into anthropological observation: the post-bomb generation communicate only in a few mangled phrases ('Gissit!' 'C'mooan!') and are routinely gunned down by the remnants of martial law for looting hunks of mouldy bread.

This New Stone Age contains odd, almost mocking relics of the twentieth century: a Casio computer game and Sainsbury's carrier bags have somehow survived the holocaust. With power generation making a ramshackle return, kids and pensioners gather in a dere-lict school to mouth inanely along to the last shred of twentieth century learning – a VHS of BBC literacy programme *Words and Pictures*. The jarring nature of these mundane remains help the viewer relate these fantastical scenes to the real world, in a way the sometimes hastily-sketched protagonists don't quite manage. In the closing scenes, Ruth's adolescent daughter, impregnated by sexual assault, gives painful birth alone in a derelict farmhouse to a hideously deformed homunculus. Championship darts from Redcar follows after the news.

*Threads* was broadcast on 23 September 1984 – although nobody knew it at the time, almost a year to the day that a catastrophic failure in the Soviet Union's early warning system mistook a NATO exercise for the start of the third world war, and came within a whisker of retaliation. The world remained blissfully ignorant of this incident, and the main charge against *Threads* came from those who felt such ignorance should be maintained. What good could come of rehearsing the end of civilisation, they asked, other than to alienate an already fearful public even further?

If anything, *Threads* had a unifying effect, both on those who girded their stomachs to watch it (it proved very popular with children, whose minds could take more blowing than Mrs Whitehouse anticipated), and those who took part. When Jackson and Hines held auditions for post-apocalyptic extras, they expected a few dozen volunteers for what would be a gruelling few days' work. Over a thousand turned up, and startled the filmmakers with their enthusiasm. 'They have acted marvellously,' said Hines. 'I've been both touched and depressed.'[389] Enlightened if not uplifted, viewers could only say the same thing.

# EVER DECREASING CIRCLES (1984–9)
## BBC One

### The sitcom becomes, in the best sense of the word, pathetic.

THE RISE OF ALTERNATIVE comedy brought many liberating bonuses to the craft, along with a few limiting stereotypes. Chief among these was the division of light from darkness. On the one hand, went the code, you had the jokey fluff of the old school sitcom; the polite clichés of a retrograde middle-class fantasy world that seldom generated controversy except by accident. Against this was the New Wave: cleansed of taboos, alert to modern life, and unafraid to explore – in the vernacular of the time – 'adult themes'. There was no mistaking one camp for the other, nor any question of mixing the two styles: old was old, and new was new, and *Never the Twain* was crap.

There were problems with this doctrine from the start. For one, 'adult themes' more often than not meant 'adolescent obsessions', which slightly offset any claim to maturity. More troubling was the old school sitcom's resolute refusal to conform to its new twee image. A close examination saw 'adult themes' – in the adult sense of the phrase – cropping up everywhere. There was no better illustration than the work of John Esmonde and Bob Larbey.

Their biggest hit, *The Good Life*, became shorthand for the lovely old guard when Adrian Edmondson's Vyvyan verbally and physically shredded it on *The Young Ones*: 'They're nothing but a couple of reactionary stereotypes, confirming the myth that everyone in Britain is a loveable middle-class eccentric and I hate them!' Richard Briers's Tom Good did exhibit a can-do cheerfulness that would have had Lulu reaching for the Valium, and a programme that recorded an edition in the presence of the Queen couldn't have been less anti-establishment. But the series ended on a jarringly bleak note, as the Goods return to their home after an evening out to find it trashed by vandals. They bravely soldier on, but the sitcom justice of niceness duly rewarded gets a sound kicking.

Esmonde and Larbey's next collaboration with Briers began at this level of desolation, and went downhill rapidly. *The Other One* packed Michael Gambon off to Spain as meek, lonely travelling salesman Brian Bryant in desperate search of fun, but finding only Briers's Ralph Tanner – equally sad, but possessing ironclad delusions of adequacy. He captivates his new-found posse of one with tall tales of a full life, but as Gambon probes deeper, ever more outlandish whoppers are needed to keep true intimacy, and the awful truth, at bay. This was a brave tone for a sitcom to take: Alan Bennett meets Samuel Beckett in a derelict Berni Inn. It worked its chilly trick for two quietly magnificent series, but two drips yoked together in chronic isolation would never match the audience of *The Good Life*.

For their third Briers vehicle, Esmonde and Larbey created a character somewhere between these two poles. Martin Bryce is, like Tom Good, an eternally busy chap with a boyishly chirpy disposition. Like Ralph Tanner, he's status obsessed, running the Rotarian social whirlpool of Horsham with military precision and childishly resentful if his achievements are outshone. The two sides combine to make the finest man-child role in British TV comedy. Permanently drunk on community spirit, Bryce fields enough displacement activity to win fifty Duke of Edinburgh awards a day. What he lacks in charisma he makes up for in fête organising. As he admits in a rare moment of self-awareness, 'for somebody like me to be centre stage, I have to write the play myself.'

Martin's position as de facto president of The Close's

highly-drilled leisure time is upended by the arrival next door of the easy-going Paul Ryman, a Cambridge blue with an address book to rival David Frost. Without trying, Paul knocks Martin off his pedestal in every activity, from cricket to snooker to breath-holding. A sweater idly tossed over the shoulder in a world of cardigans buttoned to the top, Paul gains the admiration of all in The Close, in particular Martin's multifariously frustrated wife Ann, while Martin hammers himself into the ground trying to match his idle feats.

Most suburban sitcoms have suburban normality visited by some stock crisis, of which the boss suddenly coming to dinner is only most widely parodied. *Ever Decreasing Circles* had a far more inter-esting premise: suburban normality is already a crisis, only just kept from disintegrating by the protagonists' desperate industry. For this to work, characters were kept within the bounds of credibility. Ann was granted just enough patience to keep her continuing marriage to Martin plausible, without making her a saint. Similarly, Martin occasionally let slip the odd intimation of an inner life, though it comes in touchingly infantile language. ('I've got a smile starting inside, Ann, but I'm not sure if I can make it come out of my face.') Even Howard and Hilda Hughes, an existential Janet and John in matching knitwear who spoke their innermost thoughts as if they were running their fingers underneath the words, occa-sionally exhibited enough backbone to explain their continued existence outside a secure institution.

Over four series, the characters were filled in, but rather than knock off the rough edges, the writers explained how they got there, making comic types into living creatures while keeping up the eccentricity. Martin slowly began to wise up, but only on his terms. We learnt the tragic nature of his proposal to Ann ('Why bother to cope? Let me do it'), and Paul's ex-wife spilled the beans on his less than heroic status outside The Close. Even Howard Hughes could occasionally silence Paul with a look somewhere between a baby's innocent ogle and a war veteran's thousand-yard stare.

Parts of such grotesque subtlety needed, and got, skilled actors. Nottingham Playhouse veteran Penelope Wilton made Ann a tragic heroine at bay, stoically channelling the rage of Lady Macbeth into a long, hard stare at a Laura Ashley table mat. Peter Egan, hitherto best known as the eponymous East End thug in notorious gangster drama *Big Breadwinner Hog*, worked brilliantly against type as the planet's most affable man. Most satisfying of all, Briers relished every moment as Martin Bryce, never happier than when he was undermining the 'sugar-flavoured snot' image he'd attracted with *The Good Life*. 'I hate the vacuous, the cheap,' he said, 'and [Esmonde and Larbey] aren't like that.' *Ever Decreasing Circles* contained scenes of such exquisite agony that his youngest daughter couldn't bear to watch. 'I was rather pleased, secretly.'[390]

# HEIMAT: EINE DEUTSCHE CHRONIK (1984)

## WDR/SFB (Edgar Reitz Film)

### The TV novel reaches epic proportions.

*The Americans have stolen our history.*
Edgar Reitz on *Holocaust, Liebe zum Kino*, 1983.

*HOLOCAUST*, NBC's LAVISH ANSWER to ABC's *Roots*, an eight-hour chronicle of one Jewish family's persecution in Nazi Germany, provoked every kind of response from worthy plaudits to concerned voices over Hollywood's trivialisation of Europe's darkest hour. In West Germany, its broadcast had solid effects: the sudden mass release of repressed memories it triggered was a decisive step toward the government lifting the statute of limitations for war crimes. But Edger Reitz, one time leading light of the New German Cinema movement, now licking his wounds over the grisly notices for his recent period drama *The Tailor of Ulm*, was unimpressed by Meryl Streep's martyrdom. He decided that, after decades of wilful suppression, it was time the German experience of the war was televised. Reitz began working on his contribution, *Heimat*, in March 1979.

*Heimat* began with *Tales from the Hunsrück Villages*, a compilation of real life stories, gathered by Reitz and co-author Peter

Steinbach over a solid year of research among the people of the Hunsrück Mountains, an oral history documentary reaching from the end of the Great War to the present day. Steeped in folk memory, they devoted another four years to writing, casting over a hundred parts from the local population and filming a fifteen-and-a-half hour chronicle of the fictional village of Schabbach and its citizens, from matriarch Maria Simon and her prodigal husband Paul to the scarred outcast Glasisch-Karl. Shown in art house cinemas as two mammoth epics, or one all-dayer with lunch included, *Heimat* was a daunting prospect for all but the most seasoned aesthete. Televised in eleven ninety-minute chunks, however, with catch-up prologues courtesy of Glasisch-Karl, it beguiled an entire continent.

The TV audience did have to make some allowances, however. Reitz set a demand not usually asked by a television programme of its audience. 'Don't make other plans while this film is showing,' he asked, 'stop the hectic pace of your daily life and enjoy the beauty.'[391] The pace of the early episodes was laggardly even by continental TV standards. Even with fifteen hours to cover sixty years, did we need quite so much detailed footage of blacksmiths at work? The direction would slowly pick up as the technology of the twentieth century – and the agency that made use of it, the Third Reich – invaded Schabbach and brought the world with it, ending a centuries old rural idyll for ever.

Whenever TV gives birth to something strange and new, snobbery is never far away. With *Heimat* it came in two flavours. The first was a blanket refusal – still doggedly intoned after a good thirty-odd years of constant refutation – to admit that television could work on such an exalted level. Film critic Derek Malcolm thought *Heimat* 'originally made for television but very much a piece of cinema.'[392] How else to explain it? Then there were misgivings over the format. Domestic, family-oriented, a celebration of life for life's sake – it all sounded horribly like those two words that traditionally signified the trashiest genre in all television. Richard Combs, early on in the UK screening, worried about the 'danger of *Heimat* becoming one more mammoth soap opera, in which respect for the mundane, the texture of everyday living, is also susceptible to mundane, conventional and trivial thinking.'[393]

The quality of the programme soon knocked these prejudices aside, as critics discovered how soap addicts felt, knowing the life stories of characters so intimately they began cropping up in their daily thoughts. One of the most derided aspects of the soap – its ability, by sheer weight of material, to swamp the viewer's attention – had been put to a higher use. *Heimat* came closer than any film to the *modus operandi* of Marcel Proust's *À la recherche du temps perdu*, the unparalleled depiction of *fin de siècle* Parisian high society which built a literary cathedral from a million tiny observations, thoughts and gestures; a timeless social panorama made up of countless trivial moments.

Too trivial, some argued. Just as Proust's world remains largely untouched by history until the Great War is well under way, so Schabbach seemed to have a relatively cushy time of it during the Second War. Local dignitaries converted to National Socialism out of opportunistic ambition, often laced with buffoonery, and the village held a Führer's birthday party while the Holocaust took place somewhere else. 'What about the other side?' demanded US critic Timothy Garton Ash. 'What about Auschwitz? Where is the director's moral judgement?'[394] Reitz was unmoved. 'If we are to come to terms with the Third Reich,' he wrote, 'it has to be by the same means we use every day to take stock of the world we live in.'[395] *Heimat* refused to streamline its characters' lives into the simple narratives expected of a war film. They were individuals with diverse motives and, much as it might have wished otherwise, even the Third Reich was powerless to change that.

*Heimat*'s success on German TV was immense. Repeat screenings had to be hastily arranged so haughty viewers who'd avoided the early episodes could catch up. Other European countries were similarly smitten, including France, usually resistant to Germanic cultural exports. It didn't reach the UK until spring 1986, where it took up Saturday night peak-time residence on BBC Two, heralded by 'a fanfare of ludicrous pre-publicity, in which continuity announcers went hoarse reading excerpts of rave reviews.'[396] Very unlike the understatement and humility of the programme itself.

*Heimat* wasn't the first of its kind: *Matador*, Lise Nørgaard and Erik Balling's study of a Danish town from the Great Depression to the aftermath of war, had already kept northern Europe rapt from 1978 to 1982. It wasn't the first German giant to leap the channel: Britons had already lapped up white knuckle submarine misadventure *Das Boot* and gruelling lowlife promenade *Berlin Alexanderplatz*. But *Heimat*'s ambitions and successes were of a different magnitude, and in its wake more European blockbusters arrived. *The Octopus*, Italian television's answer to *The Godfather*, was a high-end example. Lower down the ranks were German medical soap *Black Forest Clinic* and *Chateauvallon*, a French *feuilleton* whose two rich warring families bore more than a passing resemblance to certain rival dynasties in real life Toulouse, and which was marketed in English as '*Dallas-sur-Loire*'.

If that wasn't enough, rumours were abroad about the EEC imposing a minimum quota for European programmes on British channels, setting the tabloids on a gleeful panic spree. 'LATIN LOVELIES COULD ELBOW OUT DALLAS!' shivered the *Daily Express*, anticipating a Brussels-imposed hell of pretentious French discussions, naked Italian housewives, farting Finnish comics and worse. 'The language barrier alone makes it extremely difficult to enjoy some Austrian folk singer warbling about his herd of goats.'[397] The supposedly worldly British press could act like the most obtusely isolationist residents of Schabbach at times, but millions had their curiosity piqued and, in the case of *Heimat*, rewarded with one of the most complex, finely crafted and emotionally scrupulous programmes ever seen on television.

# MOONLIGHTING
# (1985–9)
## ABC (ABC Circle Films)
### The quirk factor goes through the roof.

IN TELEVISION MORE THAN any other entertainment industry, and American television most of all, the mainstream runs swift and shallow. Shows turn over rapidly and fashions change with the seasons, but depth and sophistication rarely intrude. When they do, when a series turns up in prime time bearing its nonconformity high and proud, a couple of seasons is often all it takes for it to either fall in line or completely drop out. Network caution, endless audience profiling and general creative exhaustion all contribute in various amounts, but however it happens, assimilation is almost inevitable.

Almost. Sometimes favourable conditions arise, often by accident, that let a singular series flourish. In 1985, ABC was in the doldrums, idling at a constant third in the network pecking order while NBC flew ahead in both popular and critical acclaim. Only when a network thinks it has nothing to lose does it give its producers carte blanche, and ABC were desperate enough to announce an experimental 'hands off' policy. Entertainment head Lewis Ehrlicht set up ABC Circle Films to produce a series of pilots, hiring fresh talent including Glenn Gordon Caron, a writer with a slim CV including *Taxi* and *Remington Steele*, taken on because Ehrlicht thought his work 'weird'[398] – possibly the first time a television boss had invested that adjective with approval. After two ideas floundered, ABC revoked a little of Caron's creative freedom by insisting the third pilot be a 'boy-girl' detective story.

This was hardly uncharted territory, and at the time already something of a crowded market. As well as *Remington Steele*, the schedules had recently been home to marital murder mystery *Hart to Hart* and secret agent romance *Scarecrow and Mrs King*. Looking for a way to differentiate the new pilot, Caron instinct-ively accentuated the part of the premise that interested him – the romantic comedy angle. Making the show predominantly a comedy created problems – sixty-minute comedies were practically unknown in prime time – but ABC gave him the benefit of the doubt.

What Caron was doing – unconsciously, as it took Cybill Shepherd, the first actor cast, to point it out to him – was restoring the screwball comedy to the American screen. Occupying a short but plentiful niche in the late 1930s and early 1940s, screwball was a brilliant, giddy cessation of American cinema's normal rules of combat. The standard issue square-jawed hero and sighing ingénue were jettisoned in favour of witty, fractious and above all equal partnerships between men who were not quite as cool as their sauntering suggested and women less haughtily unworldly than their bluestocking diction made out. They fell in and out of love as they stumbled from peril to peril, often having trouble taking deadly danger seriously. For a few glorious years silver screen romance was liberating, funny and empowering for both parties, until Doris Day turned up and schmaltz returned with depressing haste.

Shepherd and Bruce Willis became a Hepburn and Tracy for the Armani age. Shepherd's fashion model, fallen on hard times, investigates a deadbeat detective agency she set up as a tax dodge, finding only Bruce Willis's indolent detective David Addison, a frazzled receptionist and a non-ringing phone. ('Any appoint-ments?' 'John Gavin was made ambassador to Mexico again.') With the minimum of ceremony, the reluctant sophisticate and the gung-ho oaf tackle cases from the pitiful to the squalid, the crossfire of antagonistic crosstalk only letting up in moments of utmost jeopardy.

Within a few episodes, the order of importance of the show's constituent parts became clear. Way out at the top was the chemistry between Willis and Shepherd: the shouting, the screaming, the slamming of doors, the way his ill-judged quip would be met with her well-bred disgust, which gradually softened into a condescendingly amused admiration. The promise of romance is always central to this kind of entertainment, but the appeal of the two leads, and the relish and skill the writers lavished on putting words in their mouths – rapid fire words at that, often delivered simultaneously – went beyond anything Robert Wagner and Stefanie Powers had previously clocked up.

Growing out of the stars' charisma came the second pillar of success: conversing with the audience. Not since George Burns stepped through his kitchen wall had fictional characters demonstrated such self-awareness. The first moments of the second series featured a minute of the leads bickering to camera to fill time, as 'the network says the show's a minute too short'. This soon became a semi-regular feature, as did the ending of shows with the characters walking off the set and driving home. Then, somewhere a few fathoms beneath all of that, came the need for a tangible mystery plot – nice to have, but it was no big deal if one didn't happen to turn up that week. This was television about television – by comparison, *St Elsewhere* was a paragon of production line realism.

Still, who needed realism when everyone was having so much fun? By the second series the show had reached that critical velocity which enabled any obstacle flung at it by the network to be absorbed and transmuted into an asset. 'The Dream Sequence Always Rings Twice' was the first episode to wander playfully away from the original premise, featuring two long scenes pastiching MGM showbiz musicals and Warner Brothers gumshoe adventures in every detail, right down to real black and white film stock. This gave ABC the fear; they insisted on the addition of an upfront warning to reassure the simple viewer that their set wasn't going on the blink. The producers made the warning, and got Orson Welles, in his last TV appearance, to deliver it.

The third season was yet more extravagant. A parody of *The Taming of the Shrew*, performed in period costume on a huge medieval backlot and written in iambic pentameter, trod a fine line between flash precocity and grating conceit (and admitted as much). Stunts like this made *Moonlighting* a stupendously costly show, regularly ringing up over $1.5 million an episode. Lavish production values and an all-consuming attention to detail often led to close runs with the show's broadcast deadlines: several times repeats had to be called up to fill in the gaps (with sheepish references to the hiatus tacked onto the start of the next episode when it finally arrived). Scenes were being shot and dropped into the show on the day of transmission.[399]

With such a fragile grip on its resources and its internal logic, *Moonlighting* couldn't last forever. The 'will they, won't they?' tease came to an abrupt end with the close of season three as Maddie and David consummated their relationship. Season four began in confident mode, with the cast larking about in a parody of *The Honeymooners* and a guest appearance from Ray Charles, but things were disintegrating fast. Shepherd, pregnant and increasingly at odds with the producers, appeared less and less. Willis, preparing for the first *Die Hard* film, had one foot out the door himself. Scenes featuring Willis and Shepherd together, the lifeblood of the series, became increasingly rare. Eva Marie Saint guested as Maddie's mother. David was put on a chain gang. Shepherd appeared in Claymation. As the heart of the show went AWOL, these cute bits of business lost their charm.

The fifth season opened with a jaunty musical number. 'Another season, another try/ To make twenty-two shows before we die/ A chance for critics to stop and sneer/ "We know they'll only make sixteen this year".' Despite a concerted effort to ditch the experimental fripperies and return to the original screwball exchanges, they managed just thirteen. The last of these trundled to a close with the dismantling of the detective agency set, and a fictional producer telling the fictional pair just why their fictional lives had to come to a real end – people had tired of it. At the outer limits of American television's long tradition of exhaustive self-reference, *Moonlighting* proved a series really can be too clever for its own good.

# POB'S PROGRAMME (1985–7)
## Channel Four (Ragdoll)

### The threadbare origins of a children's television empire.

IT'S OFTEN SAID THAT children's television took a wrong turn somewhere: it began as an array of magical, prelapsarian programmes hand-crafted in potting sheds by committed artisans with an instinctive ability to think and feel like a child; and ended up as committee-designed, lifelessly loud franchises that exist primarily as a Trojan horse for branded lunchboxes. The only argument is when precisely the balance tipped from the first type to the second – it usually turns out to be when the person making the judgement hit puberty. Looked at more objectively, things aren't quite that simple – indeed, one producer achieved global domination with an equal mixture of commercial nous and childlike otherworldliness.

Anne Wood was an English teacher at a secondary modern school in 1965 when she founded child literacy magazine *Books for Your Children*. The campaign to encourage children to read slowly grew until she moved first to Tyne Tees, then Yorkshire Television in the late 1970s. Her first programme as producer, 1979's *The Book Tower*, continued the literacy-building theme and introduced Wood's signature style: an unabashed oddness. Few others would have set a programme designed to encourage reluctant junior readers in a forbidding stately home stalked by Tom

Baker, who would spy on children 'testing' new books through peepholes and secret panels. But adult expectations of what children might find off-putting are often wildly wrong, and the programme and attached library campaign were a great success.

Wood cemented her reputation as consultant children's editor to nascent breakfast channel TV-am. As the main breakfast programme plunged in the ratings, her *Shedvision* segment, hosted by puppeteer David Claridge's egomaniacal creation Roland Rat, was another offbeat hit. In turn she became an independent producer under the guise of Ragdoll Productions, with a company philosophy borrowed from Carl Jung: 'Without this playing with fantasy, no creative work has ever yet come to birth'.[400] Channel Four, looking to explore the undiscovered country of preschool entertainment, were the first to seek out her talent for high-rating oddities. Wood gave them *Pob's Programme*.

In the time-frozen landscape of snooker, old westerns and farming news that formed the typical British Sunday afternoon, Pob, a part-sock, part-monkey puppet with the public speaking skills of Joe Pasquale undergoing heavy root canal work, stood out somewhat. The concept, as ever with Wood, was both highly specific and difficult to grasp. Pob lived inside your TV set, choosing two o'clock on a Sunday to make his presence felt by semi-communicating to the very young through the screen. At the same time, friendly celebrities (Roy Castle, Hannah Gordon) were mysteriously inducted by following a trail of wool through a garden (which proved to be Pob himself unravelling) and reading a story specially commissioned from respected children's writers like Catherine Storr and Alan Garner.

Then there was the 'spitting'. To put his garbled message across, Pob would often breathe onto his side of the screen and write or draw diagrams in the resulting mist. Unfortunately the effect used for this illusion made the mist seem more like foaming snow white phlegm. Parental concerns about children responding in kind, at a time when TV sets were still a) mainly rented and b) regarded as only mildly less dangerous than Three Mile Island, were rife. Add to all this some elaborate contraptions made by Alan Dart, and a confusing assortment of melancholy Victorian etchings, and you had a show that looked thrown together on a series of conflicting whims. But logic, as Wood knew, carries little weight with the under-fives. Having put up her Surrey house as security to start Ragdoll, she took Pob seriously. Unable to afford a replacement, she stored the precious puppet carefully away between filming sessions in a deposit box.

So much children's TV is created by adults mired for too long in business mode, trying to deduce from first principles what children want, like bewildered babysitting Aristotles. The end product can often seem a strange interpretation of youthful desires, especially to children. Wood got the concept of *Pob* from real world observation: 'I really got the idea from watching children in Tesco's – you see them trapped in those supermarket trolleys, trying to communicate.'[401] The idea of an unintelligible children's protagonist, communicating on a level below language to those who were yet to master it, became a Wood trademark, despite the trouble it caused.

Wood was one of the first children's producers to embrace that elusive quality: cult status. At Yorkshire Television she noted the ability of *Ragdolly Anna* to turn the Leeds flat where the title character supposedly lived into a place of parent-child pilgrimage. Wood was less interested in the other, ironic, kind of cult status enjoyed by *The Magic Roundabout*, but her work had this too: a survey of the most popular programmes with sixteen to twenty-four-year-olds in August 1989 placed *Pob's Programme* at number seven, amid more obviously teen-friendly shows like *The Chart Show* and *4 on the Floor*.[402]

Ragdoll's star rose through the nineties. *Rosie and Jim*, the adventures of two knitted puppets aboard a narrow boat captained by *Postman Pat* creator John Cunliffe, was Ragdoll's first step into the emerging sell-through video market, and a successful one, shifting two million copies. Its second cousin, the multi-lingual *Tots TV*, won that most lucrative goal, an American franchise. In 1996,

Wood channelled the money from this into her biggest, and most outlandish, venture.

Employing a lavish, purpose-built permanent outdoor set, equally extravagant mechanically assisted costumes and a battery of Day-Glo effects, *Teletubbies* transformed the BBC's venerable *Play School* slot into a Fisher Price hangover seemingly designed specifically to enervate fastidious parents. But wary tuts over its retrograde baby talk turned first to thankful sighs over its hypnotic power to keep toddlers quietly stationary, and finally to full-blown cult membership. With *Teletubbies* and its successor, *In the Night Garden* – a *Finnegans Wake* to the Tubbies' *Ulysses* – Wood established a highly marketable pre-school style, a visual Esperanto spoken in over seventy-five countries, defiantly unintelligible to anyone over six.

# THE MAX HEADROOM SHOW (1985–7)

## Channel Four/HBO (Chrysalis Visual Programming)

### Enter the pop video, exit the pop presenter.

VIDEOS, OR TO GIVE them their original handle, 'promo clips', have been made, usually on a shoestring, since the sixties, but by the eighties they'd become an industry in themselves. In 1980, Blondie released *Eat to the Beat*, the 'first full-length album videocassette' with production costs of $100,000. 'Video tapes of rock acts may some day be a hot item,' the *NME* speculated, 'if enough directors with imagination move into the field.'[403] The current state of the art certainly seemed to offer dizzying possibilities: 'You can now walk into a record shop and buy an hour-long Boney M concert for £37.75.'[404]

Video would soon become synonymous with corporate marketing might, but in its earliest days a relatively modest outlay could get you a workable promo, and there was plenty of indie experimentation. The first video-only album, *Emotional Warfare* by The Gas, arrived in 1981 on a budget of £300. The following year Scottish band Strutz released *Start/Stop*, the first video single, available only by mail order. Punters sent a blank cassette which was returned with the video dubbed on, 'leaving the rest of the cassette free for further taping'. This was all technically, though not necessarily visually, exciting. 'Not a verse goes by without someone furiously twisting the zoom lens,' opined Phill McNeill of a typical early video, 'or shoving a black and white image across the colour one and then, even more irritatingly (cos it's a good effect) flashing it off again.'[405] These off-the-peg tricks would form the backbone of indie video making for the next decade.

Perhaps the most commercially successful early 'video artist' was Toni Basil. Her 1982 album *Word of Mouth* – white backgrounds, kaleidoscopic costumes, legs-to-the-sky choreography – came out on both LP and VHS/Beta via video label Radialchoice ('music you can see on records you can watch'), and appeared on TV as *The Toni Basil Special*. Though her success was rapid, Basil became an early victim of the video credibility gap. 'I don't consider what I do as showbiz,' she protested. 'It's not insipid Broadway stuff. It's rock 'n' roll!'

In what would become a familiar pattern for the music industry, the sell-through video market began to struggle once someone invented a way to disseminate the product for free. Ex-Monkee Mike Nesmith, who knew a thing or two about the video credibility gap, had just inherited a small fortune from his mother, the creator of Liquid Paper. With it he made esoteric 1981 video-album *Elephant Parts*, mixing music videos with freeform comedy bits perched somewhere between Ernie Kovacs and *Saturday Night Live*. (The Monkees had form in the rambling oddity stakes, both in the cinema with psychedelic consumer satire *Head*, and on TV with pantomime music business satire *33 1/3 Revolutions Per Monkee*, the latter authored by Jack Good.) Nesmith also made *Popclips* in 1980, the first music video show, for Warner Brothers' fledgling cable channel Nickelodeon. In between unenthralling promos for Poco and Huey Lewis, assorted comedians would improvise links while pretending to DJ with prop laserdiscs, on a set constructed from polystyrene electrical goods packaging. Rickety as they were, the links often held more interest than the videos.

Spotting the germ of great things in this video lean-to, Warners poached the concept and launched MTV in 1981, with more graphical pizazz but less presentational wit. Not that it mattered: within two years sixty per cent of North America's cable-ready homes were consuming over an hour a week. By then much of the old DIY chaos had been replaced by efficient content delivery, with just enough quirk to avoid youthful ridicule. Conversely the videos, especially those made in the UK, reached new heights of invention. The all-American channel inadvertently facilitated pop's second British invasion.

While the UK's artists stormed America, their fellow countrymen, slow to change viewing habits, resisted music television's charms. Virgin attempted to kick-start the revolution in 1983, hooking up with major video producers Palace Pictures to create Cable Music, a channel mixing videos with 'proper' interviews and magazine programmes. Instead of Mike Nesmith it had Ringo Starr. Still, reworked for pan-European satellite transmission and renamed Music Box, it was picked up by various ITV regions hungry for cheap content to fill the newly deregulated broadcasting hours after midnight. Timmy Mallett, Gaz Top, Gary Crowley, Nicky Campbell, Anthea Turner and John Leslie were among those whose careers were sustained or created by the station. Later still BSB, Sky Television's foredoomed opponent, advertised its music outlet The Power Station by painting its other channels as 'four ways of persuading your parents to pay for a TV channel they'll hate!' Few kids took the bait.

The credibility gap closed slightly when video makers graduated to programme production. Peter Wagg, whose promo CV included everyone from Blondie to Billy Connolly, had been toying with the idea of a non-human linkman for a pop video showcase since 1981, on the basis that 'it's hard to find a human being who won't irritate most of the people most of the time.'[406] Rocky Morton and Annabel Jankel, whose Cucumber Studios created memorable promos for Elvis Costello and Talking Heads, moulded the very man – a sharp-suited amalgam of every arch show business tic and smooth line of patter, saved from cold super-efficiency by the occasional glitchy 'stutter loop' and a nice line in esoterically egocentric chat courtesy of Paul Owen and David Hansen, fugitive writers from *Russ Abbott's Saturday Madhouse*.

Max Headroom, self-proclaimed *bon vivant, gaucho amigo*, goombah, mensch and fifth musketeer, was introduced to the public via that venerable television institution, the po-faced April fool. The earnestly-titled *Channel Four Investigates . . . A Leap Forward In Television?* pitched Wagg against various concerned pundits debating the ethical implications of entirely artificial talent. The gag was blown three days later with the screening of *Max Headroom: 20 Minutes Into the Future*, a slice of dystopian science fiction which was very much in the current style: all shadows and fog, urban no-go zones and pre-stressed *Face* magazine clobber. Amongst the forest of angular black hardware was a wryly cynical take on pressure cooker advertising, consumer docility and the barrel-scraping possibilities of multi-channel television. TV was an amoral pap factory, and its salvation a sarcastic CGI lounge lizard with the diction of Porky Pig.

Two days after that, Max himself (i.e. actor Matt Frewer in a prosthetic skull cap) hosted the real *Max Headroom Show* (i.e. the fictional show within the previous show). Combining the shopworn professionalism of Bob Hope with the snippy camp of Russell Harty, Max was a true transatlantic creation. With his supercilious introductions, microsecond mood swings and complete lack of interest in anything beyond shoes, golf and pine furniture, he exposed the lacquered shallowness of the mainstream, even as the accompanying videos, grab-bags of electronic effects, silent movie footage and papier-mâché Rene Magritte rip-offs were frantically trying to dress it up.

The result was either a neat symbiosis or a zero-sum game, depending on where your interests and investments lay, but it worked. When TV tried to match pop for glamour or danger, it just looked gawky and cheap. But by playing the fool in the rock business court, it could boost both itself and its guest stars with a wit and humility so often absent from the music itself. Sting was just one of many to realise that arguing with a visual effect over a pair of golf shoes went a long way to atone for the lyrics of 'Synchronicity II'.

# A VERY PECULIAR PRACTICE (1986–8)
## BBC Two

### Allegory goes peak time.

TV DRAMA HAS ITS fashions. Every few years certain subjects, styles and themes colonise the schedules: psychiatric soul searching in the late sixties, tricksy self-awareness in the seventies, roving-camera street realism in the early eighties. The late eighties hosted another sub-genre, identified by Hugh Herbert as 'bastard forms that draw on Gothic romance or that flirt with surrealism.' They took a dramatic genre, twisted it out of whack and decorated it with moments of supreme weirdness. In Herbert's judgement, 'often they reach for a deeper significance and almost as often they fall flat on their fancy.'[407]

Representing harsh reality with fantastic means was a strategy born of the Cold War. The threat of global destruction felt simultaneously very real and absurdly abstract. A realistic treatment, *à la Threads*, could only be done so many times before repetition set in and depression descended. *Z-Cars* creator Troy Kennedy Martin set realism aside to adapt *The Old Men at the Zoo*, Angus Wilson's 1961 conflation of international apocalypse and zoological administration, updated to 1983. Two years later came Kennedy Martin's own study of nuclear power, corporate greed and government cover up in the revered *Edge of Darkness*. For many, it was a smart melding of conspiracy thriller and environmental polemic. For others – well, for Hugh Herbert – it was 'the biggest collection of thriller clichés and trendy Thoughts for the Day you could sweep off a committee room floor'.[408] But *Edge of Darkness*'s 'clichés' were a means to an end, and it heralded a clutch of programmes that bent dramatic conventions to examine the modern world in oblique, dreamlike and often outrageous style.

Many big names entered this social hall of mirrors. In 1986, Fay Weldon's female revenge fable *The Life and Loves of a She-Devil* was burnished by director Philip Saville into high Greek tragedy with shoulder pads. Howard Schuman's *Up Line* refracted recession Britain through the prism of a cultish pyramid selling scheme. (Motto: 'shitty jobs for shitty times'.) *The Romans in Britain* writer Howard Brenton crammed diatribes on class and imperialism into *Dead Head*, a conspiracy film noir shot in what Julian Barnes dubbed 'super-murkovision',[409] which achieved notoriety for a highly symbolic rope-and-wellies sex scene.

Lower down the ladder of prestige came the psychotic pop video dystopias. *Brond*, a 'hallucinatory political thriller', brought *Z-Cars*'s Stratford Johns out of retirement to push kids off Glaswegian bridges and submit to a cattle-prod-wielding dominatrix in his underpants. That old favourite, the fascist future Britain where bedraggled hordes huddle round braziers while armoured vans full of rubberised riot police thunder down the overpass, was unpacked for *Boogie Outlaws*, a stilted rock-band-versus-the-state fantasy directed by Keith Godman, graduate of the 'Pick Up a Penguin' biscuit ads. At barrel's bottom, ultraviolent musical *Body Contact* boasted members of the Human League on the soundtrack, Timothy Spall as a Kalashnikov-toting gangster and Jack Shepherd as a hang-gliding, rapping sado-masochist priest. As sub-genres go, it was rarely dull.

The thriller wasn't the only genre that could be satirically super-charged. Andrew Davies, a lecturer at Warwick University who augmented his salary by writing children's programmes and period adaptations, worked the trick on that perennially unpromising format, the campus farce. Lowlands University was Davies's redbrick microcosm, a moribund seat of learning barely governed by vice chancellor Ernest Hemingway (John Bird), whose main priority was working out which bits to sell to Japanese corporations. Into this pit of despair Davies dropped Dr Stephen Daker (Peter Davison), a pleasant, open-minded new recruit to the campus clinic.

Daker's fellow doctors occupied various positions on the spectrum of acrimony: vampish, surname eschewing arch feminist Dr Rose Marie; head doctor Jock McCannon, a cynical ex-radical composed of equal parts R. D. Laing and Famous Grouse; and Bob Buzzard, a spineless, opportunistic entrepreneur, the free market incarnate in outsize Saatchi specs. Davies called them his 'sacred monsters': people who 'carry on as though they rule the world,'[410] the academic hothouse having distorted their fractious personalities into psychic gargoyles. Even Daker's one ally, down-to-earth behavioural psychologist Lynn, could intimidate him with, if anything, an excess of relaxed normality. In the background hovered staff and students varying in amiability and sanity, and two entirely unexplained feral nuns.

Having built the academic equivalent of a model train set, Davies put on his stationmaster's cap and began inventing ways to derail it. STD outbreaks, impotent professors, intrusive security measures and student riots assailed Daker and company week after week. Davies drew on his alma mater for odd details. Warwick was a research outpost for the Sinclair C5 electric buggy, and provided several senior lecturers with freebies, in which they solemnly trundled from lecture to lecture. A low-speed C5 chase was, however, excised from an early draft: slightly too ridiculous.[411]

For the second series, the rot took hold. Lowlands was bought by American developers, with a keen interest in cybernetics and defence and no use whatsoever for the philosophy department. In the closing one-off *A Very Polish Practice*, Daker and Buzzard duked it out in Eastern Europe as capitalism awaited its chance to move into the vacuum which would soon be left by communism in retreat. Throughout, Davies diligently ensured the allegorical elements remained subservient to the human drama. Daker's story

– a congenitally nice but often ineffectual man gets shafted by a sold-out, grudge-full world – was universal. This was crucial to the show's success. You can make your model railway as exquisite as you like, but tie a real person to the tracks.

The flogging of Lowlands coincided with the flogging of Britain, and few aspects of British life were flogged harder than British television. The popular allegory, however well crafted, became an increasingly difficult proposal. Proven talents like Dennis Potter and Alan Bleasdale were still given a fair degree of freedom, but in general the unusual was kept in check. *The Cloning of Joanna May*, Fay Weldon's sequel of sorts to *She-Devil*, was a flamboyant throwback, and Michael Dobbs's *House of Cards* (adapted by Davies) stood alone in arch defiance, the offspring of a messy one-night stand between Bertolt Brecht and Jeffrey Archer. In the main, though, nineties drama went back to its generic basics, its fancy Dan meditations on the human condition subordinated to the basic need for bums on sofas. Ambition hadn't deserted popular drama, but it seldom showed itself again in quite such lurid colours.

# THE COMIC STRIP PRESENTS . . . PRIVATE ENTERPRISE (1986)

## Channel Four (Comic Strip/ Michael White Productions)

### TV gives alternative comedy carte blanche.

NOT ALL NEW WAVES break the same. Pop's New Wave, at a generous estimate, managed five years from swell to backwash. Its theatrical counterpart began a little earlier and ended a little later. The comic New Wave, while last to gather, lasted longer than its predecessors combined, mainly due to the media savvy of its practitioners.

The Comic Strip began as an alternative cabaret night, a splinter group of comedians from hip Soho club The Comedy Store. It was established in 1980 on the seedy, plastic-palm premises of the Raymond Revue Bar by writer and actor Peter Richardson, as a venue for his latest project, a William Burroughs musical. The musical was soon forgotten in favour of modern cabaret. 'It was,' reflected compère Alexei Sayle, 'quite a calculated move for us to enhance our careers.'[412] It worked: listings magazines *Time Out* and *City Limits* hailed the club; soon broadsheet hacks and TV producers were spotted in the back row. The next move was inevitable.

The TV Comic Strip centred around three double acts.

Richardson and Nigel Planer, aka The Outer Limits, were a musical comedy duo specialising in elaborate concept shows. Rival act 20th Century Coyote (Rik Mayall and Adrian Edmondson) worked at the other end of the sophistication spectrum. Keen students of *commedia dell'arte*, they combined terrible poetry with existential acts of tit-for-tat sadism. Dawn French and Jennifer Saunders completed the sextet with a roster of naturalistic character sketches, tending towards sulky sixth form strops. Other comics, notably Sayle and Keith Allen, augmented the core squad.

Their champion was BBC light entertainment production manager Paul Jackson, who after a couple of cabaret specials commissioned *The Young Ones*, a student sitcom that could switch from Chekhov parodies to farting hamsters with only the mildest crunch of gears. Richardson was the only Strip member not to feature – he was in talks with Jeremy Isaacs of the nascent Channel Four over an entirely different proposal.

The Comic Strip had already been immortalised in an eponymous 1981 short film by Julian Temple, visual architect of Sex Pistols post mortem *The Great Rock 'n' Roll Swindle*. Like that film, it was a mess of off-the-cuff doodles built around footage of the club's various acts. Sayle impersonated a Bertolt Brecht impersonator, pop-up toasters were celebrated in song, and green and magenta gels were applied to the lights with liberal abandon. It was disowned by everyone and buried for years.

What Richardson had instigated was far more ambitious than that punkish squib, but less countercultural in its pose. Channel Four's youth commissioning editor Mike Bolland called *The Comic Strip Presents* . . . 'the Ealing comedy of the eighties.'[413] Richardson himself compared it to the then profoundly unfashionable *Carry On* films, adding, 'I don't like jokes to no purpose. I like comedy that's about attitudes.'[414] This certainly applied to the first film, 'Five Go Mad in Dorset', which adorned the station's opening night schedule in 1982. The Famous Five, Enid Blyton's jolly gang of prep school vigilantes, were recast as dim, gluttonous bigots, giving the common folk and Johnny Foreigner a good lashing in between lashings of ginger beer.

The following films varied tremendously in style, content and tone. A breakneck, surreal farce would be followed a week later by a naturalistic, subtle character study. In an industry that was just starting to buy into the culture of branding this was, one critic remarked, 'a brave attack on television market research.'[415]

The stylistic jumble could be separated into a few distinct types. 'Five Go Mad . . .' headed one: the pastiches. These picked apart the visual and verbal clichés of cinema and TV: 'A Fistful of Travellers' Cheques' did spaghetti westerns; 'Consuela' filleted Hitchcock; the glam-grit cop show was skewered by 'The Bullshitters'; the fly-on-the-wall documentary skilfully aped in 'Bad News Tour'.

Chat show parody 'An Evening with Eddie Monsoon', starring Edmondson as a repellent Afrikaner TV star, had to be canned due to its extreme, potentially libellous content. Reworked as 'Eddie Monsoon – A Life?', it took its place in another fruitful category, the anarchic free-for-all. These films, though still well crafted, were closer to the team's tumultuous cabaret roots. Edmondson and Mayall enrolled Peter Cook as honorary member for 'Mr Jolly Lives Next Door', an alcoholic stagger through the junkyard of minor celebrity. Alexei Sayle's 'Didn't You Kill My Brother?' was a 200-decibel morality play combining the Kray twins, Brecht, Vittorio De Sica and a dead badger. More so even than *Monty Python*, this was a clash of the high and low brows, with little in between: cerebral satire meets brain-stem burlesque.

Somewhere between the scatological eruption and the cool technical spoof came a handful of more character-driven films. Adrian Edmondson's 'Private Enterprise' is the ideal example: a social satire populated with morally challenged characters of variously puny social standing, it's a concentrated burst of Essence of Eighties – *Only Fools and Horses* reconditioned by Ken Loach.

Keith (Richardson) is a toilet paper deliveryman on parole for God knows what, shacking up with girlfriend Debbie (Saunders) and temporarily harbouring his even dodgier pal Brian (Edmondson), who has a nicely exasperating line in dole queue philosophy. ('I do believe it's my superior intelligence that's secured my position in that small but elite body of men and women commonly known as Maggie's Millions.') Keith happens on the demo tape of Toy Department, a New Romantic band led by Mayall's fractious, boiler-suited neo-fop Ali ('So just because I dress more imaginatively than you, then I'm too fashionable to know anything about music, am I?') He punts it to the supercilious head of A&R at Hard Corps Records (Planer), who decides to release it as a tax loss. Unfortunately the anonymous drone becomes a massive hit, and Keith and Brian are tasked with conjuring a national tour out of thin air. Deceit is piled upon deceit, and desperation mounts. Keith's parole officer (French) closes in. Urgent action is required.

It was a prescient story. A couple of weeks after it was broadcast, Sigue Sigue Sputnik, a cartoon punk 'fantasy band' assembled by Tony James, released their first single, a shapeless mess of riffs, samples and posturing yelps eerily similar to Toy Department's 'Boots', a horribly catchy number concocted by the Strip's musical ace Simon Brint. James and company peppered their debut LP with paid adverts. The idealism of the musical New Wave had become a shameless devotion to private enterprise. The comic New Wave had the last laugh.

Rather like its central character, 'Private Enterprise' was a ramshackle operator, despite a solid plot, decent parts and enjoyable cameos from Roger Sloman and Lionel Jeffries. Edmondson handled his first directing gig gamely, but there's an unevenness to it that falls outside even the generous scope of rough-and-ready naturalism. When the series returned two years later, it began with Richardson's 'Strike', which couldn't have been slicker. By dovetailing a character story (Sayle's idealistic working class screenwriter pens a history of the miner's strike which gets butchered by Hollywood) with razor sharp film parody (the all-action end result of the commission), 'Strike' dragged the series far enough into the mainstream to win the 1988 Golden Rose of Montreux – despite it being screened to delegates without foreign language subtitles.[416] The Strip's constituent players duly took their places in the comedy establishment, but it was an establishment they'd helped change radically – one that was now more technically capable, more socially aware, and considerably more flatulent.

# NIGHT NETWORK
# (1987–9)

## LWT (Night Network Productions)

### British television finally gets to stay up late.

*Sniffing glue's over and Barclaycards are in.*
Stuart Cosgrove, 'The Rise and Fall of Cult TV', *Listener*,
18 February 1988

IN THE USA, NETWORK television has run from early morning to the small hours since the 1950s, with magazine programmes populating mornings, and *Tonight* and its descendants occupying the night. British television, far more regulated and reserved from the outset, approached the depths of the night in a much more tentative manner, rarely staying up past midnight unless international sport or world events made extra time essential.

One early British all-nighter was composed entirely of American material. Granada's *The All-American All-Nite Show* sprawled over various ITV regions from 2 a.m. to 7 a.m. on 5 November 1980, marking the occasion of the USA's momentous Reagan-Carter election battle with a feast of clips from the hairier outposts of US television. Humiliating game shows, possessed evangelists, mad stuntmen jumping over speeding cars and losing a foot in the process, and Oscar the Wonder Rodent were wryly introduced by

Ned Sherrin. 'Remember,' he concluded ominously, 'that everybody you've seen tonight had a vote.' Such cretinous behaviour was kept firmly off our cultured British schedules, which still ended at a reasonable hour, even if they no longer came to a close with a thoughtful poem read by a cardigan-clad actor. But for how much longer?

Independent TV was regularly pushing out the post-midnight boat by the mid-1980s. Channel Four made highbrow treks past the dead of night with the moderately successful *After Dark*, an open-ended panel discussion, and the less successful *UK Late*, the same programme with a shouting studio audience. *After Dark* was memorable for its unflinching guest policy, booking at various times a drunk Oliver Reed, Klaus Barbie's defence counsel and a self-confessed child molester (though they decided against inviting Gerry Adams). *UK Late* was memorable for the terrible mess it made during its tiny lifespan. 'It's important to be constantly embarrassed by what you do,' mused John Peel on one edition. 'I hope, when I look at this programme on video, to be embarrassed by this, too.'

Otherwise, late night TV was a drowsy procession of veteran films, pop videos and cheap imports, notably over-excited US chat show *Donahue* and *Prisoner Cell-Block H*, a scraping from the Australian soap barrel which came to occupy a perversely high position in British popular culture. On *This Morning with Richard Not Judy*, Peter Baynham invented the game of switching randomly between different episodes of *Cell-Block H* being shown on different ITV regions to create entirely new plots ('I got Vinegar Tits to have an argument with herself the other night.') When London Weekend Television launched the first bespoke night-time programming at 1 a.m. on 29 August 1987, it had the *Prisoner*, rather than the *After Dark*, audience in mind.

*Night Network* was the creation of producer Jill Sinclair, graduate of *The Old Grey Whistle Test*, with help from future *Snub TV* founder Brenda Kelly. (Youth TV was largely female-led – Sinclair joined *Network 7* bigwigs Jane Hewland and Janet Street-Porter, and Katie Lander, architect of Jonathan Ross's *The Last Resort*.) Described by

LWT's Head of Entertainment Marcus Plantin as a 'night-time pot-pourri of youth-oriented fare'[417] and a suspicious *New Musical Express* as '*Saturday Superstore* with knobs on,'[418] *Night Network* filled the small hours of Saturday, Sunday and Monday with stripped mini-programmes that aimed to captivate easily distracted, high-spending youth with minimal production costs.

Like the first explorers of an uncharted wasteland, *Night Network*'s initial settlements were simple, makeshift affairs lashed together from whatever came to hand. Logos and livery were MTV in style: spiky luminescent graphics assembled themselves in a flurry of stylish animation to the sound of soft rock power chords. Pop videos were jammed into every available nook, alongside vintage transatlantic trash like *Batman* and *The Partridge Family*. Presenters Mick Brown and Paul Thompson addressed the sleepless thousands with the studied insouciance of the hipster journalist. Every trick was pulled to convince the viewer they were part of a tiny, clued-up elite, not a shiftless diaspora of lonely insomniacs.

Nicholas Parsons launched the 'ironic dotage' phase of his career with *The All-New Alphabet Game*, showering questions and film clips on celebrity contestants like Katie Boyle and Alice Cooper in an atmosphere of knowing tackiness. Despite Parsons's attempts to inject some edginess into proceedings ('Come on, this isn't a family show!') the mood was pure sequinned kitsch, a retro Day-Glo atmosphere that would soon usurp the earnest technophilia of *Network 7* to become the default setting for youth TV.

Slightly more successful in the sauce department was *Pillow Talk*, in which Emma Freud and guest (initially the BBC's star MP-cum-daytime-star Robert Kilroy-Silk) took coyly to bed for an 'intimate' interview lifted wholesale from Paula Yates's segment of *The Tube*. Most of the other mini-programmes were interviews, too. In *Leee's Place*, singer Leee John interviewed other musicians in a mocked-up bar, while in *The Bunker Show* Rowland Rivron chatted drunkenly to random star guests in a mocked-up fallout shelter, complete with a year's supply of toilet rolls. Angie Clarke, sister of motormouth Margi, had a shopping slot. Craig Charles ran a music video gong show. In between, bite-size snippets of Californian glamour and saucy fun (like the nation's top ten condoms) pinned *Night Network* irrevocably to its late-eighties habitat.

Not quite everything went: magician-comedian Jerry Sadowitz was given a slot to air some material from his Total Abuse live show, but a combination of self-exposure (on screen) and routines about the private life of Jimmy Savile (off it) got him banned from the programme after one appearance. As the show matured, the Sunday night edition frequently resorted to mouldering old films, and occasionally the entire night's billing would consist of three deadly words like 'Belgian rock festival'.

Beyond conquering the small hours in the name of entertainment, *Night Network* was a pioneer in less noble areas. Its producers worked closely with, and had their programming decisions formed by, the sales and advertising departments. Commercial television always kept the bottom line in sight, but *Night Network* was the first British show to tie itself firmly to its advertisers. Carefully keeping on the right side of the Independent Broadcasting Authority's ruling that 'advertising has to be clear and separate from programmes,' *Night Network* was still, in the words of sales manager Richard Holliday, 'product television,' where 'advertising becomes more of a complete part of the viewing experience than would normally be the case.'[419] These were not the words of establishment-shaking guerilla programme makers, but at a surprisingly healthy £1,000 for a thirty-second advertising slot, *Night Network* couldn't help but milk its affluent demographic for all it was worth.

*Night Network* lasted barely two years, but its various regional clones and successors kept the fast-moving capsule format and the rock-bottom budgets of the pioneers. Levels of sophistication may have varied, but the *i-D* magazine cool of *01 for London*, the laddish goofiness of *MTV's Most Wanted* and the tabloid leer of *The James*

*Whale Radio Show* were cut from the same dress pattern. The wasteland may have been colonised, but only a certain type of programme could flourish there: simple, hardy and low on sobriety; a night bus riding the ether.

# MAHABHARAT
# (1988–90)
## Doordarshan (BR Films)

### All-singing, all-dancing, all-retina-burning dramatisation of the Indian epic poem.

*Full of ideal romance, mystery, thrills, suspense, chivalry, adventure, awe-inspiring exploits and spine-shilling miracles, this wonderful epic . . . provides valuable guidance to the common householder for leading a pious, plain and virtuous life.*

T. R. Bahnot, Introduction to
*Mahabharat, Part 1*, 1990

WHEN GLOBETROTTING THEATRE DIRECTOR Peter Brook staged the *Mahabharata*, the epic poem of India's mythic origins on Channel Four in 1989, he shaved a third off his open air theatrical version to leave a six-hour pageant of mysticism, ritual and deeply respectful mime. The due deference Brook gave the host culture was in turn served up to him by his fellow countrymen. There was a respectful *South Bank Show* special, an interview on *Signals*, and Channel Four published study guides and a lavish 160-page book. It was big, it was multicultural and it was deeply devout.

At about the same time, Indian television was putting its own version together, and it couldn't have been more different. Instead of respectful ritual and tasteful candlelight, the Indian *Mahabharat* was bombastic, heartfelt and epic in scope. Replicating the highly chromatic visions of the country's abundant religious murals, it pushed the medium to the limit, testing the limits of broadcastable colour saturation and seeing just how many flying demons could be superimposed on screen at any one time. It was every bit as devout as Brook's work, and fifteen times bigger, but unlike the impresario's version, this one positively romped along.

Television in India came late and grew slowly. Doordarshan, the state service, began in 1959, serving a handful of homes in a very restricted locale. The 1970s saw the partial adoption of advertising and a steady rise in audience, but full national coverage and colour only arrived in the early 1980s, bringing with them a boom in set ownership that was mainly fuelled by gargantuan serials and soaps.

From 1984, open-ended family sagas with huge casts proliferated, beginning with *Hum Log* (rough translation: People Like Us), closely based on the emotionally explicit 'Telenovela' format popular in Latin America. Focussing on a middle class extended family with the usual quota of illicit liaisons, feuds and black sheep, it reached an estimated audience of fifty million at its peak.

In 1987 director Ramanand Sagar applied the family saga format to epic Hindu poem the *Ramayana*. The series that resulted, *Ramayan* and *Luv Kush*, comprised over sixty hours of sumptuous palatial receptions, epic running battles and science fiction monster costumes as the bejewelled green hero of the piece searched for his kidnapped wife to a fully orchestrated musical commentary. It became essential Sunday morning viewing, with public screenings organised to maximise the audience – estimated at up to 100 million by the state's (admittedly not very reliable) ratings service.[420] As with many a popular fantasy franchise since, the success was milked by dragging the story out for as long as possible, and huge, seventeen-minute commercial breaks were inserted in the middle of each episode.

While India was hooked on Ram's quest, Doordarshan was already arranging a version of the *Mahabharat* to follow it. This was the big one. Weighing in at over 83,000 couplets – several

Bibles' worth of verse – this tale of the two warring families said to have founded ancient India was well-known to the vast majority of the population in all parts of the country. Some even had the entire thing off by heart. B. P. Chopra, taking a style only marginally less opulent than his predecessor, had the job of turning it into ninety-three hour-long episodes.

It was a mammoth task. In the story, heroines take multiple husbands and have innumerable sons, one of whom spends whole episodes conducting lengthy speeches while impaled on a bed of arrows. Warriors rip open their adversaries' chests and drink their blood, while ascetics stand on one toe in snowy wildernesses for years on end. Duels are conducted with gigantic spherical golden hammers, rhythmically swung by the combatants ('Hurgh!' *Doink*. 'Hurgh!' *Doink*). A hundred elephants charge into battle under hails of flaming arrows. Fifty-foot visions of Krishna spout fire and water and swallow populations. Men impregnate fish and women give birth to cannonballs of flesh. It's the most gob-smacking story ever told.

Chopra did the source material proud, marshalling episode-long battle scenes and baroque apparitions with conviction. *Ramayan*'s previous records were shattered. Estimates pushed the audience share towards ninety-five per cent of Indians with access to a television set. The government had to reschedule their Sunday briefing session after a clash with the programme's transmission led to several cabinet ministers bunking off to watch it.[421]

The series made its way to other countries, picking up a sizeable, if less strictly devout, following in each one. The BBC's regular Sunday afternoon and midnight screenings in the early 1990s became a source of unaccountable addiction for many non-Hindu viewers, who searched vainly for adequate cultural comparisons. ('*The Singing Ringing Tree* crossed with *Clash of the Titans*', said the *Listener*.[422]) Shortly after the final episode aired, a travelling stage version, complete with most of the original TV cast and some of the original elephants, played Wembley Arena, a fittingly outsize send-off for a programme that, against all good sense, took every monumental Cinemascope epic ever made and squeezed them all onto a twenty-four inch screen – something of a miracle in itself.

# DEF II (1988–94)
## BBC Two

### The last stand of 'youth' TV.

LIKE AN OLD SATURN V rocket stack, pop is powered by the combustible mixture of two fuels – youthful ferocity and establishment unease. By the late 1980s, the second ingredient was becoming increasingly scarce. The country's great and good included ever more veteran rock fans in ever more powerful positions. Shrieks of moral abhorrence gave way to tuts of amused familiarity: the Man was once a kid himself. Television in particular was all over youth like electric Biactol, and it had learned to look relaxed about it.

Pockets of the square old guard held out, but the battles they fought started looking rather silly. Late-night ITV debate *Central Weekend Live* played host to Virginian panto-metal band Gwar, whose graphic live shows were causing consternation among upright Midlanders. In a perfect distillation of the absurdity of all encounters between the citizenry and feral youth, band members Sleazy P. Martini and The Sexecutioner, resplendent in head-to-toe latex stage regalia, lolled on swivel chairs while a scarcely less visually florid sea of blowsy councillors and pork-fed aldermen heaped righteous outrage on these 'rubber teddy boys'. The punk wars were repeating themselves, this time as slapstick.

The indie wars were similarly reduced to cartoon violence at televised pre-pubie jamboree *The 1991 Smash Hits Poll Winners' Party* when, after host Philip Schofield mocked the amp-trashing antics of Carter the Unstoppable Sex Machine ('blimey, that was original!'), the band's Fruitbat wrestled him to the ground as the kids screamed on. The same year, Carter's manager, the notorious Jon 'Fat' Beast, recorded a Channel Four pilot called *Beast on the Box*, a 'music and chat show incorporating a huge vat of baked beans'. Meanwhile Vic Reeves and Bob Mortimer made *Popadoodledandy* (working title: *What a Lot of Pop We've Got! A Copper Kettle Full of Pop!*), quizzing bands in detail about their National Insurance contributions. Generational conflict gave way to general daftness.

Elsewhere on the fourth channel, Janet Street-Porter's new Sunday morning magazine gave the new cultural relativism a more serious tone. Critics said many things about *Network 7*, but nobody could argue that it didn't put in the work. Items funereal and frivolous came and went at dizzying speed. Graphics popped up all over the place. Cameras swooped and cut about seemingly at random, in an austere, Jean-Luc Godard visual style as opposed to Mike Mansfield's exuberant Ken Russell look.

Its presenters, led by Murray Boland and Magenta Devine (née Kim Taylor, former PA to the Boomtown Rats), had two moods: knowingly grave for serious items, and knowingly detached for cultural matters. The viewer was kept regularly informed of the temperature in the studio, for reasons never revealed. It was, Street-Porter explained, 'what I like to call aspirational television. That kind of show shouldn't be too easy to understand: it ought to be television you can boast to your friends that you fully understood, even if you didn't.' She wanted *Network 7* to be the '*Tinker, Tailor, Soldier, Spy* of factual television.'[423] It was a sitting duck for critical disdain, but it did have the odd champion. 'Those who complain about "distractions" are really saying that *Network 7* isn't *Panorama*,' wrote Andy Medhurst. 'Very true, but then the Pet Shop Boys aren't Ray McVay and his Band of the Day, and I know whom I'd rather dance to.'[424]

Street-Porter's grand design transferred to BBC Two in May 1988. *Def II* sprawled over Monday and Wednesday evenings, a branded collection of programmes which overruled its parent channel's livery with scratch video barcode idents and some magnifi-cently awkward rapped continuity announcements, sounding no more authentically ghetto than Central Television's Saturday night linkman did introducing milk-float comedy *Bottle Boys* in similar style back in 1984. ('They're likely lads, you can bet this lot'll/ Prove to you they've got the bottle!')

Other hip touches fared slightly better. Quirky links were obtained by allowing celebrities of the Stephen Fry variety to ramble on about *Captain Pugwash* and other bygone cultural ephemera, some of which (*The Invaders, Battlestar Galactica*) received repeat showings. 'We are watching a culture cannibalising itself and disappearing up its own backside,' noted an apprehensive Martin Walker. 'Which may not be the best place for it.'[425]

With *Def II*, however, nostalgia was part of the structure, like the corpses of victims built into an ancient despot's defensive walls. Throughout the 1980s the 'thinking man's' pop music of choice had become more and more influenced by the ideas, often half-digested, of post-structuralist philosophers, in the same way a slim volume of Camus peeped out from their predecessors' trenchcoat pockets. For these acts, inauthenticity and spectacle became plus points. Old pop music was resurrected and playfully spliced into the new. *Def II* did the same with TV history, sporting chunks of the ironically disinterred past in the form of out-of-context archive clips. (Cut from studio to Fyffe Robertson on an old *Tonight* report, standing next to a huge fish, saying 'I'm standing here with this huge fish!' Cut back to studio.)

Gradually the style, and indeed personnel, of *Network 7* resur-faced in the magazine *Reportage* and hip travel series *Rough Guide*, but music programming was *Def II*'s main strength. Three programmes came to define the strand. *Dance Energy*, a clubland *Top of the Pops*, was the most traditional, and least typical. *Rapido* was the big draw, a rock magazine boasting fifties kitsch stylings and the rapid-fire presentation of Antoine De Caunes, linking segments with suave Gallic ostentation, in the manner of a *Max Headroom* routine as retold by an espresso-fuelled Jacques Derrida.

*Rapido* sought out rising stars like the Stone Roses, but would happily accommodate big names like Paul McCartney if they deigned to appear. They often did, because, as Street-Porter explained, 'a lot of pop stars are snobs and like the idea of being done for a French show.'

The indie sector was catered for with *Snub TV*, product of artists Peter Fowler and Brenda Kelly. At the bottom of the food chain, *Snub* was initially funded by US cable channel Night Flight (where it became an unlikely favourite with veteran acid rockers the Grateful Dead), to the miserly tune of $1500 per show. Taking the DIY approach of the scene's print fanzines, Kelly and Fowler didn't bother with hosts or a studio, instead asking bands whereabouts they'd be at, say, four in the afternoon, and turning up with a camcorder. Specially shot music videos were made by independent artists, working for nothing more than national exposure. Here was a glimpse of the twenty-first century's financially exhausted music industry. In another sign of changing times, a headmaster rang the programme – not to complain of degeneracy, but to ask after a Mekons track he wanted to use in the end-of-term show.[426] Deal with a request like that and stay fashionable.

# TWIN PEAKS (1990–1)
## ABC (Lynch/Frost Productions)

### The cult blockbuster takes America.

IN THE MEDIA PECKING order, television bows to film. Actors, writers and directors, from Dench to Chayefsky to Spielberg, learned their craft on the small screen before defecting to cinema's bigger budgets and greater acclaim. Movement in the reverse direction usually meant thin times for the talent. Ingmar Bergman switched between cinema and TV, but that was Swedish TV. *MASH* the movie satire became *M\*A\*S\*H* the sitcom, and the Coen brothers' *Fargo* begat a *Twin Peaks*-style comedy-drama, but those were happy exceptions. The rule was clear: cinema was the grown-up cousin, the fully realised art form, where the cream of TV talent could only hope to finish up.

It took David Lynch, a born flouter of industry rules, to break this convention, and even he was motivated by necessity. To follow up his art house hit *Blue Velvet*, he and former *Hill Street Blues* writer Mark Frost wrote the film *One Saliva Bubble*, a wacky backwoods identity swap comedy set to star Steve Martin. Funding proved hard to scrape together, so the pair began tossing TV ideas around instead. Their first, *The Lemurians*, concerned two detectives on the trail of extra-terrestrial descendants of a lost continental civilisation (or something like that) and was knocked back by NBC. Undaunted, they took another, a *Blue Velvet*-like murder mystery called *Northwest Passage*, to ABC, then well into its five-year plan of innovation hunting that kicked off with *Moonlighting*.

A change of title, and the most unhinged prime time drama in network history was in production.

From the first moments of its long, freaky story of the death of prom queen Laura Palmer and the subsequent collapse of a peaceful lumber town as FBI agents interrogate the community, *Twin Peaks* was set against the American television grain. It wasn't the sporadic, random and – for American television – graphic moments of violence. It wasn't the systematic undermining of the wholesome myth of rural Midwestern life, formerly a backbone of comforting small screen entertainment from *Green Acres* to *The Waltons*. It wasn't the disturbing yoking together of soapy emotional outbursts with weird urban myths. More than anything, it was the pacing: soporific one-take scenes where characters took their time to haul themselves from one spot to another; ambiguous, ominous pauses in conversation, usually topped with a non-sequitur, the oddity of which was remarked by nobody. The camera made long, slow zooms into nothing in particular. The tightly cut, tightly framed, prescriptive visual grammar of network TV, with all its T's dotted and vagueness shunned, was swapped for a languid, leisurely style that took its time getting to wherever it was going. This was New Wave cinema plonked unceremoniously into the post-MTV mainstream, making the mainstream queasy.

Characters crashed out of their stereotypical roles. Seasoned police officers broke down in tears. High school girls possessed worldly knowledge well beyond what their rural upbringing would suggest, while FBI agents obsessed intensely over mundane food items. A seedy casino vied with the private lives of the town's residents for the title of most disturbing underlit scene. Odd relatives suddenly invaded the family house with half a dozen French baguettes. Norwegians deserted en masse. Best of all were FBI Agent Dale Cooper's divinatory dreams, a straight throwback to Lynch's hardcore frightfest *Eraserhead*, with reverse-speaking dwarves and psychotic spirits taking their bows on a herringbone parquet floor. Prime time drama was coming down with a severe case of post-traumatic stress.

The show was launched with huge publicity, and immediately snagged its target Yuppie market. The pilot was the highest rated TV movie of the 1989-90 season. The series proper would reach thirty-five million and held its own against venerable NBC sitcom *Cheers*. 'Something's right in America,'[427] beamed *Newsweek* approvingly. *Time* agreed, 'The medium has rarely seen anything as strange – or as superb.'[428] *The Washington Post* heralded 'the show that re-invents the [soap opera] genre and gives it class,'[429] and it became the focus of a *Village Voice* special report on 'Rad TV'.

When it landed in the UK in October, reception was more critical. Tabloids duly puffed the show with reference to its transatlantic hipness quotient. *Today* hailed 'the wacky soap you have to quote to prove you are not a philistine,'[430] and broadsheets reported, only slightly askance, on upscale America's penchant for *Twin Peaks* viewing parties fuelled by cherry pie, doughnuts and 'damn fine coffee'. As it got underway, though, it became clear that, transplanted to a country with a long history of weird peak time television, *Twin Peaks* struggled to stand out. Sheridan Morley in *The Times* compared the first episode to watching jelly set, and after watching the second issued an apology to jelly manufacturers. Andrew Goodwin in the *Listener* spotted a hollow centre. 'Rooted in a genre that will gain mass attention, while nodding and winking hysterically at the upscale audience who thought *Moonlighting* was terribly experimental, *Twin Peaks* is trying to have its formulaic cake and eat itself.'[431] James Saynor called Lynch out on a grand televisual con trick. 'He's now watching, smirking, from a safe distance, in no danger of being personally beaten up by his own art,'[432] he wrote. 'The right-hand side of the show's brain has had a stroke.'[433] Chris Dunkley in the *Financial Times* confidently predicted the show would top out at two and a half million UK viewers. In fact, combining the Tuesday showing and Saturday repeat, it comfortably broached eight million. The cult had translated. Criticism was moot.

As the show's two series unwound at different speeds on both sides of the Atlantic, the audience, many still expecting some kind of progress on the detection front, grew restless. The identity of Laura Palmer's killer came halfway through the second season, for what it was worth by then, but the show ambled on at the same sedated pace. With the nominal denouement out of the way, fans began paying attention to the man behind the red velvet curtain. Not since *The Prisoner* had so much money and prime time real estate been given over to a cosmic shaggy dog tale, the solemn guarding of a clearly empty casket. Even Frost and Lynch couldn't escape the ancient riddle: just how do you end these things? ABC didn't trust them to find an answer, and held a third series back.

Rushing to the show's defence, Lynch appeared on the Letterman show with a personal appeal for viewers to write into the ABC president pleading a stay of execution. 'If it has to end,' he said with typical eerie calm, 'that's all right. But if it doesn't have to end, that's even better.'[434] Such campaigns had worked in the past, most notably in the early years of *Cagney and Lacey*, but two series were all ABC were prepared to risk. A cinematic spin-off, *Twin Peaks: Fire Walk With Me*, took things to new depths of obscurity and squalor, but it didn't do it opposite Carol Burnett every Saturday night, which wasn't quite the same. Then, in a twist as implausible as anything in the show itself, Frost and Lynch announced that a new series, set 25 years on from the original, would be broadcast on the CBS cable channel Showtime in 2017.

*Twin Peaks* had an immediate, if localised, effect on US TV drama for the rest of the 1990s. 'Weirdness' cropped up everywhere. The *X-Files* and Oliver Stone's mess of virtual reality pottage *Wild Palms* brought disorientation back to TV science fiction. *Northern Exposure*, an Alaskan ensemble quirk from the creators of *St Elsewhere*, arrived just a few months after *Twin Peaks* but didn't suffer too greatly from superficial similarities. *Picket Fences* was a clear copy, larding its Wisconsin folksiness with decapitations and spontaneous combustion, even employing *Twin Peaks*'s 'dwarf' actor, Michael J. Anderson. It was the work of crack *LA Law* writer David E. Kelley, who would take this vanilla form of weirdness to popular heights with *Ally McBeal*, proving there was nothing so strange that the networks couldn't digest it and make it their own. But at least Frost and Lynch had given them a debilitating attack of wind on the way.

# ABROAD IN BRITAIN (1990)

## BBC Two

### The arts documentary becomes art itself.

*'It takes a clever dick to make an arse smart.'*

Jonathan Meades, 1973

NOT MANY PROGRAMMES ABOUT church architecture begin with the line, 'God has been doted on since man, in his bewildered ignorance and reverential wonder, first conceived the notion that there must be some omniscient grease monkey who fitted all the parts together.' Not many histories of the Great British pub end with St George on horseback downing a can of lager in one gaseous gulp. Very few documentaries see fit to push their presenters off tall buildings onto the roofs of Ford Escorts. But then, as they chant from the terraces of the Royal Academy, there's only one Jonathan Meades.

The arts documentary comes in two distinct varieties. The most common is no-frills vanilla, bringing nothing to the screen that might distract from the subject, except maybe a tastefully chosen soundtrack. 'We're TV journalists,' Melvyn Bragg reminded everyone on the launch of archetypal pie-and-peas culture strand *The South Bank Show* in 1978, 'not arty-farty film-makers.' He was referring to the alternative, poetic flavour, which took boundless liberties with image and sound, as incubated during the 1960s on shows like Huw Weldon's *Monitor* – 'the only British experimental film school, ever,' according to its most notable graduate, Ken Russell.

The 'arty-farty' approach survived the eighties through the more playful entries in Alan Yentob's presenter-free arts slot *Arena*. In the early 1990s it assumed the shape of Nicholas Barker's *Signs of the Times*, a bone-dry cavalcade of domestic interiors of dubious taste, with their inhabitants musing stiffly on their choice of soft furnishings. More arch than a Victorian viaduct, it ostensibly withheld editorial judgement on its subjects while the camera trussed them up in their own awkwardness like an unwitting Gilbert and George, especially in the notorious shots where they stared blankly into space for seemingly minutes on end. Barker's work was, wrote one critic, 'packaged in the knowing, post-modernist manner . . . it hides behind a Sarah Dunant-style oleaginous irony.'[435]

Other approaches were available. Jonathan Meades, *Times* restaurant critic and RADA contemporary of Robert Lindsay and Stephanie Beacham, came to television in 1987, presenting Channel Four's *The Victorian House*, sporting huge prescription shades and ploughing unsteadily through a conventional account of nineteenth century domestic architecture. The delivery faltered as the words were not his. He fared better as one of the pundits on *Building Sights*, BBC Two's series of ten-minute visual essays the following year. The year after that he was given six half-hours to explore the country's architectural backwaters in a series provisionally titled *A Different Britain*.

Covering such recondite subjects as houses that abhor right-angles and the bodged folk dwellings of the Severn Valley, *Abroad in Britain* gave the manicured arts documentary a new kind of droll depth. It celebrated the underdogs of building and stood against the march of gutless, corporate postmodern detachment, in finely crafted programmes stylistically set against the blithely cocked eyebrow of the new ironic regime. Form followed argument. Meades's paean to the ragged Bohemian splendour of Hastings could easily apply to his own body of work: 'It's over-ripe, blowzy.

It has a bruised amiability that only the fallen can ever achieve. It really reeks of itself.'

Meades's words were provocative but serious, focused, sober. It was the landscape to which they referred, and in which they were delivered, that was out to lunch. Army platoons charged into frame from nowhere, pigs leapt from abandoned ovens and motorised golf caddies ran amok while Meades, in his unchanging FBI get-up, quietly struggled to make sense of it all – the previously common-place seen through a freshly de-scaled eye. Some critics just saw a good, straight documentary needlessly faffed about. Why, they asked, does he have to interrupt interviews with a house's inhab-itants by strolling about behind them, 'like Hitchcock making his ritual appearance in his own films . . . is this an out-take or a put-on?'[436]

With directors David Turnbull and Russell England, Meades perfected his brand of starched anarchy over three *Abroad . . .* series. Traditional, heroically perpendicular architectural photography – 'a vast institutional lie'[437] according to Meades – was junked in favour of wide angles, queasy tilts and compositions more likely to favour a nearby patch of waste ground notorious for dogging than the cottage or abattoir under discussion. By the third, *Even Further Abroad*, the look was of Peter Greenaway directing a public infor-mation film about the dangers of playing near postmodernist grain silos. Sound was exploited and perverted as much as image. Why accompany a cathedral interior with organ music when you can get a floating choirboy to sing 'Bat Out of Hell'? And who better to soundtrack the laudanum-soaked Victorian era than the Velvet Underground?

A new century, a new visual collaborator (Francis Hanly) and new technology led to even more exquisite shots and elaborate compositions in programmes ever more jokey, more wild, more compressed, with richer photography, dirtier gags, and lashings of Christopher Biggins. While other documentaries were rapidly cutting down on information, and obsessively worrying the viewer wouldn't understand the little that was left, Meades embellished his content, layer upon layer. He'd begin in a minuscule niche and end reaching out to the world. A programme set on the Hebridean isle of Lewis and Harris was carefully built from meticulously chosen individual shots to move from a prehistoric view of crags and standing stones, slowly evolving through pastoral scenes of sheep and primitive churches, to the eventual appearance of modern humanity, bathetically throwing up in the streets on a Saturday night.

With mainstream documentaries striving for ever more cloying inclusivity, Meades, the boy least likely to 'go on a journey' or be filmed studying archive footage on an iPad with mock intent, becomes ever more precious. In a schedule full of determinedly inoffensive steel-and-glass heritage interaction spaces, his programmes remain welcome intrusions of baroque, brutalist nonconformity. If it didn't go against his principles, he should be listed.

# THE REAL WORLD (1992–)

## MTV (Bunim/Murray Productions)

### Reality television takes off.

'THE *AVANT-GARDE* OF TELEVISION, way out along the boom, always tell you that the purest use of the medium should be unconscious. They would like to plant hidden eyes and ears all over the place and orchestrate by cross-cutting huge symphonies of social reality. It could be, but for reasons of humanity it obviously cannot be done.'[438] Despite that 'obviously' putting the very idea beyond the pale, Maurice Richardson, writing in 1960, was one of the first to set down the temptation for television documentary to do away with intermediaries and present the world to itself unmoderated, straight, complete – to serve up, in a word that steadily lost its meaning the more ubiquitous it became, reality.

The journey from ordinary fly-on-the-wall to full-blown reality began with a case of bad timing. Associated-Rediffusion's documentary crew built a reputation in the early 1960s for making smart, up-to-the-minute investigations into Britain's burgeoning youth culture with such films as *Living for Kicks* and *Beat City*. By the time they got themselves down the King's Road in 1966, however, they found it was swinging off its hinges, the groovy vibe long departed for pastures new. All they had left to point their cameras at was the well-manicured vacuity left behind, which they duly recorded and presented to the nation in shambling *cinema verité* study *Go, Go, Go, Said the Bird*.

The title, which sounds like a vacuously hip catchphrase until you realise it's a line from T. S. Eliot, pointed to a controlling intelligence behind the camera, which in turn pointed the camera at pure dumb chaos. You could tell by the dialogue that this was modern youth in all its splendour. 'I don't know what I feel at the moment, y'know, but one day I want to feel very calm, y'know, and next day I want to wear something ridiculous, y'know.' The beautiful people spoke their own private language: meandering nuggets of nothing. A fashion designer tried unsuccessfully to obtain a number from directory enquiries. 'They ought to be in concentration camps,' she huffed, hanging up in despair. The film-makers politely pointed out that she could just as easily look up the number herself in the phone book. 'If you've got to labour at anything it becomes too much,' she protested, 'and your thinking just dwindles away.' The temptation to sneer was there on a platter, but British viewers still felt uncomfortable doing this. 'I didn't like hearing myself making reactionary noises,' wrote George Melly, 'but I made them.'[439]

The next advance came in the USA in 1973, when PBS broadcast a twelve-part close study of the affluent Loud family from Eugene, Oregon. Produced by Craig Gilbert and filmed by Alan and Susan Raymond, *An American Family* presented the staid reactions of parents Bill and Pat Loud to the tumultuous activities of their five children, most famously Lance, who sensationally came out to his parents on screen. (Homosexuality was still officially treated as a mental illness in the States when the programme was filmed.) Antagonistic to his parents and camp beyond cliché, Lance emerged as the star of the show, a tempest of compulsive honesty in a mire of middle class repression. He also had the sharpest line on the show itself when he described it as 'the fulfilment of the middle class dream that you can be famous for being just who you are.'[440] Paul Watson's anglicised version made for the BBC the following year, *The Family*, took the lower-middle-class Wilkinses of Reading as its quarry and was several degrees more humble in every department, swapping pony riding and garage band jamming for brown Vymura wall coverings and earnest discussions about supplementary benefits over plates of crispy pancakes.

Though both these programmes became national obsessions, they were firmly rooted in the old documentary tradition – shot on film, carefully edited and broadcast as a crafted piece of reportage. In 1992 music channel MTV presented a 'social experiment' that kept the work of the programme makers well out of sight, to give the illusion of life brought fresh to the screen. Bearing more than a glancing similarity to *Nummer 28*, which appeared on Dutch station KRO the previous year, *The Real World*'s ethos was clumsily summed up in its introductory spiel: 'This is the true story of seven strangers picked to live in a loft and have their lives taped to find out what happens when people stop being polite and start getting real.'

'Real' in this case meant photogenic, flippant and nakedly aspirational. Assorted aspiring singers, dancers, models and actors piled into a spacious loft conversion in New York's SoHo to preen, argue, sulk and swap diet tips. The seven subjects wandered about in random states of undress, communicating more at than with each other in sentences that started out full of bravado before losing both energy and direction to finish in that familiar half-defeated, half-defiant 'y'know?' Low lighting and echoing sound gave proceedings a wash of streetwise drear, punched up by MTV's trademark rapid fire video editing. It simultaneously looked both glitzy and drab, and the stars were as pretty as they were dumb. A room full of kids mocked for being all surface by a station dedicated to the perfection of that surface, masquerading under the title *The Real World*, was a sitting duck for critics, but an instant addiction for viewers. One commentator could see why: 'post-adolescent lassitude is somehow acceptable when it has good muscle definition and straight teeth.'[441]

Almost as soon as its success registered, the spin-offs and copies appeared. A British version, *The Living Soap*, arrived in 1993 as part of BBC2's *Def II* youth annex, and was once again a lowlier affair, being set in a shared student house in Manchester. (And one with poor security at that, enabling locals to actively harass the show's more controversial contestants – the sort of reality feedback loop no programme wants to get stuck in, but plenty would.)

The MTV original rolled on throughout the 1990s, the carnival pitching up in a different US city each season. By 2000, as one commentator noted, the show had utterly changed 'from anthropological study to a mecca for the attention-starved and ego-maniacal.'[442] This was also the year *Big Brother* arrived in Britain, taking *The Real World*'s format and welding game show elements onto the front. It arrived with similar boasts of sociological intent, and just as surely discreetly dropped them as the seasons rolled by.

Dwarfed by the programming dynasty it had spawned, *The Real World* shrank to the status of also-ran, but it was now an institution in the micro-history of MTV, and somehow kept going. In 2014 the ailing format was given a shameless tweak: *The Real World: Ex-Plosion* confronted the unsuspecting stars with the news that their ex-partners had come along for the ride. The promise of on-air mortification drove ratings up once more but, like every reality show, *The Real World* can only last for so many seasons before it milks its premise dry. Still, with nearly a quarter of a century on the clock, *The Real World* can claim to have outlived many of the more popular shows that came in its wake, including MTV's own family portrait, *The Osbornes*. Similarly, E4's recent 'structured reality' Sloane-basher *Made In Chelsea* carries the ancestral markings of *Go, Go, Go, Said the Bird*. These twentieth century ancestors may have been less symphonies of social reality than three-minute pop songs of social awkwardness, but they had a tune that producers the world over can't stop whistling.

# COME ON DOWN
# AND OUT (1993)

## Channel Four
## (Kudos Productions)

Television's most righteously cool channel starts
confusing ends with means.

*Hello there, all you lesbians, gays and black people!*
Message that briefly greeted callers to Channel Four's
after hours Ansaphone, 1982

A COMMERCIAL STATION WITH a public service remit, the young
Channel Four was radical in every department, but especially the
factual. Series like *The Friday Alternative, 20/20 Vision* and *Bandung
File* wore their agit-prop hearts on their sleeves. Founding controller
Jeremy Isaacs was famously asked by an irate Norman Tebbit why
the minority channel the government had created for him was full
of stuff about gays and Northern Ireland, rather than the sort of
minority interests Tebbit had in mind: golf and yachting. Chris
Dunkley of the *Financial Times* posited the stereotypical Channel
Four documentary, a hopelessly obscure minority subject 'made
exclusively by women of a certain sort (you know the sort)'.[443] This
sort of criticism would only encourage them.

The channel's first problem was to snare a nation whose viewing
habits had been largely unchanged for nearly two decades. Early

efforts like earnest debate *Voices* dipped below 200,000 viewers, then the lowest measurable amount, thus earning the ignominious 'zero rating'. *Channel Four News*, Britain's first in-depth early evening bulletin, had similar audience issues in its first year. 'It would be cheaper to phone the news bulletins to people,' reckoned presenter Peter Sissons.[444] Under the editorship of ITN's Stewart Purvis it grew into Britain's most respected serious news programme, but anxieties remained. On laying out his heavyweight plan, Purvis was buttonholed by the channel's deputy chairman Richard Attenborough, who pleaded, 'darling, you will remember we are all in show business, won't you?'[445] As the channel grew larger on the landscape, and the British government less tolerant of televised dissent, big scoops got the chop. Ken Loach's union broadside *Questions of Leadership* and *The People's Account*, a look at the 1985 Broadwater Farm Estate riots from the residents' point of view, were just two high profile shows written off in the name of that mysterious entity, 'balance'.

In the latter half of the 1980s, Channel Four entered a new phase. *The Comic Strip Presents . . .* and *Saturday Live* put alternative comedy front and centre. Jonathan Ross threw out the last lingering formalities of the chat show. Entertainment elbowed its way to the front and came to define the channel with a new rakish swagger: less didactic, more off the wall, and far more comfortable in its own skin. Its factual output continued undaunted in the same ethical vein, but after Isaacs yielded to Michael Grade in November 1987, even that last bastion of the old guard would, slowly, be turned.

The 1990 Broadcasting Act made the previously subsidised channel a wholly self-funding body. Grade still vocally defended the old ethos, especially in the face of new threats to editorial independence, like the advent of fully sponsored programmes. 'There are two things which are absolute anathema to each other, and they are sponsorship and controversy.'[446] But then a subtle shift occurred. Politics were complex, dangerous and limited in impact to the informed and interested. Sex, meanwhile, though still a complicated and inflammatory topic, had universal appeal.

In 1991, the target was for thoughtful filth. *Dick*, a twelve-minute American film with a cast of a thousand penises, was put away on orders from the newly formed Independent Television Commission, but *WR: Mysteries of the Organism*, a psycho-sexual meditation with only a handful of penises, was shown, but with some hastily super-imposed goldfish swimming handily into view over the inappro-priate elements. By choosing material which kept to the channel's progressive, educational ideals, while still flushing out those who fancied a good gawp, Grade and friends had it, so to speak, both ways. Two years later *Love Weekend* repeated the trick, but with a noticeable shift towards untrammelled smut. *The Naked Chat Show*, a randy quiz and a 'snogging contest' hosted by Richard Jobson jettisoned the high-minded fig leaf of previous seasons.

In the spring of 1993, the Rubicon was crossed. *Come On Down and Out* was a purposefully crass game show in which three home-less contestants competed to win their dream prize: a home. Andrew O'Connor, ably assisted by Annabel Giles, put the hopeful down-and-outs through three gruelling rounds. First, a conventional quiz on the subject, naturally, of homelessness. What was the most common cause of death amongst the homeless? Suicide, guessed one contestant correctly. So, a bit of consciousness was raised. Immediately, however, O'Connor quipped, 'And that's why we removed all sharp objects from your dressing rooms tonight!' Humiliation was heaped on the hapless threesome in further rounds in which they had to 'build a bash' from assorted street detritus, and were subjected to demeaning hidden camera pranks while out and about. Scouse Jimmy made it to the final round, in which a dream house lay in one of three boxes. He picked the wrong one, and won a set of patio furniture. O'Connor oleaginously soothed his crestfallen nerves over the credits.

Then came a special continuity announcement: 'The programme you have just seen was not a real game show. All the contestants were actors.' And so the nation saw what they did there. The show was part of a wider season on homelessness, *Gimme Shelter*, which featured many more sober efforts like a retracing of Orwell's down-and-out odyssey and a repeat of *Cathy Come Home*. Even so, outrage broke out days before transmission. The soothing reveal was only added at the last minute as an emergency measure to offset the attacks, but it failed to placate many critics. The ethics of this sort of stunt were debated at length. The channel was accused of becoming too populist, indulging in controversy for ratings' sake, and abandoning its public service remit.

Such tactics were also being adopted by advertising agencies, unveiling 'shock campaigns' with relentless regularity, each one trying to go that bit further to offset the diminishing returns. In the process, shock value became an end in itself. A blood-soaked anti-fur campaign ad and a blood-soaked Benetton ad may differ in intent – one has real anger behind it, the other merely an eye on maximum publicity – but their effect is more or less the same, and it's the effect that generates the headlines. Upset becomes an end in itself.

Serious stuff was still being produced, but as the century turned, the channel's symbiotic relationship with tabloid consternation became one of co-dependence. Commissions like *When She Died*, an opera about the death of Princess Diana, were seemingly made with an eye for maximum free press advertising. ITV, of all institutions, criticised Four's populism. Even their own independent producers knew it. 'They're very safe,' admitted one, anonymously. 'They say they're radical, but it's all tits and willies, nothing very difficult.'[447]

Offence is a fossil fuel, requiring ever more desperate and destructive measures to extract it. When sex alone lost its power, dysfunction and outlandish peccadilloes were exhibited to attract the prurient. Extreme accidents of birth were paraded with a combination of sideshow rubbernecking and contrived compassion. Where once it was one tool among many, the ironic tone was now a mark of impregnable sophistication, a nod and a wink to help the producer disappear when awkward questions arose about motives. Assumptions were made rather than challenged. It all became a game, and a dodgy one at that, when real people were involved.

Finally, one of the station's central tenets was turned completely on its head. In 2014, *Benefits Street* catalogued the antics of a notoriously poor Birmingham neighbourhood. It was a rather old-fashioned beast, with only stylistic tics to distinguish it from the puzzled forays into the working class jungle made in television's formative years. Its publicity campaign, though, playing on the government's welfare crackdown, was a masterpiece. Viewers flocked, and kept on flocking when ministers name-checked the series in economic debates.

The old Channel Four would have been aghast at being co-opted to defend the status quo. Its mid-period incarnation might have tried to subvert the debate. Late-period Four just sat back and watched the numbers rise. In 2015 Love Productions began shooting a spin-off, *Immigration Street*, in Southampton's Derby Road. Locals, mindful of the company's previous work, organised petitions, protests and even staged disruptive direct action during location shoots. Channel Four's journey from streetwise scourge of the establishment to besieged enemy of the people was complete.

The director of Shelter, the homeless charity which collaborated with Channel Four on *Come On Down and Out*, said the game show aimed to highlight 'the hypocrisy of a society that sits in judgement, deciding who is worthy of help and who is not'. Defences of *Benefits Street* tended to skip any suggestion of intent, sticking to mollifying claims of 'getting a debate going', while naturally calling up the channel's long history of unimpeachably worthy programmes as a humanitarian shield. This wasn't tabloid telly. How could it be? It was on Channel Four, the thrusting young radical broadcaster that made minorities cool and compassion groovy. Once upon a time.

# FRASIER (1993–2004)
## NBC (Grub Street/Paramount)

### Highbrow America in all its glorious stupidity.

THE HISTORY OF THE American sitcom since at least the late sixties is largely the history of smart kids from Harvard, Berkeley and Yale acting dumb for a paycheck. In the early days, when television was a suspicious little sideline for adventurous vaudevillians, gags were the product of tenement smarts, of blue-collar minds that had to be one beat faster than their fellows to stay on top.

Paul Henning was an exception to this rule. Born in a small Missouri town, he graduated from *The Burns & Allen Show* to create some of the most successful sitcoms of the sixties – *The Beverly Hillbillies*, *Petticoat Junction* and *Green Acres* – all based around the clash of urban and backwoods American lifestyles. When advertisers took to measuring audiences by demographics instead of raw numbers, Henning's creations were first against the wall. The college-educated, eighteen-to-thirty-four-year-old 'blue jean' set became television's prize quarry, and they demanded sophistication and social relevance. That the same generation would later wax nostalgic over soufflés such as *Gilligan's Island* and *The Brady Bunch* was a point slightly too sophisticated for the advertisers to measure.

For the best part of a decade, sitcom was dominated by two houses. MTM provided the upwardly mobile wit, while Norman Lear (with more than a little help from British writers like Ray Galton, Alan Simpson and Johnny Speight) put articulate, angry working class voices on screen. In 1978 a breakaway quartet of

MTM writers formed their own company to make a fusion of the two styles in *Taxi*. Though its nominal main characters were MTM types – a struggling actor and an art gallery receptionist – they languished in an authentically filthy yellow cab depot and were augmented, and soon upstaged, by their earthier cab-driving colleagues: a hyper-aggressive Italian, an otherworldly European immigrant, a dim boxer and a messianic space cadet. White and blue collars alike turned an indistinguishable oily black. It was a vibrant cross-section of American failure.

In turn, three star *Taxi* writers – James Burrows, Glen and Les Charles – refined this dead end melting pot formula with *Cheers*, the internecine affairs of staff and assorted hangers-on in a Boston bar. A broad social spectrum cohered through the magic of boredom and beer, with one sore thumb in the shape of frustrated intellectual waitress Diane Chambers (Shelley Long), a la-di-da graduate with pretensions that are mercilessly mocked by the rest of the gang. Taking charge of a home movie made for naive barman Woody to send to his concerned folks back in Indiana, she lards it with portentous symbolism, atom bomb footage and a Wagner soundtrack, titling it 'Manchild in Beantown Redux'. Her crass precocity leaves the bar agog, and we later learn Woody's dad wasn't keen on the film: 'He said it was too derivative of Godard.'

In the third season, Diane gained a partner in bookishness in the form of insecure psychiatrist Dr Frasier Crane (Kelsey Grammer), introduced as a foil to the show's central stop-start romance between Diane and bar owner Sam Malone, a smart but romantically feeble second banana based on Ralph Bellamy's roles in screwball comedies like *The Awful Truth*.[448] Long disliked the new character, but he proved popular enough to become a regular, acquiring an icy, bloodless wife and son over the next eight years. *Cheers* begat two spin-off shows: *The Tortellis*, focussing on acerbic waitress Carla's ex-husband, lasted just one season; *Frasier*, the second choice, had legs.

*Cheers* and *Taxi* avoided domestic situations, preferring to hint at characters' home lives rather than show them wherever possible.

*Frasier* was domestic to the point of imprisonment. His Seattle bachelor pad-cum-epicurean comfort zone is invaded first by his invalid ex-cop dad Martin, dragging a homely battered recliner in amongst the 'eclectic' array of Eames chairs and Chanel sofas, then by textbook kooky home help Daphne Moon, 'originally from Manchester, England' (though to British ears she was closer to Rochdale, Mars). Niles, Frasier's even more priggish brother, alternately ameliorated and added to the familial claustrophobia. Martin's role was to remind 'the boys' of their less than high flown origins, of the fact that brash wisdom will outclass well-spoken whimsy every time, and to throw their attenuated masculinity into sharp relief. Daphne and brazen radio producer Roz were there to point up their pampered lack of purpose and to throw their attenuated masculinity into sharp relief. Frasier's job as local radio shrink is consistently unrewarding and often downright humiliating; brother Niles, trapped in a marriage even more anaemic than Frasier's used to be, unspools a ceaseless litany of first world problems. Like Diane, he sees every flat farce as a Greek tragedy, constantly pleading that he surely deserves better than this, the answer always 'no'.

The pretensions of the brothers are a writer's gift. Their shared humour is an allusive, highbrow patois that, like most avowedly intellectual attempts at comedy, seem mainly restricted to bad puns about composers and European novelists. They chuckle indulgently at their immense erudition (Niles, at age six, drew not his parents but scenes from *Aida*) while everyone else looks on with an expression of, at best, muted pity. The sitcom itself had 'classy' touches – Grammer's ersatz blues theme tune, the gnomic captions between scenes, the roll-call of uncredited stars playing Frasier's phone-in patients from Cyd Charisse to Mary Tyler Moore – but snobbery and grandiose aspiration were always comic targets, not comic means.

At its best, the show was meticulously plotted. A satisfying comic plot requires greater precision, less wastage, than a decent drama. 'A concert pianist is allowed a wrong note here and there,' wrote

Kingsley Amis. 'A juggler is not allowed to drop a plate.'[449] The show took pride in its ability to lay out a wide range of stories, taking old chestnuts like mistaken identity or an unsolved murder and adding a fresh comic spin. Frasier was sent running in frantic circles by a recurring homoerotic dream ('were there any cigars, bananas or short, blunt swords?') or an amateur revival of old fashioned live radio drama sinking under the weight of its company's incompetence and infighting. The obligatory minimalist episode, which all great sitcoms must foist on themselves on a point of technical honour, took the shape of a fractious, real time head-to-head chat in the Café Nervosa. The fourth season, capping half a century of television sitcom progress, represented the peak of the genre's wit and ingenuity – a long tradition taken to vertiginous heights.

Very rarely did *Frasier* experiment with sitcom's traditional self-reference, but one small indulgence stood out. Diane Chambers turned up like a bad penny, subjecting Frasier to a rehearsal of her theatrical atrocity *Rhapsody and Requiem*, a self-aggrandising *roman-à-clef* set in a suspiciously familiar-looking bar that made *Long Day's Journey Into Night* look like *Hellzapoppin'*. It was a scene that played clever games with the show's history, took a cheeky swipe at Long's original dislike of the Frasier character, and brought a long-standing emotional cliffhanger to a well-judged conclusion all at once. This was the smart sitcom in its element – throwing a perilously narrow bridge across the gap between its protagonists' formal intelligence and their emotional ignorance: then, when they're halfway across, giving them an encouraging sideways nudge. Gets 'em every time.

# OUR FRIENDS IN
# THE NORTH (1996)
## BBC Two

### Drama thinks big.

BY THE 1970S TALES of northern deprivation, whether romanticised by Catherine Cookson or polemicised by Jim Allen, claimed so much British screen time they constituted a genre in themselves, and thus awash with cliché. Clive James lamented the regularity with which the hero's father would become trapped underneath a collapsed pithead, and Nancy Banks-Smith noted that 'Yorkshire seems infested with iron-fisted father figures much given to shouting "Tha's nobbut nowt" and thus wounding the susceptibilities of their sensitive southern sons.'[450] *Monty Python* made the modern, media-savvy northern writer a rough-hewn D. H. Lawrence hero, lamenting a life of backbreaking creative toil. ('There's nowt wrong wi' gala luncheons, lad! I've had more gala luncheons than you've had hot dinners!')

It had come to the point where the mere sight of a colliery on the horizon or a clog-sparking child capering in front of some back-to-backs provoked pre-emptive sniggers. Meanwhile the breakdown of the British social contract dragged the north further into debt. For jaded viewers still hooting at t'mill and its manifold troubles a new language was needed; one compiled from the bottom up.

Peter Flannery, a playwright from Jarrow-on-Tyne and grandson of one of the Jarrow marchers of 1936, was a politically engaged writer who wryly described his work as 'mainly about housing'.[451] His magnum opus *Our Friends in the North* had, even by the standards of most ambitious plays, a troubled genesis. It began as a stage play, slated to run at Stratford-on-Avon in December 1981 but was postponed for six months, finally surfacing to christen the Royal Shakespeare Company's new Pit theatre at the Barbican in the summer of 1982. It was ambitious stuff: a three-and-a-half hour epic in the style of recent broad Brechtian history plays like David Hare and Howard Brenton's *Brassneck* and David Edgar's *Destiny*, plays which started from current events and extrapolated backwards into Britain's ignoble imperial past.

Flannery's play took its four protagonists from Harold Wilson's 1964 election victory to Thatcher's in 1979, watching their youthful ideals slowly perish under the weight of establishment corruption, centring on the Newcastle of city councillor T. Dan Smith but reaching out as far as Rhodesia. It was a play firmly in the didactic mould, ending with a female character shooting smack, brandishing a machine gun and beseeching the audience to 'seize the power!' Flannery offered a hard-headed interpretation of post-war history, but not everyone was convinced. 'You don't prove a case simply by piling up incidents in a mountainous heap,' countered Michael Billington. 'What weakens the play's dramatic impact is the assumption of some mystical link between these specific, individual acts of corruption.'[452]

*Our Friends* was rewritten into a series for the BBC in 1984, and turned down. A second version returned to the controller's office in 1991, where Flannery's work was once again in good company. Controversial dramas based on real people and events were all over the news at that time: the BBC's Falklands War drama *Tumbledown* and Alan Bleasdale's Derek Hatton-inspired *GBH* grabbed as many headlines as they did awards. The Beeb's lawyers blocked production, uncomfortable over its reference to real events (the Poulson housing scandal, and the possible identification of several lightly fictionalised senior police officers). One lawyer suggested Flannery distance the play from reality by setting it in a fictional country called 'Albion'. Flannery hit back by sarcastically suggesting in turn that, to show it really was a work of fiction, all the policemen should be black.[453] This wasn't a good working relationship. 'It is making dealing with public life and real events in dramatic form impossible,' said Flannery. 'If my experience is typical, [we] should be concerned about the future of drama writers at the BBC.'[454]

Finally a nine-part series of Flannery's 'political *Heimat*' was green-lit in 1993, and the £8 million production was announced as part of a £174 million drama package attacked by the *Daily Mail* as a festival of 'under-age sex, lesbianism, violence and swearing.'[455] In an increasingly conservative dramatic landscape of bonnets, breeches and Darling Buds, *Our Friends* felt like something of a throwback to a less cowed televisual age. On the other hand, with a revamped Labour Party poised to take over the clapped out Tory government, it was as of the moment as ever. (Ironically, one prescient plot strand about the rise of spin doctors within the Labour ranks was removed from the drama during those protracted negotiations. The characters based on John Poulson and Reginald Maudling remained, as their originals had since passed on.)

The wait was more than worth it. Flannery had expertly integrated the countrywide, decade-spanning hauteur of the stage original with the material and emotional minutiae of individual life. (He admitted it was the protracted gestation that allowed him to convincingly age his characters, having aged along with them.) The four leads were, aside from being slightly too old to pass for students in the first episode, uniformly strong: Christopher Eccleston's political activist Nicky; Mark Strong's rocker-turned entrepreneur Tosker; Gina McKee's Mary, who vacillates between the two of them; and Daniel Craig's Geordie, going from Soho porn merchant to broken vagrant. All of them were caught in Flannery's web of corruption, now running up to the present day, but as strongly delineated as ever.

The look and feel of the programme may have been modernised, but the message came straight from the adversarial 1970s. A week after it came to an elegiac close, BBC Two began showing *This Life*, a thoroughly modern drama of liberal aspiration and déclassé identity politics. The odd politically committed exception like Jimmy McGovern aside, this would be the model for British drama from now on; *Our Friends* was a last hurrah. Even the conservative *Daily Telegraph* lamented the fact: 'We are not likely to look upon its like again.'

# THIS MORNING WITH RICHARD NOT JUDY (1998–9)

## BBC Two

### Existential satire and blasphemy finally reach Sunday afternoons.

> *Don't you realise you're participating in a sophisticated satire on your own low expectations?*
>
> Stewart Lee to audience, *Lee & Herring Live*, Ashcroft Theatre, Croydon, November 1996

WHEN ALTERNATIVE COMEDY'S SECOND wave showed its colours on TV in the early 1990s, its distinctions were easy to spot. Politically they were just as far to the left as their predecessors, but the second wavers made politics less central to their act, partly because a left-wing stance had been ingrained over the past decade as the default consensus of the young comedy crowd (which meant conservatism would inevitably die through natural wastage within a couple of decades). Instead there was a more wide-ranging – all right, rambling – preoccupation with other social matters: religion, sexual acceptance or lack of it, and forensic poring over the detritus of recent pop culture.

It was more decadent, and more childish, in a way. *The Mary Whitehouse Experience* might start a sketch about Saddam Hussein, but within thirty seconds it became a philosophical enquiry into the significance of *Captain Pugwash*, forsaking the demolition of the realpolitik of late capitalism for some whimsical riffing on Peter Purves's World Cup electricity board adverts or the ontological implications of Baccara's 'Yes Sir, I Can Boogie'. A lot of it would later constitute the backbone of the new comedy establishment, full of well-scrubbed middle class male stand-ups with powerful agents declaiming inoffensive, banal observations to packed arenas. Some, though, married a head-banging obsession with mindless trivia to sharp social insight.

Stewart Lee and Richard Herring formed as a double act in the traditional way, bonding at an Oxford University student revue. Their roles were settled early on. Herring was the gleeful man-child whose world-view swung wildly from the touchingly credulous to the shabbily perverted; Lee the supercilious eternal sixth-former operating with absolute certainty that his opinions, tastes and achievements were superior to those of everyone else. Together they stumbled through pop culture, Herring getting the wrong end of every stick, Lee calmly disabusing and disparaging him. After years of work on the live circuit, they got into radio through milestone current affairs satire *On the Hour* before graduating to their own radio shows and, by 1995, television with the sketch show *Fist of Fun*.

Growing out of an improvised chat show the pair hosted at the Edinburgh Fringe, *This Morning with Richard Not Judy*, or *TMWRNJ* (pronounced 'Terwumwunjuh!'), was a forty-five minute sketch show nominally modelled on ITV's afternoon magazine *This Morning*, performed live at Sunday lunchtime. Even allowing for the annexation, in the wake of *Network 7* and *Def II*, of that previously fallow slot for various youth-oriented shows, this was risky in its conception to the point of mania. Lee and Herring threw everything into it, packing the long running time with a wealth of material, organising complex live routines and recorded items full of recondite references and elaborate premises in total contravention of what was normally considered easily digestible by the average viewer at that particular time.

Items were built on in-jokes and caprice, then fleshed out with the help of the BBC props department and a skilled repertory company including Paul Putner and Kevin Eldon. A pun on the title of a song by The Fall brought forth 'The Curious Orange', an outsize fruit with the mind of a small child. 'Sunday Heroes' was their attempt to represent religion, as was right and proper for the timeslot, in reconstructions of the gospels which ended up revealing Jesus as an obscurantist riddler, keeping his dimmer disciples in their place with wilfully ambiguous parables. Although these brief sketches contained a more thorough dissection of Christian teaching than had been aired in that time slot for decades, the devout were slow to show their appreciation.

Their skewering of the unsophisticated dogma of early alternative comedy was something entirely new. Herring, accused of some convoluted, shameful private act, pleads to the gallery: 'Who's the real sick man in our so-called society?' He argues – with textbook debating society rhetorical emphasis – it's not him, but 'the *busi*ness*man. In his *suit* and *tie*.' Later, the alternative establishment was forensically undermined in the sketch 'Angus Deayton's Authorised History of Alternative Comedy with Angus Deayton', parodying a recent clipshow on the subject with a series of thinly-disguised impersonations of New Wave acts intercut with their sadly wistful present day reminiscences of those 'amazing times' while nursing a commemorative SDP mug.

This was no reactionary attack. Equal scorn was poured on the trend, still fairly new but rapidly catching on, of post-political, self-reflexive controversy building. 'The Ironic Review' was a spoof fly-on-the-wall documentary of office life in a hip metropolitan magazine, not terribly loosely based on *The Modern Review*, a painfully arch culture compendium run by Julie Burchill and Cosmo Landesman in the first half of the 1990s. The staff's *raison d'être* was to manufacture opinions which were the opposite of what they assumed their peer group deemed acceptable, delivered with a childishly whinnying 'aaa-*aaah*!' At the time this niche target brought a muted response from the studio audience, but two decades on, with practically the whole of the opinion columnist's trade reduced to mindless contrariness in the desperate search for online ad revenue, it looks remarkably prescient.

This goes double for the throwaway gag that opened the show on the morning of the 1998 London Marathon, with Lee and Herring dressed as (the as yet undefiled) Jimmy Savile, cheerily looking forward to the race. 'I hope nobody dies!' 'If they do, bagsy I take them to the mortuary!' The programme's profile, low to begin with and rapidly diminishing, enabled this joke (again, to almost total silence in the studio) to be casually flung out without major controversy. 'Because we knew no-one [at the BBC] was interested in it,' Lee explained, 'we were able to do whatever we wanted.'[456]

As the second series progressed, a heady combination of the duo's obsessive industriousness and BBC management's almost total abandonment of the show meant that each of the already complicated running characters and sketches developed their own storylines, mutated out of shape, cross-bred and generally collapsed into a broiling, end-of-term chaos. This was what marked their act out in an increasingly mainstream, career-minded alternative comedy world where maximum acceptability and the thrifty re-use of material were standard practice. Lee and Herring's idea of a crowd-pleasing gesture could be summed up by the end of one especially abstruse *TMWRNJ* escapade, when Herring apologised to first-time viewers for any bewilderment caused, 'but hopefully you still enjoyed the colours and shapes'.

# THE SOPRANOS (1999–2007)

## HBO (Chase Films/ Brad Grey Television)

### US drama finally reaches critical mass.

TAKE A LOOK AT the television coverage of the quality press on both sides of the Atlantic in the early years of the twenty-first century, and you'll notice a minor miracle. For the first few years of the hopeful third millennium, television was following a slow spiral into an inescapable chasm of facetious self-assembly reality formats and drearily third-rate fiction. A few years on, however, and a new Golden Age had suddenly dawned, brought forth on a raft of original drama of unprecedented seriousness and ambition. *The Sopranos, Breaking Bad, The West Wing, The Wire* . . . series after series broke envelopes, pushed moulds and tipped points wherever you looked. The tube's sucking void was suddenly a horn of plenty. What happened?

There was, of course, no spontaneous generation of genius, more another step on the evolutionary trail that began with Paddy Chayefsky. Quality and complexity are nothing new. Innovation is continuous, but occasionally enough quality specimens clump together for the coarse filter of media journalism, and a Golden Age is solemnly declared.

Drama in the 1990s was a jumble after the self-aware MTM era. Upmarket soaps like *thirtysomething* brought drama back into the domestic fold. Meanwhile, cops and docs continued to dominate evenings with *NYPD Blue, Homicide: Life on the Street, Chicago Hope* and *ER*. Good shows, but together they didn't make something the glibber end of media journalism could rip an easy headline from. Into this network soup rode fast-rising cable channel HBO with a show that combined the crime and the domestic with the story of a middle-aged New Jersey mob boss under pressure from both his empire and his errant family – all inspired by *Goodfellas*, Martin Scorsese's filmed life of gangster-turned-witness Henry Hall.

*The Sopranos* worked the highly desirable trick of stuffing the scope of a novel into a popular weekly series. In most series a few main characters have full histories, with everyone else a cipher working in aid of the plot. In *The Sopranos* everyone, from Tony's therapist to the strippers in his 'office', was a rounded, living creation. The weekly doses kept it in the popular imagination, and when a series was over the boxed DVD version could stand there, like *War and Peace*, on the correspondent's coffee table.

With the 'literary' end of television drama – most conspicuously those beloved single plays of increasingly distant memory – drying up, innovation has to come from genre, of which the crime or police thriller is by far the most prevalent. Forty-odd years ago an ambitious writer would most likely not be drawn to genre television, though he would likely have learned his craft in it. A genre show was most often an assemblage of previously successful parts, sometimes animated by a guiding creative intelligence which clicked them into place in ways no-one had thought of before, but more often than not lashed together just well enough to weather a season or two. The network economy could operate in no other way.

The cable economy, on the other hand, could foster a show with comparatively little executive tampering, and few if any name actors demanded up front, where the creator/writer was king. (It's worth noting that only a macro-economy as big as the USA's can comfortably contain a micro-economy of this type big enough to make an impact, so critics from far smaller nations are being obtuse when they demand why their compatriots haven't come up with something similar.)

*The Wire* is far more than a police procedural, as *Battlestar Galactica* is more than space opera. With shows like this, genre is an emphasis, a lens through which the world is refracted rather than a set of rules for a game through which life can be endlessly avoided. Great things had always come from generic roots. Dickens wrote serialised stories for popular entertainment, and happened to over-fulfil his brief several times over. Tolstoy began *War and Peace* with no greater ambition than to write a Russian version of the English 'domestic chronicle' in the style of Anthony Trollope, but expanded to encompass Russian history and moral philosophy, the generic boundaries swelling to encompass 'the ever-changing, ever-great, unfathomable, and infinite life around him.'[457]

The auteured TV dramas of the 1990s and 2000s were similarly alive to the richness of the everyday as it's experienced, rather than the routine of the adventure as it's so often fictionalised. David Chase, creator of *The Sopranos*, aligned what he'd learned of crafting a TV script from his apprenticeship on quirky series like *The Rockford Files* and *Northern Exposure* with influences from beyond the Burbank backlot. For one episode involving Tony Soprano's hallucination of a beautiful Italian dental student, Chase pointed the director to the matter-of-fact surrealism of Luis Buñuel as a cue for the handling of the fantastic plot.[458] A committee-steered network series would have run a mile from that kind of influence in the unlikely event it even occurred to them.

Creativity needs freedom to work, and freedom has always been in short supply. In 1737, British spoken drama was segregated by parliamentary decree. Robert Walpole instigated the theatrical crackdown to curtail the many satirical broadsides against his government, introducing mandatory censoring of all plays. In the early twentieth century, modernist artists enforced the idea of 'literary' work as above and beyond the run of the fictional mill, focusing critical eyes on a small group of writers and leaving the mainstream to stew in its self-policing, market driven genres.

Walpole's Regulation Act was finally completely rescinded in 1968, about the same time that critics began to admit that the best practitioners of genre fiction could rival the highbrows. Television, as subject to the control of snobs and politicians as any medium, entered its most extraordinary period at about this time. From the mid-1960s to the early 1980s, British and American screens teemed with intelligent, lively, outlandish and fabulous comedy, drama and documentary. The excitable predictions of the twenties and thirties began to look like they had a point with their prognostications of a world forever changed by the UHF transmitter.

Unfortunately there was a third source of repression, which wasn't going away. In fact, it began to reassert itself to an ever greater degree. Economic necessity took hold in the 1980s and never let go. Privately owned broadcasters planted themselves across the TV landscape while state subsidised television was steadily pruned back. A profusion of new channels struggled to cover themselves with a dearth of old programmes. Market research and governmental compliance meant the making of new programmes became progressively less of a madcap art and more of a dismal science. Common denominators began burrowing their way to the Earth's core. After the briefest of spells in the ascendant, TV was hounded once more.

The melting pot of the new medium, with shows of different types and tones clashing every evening, gave birth to countless new dramatic shapes and gradually wore down the barrier between high and low. The single play – the aloof, often difficult work that stands alone – is a thing of the past. Any future innovation will come from the series, and the genre series at that. The concentrated art and wit of *The Sopranos* and many of the broadsheet-wetting prodigies that followed it show this is not necessarily the disaster twentieth century critics used to fear.

Perhaps the HBO microclimate is so celebrated because it feels like a last stand, the old forests of memory lovingly revived as a perfectly trimmed bonsai plot. At the same time, banishing these shows to subscription services and online niches away from the mainstream runs the risk of another kind of segregation. Among the genuine fans of the cable dramas, a new group of highfalutin dunces gets to feel superior to the reality-swilling masses just for being in the know. The single play flew too far from its roots and found itself starved of funds when the financial reckoning came. Today's Emmy-laden showrunners must ensure their rarefied end of the new, disconnected television system doesn't become a similar intellectual ghetto.

# PEOPLE LIKE US
# (1999–2001)
## BBC Two

### The mockumentary at its peak.

THE FIRST TELEVISION MOCK-DOC was the 1968 *Smothers Brothers Comedy Hour* extended sketch 'Pat Paulsen: the Making of a President'. Filmed on grainy, hand-held 16mm film, this perfectly deadpan skit laid out the electoral hopes of the show's semi-detached deadbeat, with everyone from Woody Allen to Bobby Kennedy in on the gag. Instantly the golden rule was established: your words and actions can be as demented as you like, as long as the presentation remains po-faced and precise.

In 1972, satirists John Bird and John Wells created several comedy specials for Yorkshire Television, each consisting of a behind-the-scenes pastiche of an area of factual programming; as Wells put it, a 'tiptoe through the grim hinterland of television'.[459] *Return to Leeds* depicted the fractious making of a 'writer revisits roots' documentary, with Bird as the left-wing subject and Wells as the metropolitan producer; while *Deadline Leeds* evoked a disintegrating current affairs programme, with the two Johns playing every character in front of and behind the cameras. The depiction of what gets shown and said on these programmes, and the thinking that makes them that way, was diabolically accurate, but real life behind-the-scenes problems meant the shows were transmitted piecemeal, with up to a year between episodes, dooming them to obscurity.

Through the next two decades, the mock-doc broadened its reach and sharpened its approach. Neil Innes and Eric Idle's fictional sixties pop group the Rutles began as a handful of Beatles pastiches with period visual accompaniment on *Rutland Weekend Television*, before having their ludicrous backstory filled in, again with a sprinkling of genuine stars, for 1978 NBC special *All You Need Is Cash*. The music business was mockumentary manna – the typical rock star's drug-flattened delivery, the insane decadence of the business and the increasing pretension of the music were a perfect combination. The *Comic Strip* depicted life at the bottom of the glorious heap with 1983's *Bad News Tour*, following a suburban metal band of honking fecklessness around Britain in a leopardskin-trimmed van. The following year, Rob Reiner's cinema release *This Is Spinal Tap* covered the same territory, creating a sleeper cult hit.

Politics and news, the beachhead of media pomp, took their lumps from the genre. In the US, HBO's miniseries *Tanner '88* allowed Robert Altman to refine the roaming, overlapping style he'd popularised with *MASH*, trapping satirist Garry Trudeau's hopeful Democratic candidate in a web of pregnant pauses and fumbled rhetorical stabs. In Britain current affairs were demolished by the dynasty of radio and TV programmes marshalled by Armando Iannucci and Christopher Morris. *The Day Today*, their first TV manifestation, dressed as a news bulletin but impersonated everything. What looked like blunderbuss fire from a distance proved on close inspection to be a blitz of trained snipers. Picture, sound, style and speech of eras from the fifties to the present, and countries from the USA to France, were forensically restaged. A three second clip of a forgotten drama brought the sense of an entire series, even generation, with it – believable and familiar, but somehow fundamentally ajar. Countless delicately wrought moments piled up on each other to give the cumulative effect of television itself cracking up.

*Brass Eye*, Morris's demolition of the self-righteous *World in Action* crusading tradition, went even further, showing sanity a clean pair of heels from the interminable opening titles onward. Director Michael Cumming, who'd served an apprenticeship on sober science programmes like *Tomorrow's World*, was instrumental in keeping the wild script in contact with reality by furnishing the madhouse with authentic visual bric-a-brac. Cumming didn't direct the *Brass Eye Special*, the show's slight return in 2001, and the look of it suffered from the lack of visual unity: faked archive footage looked mannered, graphics too obviously wacky, and clips from supposedly different programmes not quite distinct enough. In this game the details matter.

The format reached its limit in writer John Morton's debut broadcast work *People Like Us*. It began on Radio Four in 1995 as a pastiche of the BBC's long tradition of earnest explorations of everyday life, which had grown into a recognisable formula. An everyday situation – a market stall, an accountancy firm – was visited by a reporter with a lugubrious, earthy, borderline sarcastic manner (Ray Gosling, Bernard Falk, and especially John Pitman) resulting in a half-elegiac, half-melancholy portrait of honest, humdrum Britain. Knowingly mundane titles like *The Beaminster and District Gardens and Allotments Society Goes to Chelsea* abounded. This had already been parodied in a running sketch on *Victoria Wood: As Seen on TV*. Authentic documentary reporter Paul Heiney and authentic documentary cameraman Philip Bonham-Carter were placed amongst characters created by Wood and her company of actors, creating a believably textured world that slowly but surely turned fully absurd.

In *People Like Us* Chris Langham was dogged interlocutor Roy Mallard, a distillation of the Gosling-Pitman manner with the bathos multiplied tenfold and the self-awareness stripped out, following honest working types through a typical day. ('Thursday.') His lugubrious voice plods through endless dollops of vapid scene-setting prose. ('Whilst those around him are bound for jobs in offices, shops or other offices, Rob's day may well take him to places he doesn't even know about yet, although equally it might not, in which case he doesn't know about that either.')

Mallard's inane questions, his subjects' only marginally less inane responses, and the tendency of both parties to become easily distracted from the task in hand, give the meandering format a deceptively quick-fire gag rate. Unusually for a sitcom, the director's main job was to make it look like it contained fewer jokes than it actually did.

Translated to television, the documentary conceit opened up further opportunities for self-sabotage. The visual constantly exposed defects in the verbal. Gaps in the film were arbitrarily plugged with Mallard's half-awake platitudes. ('Acting is a profession of extremes on the one hand, and on the other hand, too; an all-or-nothing world in which triumph and rejection, comedy and tragedy, go hand in glove like two halves of the same puppet.') The supposedly invisible filmmaking process becomes so gummed up in its own ineptitude it threatens to push its subject off the screen. The lives of dull fools are proudly explained by even duller fools, who still tell us plenty about life nevertheless, by sheer galumphing accident. It's a feeling every TV viewer knows well, so to have it intentionally replicated works as a welcome release: there's someone with brains in the zoo after all.

What followed *People Like Us*, though, was very odd indeed. The basic technical trappings of the fake documentary need a degree of observation and skill to pull off, but they're not that difficult to do. Unbolt the camera from the tripod, chop the dialogue into awkward, overlapping chunks and you're superficially halfway there already. The *Hill Street Blues* style of shaky realism becoming a one-stop application of grit for your drama output might seem logical, but its equally pernicious takeover of comedy a few years later (and soon everything up to and including ads) was more surprising.

Producers spotted that, just as the *Hill Street* technique could 'sell' a drama that might be lacking in other areas, it also added credibility to an undernourished comedy, soap or workplace injury advocacy commercial. Used cynically, it's an easy-to-apply prophylactic protecting the script's gaping holes from close inspection.

Suspend the camera from a woozy gimbal and the viewer's disbelief will follow. Until, that is, it becomes the default visual style and starts to count for nothing. 'In an age of naturalism,' wrote Eric Bentley, 'a writer's courage sometimes fails him and he tries to pass off a tame duck as a beast of the jungle.'[460] With their rag-bag of naturalistic tricks toted shamelessly up front, some programmes of the early twentieth century couldn't half quack.

John Morton addressed the courage deficit in *W1A*, his 2014 dissection of the BBC's bloated management culture. Given the run of the Corporation's spanking New Broadcasting House, Morton made it an anthill run by grasshoppers: uneasy, status-obsessed folk guarding their jobs with a jealousy that matched their inability to define what those jobs actually were, passing responsibility back and forth in a fugue of freshly-minted buzzwords that carried as little meaning as possible. Some critics dismissed it as a cosy dig in the ribs. As Morris and Iannucci discovered, satire's targets possess a sublime ability to mentally exempt themselves from attack. But at its best, the mockumentary lobs a message to the viewer over the social barrier – a valuable service when the official channels, as in *W1A*, aren't willing to offer anything more than an obtuse, 'No, yes. Right. Brilliant.'

# BATTLESTAR GALACTICA (2004–9)
## Sci Fi (NBC Universal)

### Big, dumb science fiction smartens itself up.

NO ENTERTAINMENT GENRE IS more patronised, in both senses of the word, than science fiction. Done right, it promises instant access to an audience large, loyal and lucrative enough to make crime writers retreat into their locked rooms and pull the trigger. And yet, even with a hit on their hands, TV people seem oddly ill at ease pushing space-age kicks. It's not . . . 'proper' drama, really, is it?

In literature, where it's been responsible for some of the most important and experimental works of the last century, science fiction enjoys a grudging tolerance. In the cinema it can choose between cultish esteem and mountains of cash, but almost never gets both. On television its reputation has long been lower still: an endless parade of beetle-browed men in one-piece polyester romper suits bellowing co-ordinates into silver hairdryers to a backing chorus of microwave oven alarms. It veers between the infantile and the psychedelically incomprehensible, often from minute to minute. Or at least that's the received opinion, and as a result it's generally the first thing to get the chop when a station tightens its purse strings.

Science fiction seems to come in three types. At the top there are the smoky fascist dystopias, which gain a few brownie points for fumbling at would-be 'adult' themes to the sound of rubber on brushed concrete. (This is the genre most 'proper' writers are likely to have a crack at – it seems easy enough.) Then come the one-shot plays with the dimension-warping twist in the tail, which are lauded for their wit, economy and cleverness, and then never referred to again. At the very bottom come the space operas, floating foil palaces full of jut-jawed men and well-proportioned women whose constant frowns are only there to prevent every meaningless speech dissolving into a fit of RADA giggles. All three are strapped for cash and drained of emotion. Brian Aldiss spoke of the bifurcation of fiction into literature (kosher) and genres like science fiction (suspect) some time after the war. Many practitioners of the TV variety have looked at the reputation of their trade and wondered if they didn't take the wrong turning.

It's a rough deal all round for the off-worlders. Come the twenty-first century, however, and American television caught the space bug again, even if the raw material it chose looked far from promising. Soon after the release of *Star Wars* (which was in turn shamelessly lifted from old movie serials – premise from *Flash Gordon*, helmets from *Fighting Devil Dogs*) producer Glen A. Larson had adapted a long-cherished pet project into a thirteen-part, million-dollar-per-episode George Lucas clone for ABC.

With its blonde hero, cute robots and evil, faceless Cylons, the original *Battlestar Galactica* was Lucas listlessly retrod: a slavish visual copy of its cinematic counterpart spiced with a gratuitous dash of Mormon theology and Lorne Greene in a purple cape. Mick Farren called it 'the product of Hollywood huck, jive and money shuffle.'[461] It was to *Star Wars* what another Glen A. Larson production, *Alias Smith and Jones*, was to Butch and Sundance – a luncheon voucher to a hundred dollar bill.

The show was the most perverse possible choice for a twenty-first century remake, but David Eick, producer of *Hercules: The Legendary Journeys*, and Roland D. Moore, writer for various reactivated branches of the *Star Trek* franchise, set upon it with the aim of fashioning a fully shaded drama that would take them out of 'the science fiction ghetto'.[462]

A two-part pilot cleared the decks of kitsch. Moore's remake was 'a character story about people who happen to be inside a science fiction universe.'[463] The cultural references to other TV shows, by now a network tradition, were still there – the station is introduced with a *M\*A\*S\*H*-style camera sweep around the ensemble cast, much-cloned blonde female Cylon Number Six is named after McGoohan's Prisoner, and the *Hill Street Blues* cry 'let's be careful out there' makes several appearances. This time, though, the playfulness was kept in check – the story itself was too good to upstage.

Sci Fi, the show's host channel, had a chequered reputation among genre devotees. When *Galactica* came their way, they were bogged down with several unsuccessful adaptations of hard science fiction; an adaptation of Philip José Farmer's lauded *To Your Scattered Bodies Go*, set on an endless, alien-manufactured river valley where every human who ever lived is reincarnated, got no further than pilot stage, while a series based on Roger Zelazny's elephantine parallel world *Amber* series never escaped development. Grandiose ideas became inelegantly stuck in their tiny niche of appeal. Something altogether less esoteric was needed.

*Galactica*'s budget had hardly swelled in the last quarter century to $1.5 million per episode: relative chickenfeed. Making the Cylons humanoid was first a money-saving choice, but took the show in a new, more fruitful direction; pouring off the spacey trappings expanded the possibilities. Flat broke and ghetto-bound, *Battlestar Galactica* stole a march on the mainstream of its cinematic sisters, where if something the size of Manhattan hasn't crashed into something the size of Belgium in the first reel, the film walks. For all the capable CGI battle scenes (framed in synthetic 'wobblyscope' for extra impact) the most memorable interludes consisted of two faces, talking.

Ever since Stanley Kubrick ended his space odyssey in an oak-panelled dining room, visual science fiction has delighted in spinning viewers' heads with the sudden appearance of retro props amongst the brushed chrome and pink perspex. *Battlestar Galactica*'s conceit – that these are humans from our distant past, who will eventually colonise Earth – was the one bit of Mormon detritus from the original that could be put to good use. With everything set in the past, the decision to go for rusting rivets, clockwork clocks, chunky buttons, sturdy ring-bound flight manuals and phones with flexes makes story sense and gives battle scenes a welcome physicality that virtual displays lack.

The commander can barely talk to his son, the Vice President is a duplicitous delusional paranoid and the President has cancer. Everyone from the top down is hugely vulnerable, becoming more wearied and brutalised as the series unfolds. They swap allegiances, question the point of it all, sometimes just give up. Religious conversions, class war, domestic violence and post-traumatic stress abound. It's no arid fantasy but a rich, living mess, rooted in the mundanities of life – characters endure vehicular breakdowns, act awkward with estranged relatives and eat mashed potatoes.

They also have sex. The two-episode pilot opened with a diplomatic human-Cylon snog. Sex in space opera was nothing new, but instead of Clark Gable clinches and girl-in-every-port fantasy, here it led to unwise relationships, betrayal and childbirth in every messy, complicated permutation. The often unacknowledged sexual tension that made RSC stalwarts collapse with mirth during futuristic speeches was thrust – or rather delicately placed – into the thick of the script. Wives and husbands populated the fleet, and the unisex crew were an army of sweaty-vested lovers from the start.

To get the general audience watching, smart science fiction needs a good reason for the effort and distraction of its whole invented world, when the real one seems to do well enough for others. *Battlestar Galactica* had a fine one: America's post-9/11 complex of fear, jingoist rancour and guilt was still too raw and inchoate to be addressed directly. Trussing it up in a prophylactic metaphor and bunging it to the other end of time and space allowed the writing team to treat recent events close-up. Though nominally set hundreds of millennia in the past, it was firmly attached to the times.

But War on Robo-Terror was only the most journalistically saleable angle of a complex scheme. The Cylons, who come in twelve flavours from hot blonde to sarcastic atheist priest, are mystically inclined, ultra-repressed and occasionally childishly vulnerable when the gaps in their emotional make-up come to light. According to Moore, 'They have aspects of Al Qaeda, and they have aspects of the Catholic Church [the Cylons worship one God, humans a selection box from Greco-Roman antiquity], and they have aspects of America.'[464] The allegory was turned on its head halfway through, as humans fought back against Cylon occupation with suicide attacks. The series grew deeper, not just more convoluted, as it grew longer.

Over four series *Battlestar Galactica* managed, more or less, to stay on top of its huge, ever-growing, pulsating agglomeration of mystical baggage to bring television science fiction back into favour. Many times in the past, whether through incomprehension or incompetence, producers have sorely underestimated the difficulty of the genre. The *Galactica* team not only got that right, they managed to marry science fiction's intellectual peaks with its trashy bottom line, in one Möbius strip of a serial. It's good science fiction; it's good drama. That's all.

# FORBRYDELSEN (2007–12)
## DR1 (Danmarks Radio)

### European drama finally takes on the world.

IF THIS HAS BEEN a very Anglophone story, that's a symptom of the way television has enabled the culture with the most financial clout behind it to bulldoze the television of others into pidgin clones of its native formats, plus a few charmingly rustic local aberrations: emotionally incontinent Latin American soaps, impenetrably austere Albanian cartoons and childishly sadistic Japanese game shows. (It was chauvinistically assumed that these heightened qualities said more about the population of the programme's parent country than the genre it belonged to.)

When the original eight-nation Eurovision network started up in 1954, technical obstacles were soon dwarfed by language issues: 'a deadly self-criticism of what ought to be a mainly visual art.'[465] But it wasn't a mainly visual art; that pipe dream had died with silent cinema. Television was nearly all talk. The language barrier in television became high and immovable, but occasionally a show of sufficient cunning could still cross over.

For a long time, British productions used Europe primarily as a backdrop for middle class dramas with a holiday vibe. For the BBC, Michael J. Bird toured the islands of the eastern Mediterranean for exotically decorated thrillers such as *The Lotus Eaters* and *Who Pays the Ferryman?* Bird's Mediterranean, according to Jonathan Meades, was a place 'where the natives spout purplish aphorisms and specialise in looking meaningfully at strangers through eyes narrowed against the spitting fat of sheftalia.'[466]

In 1985, Bird relocated to Norway for the rural Gothic of *Maelstrom*, a psychological shocker stuffed with art-house longueurs, impenetrable plot twists and a surfeit of information about the salt fish industry, which became something of a public running joke. 'I would not want this to get around,' confessed Nancy Banks-Smith, 'but I have been following *Maelstrom* surreptitiously behind locked doors claiming defensively, when challenged, to be watching blue movies.'[467] Noting the package holiday landscape photography, Julian Barnes added, 'You half expect Cliff Michelmore or Frank Bough to turn up and explain about ferry bookings.'[468] But the gag was already reality: ferry firms were advertising exotic excursions to 'Norway: Land of the Maelstrom'.

Scandinavian countries built TV networks at various speeds in the early 1950s, with the single state broadcaster dominating. Sveriges Radio, Stockholm's answer to the BBC, exported Ingmar Bergman's six-part divorce study *Scenes from a Marriage* as far as the USA in 1973, albeit with Liv Ullmann dubbed by Annie Ross. National stereotypes informed the attendant press speculation that the 'gloomy' series might be responsible for the hefty recent increase in the Swedish divorce rate. On a lighter note, it was cited as a major influence by *Dallas* creator David Jacobs in the development of *Knots Landing*. But the general picture was of a TV landscape as bland as they came. Anthony Burgess, visiting Stockholm in 1981, noted that peak time was devoted to 'a highly instructive though sedative film on shoemaking in a remote Swedish village'.[469]

In 2009 Norway's national broadcaster NRK2 subverted this dreary reputation with a marathon broadcast of an uninterrupted live train journey in *Bergensbanen: Minutt for Minutt*, followed by *Hurtigruten: Minutt for Minutt* – live coverage of a five-day coastal cruise. 'Slow TV' was born, and quickly added to with live salmon fishing, close-up knitting and National Firewood Night. There was nothing new here: in TV's infancy, the BBC's intermission films of potters' wheels and kittens playing with wool were often eulogised as superior to their actual programmes. In the US, pioneering shows like *Garroway at Large* would rig up a camera on the studio roof and offer leisurely shots of the Chicago skyline, while in the mid-1970s a New York cable channel offered a constantly burning Yule Log service over Christmas, cited as 'evidence that daily life in America has surpassed surrealism and broken through into science fiction.'[470] Norway's programmes, though, amounted to a cult, with everybody in on the joke yet deadly serious about its telling. 'TV has mostly been produced the same way everywhere with just changes in subjects and themes,' claimed Rune Møklebust, the producer behind the movement. 'This is a different way of telling a story. It is more strange. The more wrong it gets, the more right it is.'[471]

The UK and US, with little to go on, were still getting Scandinavians wrong. Stereotype dictated that, though they themselves are incorrigibly morbid, their society was superhumanly idyllic, ordered and egalitarian. A new wave of crime writing, which explored the personal cliché and questioned the truth of the national one, took root in the 1990s with Henning Mankell's *Wallander* books. The brusque Swedish detective with an excessive love for opera and alcohol took a single murder and from it extrapolated a mare's nest of Mafia, drug cartels, far-right groups and corrupt politicians. Its TV adaptation in 2005 proved a surprise hit outside Sweden. British viewers especially couldn't get enough of 'Inspector Norse', and the quality channels started looking for more Nordic crime to import.

Denmark's public broadcaster, Danmarks Radio, was the first to go live in Scandinavia, but its creative peaks failed to travel. *Matador*, a huge saga of two influential families set during the Depression and WWII, remained a well-kept domestic secret, despite pre-empting *Heimat*. There was little else on Danish TV to challenge it, until Søren Sveistrup put a new crime series together for DR1. Like *Wallander*, it featured an emotionally reticent, case-hardened detective, and murder inquiries that touched on social problems. Instead of a new case every week, one incident was the trigger for twenty episodes of internecine connections and chilling discoveries.

*Forbrydelsen* ('The Killing') took the international language of crime literature and added Danish touches, from the murky half-light that pervaded every space to the co-operative nature of its production. Sveistrup, producer Piv Bernth and director Birger Larsen collaborated as the sort of free-associating team that used to be behind nearly every British TV production before managerial protocol swamped the process. In particular, Sveistrup worked closely with lead actress Sofie Gråbøl in the construction of DI Sarah Lund's personality. The pathologically taciturn inspector, fumbling male relationships from her estranged adult son to the assorted male colleagues she's teamed with, was a new and fascinating creation after a long line of similarly pensive male cops. A mystery as impenetrable as the motives of the mayor, it helped *Forbrydelsen* gain international status. For light relief, the Faroe sweater she constantly wore became a handily saleable signifier.

Sveistrup started from the personal. He was suspicious of what he claimed Mankell's books did, attacking social problems full on, preferring a subtler initiating incident whose repercussions affect all levels of society. 'It starts with an emotion,' he maintained, 'otherwise I don't see the point.'[472] That he could go from a single murder right up to the prime minister was down to the compact and bijoux nature of his homeland. *Forbrydelsen* could get its murder investigations to touch the depths of Danish society and still remain credible because Danish society, at around five and a half million strong, was so tight knit. Small countries work differently. As Bjork said of Iceland, 'if you go to the geothermal baths the prime minister is naked in the shower.'[473] Which sounds quaint, but with no-one deemed untouchable, a strangely sparse claustrophobia takes hold, a quiet village menace ideal for conspiracy's slow release.

British TV used to be able to capture the stillness and the mystery of its native countryside, but decades of period drama suffused fields and hedgerows with the soapy odour of the National Trust. The wilds were domesticated – even the most forbidding landscapes had to be shot imaginatively to remove the strong suspicion that there was a sizeable gift shop just out of view. Nordic scenery was wilder and free of 'Haywainification'. The people, too, were just exotic enough: though steeped in Americana, Danish culture was a lot less Americanised than the UK, retaining its own peculiar identity – both somewhere very vivid and nowhere in particular.

The Nordic incursion into the great Anglo-American TV narrative gathered steam with *Borgen, The Bridge, Mammon, Unit One* and more. Naturally they weren't allowed to do it all themselves; America demanded remakes. AMC's version of *The Killing* relocated the original's tranquil unease to the Pacific north-west and was compared by many to *Twin Peaks*, though without the 'metaphysical whimsy'[474] with which that show sabotaged itself. Though translations still had to be made, the Nordic renaissance was a harbinger of the new, more interconnected TV market. Where once subtitles signalled the presence of an obscure avant-garde film, they now adorn a much more accessible collection of international drama, from Sicilian procedural *Montalbano* to Parisian legal thriller *Engrenages*. The language barrier hasn't shifted, but world television becomes more accessible by the day, and the more we get, the more we'll watch it for edification and entertainment, not just to chuckle at funny customs or plan a fortnight's self-catering jaunt to Malmö.

# APPLE ACTION NEWS
# (2009–)

## Apple Daily/YouTube
## (Next Media Ltd.)

### The slightly silly dawn of virtual journalism.

IN THE 1990S, TOPICAL comedy underwent a change in emphasis. Instead of mocking public figures and social convention, many satirists turned their attention to society's reporters and pundits. In America, satirical paper *The Onion* used American journalism's bone dry verbal conventions to pull apart the self-generating forms and irrelevant content of much of its output.

In 1994 in the UK *The Day Today*, built from radio origins by a nexus of comedians centred around Chris Morris and Armando Iannucci, took the increasingly bombastic and tech-heavy direction British television news had been taking for the previous decade and projected it into idiotic space. One skit, a report on the NASA Space Shuttle's exhilaratingly pointless upcoming mission to leap over a line of twelve other shuttles in orbit, was illustrated with a 3D animation that looked exactly like a genuine news bulletin graphic, nudged just slightly into the realm of digital camp. Fifteen years later, that one-shot gag would be echoed in the birth of a new and rather suspect information industry.

Taiwanese animation studio Next Media began by creating 3D animated diagrams of serious news stories that needed detailed visual information: plane crashes, tanker spills and military manoeuvres. They did this in a style not too far removed from mainstream television news's in-house graphics departments, with perhaps a little more directorial licence on camera angles and the odd sound effect. With a huge bank of visual assets, slightly stiff but reasonably polished capsule reports could be turned out on their production line in a few hours. Hundreds of companies worldwide offered similar services, but Next Media quickly became one of the biggest in the field.

In 2009, they began branching out into stories on a more human scale. In a fast-growing and increasingly borderless video news market, it was becoming clear that the spoils were going not to the hack with the sharpest analysis or the inside line, but the organization with the most footage. For many stories, particularly those involving reports of personal indiscretion by celebrities, a fuzzy CCTV image was as good as it got, leading to a glaring gap between the breathless tabloid descriptions of Star X's crazed drug-fuelled antics and the solitary blue-grey blur viewers were assured was them caught mid-freak-out. Something was needed to bridge that gap, and CGI was the answer.

With a few additions to their basic set-up, Next Media began making human stories. Because of the lightning production schedule, results were far from polished. What was fine simplification with vehicles and buildings looked humorous, even grotesque, on people. Faces were realistically proportioned and textured, but lighting, expressions and motion were only half there, creating an overlit world of glassy-eyed, karate-chopping stock figures bearing only the most basic similarity to whomever they were meant to be impersonating. It looked clunkily unreal to the point of demonic possession, but it put the story across in a memorable way.

Next Media's work initially appeared on two outlets – sister company Apple Daily's news website, and their own NMA.tv domain, though most of their international traffic naturally came via YouTube, helpfully showcased on traditional press and television reports. The first report to gain worldwide attention focussed on Tiger Woods's mysterious midnight altercation with his wife and subsequent low-speed car crash, recreated in glorious glassy-eyed, joint-popping 3D. Bits of dramatic emotional shorthand borrowed from Japanese *animé* – torrents of tears to indicate an upset protagonist, head erupting in flames for anger – added to the oddity.

Questions of taste that would trouble most mainstream TV outlets were brushed aside. To illustrate the Jimmy Savile scandal, what could be more appropriate than having a jogging, shell-suited avatar transform into the Child Catcher from *Chitty Chitty Bang Bang*, while children run away in all directions? Quite a lot as it happens, but as the lower end of print journalism had known for decades, the crass and the obvious get people's attention.

This new media was received with some very Old World attitudes. American and European pundits leapt on the viral success as a comprehensive dumbing down of core journalistic values by those inscrutable, childlike orientals. 'If this is the future of tabloid journalism,' thundered CNN's Howard Kurtz, 'then I want no part of it.'[475] Next Media intended it to be nothing of the sort, of course – the 'zanies', as they called them, were treated as the hi-tech equivalent of newspaper op-ed cartoons, with all the visual metaphor and irrelevance that came with it, rather than a news source in itself. It was a massively successful international calling card that initially helped to plug, and eventually overtook, their diagrammatic meat-and-potatoes work. By early 2014 their videos were averaging forty million views each.

The problem was that the wackiness was indeed starting to get confused with the serious reporting. TV news, especially in the English speaking world, was shedding the responsible restraint it had kept up for decades. In America, proprietary news outlets like Fox gave blocks of airtime to opinionated and animated pundits from the sweaty end of the far right, who manically outlined elaborate liberal conspiracies unchallenged for hours at a time. Britain had the opposite problem, a retreat into a kind of detached patrician superciliousness, looking askance at events through narrowed eyes as if the latest government initiative was a smudged drawing of a three-armed Santa from an unloved nephew. One took itself ultra-seriously, the other found it hard to respond to anything except as a bad joke. The two vastly different sicknesses produced the same symptom: prancing trivia.

This strangely wilful decline was encapsulated when, in 2013, editorship of BBC Two's flagship heavyweight news programme *Newsnight* went to Ian Katz, former *Guardian* deputy editor and complete television ingénue. Citing the very real lack of public engagement with contemporary politics, Katz loaded the analytical pantechnicon with gimmicks and stunts – anything to leaven that tedious political discussion, summed up by Katz's injudicious Tweet on Labour shadow minister Rachel Reeves's 'boring snoring' performance on the show.[476] The editorial tone fell somewhere between the world's oldest cynic and a ten-year-old child who'd won a competition.

The wall between serious news and mucking about, which had just about held up since Angela Rippon stepped out with Eric and Ern, collapsed. The 'and finally' item turned into a nugget of forced, end of term jollity – Kirsty Wark danced like a zombie on Halloween and a clearly reluctant Emily Maitlis covered children's channel CBeebies' collaboration with the makers of *Sesame Street* by interviewing the Cookie Monster. Serious reporting remained the programme's *raison d'être*, but the daft stunts got people's attention. As with *Apple Action News*, the objective was to generate a viral internet success by any means necessary. In a world faster, more connected and fractious by the day, reliable and quick news services were more important than ever. Perhaps it was in an honest reflection of the times that they spent so long goofing off.

# LOUIE (2010–)
## FX (Pig Newton Inc)

### Comedy reaches new heights of philosophical rigour and infantile seediness.

'COMEDY IS THE NEW rock 'n' roll.' It's a sentence so corny and demonstrably wide of the truth (a large part of rock 'n' roll's impact relies on the wilful denial of absurdity) that it's amazing it hung around for a few months, let alone decades. It first surfaced in the USA in the late 1980s to help journalists crudely bracket an assortment of smoking, swearing truth tellers – most notably Sam Kinison and Bill Hicks – who provided welcome relief from the mass of jobbing actors in open-necked shirts cynically sliding behind the mic with the sole intent of securing a sitcom deal. The new breed eschewed network TV for raw cable channels and sweaty-walled basement clubs, firing out painfully honest material in assorted shades of adversarial rage. Skirting mainstream TV removed the cred-busting taint of show business from the acts, aligning them with Lenny Bruce rather than Bob Hope.

But TV comedians were often outsiders, fighting the medium and mocking its wares, ever since Ernie Kovacs and Spike Milligan pulled television apart when it had barely got itself together. Just as vaudeville troupes like the Marx Brothers filled theatre owners with as much trepidation as they did audiences with joy, the list of comedians who've properly embraced TV and of those who reduce channel executives to low, apprehensive mutterings are almost identical. Provide alternative comics with an hour of peak time and they'll blow it up. Give a whimsical folk duo their own comedy show and they become enemies of the state. Give a forty-something divorcee his own series and he'll show you the world. After a fashion.

Louis C. K. (real name Louis Székely) started out as a stand-up comic on the Boston circuit, but always had designs on television. 'It made me mad that the shows were so bad,' he recalled of his youth in front of the networks. 'People have a right to relax and watch theatre about themselves that makes them reflect and feel and have a good time doing it.'[477] He made a few art house films with his wife, but disliked the aloofness of the independent film scene, preferring the 'low self-esteem' of television.[478] His first sitcom for HBO, *Lucky Louie,* was a conscious attempt to slap a modern comic sensibility on *The Honeymooners'* old three-camera, dirty-walled kitchenette set-up. It passed through the 2006 summer schedules without touching the sides. The follow-up dropped conceptual gimmickry for street-level introspection.

*Louie* did things the modern way, taking a single camera out into New York for a mix of extended sketches 'from life' interspersed with stand-up bits based on their contents. Gradually themes took over whole shows, and Louie's fictionalised domestic life (divorced, two precocious daughters, struggling on the club circuit, shares an apartment block with a cast of oddballs) grew into a kind of half-sitcom with a running meta-commentary and, miraculously, no commercial break.

'The show we're doing has no precedent in American television history,' he claimed with mock grandeur, carefully adding, 'I can't speak for British TV.'[479] Something like it had been done in the UK before: Kelly Monteith, a Canadian comic working at the BBC, created a sitcom cutting between his slick act and the messy personal life that informed it a quarter of a century earlier. And just to dispel any hint of sophistication, Paul Squire, old school Mancunian comic who stormed the 1980 Royal Variety Performance, used the sitcom-about-making-comedy shtick for his TV début the following year. In formal terms, this postmodern nag had been ridden before.

The content, though, was another matter. 'Middle-aged man versus the modern world' had never been done with this level of raw honesty before. No plots where the hero takes up jogging and gets a hernia here. Instead, a curious Louis goes in search of an anal sex toy, only to put his back out in the shop pointing to the one he's after. Rock 'n' roll edge and middle-aged domestic farce collide, cruelly cancelling each other out. His regulation will-they-won't-they female buddy, played by Pamela Adlon, appraises him in terms varying from 'You're so afraid of life that you're boring' to 'You can't even rape well'. On the street, he's assailed by the randomness of the modern city. He goes apartment hunting and finds one with a toilet in the kitchen. He spots government agents swapping homeless people around on street corners. Another homeless ranter gets decapitated by a truck as he's on his way to a date: the ultimate visitation from blind fate. Incidents take on a fantastic turn, adding to the feeling of a dreamworld – a largely mundane and shitty dreamworld at that.

The show evolved from season to season. For the third, stories broke out of their twenty-three-minute confines and spread over several episodes. One three-part story brought the new and old ways of making television into a fantastic pileup. Louis gets, seemingly from nowhere, a chance to audition as a replacement for a supposedly retiring David Letterman. This biggest of big breaks turns into a nightmare as he finds himself in the starched throwback hands of Jack Dall, a veteran producer of Pre-Cambrian heritage. C. K. cast about the nation's entertainment grandees for the role: Jerry Lewis, Woody Allen and Martin Scorsese politely turned him down. Eventually David Lynch said yes.[480]

Remote and stilted, yet confident in an otherworldly way, Lynch proved the perfect choice to embody C. K.'s vision of the TV pioneers, being impossibly out of date to the point of total alienation, yet possessing a weirdly unflappable confidence and experience sorely lacking in the current generation. Louis is in awe of Dall, a buttoned up stiff working to cast iron show business laws only he can access; the wisdom of the ancients. The new rock 'n' roll rubs up against a wartime big band and finds its musical chops sorely lacking. It's the relationship modern TV has with its past – alternately raiding it for ideas and patronising it with smug nostalgia – in a nutshell of professional awkwardness.

Modern Jack Dalls are legion, but their collective usefulness is a matter of debate. Twenty-first century TV is subject to a ping-pong development process far more intensive and protracted than before, with each circle of development hell progressively more removed from the light of the studio floor. Mirages arise from endless boardroom table talk and budgets shrivel by the hour. Merely getting a programme on air is a triumph for the production team against an executive army that can seem endless, like Ray Harryhausen's regenerating skeleton brigades.

*Louie* was made in an uncommonly efficient way. Louis C. K. wrote, produced and directed the vast majority of the series, even editing early episodes himself on a Macbook Pro, before drafting Woody Allen veteran Susan E. Morse for the third season.[481] With a decision making chain that short, crises could be dealt with and on-the-hoof changes made in an instant. While the economic and distributive knots of television – channel, network, studio or online platform – can change with the seasons, the unit of production, the size of the crew who actually get the show made, is only as big as it needs to be. The numbers should stack up in descending order: an audience of millions for the labour of a dozen, working to the vision of one. Smaller, swifter and knowing all the angles, the makers will always get the last laugh.

Comedy, as much as any branch of the entertainment industry, has become a global leviathan. World tours and arena venues are the signs of stand-up success, and scale can't help but affect content. The restriction of British theatre to larger, approved venues like Drury Lane in the nineteenth century meant that Victorian acting, to fill the cavernous space, tended toward the loud, the unsubtle: literally playing to the gallery. Arena comedy has a similar effect: subtlety gets lost, and the size of the crowd means stand-ups metaphorically play to the gallery, going for laughs of easy recognition and steering well away from ambiguity, obscurity and offence. Treble-checked and hyper slick, arena shows are slow, lumbering beasts, at the mercy of the small club comic's instantaneous powers of reinvention. The close-up conjurer can work twenty tiny miracles while David Copperfield's still pouting through the overture to his set piece.

If Louis C. K.'s basement clubs were the opposite of arena shows, his FX show ran counter to the prevailing trends of TV comedy in many ways. *Louie* uses 'dark' comedy (the adolescent glee in gorging on childhood taboos) as decoration, but its bricks and mortar are the randomness of life, the terror of chance (what Anthony Burgess called 'the black borders of comedy').[482] There are no easy villains, no cardboard enemy for the crowd to round on, just one poor sap and his dumb luck.

Modern media make wild claims to girdle the Earth and serve huge populations. TV has been the most successful in doing this, but it did so by working on a small, human scale. Screens may now measure sixty inches or more, but they're also six inches or less. Like all great comedy, *Louie* shows the directionless mess of modern life can be redeemed through tiny pleasures. And if television isn't the biggest collection of tiny pleasures and telling details created by man, what is?

# HOUSE OF CARDS (2013–)

## Netflix (Media Rights Capital/Panic Pictures)

### Television outgrows the television set.

To PREDICT THE FUTURE direction of television with any degree of confidence takes either extreme gumption or exquisite gormlessness. The traditional set-up of a handful of national terrestrial broadcasters per country, one of them funded by the state, has, after several decades under siege from the robber barons of cable and satellite, become critically enfeebled. The Internet has shown it can encompass television just as television could encompass cinema, and do a hundred other things besides. Doomy punters envision the death of TV just as they saw cinema's imminent demise when television first arrived, but they're no more likely to be right this time round. It is, however, changing shape drastically. The television of 2020 will differ massively from that of 2010.

Reality television is not so much a genre as a coalition of prurient documentaries and immense, season-spanning game shows engineered by producers who mould the gamely gullible as Isambard Kingdom Brunel manipulated cast iron. This is television as science, every element precisely calibrated to chime with the press and social media, expanding the reach of the franchise. As fewer and fewer people watch TV as it happens, these gilded tent-poles support the old broadcast channels for entire evenings, even weekends. But reality shows yield steadily diminishing returns, despite the dexterity of producers adept at shuffling and recombining the chunky building blocks of the trade (snap the community spirit factor off that old choir-in-a-council-estate singing show, clip it to the underside of this recreation of a wartime primary school syllabus, get an endearingly bumbling former home secretary to present, job done).

For anyone attempting to divine the future of broadcasting fifteen years into the twenty-first century, the interface between broadcast television and social media provides a damp set of tea leaves indeed. 'Live tweeting' takes television right back to the Victorian stage, when heckling and hissing were the audience's right, and the poor players targets for well-aimed veteran groceries. Producers scamper to social media portals, optioning the sensation of last Tuesday afternoon for a hastily bodged two-season package, but once they get down to business it all looks rather familiar. Musical YouTube sensations collapse under the pressure of that difficult second single; comic flavours of the month generate material that would shame a Basildon stag night from 1973. After a decade of this tentative symbiosis, social media has turned the 'and finally . . .' news item into an autonomous collective, but programmes proper are another matter.

This stand-off between frantic technological innovation and retrograde content is perfectly embodied by *House of Cards*, Beau Willimon's adaptation for Netflix of Andrew Davies's adaptation for the BBC of a political thriller written by Michael Dobbs, former chief of staff to Margaret Thatcher. Davies's version was of its time and place – Francis Urquhart, the Machiavellian chief whip, indulged in bloodless postmodern confessions to camera. Ian Richardson gave Urquhart a supercilious detachment to match the chilling words, becoming the charismatic presenter of a 'how to' guide for the power-crazed sociopath.

Frank Underwood, Urquhart's American avatar, was a Democrat with the ambition, guile and dark mental hinterland of Lyndon Johnson, but the dangerous aloofness remained. The main alterations involved the transposition from Westminster to Washington, and an expansion: the BBC's compact yet commercially inadequate four-hour series was expanded to a standard thirteen.

Netflix, having gamely commissioned two series without even a pilot, respectfully left the production well alone. (Still essentially a distribution company, they lacked the staff and the kind of corporate structure where meddling executives thrive.) David Fincher was tempted out of the cinema to direct by the simple advantage television has always had – more time than a feature film, and potentially more depth. Kevin Spacey was lured from the stage to play Underwood for similar reasons. With television's dramatic renaissance now widely acknowledged, neither saw it as a step down. *House of Cards* made history in 2013 when it became the first television show to win Emmys without a single episode being broadcast in the traditional sense. 'TV will not be TV in five years' time,' predicted Willimon in 2012. 'Everyone will be streaming.'[483] By early 2015 the prophecy looked solid as Netflix, broaching fifty million subscribers worldwide, was joined by other non-broadcast studios including an offshoot of cyber-vending behemoth Amazon, which commissioned pilots on spec, released them online and made series from the winners.

A future where television drama is released like multi-part films sounds grand: with programmes not only resembling but being distributed the same way as films, TV drama's unwarranted inferiority complex could easily vanish for good. Documentary, too, has outgrown the box. Adam Curtis, auteur of a series of left-field factual programmes that used found footage to demolish received wisdom, debuted his 2015 opus *Bitter Lake* on the BBC's iPlayer online service, bypassing broadcast entirely. 'I wanted to create something you wouldn't put on television,' he explained. 'It's a deal I have with the BBC: you can experiment, but don't cost any money.' Curtis could see where the talent was heading: 'in five years' time, everyone's going to watch everything on iPlayer, so let's get in there before the bureaucrats do.'[484]

Tales of digitally-distributed creative liberation abound, but with the fertile ecosystem of broadcast television gone – the wild cross-pollination that comes from all types of programming sharing the same transmission and production space, to which many of the shows in this book owe their existence – it could be at the expense of the biggest change of character ever undergone by a mass medium.

It will all depend on the speed and extent to which the original, mixed broadcasting model disappears. The current state of play suggests a future of straight-to-box-set prestige shows plus specialist channels for news, sport and the like funded by rental and subscription fees – economically lean, but shorn of its potential for creative chaos. State broadcasters will almost certainly continue to be cut down both financially and existentially, through targeted campaigns by rival commercial interests and the indifference of a public increasingly forgetful of the vital role they continue to play. Those rival commercial interests themselves will see their advertising revenue fall as the novelty of big top reality television wears off.

Television has fallen back on its past output in a big way, but perhaps not the right way. Instead of selecting well-remembered programmes to simply update and relaunch, it might be more profitable to try to rediscover the ideas, techniques and tricks it carelessly discarded on the way from there to here. Most of all it needs to recover the adventurous experiment of the pioneering decades, when the definition of television was still only half-written. Producers should stop timidly holding each other's hands and strike out across new terrain. They need to widen their search for talent of all kinds, especially writers, instead of waiting for other media to serve up ready-made stars. It might even be beneficial for TV to completely lose its head again once in a while, even if it results in the odd baroque flop. When everything's focus-grouped nothing surprises, and television's great power is its ability to shock and delight you in your own front room.

The global cottage industry of the late twentieth century is never coming back, but there's no reason why its tradition of intelligent risk-taking can't be salvaged and refashioned into exciting new shapes. Television's past isn't just good for a smug chuckle over atavistic attitudes and shapeless trousers, it's an education in making some of the most potent popular art ever created, and never was an industry in more desperate need of some last-minute revision.

Even yesterday's garbage can teach us something. In 1955 Associated-Rediffusion transmitted *You've Never Seen This!*, a 'series of canned filmlets' shot by a jobbing Gerry Anderson, in which sideshow organiser Pete Collins paraded human oddities in front of the camera – including dwarfs, giants and a 'human gasometer' – for the gawping amusement of the capital's early TV adopters. Bernard Levin was not impressed. 'It is not at all simply putting freaks in front of a camera and hoping the audience will stand up and cheer,' he claimed, and offered a piece of TV wisdom as true today as it was sixty years ago: 'No machine, as I believe the First Law of Thermodynamics tells us, will enable us to get more out of it than we put in.'[485]

# ENDNOTES

1 'Coming "Frightfulness": America to see Cocktails by Wireless', *Manchester Guardian*, 28 February 1924.

2 'New Threat to Liberty', *Manchester Guardian*, 6 February 1926.

3 'Wireless and the Future', *Manchester Guardian*, 6 January 1924.

4 *Ibid.*

5 'A Liberal's Views on Sponsored TV', *Manchester Guardian*, 10 August 1953.

6 *Report of the Broadcasting Committee of Lord Hankey*, HMSO, 1945.

7 Mike Lloyd, quoted in *TV Times*, 1970.

8 'John Osborne Talks to Kenneth Tynan', *Guardian*, 30 June 1968.

9 Hamish MacRae, 'When it Comes to TV Viewing, Staring at Words or Figures Takes a Back Seat', *Guardian*, 25 August 1982.

10 Peter Fiddick, 'Human Brain', *Guardian*, 1 June 1982.

11 Philip Hope-Wallace, *Listener*, 5 June 1952.

12 Grace Wyndham Goldie, *Listener*, 18 August 1938.

13 Grace Wyndham Goldie, *Listener*, 2 March 1939.

14 Reginald Pound, *Listener*, 5 November 1953.

15 *Daily Express*, 21 May 1954.

16 'TV Cook Attacks Sparrow-Sized Breakfasts', *Daily Express*, 11 October 1949.

17 *Daily Mirror*, 26 April 1957.

18 Philip Harben, 'All For the Love of Good Food', *TV Times*, 1964.

19 *Manchester Guardian*, 16 May 1934.

20 Harry Castleman and Walter J. Podrazik, *Watching TV: Six Decades of American Television*, Syracuse University Press, 2003.

21 Keith Scott, *The Moose That Roared*, Thomas Dunne, 2000.

22 *Ibid.*

23 Donna Rico, *Kovacsland*, Harcourt Brace Jovanovich, 1990.

24 NBC script, quoted in Donna Rico, *Kovacsland*, Harcourt Brace Jovanovich, 1990.

25 Shaun Considine, *Mad as Hell*, Random House, 1994.

26 Paddy Chayefsky, *Television Plays*, Simon and Schuster, 1956.

27 Shaun Considine, *Mad as Hell*, Random House, 1994.

28 Paddy Chayefsky, *Television Plays*, Simon and Schuster, 1956.

29 Shaun Considine, *Mad as Hell*, Random House, 1994.

30 Oliver Postgate, *Seeing Things*, Sidgwick & Jackson, 2000.

31 John Crosby, *New York Herald Tribune*, 26 September 1955.

32 David Everitt, *King of the Half Hour*, Syracuse University Press, 2001.

33 *Ibid.*

34 *Ibid.*

35 C. A. Lejeune, *Observer*, 27 November 1949.

36 Peter Black, *Daily Mail*, 25 February 1956.

37 Peter Black, *Daily Mail*, 10 May 1956.

38 Bernard Levin, 'The Goons Give a New Dimension to Television', *Observer*, 12 May 1956.

39 Peter Black, *Daily Mail*, 17 May 1956.

40 Bernard Levin, 'The Goons Give a New Dimension to Television', *Observer*, 12 May 1956.

41 Philip Purser, *Daily Mail*, 31 May 1956.

42 Bernard Levin, 'Elephants Low Down – and The Only Treatment for Them', *Observer*, 19 May 1956.

43 *Person to Person*, BBC1, 2 August 1979.

44 'Broadcasters' Fees', *Hansard*, 11 February 1942, Vol. 377, cc1508-9.

45 'BBC Panel Game for American TV', *Manchester Guardian*, 10 July 1954.

46 James Laver, *Radio Times*, 17 October 1952.

47 David Attenborough, *Life On Air*, BBC Books, 2002.

48 'BBC Plan for Television', *The Times*, 30 August 1955.

49 *Manchester Guardian*, 30 May 1956.

50 *Manchester Guardian*, 16 May 1956.

51 *Ibid.*

52 'Youth Not Afraid to Ask', *Manchester Guardian*, 27 June 1956.

53 Clive James, 'Bernard Levin: Book Two', *London Review of Books*, 1979.

54 Bernard Levin, 'Opportunity Knocks – But No-one is at Home,' *Manchester Guardian*, 21 July 1956.

55 'Man With a Lemon in His Ear', *Manchester Guardian*, 16 January 1957.

56 Peter Fiddick, 'The Shows that Died of Embarrassment', *Guardian*, 20 March 1978.

57 *TV Times*, 6 November 1976.

58 Monica Sims, *The Singing Ringing Tree: a Cold War Fairytale*, BBC Radio 4, 28 December 2002.

59 *Evening Standard*, 23 January 1992.

60 *Radio Times*, 15 February 1957.

61 *Radio Times*, 22 February 1957.

62 Alley Cat, *New Musical Express*, 12 December 1958.

63 *Daily Mirror*, 23 May 1959.

64 Garth Bardsley, *Stop the World*, Oberon Books, 2003.

65 'Gurney May Be Dead . . .', *Daily Mail*, 28 November 1960.

66 'A "Diggable" Life for Anthony Newley', *TV Times*, 3 April 1960.

67 'The Strange World of Gurney Slade', *ATV Star Book*, 1961.

68 J. Piper, letter, *TV Times*, 27 November 1960.

69 Cecil Wilson, 'When a Teen Idol Hits his First Snag', *Daily Mail*, 29 November 1960.

70 Michael Wale, 'David Bowie: Rock and Theatre', *Financial Times*, 24 January 1973.

71 W. J. Weatherby, 'Anthony Newley', *Guardian*, 12 June 1961.

72 Michael Billington, *Harold Pinter*, Faber and Faber, 1996.

73 Letter, *TV Times*, 10 April 1960.

74 Letters, *TV Times*, 14 April 1960.

75 Philip Purser, 'The Landscape of TV Drama', *Contrast*, Autumn 1961.

76 *TV Times*, 24 April 1960.

77 Irene Shubik, *Play for Today*, Davis-Poynter, 1971.

78 'Tangled Quartet of TV Play', *Guardian*, 2 November 1960.

79 Roger Wilmut, *Tony Hancock – 'Artiste'*, Eyre Methuen, 1978.

80 *Radio Times* interview, 18 May 1961.

81 *Ibid.*

82 Roger Wilmut, *Tony Hancock – 'Artiste'*, Eyre Methuen, 1978.

83 *Omnibus: From East Cheam to Earl's Court*, BBC1, tx. 26 April 1985.

84 Anthony Cookman, Jr., *Listener*, 8 September 1960.

85 *Radio Times* 28 December 1967.

86 Martin Amis, *Experience: a Memoir*, Vintage, 2001.

87 Kingsley Amis, 'The World of Jazz: Rhythm and Blues', *Observer*, 21 October 1956.

88 Kingsley Amis, Letter to Philip Larkin, 19 April 1969.

89 *Daily Mail*, 14 September 1962.

90 Peter Black, *Daily Mail*, 15 November 1962.

91 M. Stowers, letter, *TV Times*, 2 December 1962.

92 Simon Reynolds, *Rip It Up and Start Again: Postpunk 1978-1984*, Faber & Faber, 2005, p524.

93 T. S. Eliot's personal note on *Beyond the Fringe* programme, Alan Bennett's Diary, *London Review of Books*, 3 January 2013.

94 *TV Times*, 25 October 1962.

95 'Satire in the Age of Television', *The Times*, 15 December 1962.

96 Peter Green, *Listener*, 29 November 1962.

97 'Satire in the Age of Television', *The Times*, 15 December 1962.

98 Anthony Burgess, *Listener*, 3 October 1963.

99 Peter Green, *Listener*, 13 December 1962.

100 Peter Green, *Listener*, 17 January 1963.

101 Peter Green, *Listener*, 10 January 1963.

102 *Private Eye*, 29 November 1963.

103 Interview, *New Release*, BBC Two, 22 November 1966.

104 David Mercer, *Radio Times*, 23 November 1972.

105 David Mercer, 'Birth of a Playwriting Man', *Theatre Quarterly*, Vol. 3, No. 9, 1973.

106 Don Taylor, *Days of Vision*, Methuen, 1990.

107 Derek Hill, *Listener*, 25 October 1962.

108 Michael Overton, *Plays and Players*, December 1962.

109 Don Taylor, *Radio Times*, 18 October 1962.

110 Michael Billington, *Harold Pinter*, Faber & Faber, 1996.

111 Kenneth Tynan, 'Sir Ralph Does it all by Numbers', *Evening Standard*, 13 June 1952.

112 John Russell Taylor, *Listener*, 7 December 1972.

113 Clive James, 'Lobbing-match Over a Cat's Cradle', *Observer*, 3 December 1972.

114 Mervyn Johns, *Listener*, 11 December 1980.

115 Laurence Leamer, *King of the Night*, William Morrow, 1989.

116 Kenneth Tynan, *Show People*, Weidenfeld & Nicolson, 1979.

117 Gordon, Corner and Richardson, *Public Issue Television: World in Action 1963-98*, Manchester University Press, 2007.

118 *Ibid.*

119 *TV Times*, 6 February 1965.

120 Peter Hillmore, *Guardian*, 15 August 1978.

121 Robert Waterhouse, 'Obituary: T. Dan Smith', *Guardian*, 28 July 1993.

122 Peter Fiddick, 'When the Action Replay isn't the Real Thing', *Guardian*, 17 November 1977.

123 Gordon, Corner and Richardson, *Public Issue*

*Television: World in Action 1963-98*, Manchester University Press, 2007.

124 *Ibid.*

125 Anthony Davis, *TV Times*, 9 June 1979.

126 Peter Fiddick, *Guardian*, 2 June 1981.

127 Andrew Culf, *Guardian*, 4 October 1995.

128 *A Fresh Start for ITV Current Affairs*, Granada, 1999.

129 Catherine Stott, 'I Kid You Not', *Guardian* 10 September 1971.

130 *Ibid.*

131 Maureen O'Connor, 'Humpty Dumpty's Big Break', *Guardian*, 27 April 1970.

132 *Ibid.*

133 Harold Jackson, 'Jackanory & Co.', *Guardian* 21 December 1966.

134 Angela Neustatter, *Guardian*, 23 December 1976.

135 George Melly, 'In McLuhan's Seat,' *Observer*, 3 September 1967.

136 *Children and the Mass Media* seminar, Hellebaek, Denmark, May 1973.

137 *Crossroads Revisited,* Central Independent Television, 1985.

138 Nancy Banks-Smith, *Guardian*, 30 March 1971.

139 Peter Fiddick, 'Signposts Point One Way for Crossroads', *Guardian*, 11 September 1981.

140 Alan Rusbridger, 'Meg Fans Crossroads' Embers', *Guardian*, 5 November 1981.

141 Tom Stoppard, 'Festival of Soap Opera', *Observer*, 29 September 1974.

142 Catherine Stott, 'Doggone', *Guardian*, 2 August 1972.

143 'A Dog for All Seasons', *Observer*, 23 April 1967.

144 Mary Samuel, letter, *Guardian*, 14 November 1966.

145 *Daily Mirror*, 7 December 1972.

146 'Puppets to the Tune of £250,000', *Financial Times*, 3 March 1969.

147 '2m More Watch Television', *Financial Times*, 21 July 1961.

148 'Paret Fight Not on TV', *Guardian*, 29 March 1962.

149 G. Reichardt, letter, *Financial Times*, 24 July 1968.

150 Dave Lanning, *TV Times*, 2 January 1965.

151 *Ibid.*

152 Mick McManus, *TV Times*, 3 May 1974.

153 Kenneth Tynan, 'West End Apathy', *Observer*, 31 October 1954.

154 Michael Billington, 'The Industry of John Hopkins', *The Times*, 23 March 1968.

155 George Melly, 'The First Masterpiece', *Observer*, 30 October 1966.

156 *Ibid.*

157 Edward Mace, 'Taking Telly

Seriously', *Observer*, 30 October 1966.

158  J. C. Trewin, *Listener*, 3 November 1966.

159  *Ibid.*

160  *Ibid.*

161  Clive James, *Listener*, 9 March 1972.

162  Nancy Banks-Smith, *Guardian*, 1 March 1972.

163  Linda Christmas, 'The Mourning After', *Guardian*, 4 March 1972.

164  David Bianculli, *Dangerously Funny*, Simon & Schuster, 2009.

165  Harlan Ellison, *Los Angeles Free Press*, 21 February 1969.

166  David Steinberg, interview, *The Smothers Brothers Comedy Hour: The Best of Season 3*, Time-Life DVD, 2008.

167  M. A. Jones, *Memorandum, RE: Elvis Presley*, Federal Bureau of Investigation Dockets, 4 January 1971.

168  Lee Langley, 'Dangerous but Decent', *Guardian*, 8 June 1965.

169  T. C. Worsley, 'The Leaden Touch', *Financial Times*, 25 October 1967.

170  Anthony Burgess, *Listener*, 2 November 1967.

171  Lew Grade interview, *Six Into One – the Prisoner File*, Channel Four/Illuminations/Yo-Yo Films, 1984.

172  Anthony Burgess, *Listener*, 2 November 1967.

173  Patrick McGoohan interview, *Six Into One – the Prisoner File*, 1984.

174  P. J. Nee, letter, *TV Times*, 17 February 1968.

175  Andrew Billen, 'Come in Number 6', *Observer*, 15 December 1991.

176  Johnny Speight, *For Richer, For Poorer*, Penguin, 1991.

177  Tom Stoppard, 'Fact, Fiction and the Big Race', *Observer*, 11 August 1968.

178  Robert Pitman, *Daily Express*, 6 August 1968.

179  Robin Thornber, 'Blacks and the Prostitute', *Guardian*, 12 November 1969.

180  Dennis Barker, 'Changing Views Overtake Speight's TV Play', *Guardian*, 18 June 1973.

181  Johnny Speight, *For Richer, For Poorer*, Penguin, 1991.

182  Joan Ganz Cooney and Dr Edward L. Palmer, remarks before the Regular Education Subcommittee of the House Committee on Education and Labor, 2 October 1969.

183  Melanie Perrin Berson, 'Ali Baba! What Have You Done?', *Childhood Education*, March 1970.

184  Linda Christmas, 'Sesame Street Cul de Sac', *Guardian*, 24 November 1971.

185  'For Adult Children?', *Guardian*, 11 August 1967.

186  Alan Garner, *The Edge of the*

*Ceiling,* Granada Television, 1980.

187 Robert Nye, 'A Question of Form', *Guardian,* 19 October 1973.

188 'For Adult Children?', *Guardian,* 11 August 1967.

189 Jenny Rees, 'Tea-Time Terrors', *Daily Mail,* 1 July 1978.

190 Peter Black, *Daily Mail,* 10 September 1969.

191 Mary Malone, 'A Glorious Bag of Disasters', *Daily Express,* 11 September 1969.

192 Richard North, *Listener,* 30 September 1976.

193 *Ibid.*

194 *Ibid.*

195 John Naughton, *Listener,* 21 July 1977.

196 *Ibid.*

197 'Teatime Treats,' *Listener,* 25 February 1982.

198 Robert S. Alley and Irby B. Brown, *Love Is All Around: the Making of the Mary Tyler Moore Show,* Dell, 1989.

199 Sally Bedell, *Up the Tube,* Viking 1981.

200 Robert Kubey, *Creating Television,* Routledge, 2009.

201 Ian Hamilton, *Listener,* 26 November 1970.

202 Nancy Banks-Smith, 'Miss TV Times', *Guardian,* 24 May 1973.

203 Reginald Pound, *Listener,* 25 October 1956.

204 Hilary Corke, 'Critic on the Hearth', *Listener,* 19 November 1954.

205 *Ibid.*

206 Christopher Walker, 'Miss World Was Not Amused', *Observer,* 22 November 1970.

207 *It's Your Time,* BBC Radio 4, January 1971.

208 Veronica Horwell, James Garner obituary, *Guardian,* 20 July 2014.

209 Fyodor Dostoyevsky, *Crime and Punishment,* Russkiy Vestnik, 1866.

210 Peter Brook, *The Empty Space,* McGibbon & Kee, 1968.

211 Henry Raynor, *The Times,* 12 February 1971.

212 John Gross, *Observer,* 14 February 1971.

213 T. C. Worsley, 'Familiar Faces', *Financial Times,* 17 February 1971.

214 Peter Black, *Daily Mail,* 12 February 1971.

215 Nancy Banks-Smith, *Guardian,* 12 February 1971.

216 Steven Awalt, *Steven Spielberg and Duel: the Making of a Film Career,* Rowman & Littlefield, 2014.

217 *Ibid.*

218 *Ibid.*

219 Shaun Usher, 'Enter Tom Jones, the Actor', *Daily Mail,* 13 May 1972.

220 Philip Hope-Wallace, 'Oh Dad at the Piccadilly', *Guardian,* 7 October 1965.

221 Jörg Türschmann, *TV Global: Erfolgreiche Fernseh-Formate*, Transcript Verlag, 2011.

222 'Man Alive', *Guardian*, 20 January 1972.

223 Brian Groombridge, *Television and the People*, Penguin, 1972.

224 John Ezard, *Guardian*, 9 June 1971.

225 Susan Pleat, *Pipkins Vol 2 (1973-1981)*, Network DVD, 2005.

226 Hartley Hare in Conversation, *Pipkins Vol 2 (1973-1981)*, Network DVD, 2005.

227 *Omnibus: Whatever Happened to Clement and La Frenais?*, BBC, 1997.

228 Mark Lewisohn, *The Radio Times Guide to TV Comedy*, BBC Publications, 1998.

229 Stacy Marking, 'No Laughing Matter', *Guardian* 15 March 1975.

230 *Ibid.*

231 *Daily Express*, 8 September 1976.

232 Brian Clemens interview, Network/Jeff Smart, 2005.

233 Eric Bentley, *The Life of the Drama*, Methuen, 1966.

234 'A Day with Dr Conan Doyle', *Strand Magazine* No. 20, August 1892.

235 Alix Coleman, 'The Kids Turn On to Saturday Pop', *TV Times*, 1975.

236 'BBC Chiefs Hit Back in the Children's TV War', *Daily Mail*, 4 September 1980.

237 'TV Notes', *Manchester Guardian*, 29 August 1956.

238 *TV Times*, 10 May 1975.

239 Magnus Pyke, *The Six Lives of Pyke*, JM Dent.

240 *Ibid.*

241 Michael Parkin, 'TV Shot Falls Even Shorter', *Guardian*, 18 August 1978.

242 Bart Mills, 'Box Pop', *Listener*, 12 February 1976.

243 *TV Times*, 1976.

244 Bart Mills, 'Box Pop', *Listener*, 12 February 1976.

245 Stephen Dixon, *Guardian*, 8 July 1975.

246 *TV Times*, 22–28 March, 1975.

247 *Daily Mirror*, 24 January 1983.

248 Julian Barnes, *Observer*, 27 February 1983.

249 Julian Barnes, *Observer*, 13 March 1983.

250 'Cassius Clay Walks off Sportsview', *Guardian*, 30 May 1963.

251 Bernard J. Mullin, Stephen Hardy, William Sutton, *Sport Marketing 4th Edition*, Human Kinetics, 2013.

252 Jonathan Lemire, 'Original Cable Guy', *Columbia College Today*, January 2005.

253 Paul Kane, *Australian Poetry: Romanticism and Negativity*, Cambridge University Press, 1996.

254 'ABC Plans a Vivid Colour', *Australian Women's Weekly*, 2 April 1975.

255 Roger Wilmut, *Kindly Leave the Stage!*, Methuen, 1985.

256 James Murray, 'Your Host, Gormless Gunston!', *Daily Express*, 18 November 1976.

257 Dennis Potter, *Radio Times*, 3 April 1976.

258 Dennis Potter, *Daily Herald*, 22 May 1964.

259 Dennis Potter, *Daily Herald*, 13 February 1964.

260 Dennis Potter, *Daily Herald*, 19 February 1964.

261 Dennis Potter, *Daily Herald*, 14 February 1964.

262 Dennis Potter, *Daily Herald*, 1 May 1964.

263 Dennis Potter, *Daily Herald*, 28 February 1964.

264 Dennis Potter, *Daily Herald*, 14 May 1964.

265 Dennis Potter, *Daily Herald*, 7 May 1964.

266 Dennis Potter, *Daily Herald*, 21 February 1964.

267 Dennis Potter, *Daily Herald*, 9 March 1964.

268 Dennis Potter, *Daily Herald*, 3 March 1964.

269 Letters, *Radio Times*, 1 May 1976.

270 Richard North, 'A Tricky Business', *Listener*, 8 February 1979.

271 Alan Coren, *The Times*, 30 November 1976.

272 *Daily Express*, 2 December 1976.

273 Nancy Banks-Smith, *Guardian*, 8 December 1976.

274 Reginald Whiteley, 'Charles Laughton Practises Stutter', *Daily Mirror*, 23 February 1937.

275 'Claudius to Reign . . . at Last', *Daily Mail*, 13 September 1976.

276 'J. M. Osborn, Public Opinion', *Daily Mirror*, 13 December 1976.

277 *I, Claudius: A Televison Epic*, BBC, 2002.

278 Peter Fiddick, *Guardian*, 19 October 1976.

279 Robert Giddings and Keith Selby, *The Classic Serial on Television and Radio*, Palgrave, 2001.

280 Clive James, 'Last of the Romans', *Observer*, 12 December 1976.

281 *Ibid.*

282 Harriet van Horne, 'The TV Week', *New York Post*, 5 November 1977.

283 Arthur Unger, *Christian Science Monitor*, 4 November 1977.

284 David Nobbs, *I Didn't Get Where I Am Today*, Heinemann, 2003.

285 *Ibid.*

286 Robert Tyrrell, *The Work of the Television Journalist*, Focal Press, 1972.

287 Jeremy Bulger, 'Battle of the Bulletins', *Listener*, 1 April 1976.

288 Public Eye, *Observer*, 24 April 1977.

289  Lesley Ebbetts, 'Be Your Age, Angela!', *Daily Mirror,* 7 April 1976.

290  Peter Fiddick, 'Not Just a Pretty Picture', *Guardian,* 8 March 1976.

291  Nicholas Harman, 'Read All About It', *Listener,* 18 March 1976.

292  Peter Fiddick, 'Not Just a Pretty Picture', *Guardian,* 8 March 1976.

293  Jeremy Bulger, 'Battle of the Bulletins', *Listener,* 1 April 1976.

294  *Ibid.*

295  Nicholas Harman, 'Read All About It', *Listener,* 18 March 1976.

296  Sue Francis, 'The Man Who Made a Goldmine Out of Trash', *Observer,* 15 April 1979.

297  Martin Amis, 'Trials of Strength', *Observer,* 28 December 1980.

298  Howard Schuman, 'Video-Mad: An American Writer in British Television,' Frank Pike (ed.), *Ah! Mischief: The Writer and Television,* Faber & Faber, 1982.

299  *Daily Mail,* 21 October 1982.

300  *Observer,* 3 July 1983.

301  David Housham, *Listener,* 29 January 1987.

302  'The Name of the Game is Audience Ratings', *Guardian,* 3 September 1984.

303  James Thurber, 'Onward and Upward with the Arts: Soapland', *New Yorker,* 29 May 1948.

304  Ellen C. Seiter (ed.), *Remote Control: Television, Audiences and Cultural Power,* Routledge, 1989.

305  Robert Kubey, *Creating Television,* Routledge, 2009.

306  *Susan Harris, Television Writer, Producer,* Paley Center for Media.

307  Robert Kubey, *Creating Television,* Routledge, 2009.

308  Martin Cropper, *The Times,* 2 August 1986.

309  Susan Harris, *Toronto Globe and Mail,* 8 January 1983.

310  Tony Schwartz, 'ABC had Adviser Known as a Psychic', *New York Times,* 13 March 1981.

311  *The Phenomenon of Roots,* The Wolper Organisation, 1978.

312  Richard Schickel, 'Viewpoint', *Time,* 24 January 1977.

313  Anthony Burgess, 'Firetalk', *Homage to QWERTYUIOP,* Century Hutchinson, 1986.

314  Mark Ottaway, 'Tangled Roots', *Sunday Times,* 10 April 1977.

315  'Getting Down to the Roots', *Guardian,* 11 April 1977.

316  Malcolm R. West, 'Black Historians Reflect on Criticisms of Roots', *Jet,* 28 April 1977.

317  *Daily Express,* 6 May 1952.

318  *TV Times,* 16 January 1965.

319 Oliver Pritchett, 'Mixed Reception for Sex Film', *Guardian* 17 April 1971.

320 Jonathan Coe, *B. S. Johnson: Like a Fiery Elephant,* Picador, 2004.

321 Peter Buckman, *Listener,* 9 May 1974.

322 Henry Fenwick, *Sunday Telegraph,* 24 September 1978.

323 Susan Willis, *The BBC Shakespeare Plays: Making the Televised Canon,* University of North Carolina Press, 1991.

324 *Ibid.*

325 Peter Fiddick, 'Burke's Steerage', *Guardian,* 30 December 1975.

326 *Ibid.*

327 Peter Lennon, *Listener,* 11 April 1985.

328 Clive James, 'The Burke and Burr Laugh-In', *Observer,* 4 January 1976.

329 *Ibid.*

330 Julian Barnes, 'Lost in a Noddy Universe', *Observer,* 24 March 1985.

331 Brian Winston, *Listener,* 7 December 1978.

332 Bella Bathurst, *The Wreckers,* HarperCollins UK, 2006.

333 JICTAR ratings, w/e 23 February 1979.

334 'Blank Shot Hits a Bullseye', *Daily Mirror,* 17 March 1979.

335 John Naughton, *Listener,* 8 September 1983.

336 JICTAR ratings, w/e 21 October 1979.

337 John Naughton, 'Barks and Whistles', *Observer,* 26 October 1980.

338 Television Notes, *Guardian,* 28 January 1958.

339 David Attenborough, *Life On Air,* BBC Books, 2002.

340 Manuel Alvarado and John Stewart, *Made for Television: Euston Films Limited,* BFI Publishing, 1985.

341 Leon Griffiths, *Minder Format,* 1978.

342 *Ibid.*

343 Cedric Cullingford, *Popular Television and Schoolchildren,* Oxford Polytechnic, 1982.

344 'Catch This If You Can', *Daily Mirror,* 9 March 1977.

345 Julian Barnes, 'View from Inside the Box', *Observer,* 25 May 1986.

346 Stanley Reynolds, *Guardian,* 27 September 1981.

347 David Hare, *Ah! Mischief, the Writer and Television,* ed. Frank Pike, Faber and Faber, 1982.

348 Herbert Kretzmer, *Daily Express,* 26 June 1964.

349 Michael Billington, *Guardian,* 10 November 1977.

350 Michael Coveney, 'Triumph of Death', *Financial Times,* 11 March 1981.

351 'Sting on a Wing', *Daily Mirror,* 28 December 1981.

352 Kenneth Hughes, 'Don't Worry . . . Just Enjoy It',

*Daily Mirror*, 29 December 1981.

353  *Ibid.*

354  Bill Pannifer, *Listener,* 20 May 1987.

355  James Murray, *Daily Express*, 2 January 1982.

356  Nancy Banks-Smith, 'Hitch in Time', *Guardian*, 30 December 1981.

357  Todd Gitlin, *Inside Prime Time*, Pantheon, 1983.

358  *Ibid.*

359  *Ibid.*

360  Feuer, Kerr, Vahimagi, *MTM: 'Quality Television'*, BFI Publishing, 1984.

361  Phill McNeill, *NME*, 9 January 1982.

362  John Craven, *Radio Times*, 14 November 1981.

363  Ian Penman, *NME*, 16 January 1982.

364  Norma Farley, Letter, *Guardian*, 2 October 1980.

365  Clive James, 'Marginally Better', *Observer,* 7 October 1979.

366  Jonathan Meades, *Peter Knows What Dick Likes*, Paladin, 1989.

367  Peter Fiddick, *Guardian*, 3 June 1974.

368  John Carey, *Listener,* 22 February 1973.

369  Peter Fiddick, *Guardian*, 6 August 1982.

370  Sean Day-Lewis, *Talk of Drama*, University of Luton Press, 1998.

371  *Daily Mirror*, 11 October 1982.

372  Joseph Turow, *Playing Doctor: Television, Storytelling and Medical Power*, Oxford University Press, 1989.

373  Scott Haller, 'Goodnight *St Elsewhere*', *People*, 23 May 1988.

374  Robert J. Thompson, *From Hill Street Blues to ER*, Continuum, 1996.

375  Max Beerbohm, *Saturday Review*, May 1906.

376  Adrian Thrills, 'Going Up the Tube', *NME*, 13 November 82.

377  Julie Burchill, *NME*, 13 November 1982.

378  Andy Medhurst, 'Def Sentences', *Listener,* 29 September 1988.

379  Jools Holland to Sean O'Hagan, 'Tube Disaster', *NME*, 7 March 1987.

380  Sally Bedell, *Up the Tube*, Viking Press, 1981.

381  Larry Gelbart, interviewed by Dan Harrison, *Archive of American Television*, 26 May 1998.

382  'Finale of *M*A*S*H* Draws Record Number of Viewers', *New York Times*, 3 March 1983.

383  Maurice Richardson, 'Third Programme?', *Observer,* 11 March 1956.

384  Sarah Bond, 'A Fair Celebration', *Daily Express*, 26 March 1984.

385  Deborah Ryan, letter, *Radio Times*, 16 June 1984.

386 John Naughton, *Listener,*
7 June 1984.

387 Mary Whitehouse, 'Shield for
Raw Minds', letter, *Guardian,*
26 September 1980.

388 Mick Jackson, 'Tearing
Threads', *Listener,*
20 September 1984.

389 Jim Crace, 'Acting
Armageddon', *Radio Times,*
22 September 1984.

390 Tim Heald, 'The Luck of the
Insecure Actor', *Radio Times,*
20 October 1984.

391 *Heimat* press kit materials,
WDR Publishing, 1 August
1984.

392 Derek Malcolm, 'Soap and
Glory', *Guardian,*
6 September 1984.

393 Richard Combs, *Listener,*
17 April 1986.

394 Timothy Garton Ash, 'The
Life of Death', *New York
Review of Books*, 19 December
1985.

395 Edgar Reitz, *Medium,* May
1979.

396 John Naughton, 'The Big
Brains', *Listener,* 24 April 1986.

397 James Murray, *Daily Express,*
15 March 1986.

398 Joy Horowitz, 'The Madcap
Behind *Moonlighting', New
York Times*, 30 March 1986.

399 *The Story of Moonlighting,*
Lions Gate, 2005.

400 Carl Gustav Jung,
*Psychologische Typen,* Rascher
Verlag, 1921.

401 Hillary MacAskill, 'Pob
Launch', *Guardian,*
4 November 1985.

402 '16-24 Year Old's Top 10 by
Index', *Listener,* 13 April
1989.

403 Richard Grabel, *NME,*
5 March 1980.

404 *Ibid.*

405 Phil McNeill, *NME,*
16 January 1982.

406 'Computer Wogan for
Channel Four', *Guardian,*
23 March 1985.

407 Hugh Herbert, 'The Perils of
Pye in the Sky Television',
*Guardian,* 22 March 1986.

408 Hugh Herbert, 'Portion of
Low Fibre Serial', *Guardian,*
5 November 1985.

409 Julian Barnes, 'Leaving the
Latex Cabinet', *Observer,*
19 January 1986.

410 Nick Smurthwaite, 'Out of
Practice', *Guardian,*
10 August 1989.

411 Christopher Kenworthy,
'What's Up, Doc?', *Radio
Times,* 17 May 1986.

412 Roger Wilmut, *Didn't You Kill
My Mother-In-Law?,*
Methuen, 1989.

413 Jeremy Isaacs, *Storm Over 4,*
Weidenfeld & Nicolson,
1989.

414 Mary Harron, 'A Strip Off
the Old Block', *Guardian,*
3 January 1983.

415 *Ibid.*

416 Edward Durham Taylor,

'Blight Strikes the Rose', *Guardian*, 23 May 1988.

417 *Listener*, 20 August 1987.

418 John McCready, *NME*, 22 August 1987.

419 *Listener*, 20 August 1987.

420 John Stratton Hawley (ed.), *The Life of Hinduism*, University of California Press, 2006.

421 Ananda Mitra, *Television and Popular Culture in India*, SAGE Publications, 1993.

422 James Saynor, *Listener*, 14 December 1989.

423 Janet Street-Porter, 'Def Sentences', *Listener* 29 September 1988.

424 Andy Medhurst, *ibid.*

425 Martin Walker, *Guardian*, 4 December 1982.

426 'More Pop and Less Champagne', *Guardian*, 23 March 1989.

427 *Newsweek*, 8 April 1990.

428 Video, *Time*, 7 April 1990.

429 Tom Shales, *Washington Post*, 12 April 1990.

430 *Today*, 20 October 1990.

431 Andrew Goodwin, *Listener*, 10 May 1990.

432 James Saynor, *Listener*, 1 November 1990.

433 *Ibid.*

434 *Late Show with David Letterman*, 27 February 1991.

435 James Saynor, 'The Condemned Sell', *Listener*, 12 April 1990.

436 Hugh Herbert, *Guardian*, 20 October 1990.

437 Jonathan Meades, *Museum Without Walls*, Unbound, 2012, p. 11.

438 Maurice Richardson, 'A Triumph of Principle', *Observer*, 13 November 1960.

439 George Melly, 'Television's First Masterpiece', *Observer*, 30 October 1966.

440 Lance Loud on *The Dick Cavett Show*, ABC, 1973.

441 Nathaniel West and Steven Daly, 'Overt, Overdone and Over Here', *Observer*, 6 June 1993.

442 Jonathan Bernstein, *Guardian*, 24 June 2000.

443 Chris Dunkley, *Financial Times*, 20 January 1983.

444 Diary, *Observer*, 9 January 1983.

445 Jeremy Isaacs, *Look Me in the Eye*, Little, Brown, 2006.

446 Emily Bell, 'Not a Word from Our Sponsors', *Observer*, 21 April 1991.

447 Andy Beckett, 'Growing Pains', *Guardian*, 23 March 2000.

448 Brian Raftery, 'The Best TV Show That's Ever Been', *GQ*, 27 September 2012.

449 Kingsley Amis, introduction, *The New Oxford Book of Light Verse*, Oxford University Press, 1987.

450 Nancy Banks-Smith, 'Railway', *Guardian*, 15 May 1980.

451 Kate Kellaway, 'Behind the

Wire, in the Money',
*Guardian,* 8 October 1989.

452 Michael Billington, *Guardian,*
11 June 1982.

453 'Friends Come in from the
BBC Cold', *Observer,*
24 December 1995.

454 Richard Brooks, *Observer,*
14 July 1991.

455 *Daily Mail,* 12 May 1995.

456 *Richard Herring's Leicester
Square Theatre Podcast,*
Episode 8, 20 June 2012.

457 Leo Tolstoy, *War and Peace,*
Vol. 4, Russkiy Vestnik, 1869.

458 Martha P. Nochimson, 'Did
Tony Die at the End of The
Sopranos?', *Vox.com,*
27 August 2014.

459 John Wells, 'Don't Get Your
Johns in a Tangle', *TV Times,*
3 August 1972.

460 Eric Bentley, *The Life of the
Drama,* Methuen, 1966.

461 Mick Farren, 'Set the Controls
for Total Media Overkill',
*NME,* 28 April 1979.

462 Gavin Edwards, 'Intergalactic
Terror', *Rolling Stone,*
27 January 2006.

463 Walden Sadiri, 'Roland D.
Moore Re-Imagines science
fiction', *Manila Reporter,* 26
June 2005.

464 *Ibid.*

465 'Our London
Correspondence', *Manchester
Guardian,* 23 April 1954.

466 Jonathan Meades, *Observer,*
6 November 1977.

467 Nancy Banks-Smith,
'Maelstrom', *Guardian,*
13 March 1985.

468 Julian Barnes, 'Misery in a
Ravaged Land', *Observer,*
2 October 1985.

469 Anthony Burgess, *One Man's
Choru*s, Carroll & Graf, 1998.

470 J. Hoberman, 'Medium Cool
Yule', *Village Voice,*
29 December 1976.

471 Mark Lewis, 'Norway's "Slow
TV" Movement: So Wrong,
it's Right', *Time,* 8 July 2013.

472 Gerard Gilbert, 'An End to
The Killing', *Independent,*
28 July 2014.

473 Lucy Siegle, Observer Ethical
Awards, *Observer,* 15 June
2014.

474 David Bianculli, '*The Killing:
Twin Peaks* meets *24* on
AMC', *NPR,* 31 March 2011.

475 Elise Hu, 'For Taiwanese
News Animators, Funny
Videos Are Serious Work',
*NPR,* 27 January 2014.

476 Ian Katz, Tweet (deleted),
9 September 2013.

477 Joe Hagan, 'Can HBO
Save the Sitcom?', *New York
Observer,* 18 April 2005.

478 Emily Nussbaum, 'One-Man
Show', *New York Magazine,*
15 May 2011.

479 Joe Hagan, 'Can HBO Save
the Sitcom?', *New York
Observer,* 18 April 2005.

480 Dave Itzkoff, 'Louis C. K. and
the Ballad of Jack Dall', *New*

*York Times*, 5 April 2013.

481 Ned Hepburn, 'Louis C. K. Fires Self from Own Show', *Death & Taxes Magazine*, 27 February 2012.

482 Anthony Burgess, *Urgent Copy*, Jonathan Cape, 1968.

483 Scott Roxborough, 'Why Netflix's *House of Cards* is the Future of TV', *Hollywood Reporter*, 7 October 2012.

484 Paul MacInnes, *Guardian*, 25 January 2015.

485 Bernard Levin, 'House That ITV Is Building', *Manchester Guardian*, 19 November 1955.

# ACKNOWLEDGEMENTS

This book reached publication via the scenic route, over the best part of a decade. Thanks to Martin Redfern, Scott Pack, Morwenna Loughman, Rachel Faulkner and Tom Bromley for helping it get there. For vital help with the whys and wherefores in this book, thanks in no particular order to John Williams, Ian Greaves, Louis Barfe, Justin Lewis, Chris Diamond, David Rolinson, Steve Berry, Nigel Plaskitt, Steve Williams, Jonathan Sloman, John Lloyd, Simon Farquhar, Jack Kibble-White, Ian Potter, Chris Hughes, Paul Whitelaw, Tim Worthington, Peter Gordon, Jill Phythian and Simon Harries. Thanks also to the British Library, BBC archives, the British Film Institute and the Archive of American Television.